Canon® EOS 5D Mark III FOR DUMMIES®

by Robert Correll

WILEY
John Wiley & Sons, Inc.

Canon® EOS 5D Mark III For Dummies®

Published by
John Wiley & Sons, Inc.
111 River Street
Hoboken, NJ 07030-5774

www.wiley.com

Published by John Wiley & Sons, Inc., Hoboken, New Jersey

Published simultaneously in Canada

For general information on our other products and services, please contact our Customer Care Department within the U.S. at 877-762-2974, outside the U.S. at 317-572-3993, or fax 317-572-4002.

For technical support, please visit www.wiley.com/techsupport.

Wiley publishes in a variety of print and electronic formats and by print-on-demand. Some material included with standard print versions of this book may not be included in e-books or in print-on-demand. If this book refers to media such as a CD or DVD that is not included in the version you purchased, you may download this material at http://booksupport.wiley.com. For more information about Wiley products, visit www.wiley.com.

Library of Congress Control Number is available from the publisher.

ISBN: 978-1-118-33593-2 (pbk); ISBN: 978-1-118-40170-5 (ebk); ISBN: 978-1-118-40171-2 (ebk); ISBN: 978-1-118-40172-9 (ebk)

Manufactured in the United States of America

10 9 8 7 6 5 4 3 2 1

WILEY

About the Author

Robert Correll is the author of several books about digital photography and imaging, including *Digital SLR Photography All-in-One For Dummies.* His most recent titles include *Sony Alpha SLT-A65/A77 For Dummies, Sony Alpha SLT-A35/A55 For Dummies, Photo Retouching and Restoration Using Corel PaintShop Pro X4,* Third Edition; *HDR Photography Photo Workshop,* Second Edition (with Pete Carr); *Canon EOS Rebel T3/1110D* and *Canon EOS 60D For Dummies* (both with Julie Adair King), and *High Dynamic Range Digital Photography For Dummies.*

When not writing, Robert enjoys family life, photography, playing the guitar, grilling, and recording music. Robert graduated from the United States Air Force Academy and resides in Indiana.

Canon® EOS 5D Mark III

FOR

DUMMIES®

Dedication

To my family.

Author's Acknowledgments

I want to express my appreciation to everyone I had the pleasure of working with on this project. Each person devoted their skills, talents, attention to detail, vision, and time. Those are valuable commodities.

In particular, I am deeply grateful to the wonderful publishing team at John Wiley & Sons. Susan Christophersen and Steve Hayes are just some of the talented editors who helped make this book possible. I am also thankful to technical editor Scott Proctor, whose insights and expertise helped keep this book on the straight and narrow.

Many thanks to David Fugate at Launchbooks.com.

Special thanks to all the folks at LensRentals.com, especially Drew and Roger. I want to encourage everyone to drop by and check out what you guys do and how. I've never had a moment's hesitation renting equipment from you. Your service is second to none.

Thanks to Michael of Michael Tapes Design for providing me with a high-quality image of LensAlign to use in the book.

A big "Thank you!" to our Pine Hills Church family. From shooting movies to photographing practices and services, your encouragement and assistance have been invaluable.

As always, thanks to my wife and children for encouraging, supporting, and sustaining me.

Thank you!

Publisher's Acknowledgments

We're proud of this book; please send us your comments at http://dummies.custhelp.com. For other comments, please contact our Customer Care Department within the U.S. at 877-762-2974, outside the U.S. at 317-572-3993, or fax 317-572-4002.

Some of the people who helped bring this book to market include the following:

Acquisitions and Editorial

Project Editor: Susan Christophersen

Executive Editor: Steve Hayes

Copy Editor: Susan Christophersen

Technical Editor: Scott Proctor

Editorial Manager: Jodi Jensen

Editorial Assistant: Leslie Saxman

Sr. Editorial Assistant: Cherie Case

Cover Photo: © technotr/iStockphoto.com

Cartoons: Rich Tennant (www.the5thwave.com)

Composition Services

Project Coordinator: Patrick Redmond

Layout and Graphics: Joyce Haughey, Christin Swinford

Proofreader: Melissa Cossell

Indexer: Potomac Indexing, LLC

Publishing and Editorial for Technology Dummies

Richard Swadley, Vice President and Executive Group Publisher

Andy Cummings, Vice President and Publisher

Mary Bednarek, Executive Acquisitions Director

Mary C. Corder, Editorial Director

Publishing for Consumer Dummies

Kathleen Nebenhaus, Vice President and Executive Publisher

Composition Services

Debbie Stailey, Director of Composition Services

Contents at a Glance

Table of Contents

Introduction

The Canon EOS 5D Mark III is a breathtaking camera. It is a full-frame beastie, which means that the sensor behind the lens is the size of a 35mm frame of film. You have to take the lens off the camera and look behind the mirror to see it. It's impressive.

Behind this full-frame goodness is a whole lot of camera. The 5D Mark III bridges the gap between the less expensive cameras in the Canon lineup and the price-is-no-object upper end. It's perfect for serious amateurs and working professionals.

This camera offers the range of advanced controls and features that experienced photographers demand (impressive high ISO performance, great top-end shutter speed, a top LCD screen, plenty of autofocus options, customizability, and more) plus an assortment of tools designed to help beginners be successful (great Quick Control screen, Live View, an easy-to-use Scene Intelligent Auto shooting mode, and more). Adding to the fun, this camera continues the Canon commitment to fielding pro cameras that can record high-definition digital movies.

The 5D Mark III is so feature packed, in fact, that sorting out everything can be a challenge, whether you're new to digital SLR photography or new to this camera. This book is about mastering that challenge. I've had terrific fun working with the 5D Mark III to create this book and wish you all the success in the world with it.

About This Book

This book's purpose is to put the right information in your hands so that you can take advantage of the technological prowess of your Canon EOS 5D Mark III. You don't need to know anything about photography before opening these pages. In classic *For Dummies* style, I explain things in easy-to-understand language and use plenty of color photos to show off the camera and make the photographic concepts easier to understand.

Who This Book Is For

The Canon EOS 5D Mark III is a serious camera. It's expensive and loaded with professional-level features. It is also Canon's entry-level full-frame dSLR. That puts the camera into a unique category and challenged me to write the book in a way that will appeal to a broad range of photographers.

In keeping with the *For Dummies* series concept (simplifying and de-geekifying hard topics), this book covers the basic aspects of working with the 5D Mark III. Topics such as attaching the lens and holding the camera are covered. The book *also* delves into some of the more esoteric features included in the 5D Mark III, such as which Case to select when you're fine-tuning the AI Servo AF mode.

If you are a beginner, my goal is to provide a friendly helping hand so that you can quickly start taking advantage of what you hold in your hands.

If you are a more experienced photographer, I have written this book with an eye toward providing you with a thorough reference that summarizes a number of the 5D Mark III's important settings, menus, and features. Use this book to familiarize yourself with the many different aspects of the 5D Mark III so that you can quickly get to work.

How This Book Is Organized

This book is organized into four parts. Each one has a particular focus. The chapters flow from what you need to start out to more advanced subjects. You can read the book from start to finish if you like, or you can jump to any section in any chapter and dig right in. Use the Table of Contents, the index, and the chapter cross-references to find sections with related information.

Here's a quick look at what you can find in each part.

Part I: Knowing Your Camera Inside and Out

This part contains two chapters designed to familiarize you with your 5D Mark III as thoroughly as possible. In Chapter 1, you get to know the buttons and dials, what they do, and how to use them. You find steps for how to decode the viewfinder and LCD displays. Chapter 2 covers setting up the camera. You read about the shooting modes, important setup menus, how to set picture quality, size, and aspect ratio, as well as which settings make the most sense for you.

Part II: Fast Track to Super Shots

This part gets you up to speed quickly for taking photos, movies, and playing them back. Chapter 3 covers using the Scene Intelligent Auto shooting mode, as well as how to use the LCD monitor as a viewfinder (called Live View). Chapter 4 is all about making movies: how to configure the camera, which options are best for you, and how to shoot and review them. In Chapter 5, you read about the ins and outs of photo playback. Review pictures, look at the settings you used, change the display to include more or less information, delete photos, rotate photos, set up a slide show, and show off your photos on an HDTV.

Part III: Expressing Your Creativity

Part III explains the concepts you need to operate your camera in the more advanced modes, which allow you to make more creative decisions on your own. You see how to make exposure and flash decisions in Chapter 6. Use the advanced exposure modes and decide what exposure settings you want to use to create the photos you like. Chapter 7 is about working with the 5D Mark III's impressive autofocus tools. Chapter 8 covers color issues such as setting the right white balance. You also see how to apply Picture Styles and choose a color space. Chapter 9 is the putting-it-all-together chapter. Review general settings, come up with a plan, and then photograph portraits, landscapes, close-ups, and more.

Part IV: The Part of Tens

Always a favorite, the Part of Tens concludes the book with two chapters of essential nonessential information. In Chapter 10, you read about how to customize your camera. Feel free to experiment with features like Custom Shooting modes and My Menu, and find out how to customize other controls. Chapter 11 concludes the book with a list of ten interesting features that you might want to check out on a rainy day. These include working with dual memory cards, using GPS, viewing the electronic level, and registering automatic dust deletion data.

A Word about Firmware

As I write this, the most current firmware available for the 5D Mark III is version 1.1.2. Occasionally, Canon releases firmware updates. You should check its Web site (`www.canon.com`) periodically to find out whether any updates are available. (Chapter 2 shows you how to check which firmware version your camera is running.)

Firmware updates typically don't carry major feature changes; they're mostly used to solve technical glitches in existing features. If you download an update, be sure to read the accompanying description of what it accomplishes so that you can adapt this book's instructions as necessary.

Icons Used in This Book

If this isn't your first *For Dummies* book, you may be familiar with the large, round art (a.k.a. *icons*) that decorates its margins. If not, here's your very own icon-decoder ring:

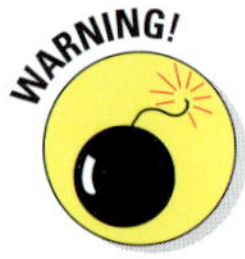

Danger is lurking. Pay attention and proceed with caution. You know, as though you were about to open a hatch you shouldn't (Locke) or be so foolish as to be a minor character lecturing people about the dangers of dynamite while wrapping an old stick of it in a shirt on a deserted island (so long, Artz).

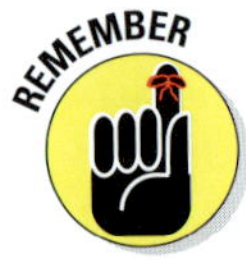

This icon should trigger an immediate data download for storage in your brain's long-term memory. The information is something important that rises above the level of a cute tip but not quite to the danger of a warning. As Spock would say, *Remember.*

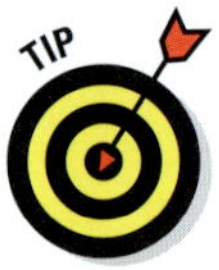

Here lies helpful information that's likely to make your life easier. It may save you time, effort, or sanity. (Your mileage may vary.) I love tips. If I could, I would make every paragraph a tip.

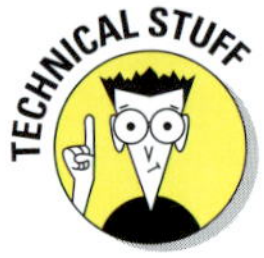

Some of the information in this book is pretty technical. If it's not necessary for you to understand, it's marked with this icon. Use the information to impress your family and friends. Or skip it completely.

Where to Go from Here

Why, get out and take loads of pictures, of course. Throw in some Full HD (1920 by 1080 pixels) movies, too!

No matter how much you fill your brain with facts and features, photography is about using the camera to capture something of your world.

If you're feeling daunted, put the 5D Mark III on Scene Intelligent Auto shooting mode, set the focus to AF, and go forth proudly with your awesomely capable point-and-shoot camera. Review what you do and learn from what you see. Progress from there to Av or Tv modes; experiment with changing the metering modes, drive mode, other modes; and so forth. Then take more pictures.

The hands-on experience that you accumulate will sink in. I know. If you practice and don't give up, you'll accomplish what you set out to do. I've put the information in this book that I think you need to get started, and then some.

If you know what you're doing, set the bar even higher. Use this book to help you uncover aspects of the 5D Mark III that you aren't familiar with. Experiment with areas of photography that you're not as good at. If you shoot landscapes, go out and try to shoot portraits, close-ups, or action. If you haven't shot Full HD movies yet, get out there and do it. Get out of your comfort zone. You'll benefit greatly.

Part I

Knowing Your Camera Inside and Out

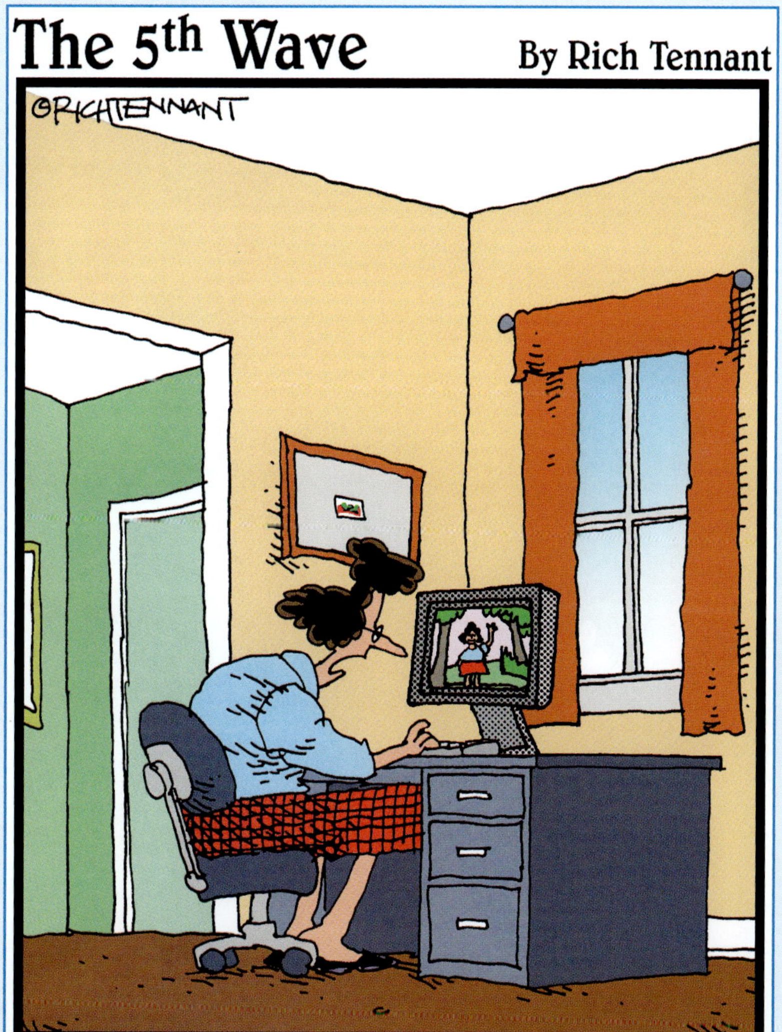

"My God! I've gained 9 pixels!"

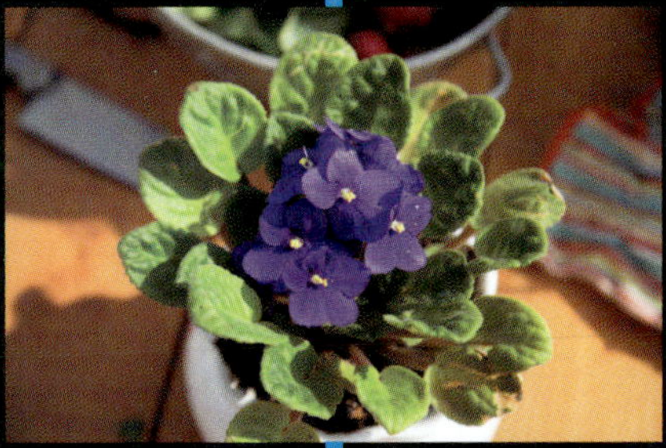

Very simply, this part gets you up and running.

Chapter 1 explains all the buttons, bells, and whistles on your Canon EOS 5D Mark III. You learn how to get at and manage the information the camera throws at you; how to work with lenses, batteries, and memory cards; how to adjust the viewfinder so that you can see better through it; and how to clean the camera's sensor.

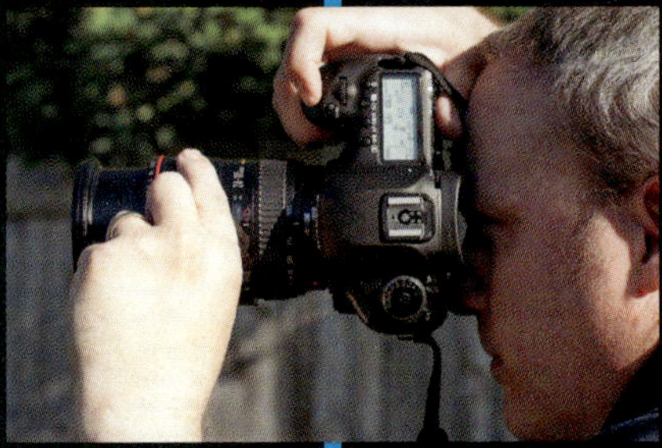

Chapter 2 walks you through how to set up the camera, including how to set the date and time, choose a shooting mode and drive mode, and set up image size, quality, and type.

It's an action-packed way to start the book, I tell ya!

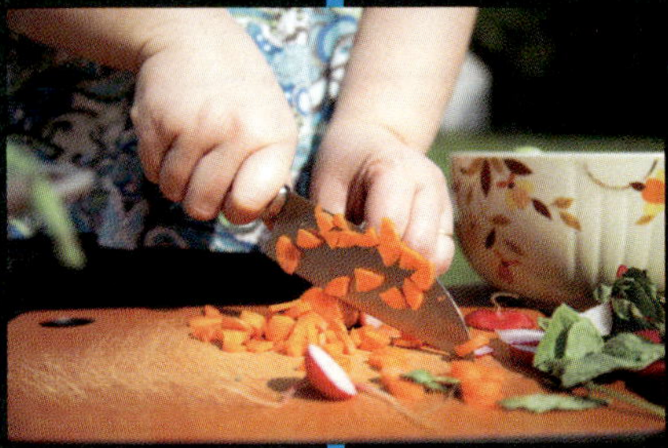

1

Surveying the Territory

In This Chapter

- Discovering all the buttons, controls, and displays that the 5D Mark III has to offer
- Learning how to manage the wealth of information thrown at you
- Reviewing how to attach and remove lenses
- Zooming in and out, and manually focusing with the lens
- Adjusting the viewfinder's focus to make images sharp and clear
- Working with batteries and memory cards
- Cleaning the camera's sensor

The Canon EOS 5D Mark III is a beautiful, powerful camera. Your assignment, should you choose to accept it, is to learn the 5D Mark III inside and out. Master it. Make it part of your arsenal. Whether you are a professional photographer or an enthusiast, the 5D Mark III should be an extension of *you* and *your vision*.

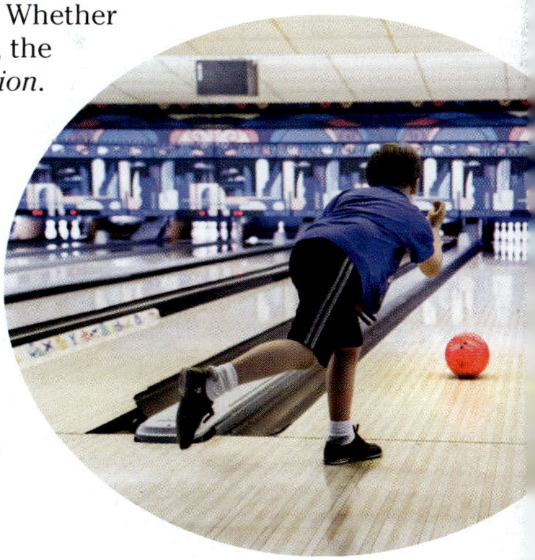

Show us the world you see.

The road ahead has some hard work, but it's an enjoyable and worthwhile trip. This chapter starts you on that road by first showing you the externals of the 5D Mark III. I show you the buttons, dials, and displays and briefly cover their function (with plenty of references to more meaty sections in the book where they are more fully illustrated). You also learn how to insert batteries, attach lenses, work with memory cards, and get a sense of how the 5D Mark III works. All important stuff.

Time to get started!

It's the Hard-Knocks Life (Not)

I named this section as I did because although you have quite a few controls and displays to learn about, it's really *not* the hard knocks life. Please, *make* me learn about a $3,400 full-frame camera with incredibly high ISO speeds. (*ISO speed* is a measure of the camera sensor's sensitivity to light; ISO is short for the International Organization for Standardization, the body, not surprisingly, responsible for standardizing these things.) Male me have to learn to shoot full HD movies with a camera that's also a workhorse in the hands of *actual filmmakers*. Yeah, torture me with it, why don't you!

As Figure 1-1 shows, the 5D Mark III is a joy to behold. This section walks you through the controls, displays, and other doodads, with brief descriptions of what they are and how they work. Use this material as a learning tool or as a reference to keep handy.

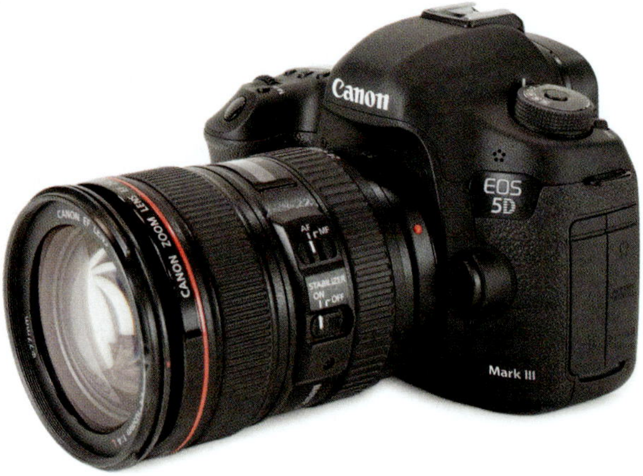

Figure 1-1: She's gorgeous, isn't she?

Full frontal awesomeness

The front of the camera has a few important controls and other gizmos (see Figure 1-2, which was taken with the lens off to make the controls more visible). Practice identifying them so that you don't have to turn the camera around to see them.

Self-timer lamp

The self-timer lamp works based on how you have set the self-timer:

- **10-second self-timer:** Blinks twice a second (yes, I counted) for the first eight seconds and then remains steady for the remaining two.
- **2-second self-timer:** Lights up but doesn't blink. Goes off just as the photo is taken.

You can find more on drive modes, including the self-timer, in Chapter 2.

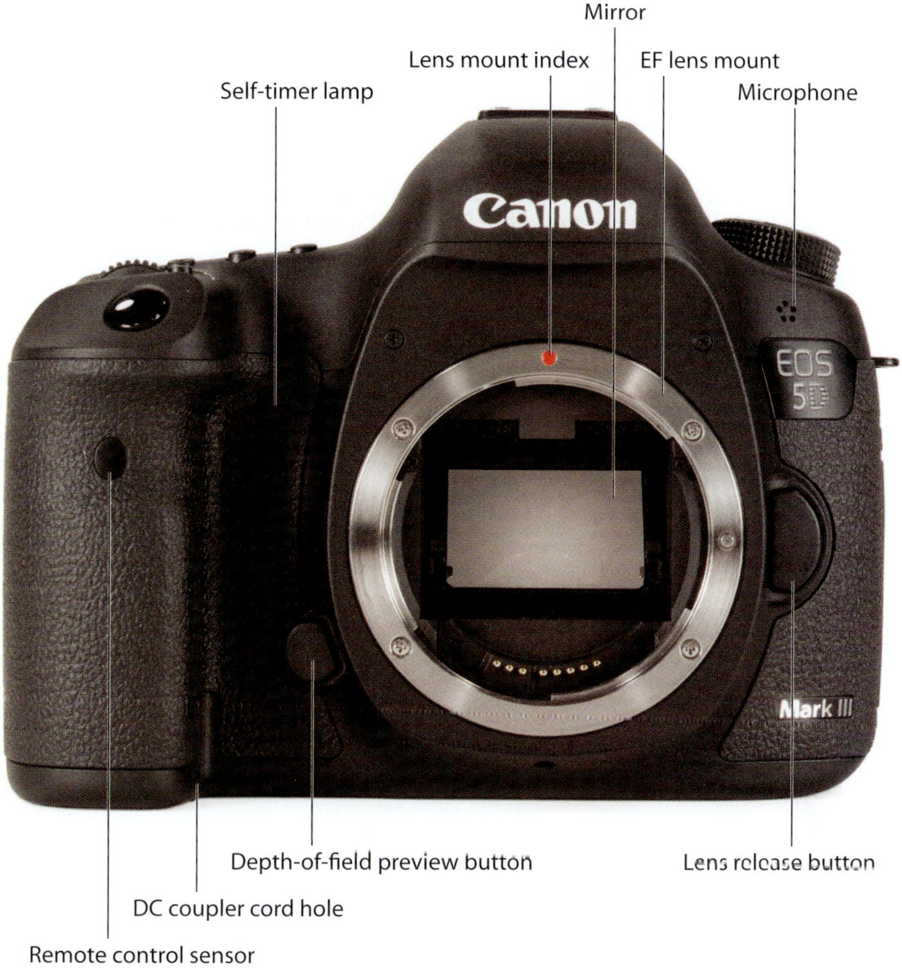

Figure 1-2: The business end of the 5D Mark III.

Remote control sensor

This sensor receives signals from the Canon family of remote controllers (Remote Controller RC-6, RC-5, or RC-1), which are all wireless. Don't cover or block the sensor if you're planning on using a wireless remote.

DC coupler cord hole

This little flap (see close-up in Figure 1-3) covers a connection for attaching an optional AC power adapter. When open, the AC adapter power cord snakes through this hole cover and down into the battery compartment, where it connects to a power coupler that replaces the battery in the compartment. Canon sells the AC Adapter Kit ACK-E6 for about $180 (you wanna play with the big boys, you gotta pay with the big boys). The alternating current (AC) that comes out of your wall is converted to direct current (DC) — the same type as the battery — so that it doesn't blow your camera up. See the camera and adapter manuals for specifics.

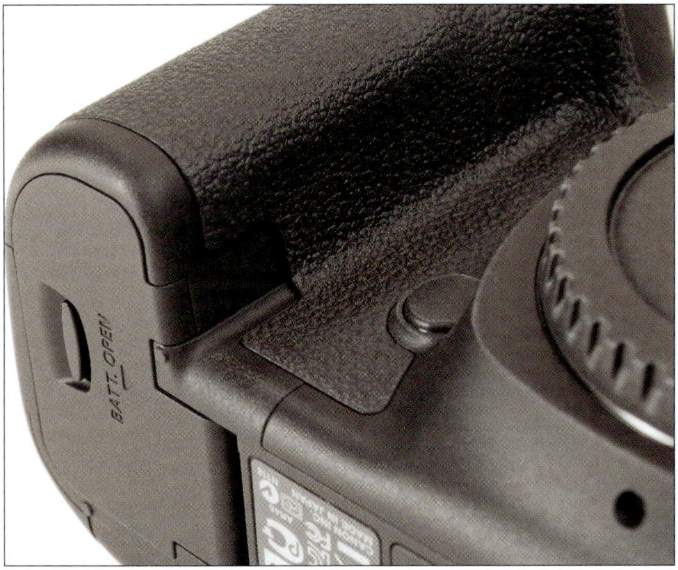

Figure 1-3: The DC coupler cord hole routes a cable into the battery compartment.

Depth-of-field preview button

Use the preview button to check the depth of field before taking the photo. (See Chapter 7 for more on depth of field.) You won't notice much of a difference between your normal view and the preview if the f-number is small (meaning a large aperture).

You can reprogram the depth-of-field preview button, as described in Chapter 10.

Mirror

This is the reflex mirror mounted inside your 5D Mark III. It is in the down position in Figure 1-2. In this position, it reflects light up and through the viewfinder. When you enter Live View or movie mode, or when you take a photo, it flips up and out of the way to expose the sensor.

EF lens mount

The Canon 5D Mark III features an EF lens mount. It is not compatible with EF-S lenses. More on the EF lens mount and how it differs from the newer EF-S mount later in this chapter, in "Your Windows to the World."

Lens mount index

The EF lens mount index is the red dot at the top of the mount. When attaching a lens to the camera body, use the index to line them up correctly.

Lens release button

Press this button all the way in to release the lens. Instructions for attaching and removing lenses are in "Your Windows to the World."

Microphone

Your 5D Mark III has a built-in mono microphone (see Figure 1-4 for a close-up). The internal microphone gives you the ability to record audio with your movies.

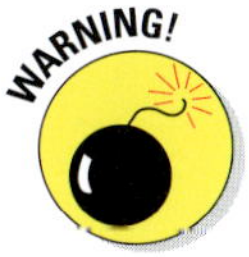

The microphone is close enough to your face, however, to possibly record every breath you take, not to mention other noises, such as your fidgeting while you try to hold the camera steady, focus, and work the controls. On the whole, the internal microphone is good enough if you don't need stereo and can keep things quiet, but for anything else, you should seriously consider attaching an external stereo mic (which happens to turn the internal mic off). Turn to Chapter 4 for more information on making movies and configuring the audio settings.

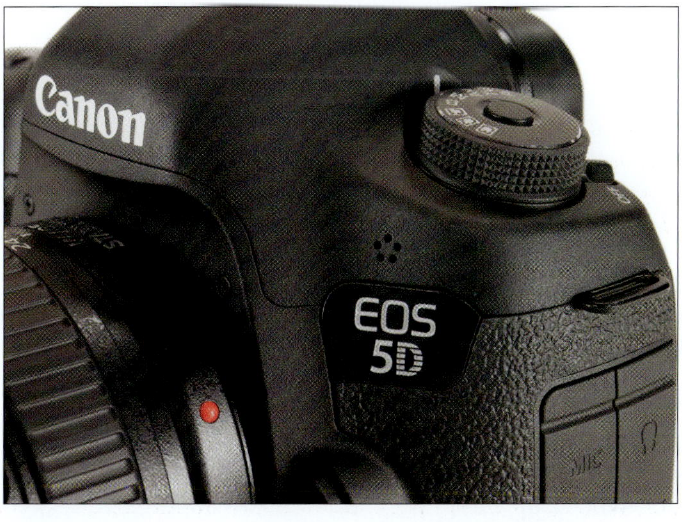

Figure 1-4: The mono microphone lies beneath those holes.

On top of the world

The top of the camera (see Figure 1-5) is where some of the really important controls are located. The Mode dial and Power switch dominate the top left, whereas the LCD panel, Main dial, and a bevy of other buttons are prominently featured on the top right.

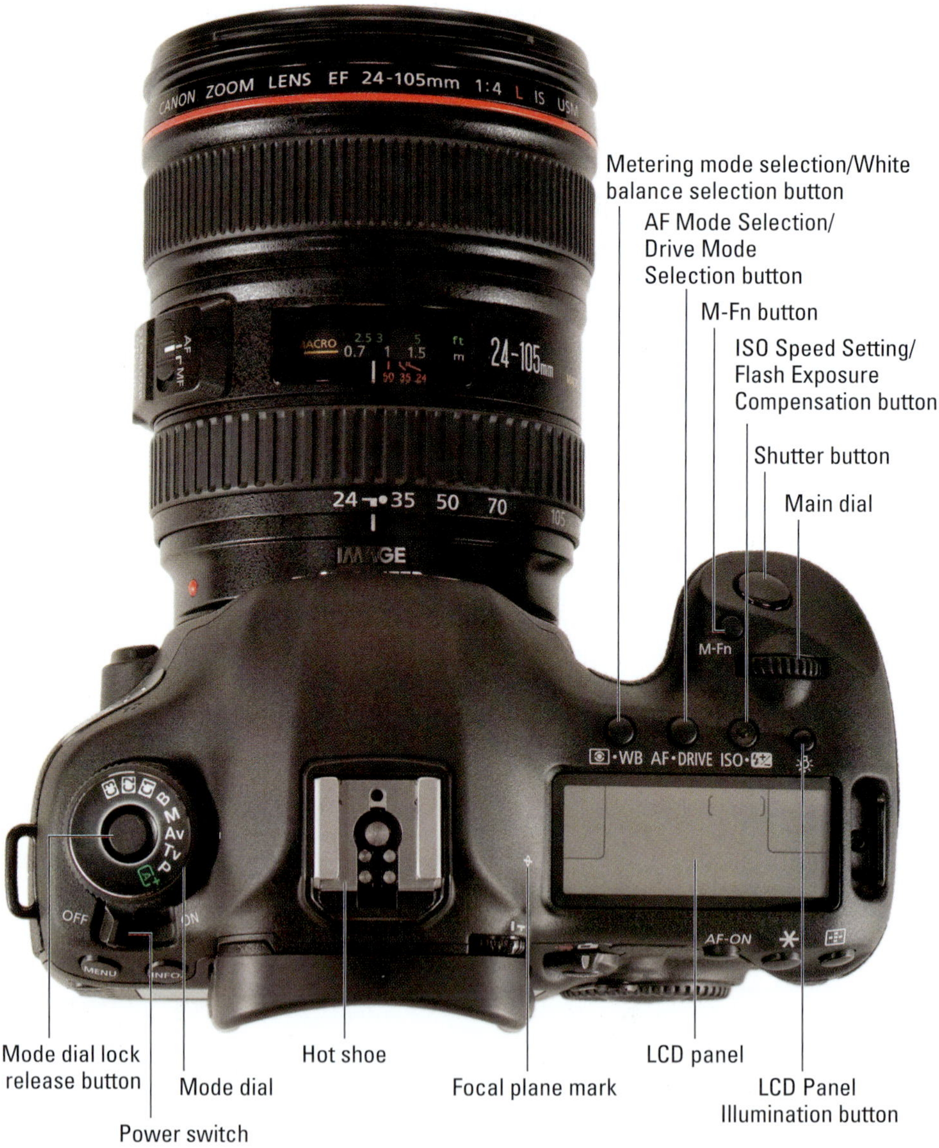

Figure 1-5: The top has the Mode dial on one side and everything else on the other.

Mode dial

Aside from the Shutter button, the Mode dial (see Figure 1-6 for a close-up) is probably the most important control on the camera. You use this dial to select a *shooting mode* (sometimes referred to as an exposure mode). Shooting modes determine how the camera operates. Different modes (discussed in Chapter 2) have different creative and practical goals.

The Mode dial is locked and cannot be turned unless you press and hold the Mode dial lock release button (discussed next). So don't force it!

Mode dial lock release button

Press this button (shown in the close-up in Figure 1-6) and hold it down while spinning the Mode dial to change shooting modes.

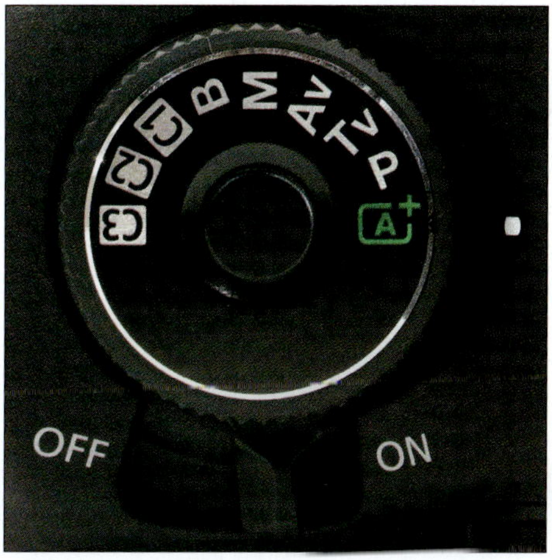

Figure 1-6: The release button is in the middle of the Mode dial.

Power switch

This one's pretty obvious.

Hot shoe

The hot shoe (known as *hot* because it can make an electrical connection between it and the device attached to it) is where you mount an external flash and other accessories, such as a beverage warmer, GPS receiver, or remote flash trigger.

Slide the external unit on the shoe fully and then lock it down by turning the lock lever to the right until it clicks in place. (The lock button will pop and get firm.) Figure 1-7 shows a close-up of the lock button. To release the device, press the lock-release button, slide the lever to the left, and then gently slide the entire contraption out of the hot shoe.

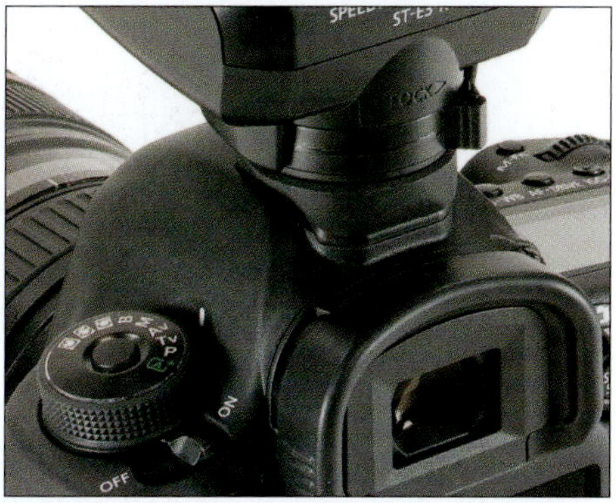

Figure 1-7: Mount and lock accessories on the hot shoe.

M-Fn button (AF Area Selection Mode/Multi-function button)

The main purpose of the M-Fn button, shown in the close-up in Figure 1-8, is to confuse you. By default, it seems to do nothing until you press the AF (autofocus) Point Selection button. Then you must press the M-Fn button to cycle through the different modes. Actually, its default assignment is FE Lock (see Chapter 6 for more on FE Lock), but you can change this behavior (see Chapter 10).

Metering Mode Selection/White Balance Selection button

Press this button to change metering modes (Main dial) or white balance (Quick Control dial). See Figure 1-8 for a close-up.

AF Mode Selection/Drive Mode Selection button

Press this button to change AF modes (Main dial) or drive mode (Quick Control dial). See Figure 1-8 for a close-up.

ISO Speed Setting/Flash Exposure Compensation button

Press this button (see Figure 1-8 for a close-up) to change ISO speed (Main dial) or dial in some flash exposure compensation (Quick Control dial). Notice that this button has a tiny little bump on top. That makes identifying it without looking marginally easier.

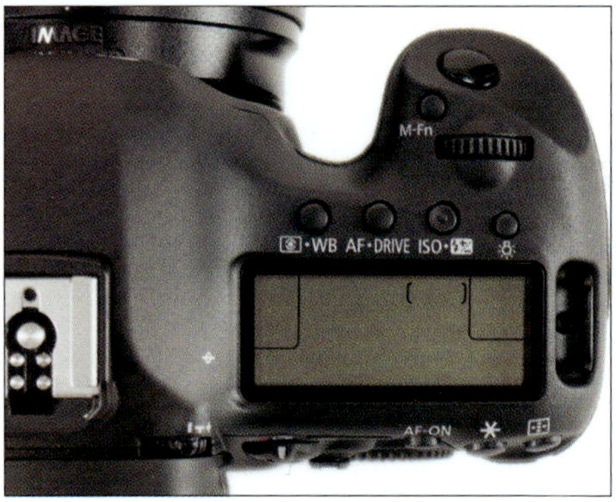

Figure 1-8: It's button soup beyond the top LCD panel.

LCD Panel Illumination button

Press this baby (shown in Figure 1-9) to light up the top LCD panel with a soft, pleasing, amber glow, also shown in Figure 1-9. Press the button again to turn the light off.

LCD panel

The LCD panel, located on the top of the 5D Mark III, gives you another way to view your camera's settings. It shows important exposure and mode information regardless of what's displayed on the LCD monitor or in the viewfinder. The display shows different information depending on the mode you're in, plus helpful reminders like the white balance; the card you are recording to; image quality settings; metering mode; and so forth. The LCD panel is covered in more depth later in this chapter.

LCD Panel Illumination button

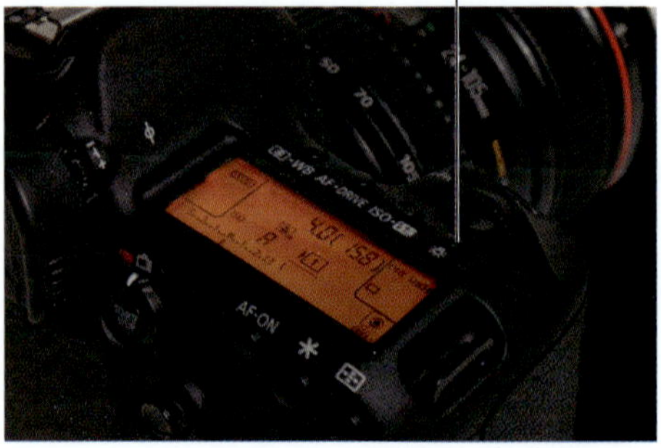

Figure 1-9: That's a pretty backlit LCD panel.

Main dial

The Main dial has a ton of uses. You use it primarily to change shutter speed and aperture, depending on what shooting mode you're in. It's also helpful to spin the Main dial to quickly scroll through menus, lists, or options.

The Main dial is associated with the first function of three of the four buttons to the front of the LCD panel. When you press the Metering Mode Selection/White Balance Selection button, AF Mode Selection/Drive Mode Selection button, or ISO Speed Setting/Flash Exposure Compensation button, change the first setting with the Main dial. The latter is changed by spinning the Quick Control dial.

Shutter button

The Shutter button does more than just take pictures:

- Press the Shutter button fully to take a photo.
- Press it halfway to start autofocus and metering. It is critical for the camera to have time to focus and determine the lighting conditions so that the photo is sharp, clear, and properly lit.

WARNING!

Don't punch at the Shutter button. Doing so shakes the camera.

Focal Plane mark

This mark tells you exactly where the focal plane is in the camera body. If you ever set up a shot that requires you to know the precise distance to the subject, use this mark as a reference point.

Behind the scenes

The rear of the camera, shown in Figure 1-10, has quite a few important controls, not to mention the viewfinder and LCD monitor.

In general, nonshooting controls that access information and the menu, as well as control playback, occupy the back left of the camera. Selection and navigation controls like the Multicontroller and Quick Control dial are conveniently located to the right of the LCD monitor. Some autoexposure and autofocus controls are located near the top on the right side of the back of the camera.

Menu button

Press the Menu button to activate the camera's menus. Through these menus, you configure the camera and change many of its settings. Menus are covered in this chapter and used throughout the book.

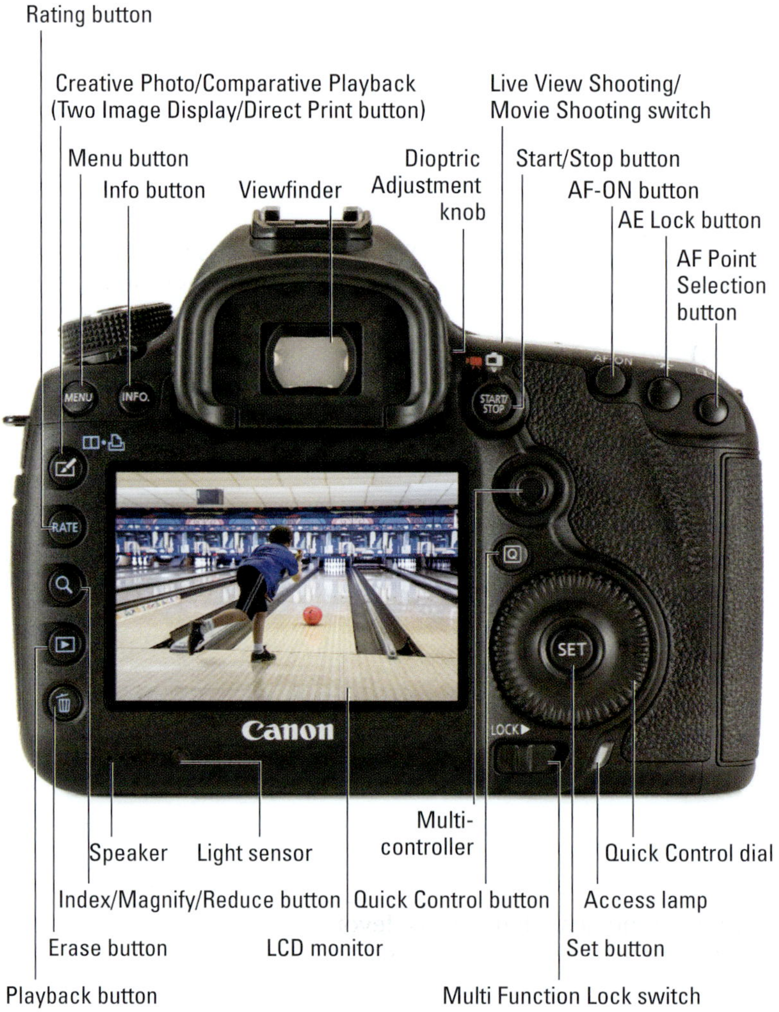

Figure 1-10: The back of the camera is clean yet powerful.

Info button

The Info button is very useful. Press it to see the Camera Settings display (discussed later in this chapter); the electronic level (see Chapter 11); and the camera's shooting settings (also in this chapter). During playback, press it to change the level of information you see associated with each photo or movie (see Chapters 4 and 5 for the details about reviewing photos and movies).

Be on the lookout for when the Info button has another purpose (the menu setting or option page will tell you). For example, when you're inputting copyright information, the Info button cancels the operation.

Creative Photo/Comparative Playback (Two Image Display/Direct Print button)

This button has three completely unrelated uses:

- **Creative Photo:** When shooting, press to choose a new Picture Style (Chapter 8), shoot with multiple exposures (Chapter 11), or shoot in HDR mode (Chapter 6).
- **Comparative Playback:** The symbol for this button is in blue and looks like two pages next to each other. When in playback, press to compare two photos side by side (see Chapter 5 for details about photo playback).
- **Direct Print:** The Direct Print button (whose symbol is in blue and looks like a little printer) is used to print directly from the camera to a compatible PictBridge printer.

Rating button

If you're into rating your photos, Canon has the button for you! When playing back photos or movies, press it to change the rating. If you like, you can change the Rate button to protect photos and movies instead (press the Menu button and look in Setup Menu 3). For more information on rating photos, see Chapter 5.

Index/Magnify/Reduce button

Use this button to change the magnification of images in playback. You can also zoom in to check focus when you're shooting in Live View. For more information on playback, see Chapter 5; Chapter 3 covers Live View.

Playback button

This button is single-mindedly focused on playback. Press it to play back photos or movies. Chapter 5 is devoted to playback as a whole. Chapter 4 has a bit more info on movie playback.

Erase button

Use this button to delete photos or movies. Check out Chapter 5 for more about deleting files. The Erase button appears (rarely) in some menu options. For example, the Erase button resets Custom Controls to their default and deletes characters when you're entering copyright information. Notice that the Erase button is concave. It's the only button on the camera shaped like this. Its shape makes it harder for you to accidentally press it and a smidgen easier to identify it without looking.

Speaker

The camera's speaker is located near the bottom of the rear of the camera, next to the light sensor. The speaker plays back movie audio, when recorded, and beeps. For example, the camera beeps when it establishes autofocus and when the self-timer is counting down. You can disable beeps with the Beep option in Shooting Menu 1. See Figure 1-11 for a close-up of the speaker.

Light sensor

The LCD monitor frame has a built-in light sensor (shown in Figure 1-11) that adjusts monitor brightness according to the surrounding light level. You can also adjust the monitor's brightness manually. (See the LCD brightness option in Setup Menu 1.)

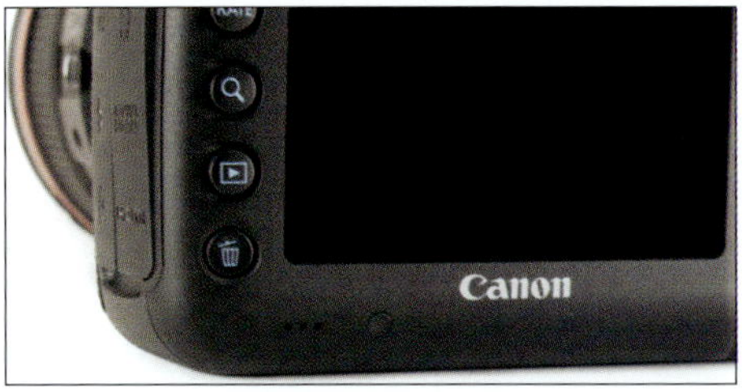

Figure 1-11: This sensor (to the right of the speaker holes) helps the monitor automatically stay bright.

LCD monitor

The large, 3.2-inch LCD monitor (with roughly 1.4 million pixels) is the main display on the camera. Use it to access menus, configure the camera, display important shooting information, play back photos and movies, and more. You can also use the viewfinder to compose shots in Live View mode and when shooting movies.

Viewfinder

The 5D Mark III has a wonderfully large, clear, bright viewfinder that boasts of nearly 100 percent coverage, which makes framing a scene and focusing a joy. (Something you would expect from a camera in this price range.) The viewfinder displays shooting and other pertinent information at the bottom, with composition, focusing, and other aids throughout. Look through the viewfinder to compose and focus when shooting still photos.

Dioptric Adjustment knob

A small but important dial is nestled on the upper-right side of the viewfinder, as pointed out in Figure 1-12. It goes by the super-technical sounding name of *Dioptric Adjustment knob*. Use it to adjust the viewfinder to your eyesight. You find instructions on how to make this adjustment later in this chapter, in "Adjusting the Viewfinder Focus."

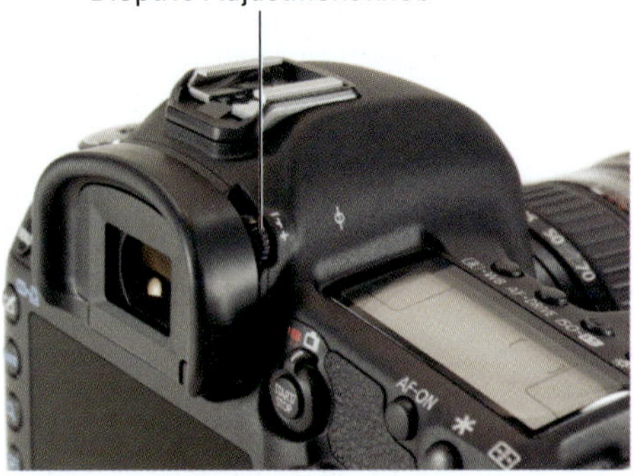

Figure 1-12: Your wheel of fortune. Use it to improve your view.

Live View Shooting/Movie Shooting switch

Turn this switch to the camera back to enable Live View shooting.

Nothing happens immediately. You have to press the Start/Stop button to activate the LCD monitor.

Turn the switch to the red movie icon to enter movie shooting mode. In this case, something *does* happen immediately. The LCD monitor shows you a live preview and you're in movie mode.

Start/Stop button

When in Live View shooting mode, press the Start/Stop button to activate the LCD monitor on the back of the camera. When in movie shooting mode, this button starts and stops recording.

Multicontroller

The Multicontroller is your camera's mouse (although it acts more like a joystick). Use it to navigate among menus and areas of the Quick Control screen; to make other selections; and to move things around the screen (such as when you pan a magnified photo during playback). You can push it in any one of eight directions. It also acts as a button (useful when making menu selections) if you press it in.

Quick Control button (Q)

You use this button to enter Quick Control mode.

Quick Control dial

The Quick Control dial is a great way to make fast selections, whether you're working with the Quick Control screen or the camera's menu system. Spin it to win it!

Now for some quirkiness.

The Quick Control dial is associated with the second function on the Metering Mode Selection/White Balance Selection button, AF Mode Selection/Drive Mode Selection button, and the ISO Speed Setting/Flash Exposure Compensation button. When you press any of those buttons, the Quick Control dial changes the *second* setting (white balance, drive mode selection, and flash exposure compensation), not the first (which is what the Main dial changes).

When you're shooting a movie, and Silent Control (Custom Function 2) is enabled, the Quick Control dial turns into a touch pad. Figuring this one out may take a few minutes, but when you get it, it's not bad at all. When Silent Control is enabled and you are in the act of shooting, press the Quick Control button and then tap the Quick Control dial as if the surface of the dial were cross keys or arrows to change exposure settings and sound recording level (if Sound Recording is set to Manual). What you can change depends on what mode you are in. More on shooting movies and setting sound in Chapter 4.

Set button

Officially known as the Setting button, the Set button is used to make choices. You'll use this button a lot.

AF-ON button

Press the AF Start button (officially known as the AF Start button) in P, Tv, Av, M, or B modes to activate the autofocus system and the meter, as well as to set the exposure.

When in Live View mode or shooting movies, you can focus by pressing the AF-ON button (indeed, it is the only way to focus when shooting a movie).

AE Lock button

Press the AE Lock button to lock the current autoexposure settings in the camera. After a few seconds of inactivity, the exposure settings will disappear from the viewfinder. When this happens, AE Lock is cleared. See Chapter 6 for more information on how to use AE Lock.

AF Point Selection button

Selecting an AF Area Selection mode is a two-step process. First you press the AF Point Selection button. Then you need to press the M-Fn button to select one of the six AF Area Selection modes. When the mode is selected, you can press this button to enter AF Point Selection mode, in which you can select individual AF points or zones. See Chapter 7 for more information on setting AF Point Selection modes and selecting AF areas.

Multi Function Lock switch

Set the Multi Function Lock switch to the right to lock down the Main dial, Quick Control dial, and Multicontroller. When these controls are locked, you can't use them to change any of the camera's settings.

But wait! There's more. You can configure which controls the Multi Function Lock switch locks from the Multi Function Lock function in Custom Function Menu 2 (see the top of Figure 1-13). Check the controls you want to lock (as shown in the

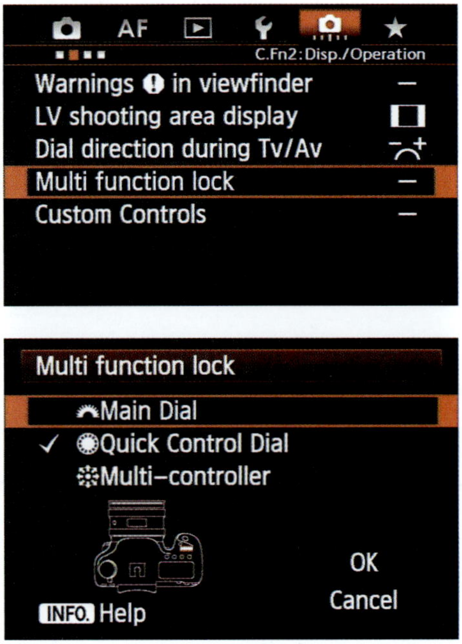

Figure 1-13: You can configure the Multi Function Lock switch.

bottom of Figure 1-13), and when the lock is locked, those controls are also locked. Chapter 10 has more information on working with Custom Functions.

Access lamp

This light shines when the camera is reading from or writing to the memory card (see Figure 1-39 below to see it lit). Don't open the battery or memory card cover when the lamp is lit.

Making camera connections

All terminals are on the left side of the camera, as shown in Figure 1-14. If you don't need them, you can ignore them.

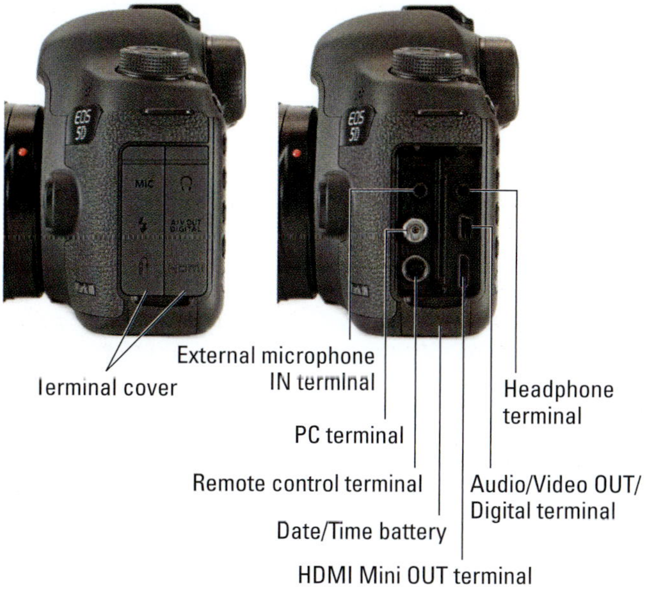

Figure 1-14: Grand central play station.

Terminal cover

The terminal cover is actually two covers in one. Gently but firmly lift up the rubber cover from the bottom to reveal the terminals beneath. The left side houses the microphone, PC terminal, and remote control terminal. The right side contains the headphone terminal, plus the USB and HDMI terminals. Icons are molded into the rubber to remind you which terminals are under which covers.

Date/time battery

The 5D Mark III has a separate battery that maintains power to preserve the camera's date and time in memory. This battery should last about five years. If you need to replace it, this here's the place to do it. Unscrew the battery holder screw and remove the battery holder. Replace the battery and then reverse the process to reinstall.

External microphone IN terminal

You have two options when recording sound with movies. You can use the internal mono microphone, which records a single audio channel. Or if you want to record in stereo (two channels), plug an external stereo microphone into the 3.5mm mini plug. More on recording sound with movies in Chapter 4.

Headphone terminal

No, the 5D Mark III doesn't double as an MP3 player (although that would be super cool). Connect your stereo headphones to the 3.5mm mini plug to listen to the sound that is being recorded when you're shooting a movie or playing back a movie.

PC terminal

This terminal accepts PC sync cords, which are used to connect remote flash units. Wireless triggers have become very popular, and many photographers have stopped using PC sync cords. Some also use wired connection with 3.5mm or 1/4-inch jacks known as mono plugs, enabling them to bypass traditional PC sync terminals. Whatever your stance on this issue, you will appreciate the 5D Mark III's support of PC sync cords if you need or want to use them.

Audio/Video OUT/Digital terminal

Use this terminal to connect the camera to a computer via the supplied USB interface cable (IFC-200U) for picture and movie downloading (although using a memory card reader is usually a better alternative).

Use the provided Stereo AV Cable (AVC-DC400ST) to connect the camera to a non-HD television. This is an interesting cable. It is terminated by a USB plug on the end that connects to the camera; also, it has RCA plugs on the other end, one each for two channels of audio (white and red) and one for video (yellow). See Chapter 5 for more information on connecting your camera to a TV.

HDMI mini OUT terminal

For picture or movie playback on an HD television or screen, you can connect the camera via this terminal, using an optional HDMI cable HTC-100 (HDMI male to mini C connectors). You'll pay about $80 if you buy the cable direct from Canon. (You can use other manufacturer's cables, but be sure they are of high quality.)

Trust me, if you haven't seen your photos or movies on a wide-screen HD TV, go out and get an HDMI cable *right now* and start. It's amazingly gratifying. See Chapter 5 for more about picture playback; Chapter 4 has information on movie playback.

Remote control terminal

As an alternative to triggering the shutter with your finger, you can attach Canon's Remote Switch RS-80N3 wired controller ($70; available from Canon) or Timer Remote Controller TC-80N3 ($210 available from Canon) here.

Controllers are a very worthwhile investment. In general, remotes eliminate the chance that the action of your finger on the Shutter button will move the camera enough to blur the shot, which is especially problematic during long exposures. A remote also frees you from having to stand at the camera and hold the Shutter button down when shooting in bulb mode. I use mine when in the studio shooting close-ups. I also use it for landscapes, at night, during fireworks, and whenever else I can.

Don't confuse this remote control terminal with the wireless remote (Remote Controller RC-6), whose signals are received via the remote control sensor on the front of the camera. If working with a wireless remote, you have to set the drive mode to 10 or 2-second self-timer/remote control. With a wired controller, you just plug it in and go.

Don't forget the memory card

The 5D Mark III's memory card slots are located on the right side of the camera. There are two, and you can use them both at the same time (see Chapter 11). A helpful graphic is located on the inside of the cover door (see Figure 1-15) that reminds you which card is which. The Compact Flash card is card number 1 and the Secure Digital card is card number 2 — and no, you can't change this assignment. Remember that. You'll need to know which card is which when selecting between them. The card icons and numbers are also displayed on the top LCD panel, the Quick Control screen, and when selecting a card or folder on a card.

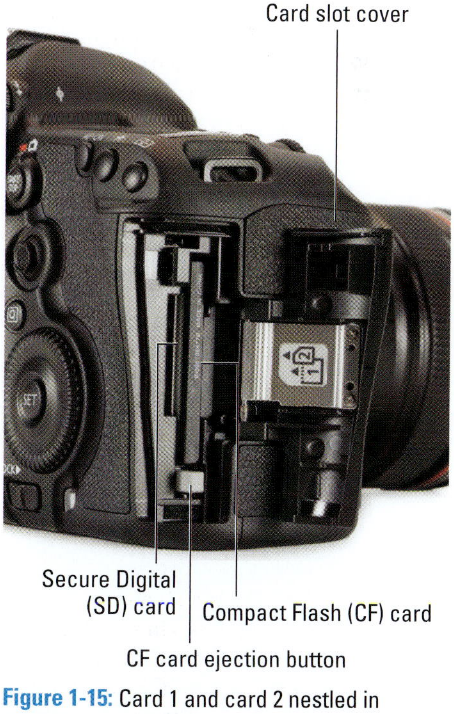

Figure 1-15: Card 1 and card 2 nestled in snugly.

Card slot cover

The memory card slides back and then flips open, revealing twin card slots (one Compact Flash, one Secure Digital). See the section "Using Batteries and Memory Cards," later in this chapter, for how to insert and remove memory cards.

CF card slot

The Compact Flash (CF) card slot is the slot located right beside the Secure Digital card slot, but more toward the front of the camera. It's bigger than the SD slot and has a gray ejection button just beneath it. It is labeled as card 1.

CF Card Ejection button

This button ejects the Compact Flash card.

SD card slot

The SD card slot is the rear slot of the two. SD cards don't require an ejection button. They are spring-loaded. The SD card is labeled as card 2.

And the underbelly

The bottom of the 5D Mark III (see Figure 1-16) has two important features. I use both all the time.

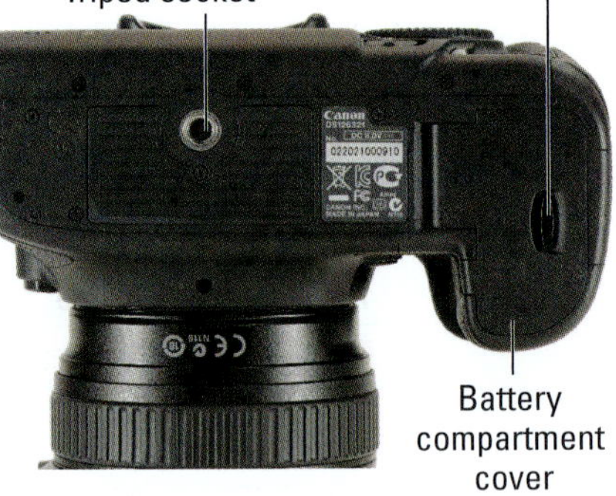

Figure 1-16: You normally never get to see this shot.

Tripod socket

The tripod receptacle is in the bottom-center of the camera.

Battery compartment cover

This cover protects the battery compartment. It's spring-loaded, which means the cover pops open when you slide the release lever toward the center of the camera.

Battery compartment cover release lever

Slide the lever toward the center of the camera to release the battery compartment cover.

Connecting with Your 5D Mark III

A large part of working a complicated piece of equipment like the 5D Mark III is managing the wealth of information available. Not only do you have to control the camera's shooting settings (such as shooting mode, exposure settings, image quality, and so on), you also have menus, options, customizable controls, displays, and other hidden gems to become familiar with.

You can't see everything or control everything at one time. Therefore, you have to know where things are, how to control the camera, access options, and use the right information at the right time to take the best photos or movies.

When the art of working with the camera becomes second nature, you will spend less time fiddling with buttons, menus, and displays, and more time being productive.

Working with menus

Press the Menu button to open the camera's internal menus, which are displayed on the LCD monitor. Use the menus to configure the camera. Navigate and select options by using the Main dial, Multicontroller, Quick Control dial, and the Set button.

Although I go into much more detail about menus in other chapters, Table 1-1 provides a handy reference of what's available:

Table 1-1 Of Mice and Menus

Icon	*Name*	*Description*
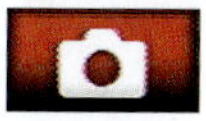	Shooting	Several pages of shooting options, such as Image Quality, Color Space, Long Exposure Noise Reduction, Live View, and Movie settings.
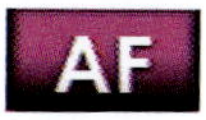	AF (autofocus)	The 5D Mark III has an entire menu section devoted to autofocus (AF) options. Choose different AI Servo cases and much more. Most of Chapter 7 is devoted to autofocus.
	Playback	This menu has three pages and includes options such as Protect Images, Slide Show, Playback Grid, and so forth. More on this in Chapters 4 (for movie playback) and 5 (still photo playback).

(continued)

Table 1-1 *(continued)*

Icon	*Name*	*Description*
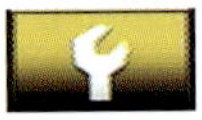	Setup	Four pages of camera configuration options, including Format Card, Date/Time/Zone, Battery Info, and Copyright Information.
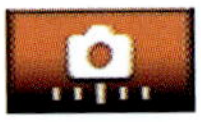	Custom Functions	The Custom Functions on the 5D Mark III are all located in these four menu pages.
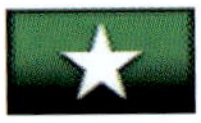	My Menu	This single page is a customizable menu. See Chapter 10 to learn how to create your own menu.

I describe the menus more fully in Chapter 2. Chapters 10 and 11 also describe quite a few menu options, including Custom Functions and other cool features.

Using yonder olde viewfinder

When the camera is turned on, you can view critical exposure settings and a few other pieces of information in the viewfinder. Just put your eye to the viewfinder and press the Shutter button halfway to activate the display. (In Live View mode, you use the LCD monitor as a makeshift viewfinder.)

The bulk of the viewfinder is taken up by the scene, as well as by focusing and other overlays such as the grid and Warning symbol. Exposure and other useful information is always displayed in bright green on a black background at the bottom of the viewfinder (see Figure 1-17). This is where you'll find the shutter speed, aperture, ISO speed, and symbols that tell you how the camera is set to shoot (FE Lock, for instance).

The viewfinder has a lot of information in it. Use the callouts in Figure 1-17 to familiarize yourself with the most important items. Others are explained as they come up in the book.

One viewfinder element, however, constantly trips people up. It's the number in brackets at the bottom right. Don't be tempted to think that this number represents the remaining number of photos you can take and record to the current memory card. No, that would be too easy. Most often, this number represents the maximum number of possible photos you can take during continuous shooting (known as the *maximum burst*). For example, if you're recording large RAW and JPEG photos, this number will drop dramatically; however, if you set the image quality to something small, the number goes up. Note that 99 is the maximum display number possible. The actual maximum burst value may be higher. You don't really need to pay attention to the number until it starts dropping toward 0, which indicates that the camera's *memory buffer* (its temporary internal data-storage tank) is filling up. If that happens, give the camera a moment to catch up. See Chapter 2 for more Image Quality and drive mode information.

To complicate matters even further, the number (just described as maximum burst) may also display the number of multiple exposures you have left in the current sequence. See Chapter 11 for more information on shooting multiple exposures.

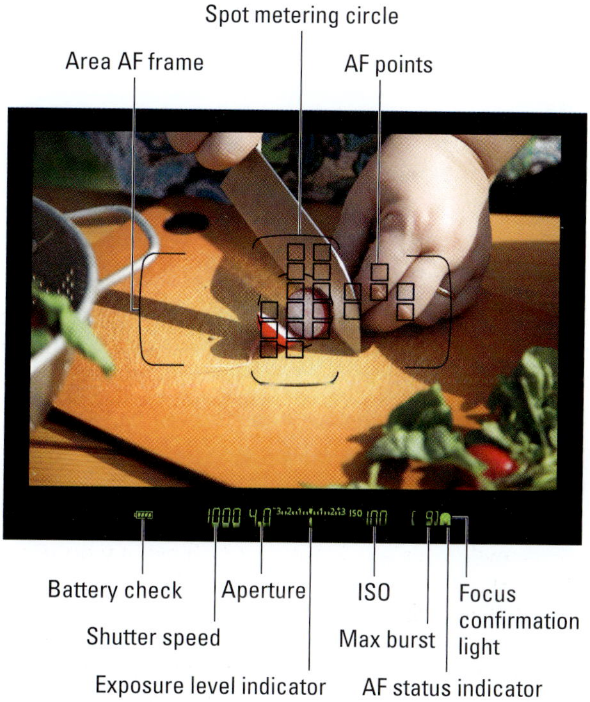

Figure 1-17: Viewing camera information at the bottom of the viewfinder.

Grokking the top display panel

Another way for you to keep track of shooting information on your 5D Mark III is by using the LCD panel on the top side of the camera, as shown in Figure 1-18. (This panel provides a lot of information, although that information is presented differently from how the viewfinder or LCD monitor presents it. (By the way, *grokking*, for those unfamiliar with *Stranger in a Strange Land*, by Robert Heinlein, means "understanding.")

As you can see from Figure 1-19, the panel is divided into several areas. Depending on how you have the camera set up, you'll see currently selected options or settings displayed in the various sections of the panel.

When you're shooting, the top-left corner of the panel is devoted to settings described in Table 1-2.

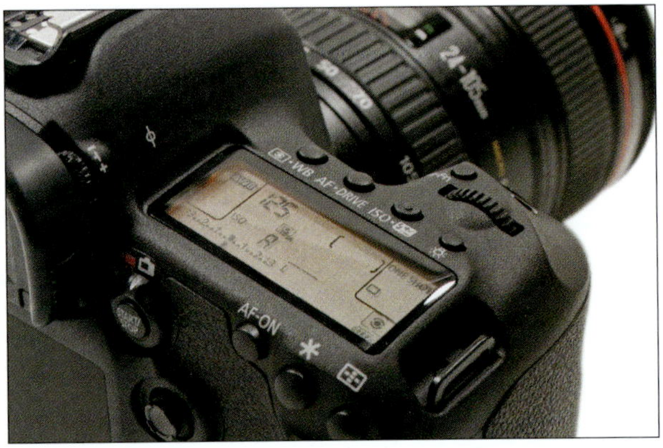

Figure 1-18: Use the top LCD panel to help you stay aware of how your camera is set up.

Table 1-2 LCD Panel Shooting Settings

Setting	*Purpose*
White balance	Displays the current white balance setting (see Chapter 8).
AF mode	Displays the current focus mode (see Chapter 7).
Drive mode	Displays the current drive mode (see Chapter 2). The number of possible shots is displayed prominently beside the aperture.
Exposure settings	Displays the current shutter speed, aperture, and ISO (see Chapter 6).
Exposure level indicator	Displays exposure compensation, AEB range, or exposure when in manual shooting mode (see Chapter 6).
Memory cards	Displays which cards are inserted and which card is active (see this chapter and Chapter 11).
Image quality	Shows the quality of the still images that will be recorded (see Chapter 2).
Metering mode	Displays the current metering mode (see Chapter 6).
Battery	Displays the current charge in the battery.

Setting	*Purpose*
Other symbols	A few symbols are scattered around the display. They indicate flash exposure compensation (by the battery symbol), highlight tone priority (by the ISO), and Auto Exposure Bracketing (AEB). Also, a central line of reminder symbols runs across the upper-middle line of the display. Chances are, these symbols will mostly be off. A symbol turns on only when the option or feature it represents is enabled. For example, the Multiple-Exposure Shooting symbol comes on only when you are using that feature.
Other indicators and text	The LCD panel also displays messages and other information when the camera is working (for example, cleaning the sensor) or you are changing the AF point selection method. These are located on the top line.

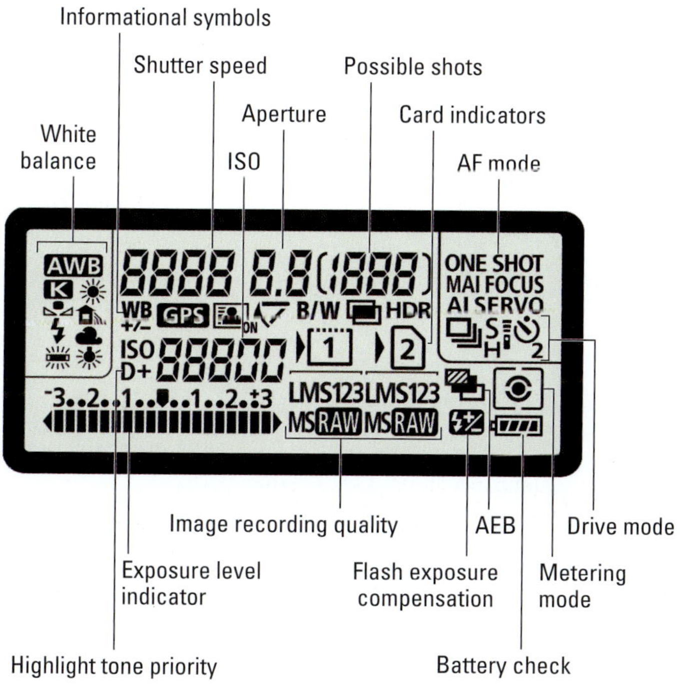

Figure 1-19: I turned everything on for effect.

Although the LCD panel displays a ton of information (some of which you can't find anywhere else, such as the Mirror Lockup indicator), it will *not* display your current shooting mode, focus or flash indicators, or the current Picture Style (unless Monochrome).

Viewing the Shooting settings display

The Shooting settings display, shown in Figure 1-20, contains the most critical photography settings: aperture, shutter speed, ISO, and the like. Note that the display is relevant only to still photography when you're looking through the viewfinder. When you switch to Live View or movie mode (see Chapters 3 and 4 for details), you can choose to superimpose some settings over the scene in the monitor, but you won't see such an LCD-dominating display.

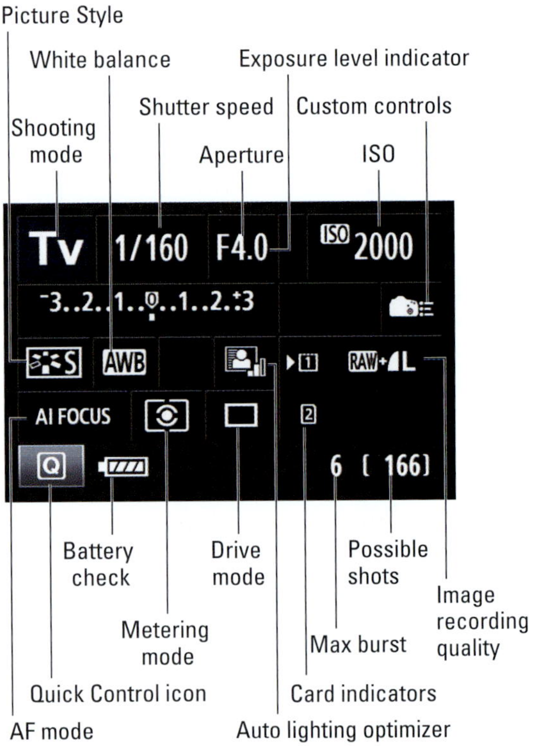

Figure 1-20: Monitoring the current shooting settings.

Figure 1-20 labels all the elements of the display. Bear in mind two key points of data that are helpful at all times:

- **Shots remaining:** This number indicates how many more pictures can fit on your memory card at the current settings. For more information on how size and quality affect the number of photos you can fit onto a memory card, please turn to Chapter 2.
- **Battery status:** A "full" battery icon like the one in the figure shows that the battery is fully charged. If the icon appears empty, you had better have your spare battery handy if you want to keep shooting.

The Shooting settings display appears after you press the Info button a number of times (how many depends on how you have configured it; see Chapter 10). Press Info again to turn off the display.

If the camera goes to sleep and the monitor turns dark, press the Shutter button halfway to wake it back up. If the Shooting settings display was visible before, it will return. Or, if you're looking at a menu, press Info or the Shutter button halfway to go back to the Shooting settings display.

If you see the Shooting settings display and want to make changes to the settings, press the Q button to enter Quick Control mode. You can immediately make changes to four settings without first entering Quick Control mode. To activate the appropriate screen in which you can change those settings, press one of the following buttons:

- Metering Mode Selection/White Balance Selection
- AF Mode Selection/Drive Mode Selection
- ISO Speed Setting/Flash Exposure Compensation
- AF Point Selection

Checking the Camera Settings display

In addition to the Shooting settings display, you can view a collection of additional settings data via the Camera Settings display, as shown in Figure 1-21. This screen is purely an informational tool, however; you can't actually adjust any of the reported settings from this screen.

To display the Camera Settings screen, press the Info button.

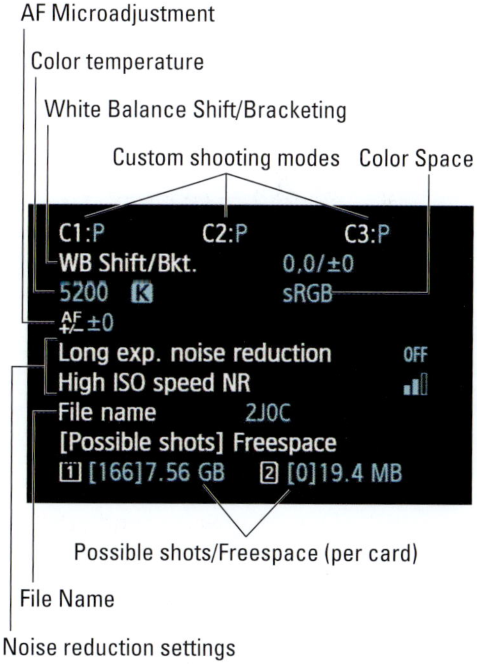

Figure 1-21: This screen displays several useful bits of helpful camera information.

Notice that the labels appear in white on the camera, whereas the information is in a cyan-looking light blue. Here are the settings listed in the order they appear onscreen:

- **Custom Mode modes:** Displays the shooting mode assigned to each Custom Shooting mode.
- **White Balance Shift/ Bracketing:** Displays the current white balance shift value and whether you are bracketing. See Chapter 8.
- **Color Temperature:** Shows you the current manual color temperature, regardless of whether you have it selected as a white balance option. Chapter 8 has more information on the topic.

- **Color Space:** Tells you whether the camera is capturing images in the sRGB or Adobe RGB color space. See Chapter 8.
- **AF Microadjustment:** This one isn't in the manual. However, if you have enabled AF Microadjustment (see Chapter 11 for information on how to use this feature), a small icon appears to remind you.
- **Image Transfer Failure warning:** Appears if a problem arose while transferring images.
- **Noise Reduction settings:** Displays whether Long Exposure Noise Reduction is on or off, and whether High ISO Speed Noise Reduction is off; if on, this setting displays a graphic indication of the level. See Chapter 6.
- **File Name:** Shows you the current filename prefix that is assigned.
- **Possible Shots/Freespace:** Indicates how much storage space remains on your camera memory card(s). How many pictures you can fit into that space depends on the Quality setting you select. Note that each card can be configured independently. Chapters 2 and 11 explain this issue further.

The Camera Settings display gives you a quick way to monitor some of the camera's critical functions without having to hunt through menus.

Taking charge in Quick Control

The Quick Control screen (whose full name is Quick Control for Shooting Functions) is a sort of one-stop shopping locale that displays your camera's shooting settings and enables you to modify them with a minimum of button presses and dial movements. The power of the Quick Control screen is that it makes it easy for you to quickly control the camera (hence, the name).

(Don't confuse the Quick Control screen with the Shooting settings screen. They are almost identical. The key difference is that you can change settings in Quick Control mode. The Shooting settings screen is just for looking.)

Follow these steps to enter Quick Control mode to change shooting settings:

1. **Switch the Live View shooting/Movie shooting switch to Live View shooting.**

   Quick Control doesn't work in movie shooting. Don't press the Start/Stop button; just make sure that the camera is not set to movie mode.

2. **Make sure that the camera is awake and then press the Quick Control button.**

   If the LCD screen is dark, you may have to wake it up before pressing the Quick Control button. You may do this by pressing the Info button until you see the Shooting settings display or pressing the Shutter button halfway. See Chapter 10 for information on how to configure Auto Power Off time.

The LCD monitor will enter Quick Control mode, and one of the options on the screen becomes highlighted. The option name also appears at the bottom of the screen, as shown on the left in Figure 1-22.

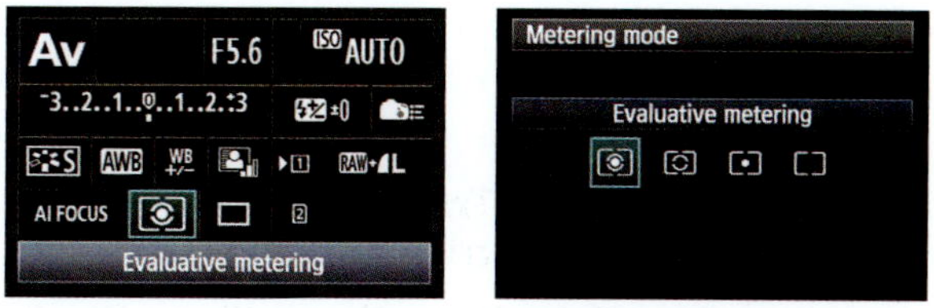

Figure 1-22: Press the Quick Control button to shift to Quick Control mode; the active option appears highlighted.

If you've activated Scene Intelligent Auto mode, Quick Control mode is much more limited. (See Chapter 3 for more about Scene Intelligent Auto mode.)

3. **Press the Multicontroller to move the highlight over the setting you want to adjust.**

   Figure 1-22 shows options presented in Av (Aperture-Priority Autoexposure) mode.

4. **Adjust the setting.**

   In general, you can use either of these three techniques:

   - Rotate the Quick Control dial to scroll through the settings.
   - Rotate the Main dial to scroll through the possible settings.
   - Press the Set button to display a screen that contains all the possible settings. In some cases, the screen contains a brief explanation or note about the option, as shown on the right in Figure 1-22. You then can choose between rotating the Main dial or pressing the Multicontroller to highlight the setting you want to use. Then press Set again to return to the Quick Control screen.

   A few controls require a slightly different approach, but don't worry; the needed steps are spelled out throughout the book.

5. **To exit Quick Control mode, press the Shutter button halfway and release it, or press the Quick Control button again.**

   You return to the normal Shooting settings display or a blank screen.

Your Windows to the World

Your camera can accept only one type of Canon or Canon-compatible lens: Electro Focus (EF) lenses. These lenses are designed to work on full-frame cameras like the 5D Mark III. The other mount that Canon currently uses is called the EF-S mount (S stands for *short back focus*), which is fitted to cropped-frame cameras like the Canon EOS 7D, 60D, and Rebel line. The EF-S mount allows the rear element of the lens to come closer to the sensor in the camera.

EF-S cameras can accept EF-S and EF lenses. However, EF cameras can accept only EF lenses. That's the cost of working with a full-frame camera. To be honest, it's largely worth it. Make sure that any lenses you buy for the 5D Mark III are EF lenses.

The lens that comes most often with the 5D Mark III is the EF 24–105mm f/4L IS USM.

All the letters are part of the lens name. EF, as already mentioned, stands for *electro focus.* L indicates it is an *L-series* lens, which are professional-level lenses (in quality and price). IS stands for *Image Stabilizer*, and USM stands for *ultrasonic motor.*

If you want to buy a non-Canon lens, check the lens manufacturer's website to find out which lenses work with Canon cameras in general and the 5D Mark III (or Canon full-frame cameras) specifically. This information is critical. For example, the Sigma 10-20mm f/4-5.6 EX DC lens is listed as being compatible with Canon cameras, but when you read the details, you find that the lens was designed exclusively for APS-C (cropped) or four-thirds cameras. Yikes! On the other hand, the 12-24mm f/4.5-4.5 DG HSM II lens *is* designed to work with full-frame cameras.

Until you get used to it, changing lenses makes you envy an octopus for its arms (still, I'll take a pass on being a floppy bag of ink-squirting jelly with a beak). You have to support the camera with one hand and use the other to hold the new lens. That leaves the need for a third to handle other lenses and lens caps.

Gripping the beast when changing lenses

The 5D Mark III is a heavy camera. You may not be able to use the same technique that you would with a smaller, lighter camera. Try both of these grips to see which one you like:

- **Grip 1 (refer to Figure 1-23):** Hold the camera's left side with your left hand and press its right side in to your body for additional support. Put your left thumb on top of the Mode dial and stretch your left pinky underneath the camera for additional grip. The camera will be facing to your right. Your left index finger will press the lens release button when necessary.

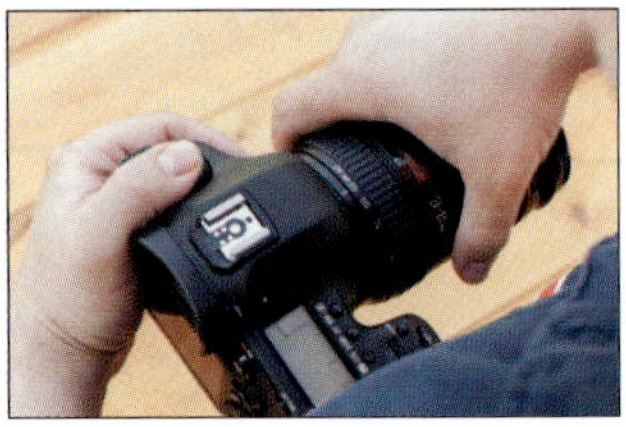

Figure 1-23: Grip 1 uses your body to help support the camera.

Use an overhand grip on the lens the way you would put your hand on a railing rail. The "C" formed by your right index finger and thumb grips the lens from the top and faces the camera body.

- **Grip 2 (refer to Figure 1-24):** This grip is similar to Grip 1 in that the camera faces to the right. However, rather than use your body for support, your left hand (repositioned) does all the heavy lifting.

  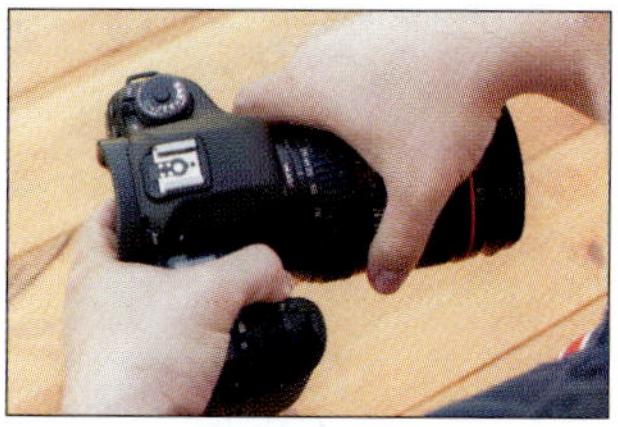

  Figure 1-24: Grip 2 uses your left hand to manhandle the camera.

  Place your left palm on the LCD panel on top of the camera. Wrap your left thumb to the front of the camera. Position this thumb to the side of the lens, about where the self-timer lamp is. Use a firm grip. The fingers on your left hand should reach down the back of the camera and grab the bottom. Your left index finger rests on the LCD monitor; use that finger for stability." (Entire sentence s/b: "Your left finger rests on the LCD monitor; use that finger for stability. You should be able to hold the entire weight of the camera with this hand.

  Now, take your right hand and place it on top of the lens, the way you would put it on a railing. Grip the lens near the lens collar (the part of the lens that's nearest the camera body). Your right thumb should be on the side of the lens nearest you. Use the knuckle on your right index finger to press in the lens release button when removing a lens. The last part sounds dodgy until you do it. Then it feels totally natural.

In both cases, try angling the front of the camera down a bit. Although it may feel awkward at first, this position helps prevent dust and other debris from getting into the camera opening. Practice so that you can attach and remove lenses without angling the camera up to see what you're doing. In fact, after some experience, you should be able to attach and remove lenses while blindfolded.

REMEMBER

By the way, if the camera is mounted on a tripod, most of the hand-holding and camera-supporting descriptions in this section are moot. The camera should be well supported by the tripod. Hold tightly to the lens, however. If you are using a lens-mounted support (monopod or other), you'll end up turning the camera instead of the lens.

Attaching a lens

Follow these steps to attach a lens to the camera body:

1. **Remove the body cap that covers the lens mount from the front of the camera.**

   Twist counterclockwise, just like you're removing a bottle cap.

This step assumes that the camera doesn't already have a lens mounted. If it does, you have to remove the existing lens first. Those instructions are next.

2. **Remove the rear lens cap (counterclockwise again).**

   The rear lens cap covers the back of the lens — the part that attaches to the camera body.

   Put this (and any other) cap in a safe, dust-free place, such as a pocket in your camera bag.

3. **Get your grip on.**

   In other words, grip the camera and lens using one of the previously described hand grips.

4. **Locate the EF lens mounting index on the camera body.**

   This marker tells you where to align the lens with the camera body when connecting the two. Your camera has an EF index, as shown earlier in Figure 1-2.

   If you buy a non-Canon lens, check the lens manual for help with this step.

5. **Align the mounting index on the lens with the one on the camera body.**

   The lens also has a mounting index. Figure 1-25 shows the one that appears on the EF 24–105mm zoom lens that Canon sells as a unit with the 5D Mark III. If you buy a different lens, the index marker may be red or some other color, so again, check the lens instruction manual.

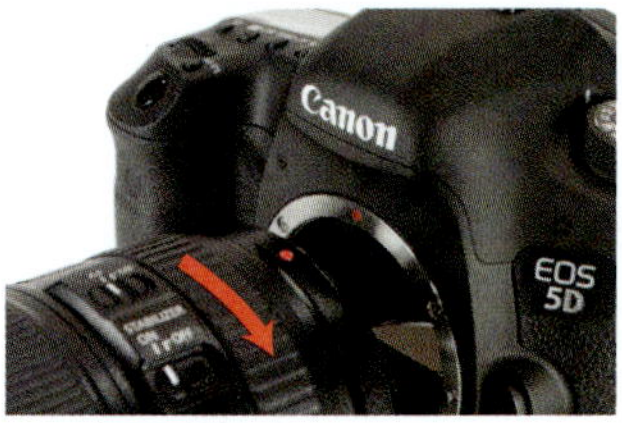

Figure 1-25: Place the lens in the lens mount with the mounting indexes aligned.

6. **While being sure to keeping the mounting indexes aligned, position the lens on the camera's lens mount.**

   When you do so, grip the lens by its rearmost collar.

   Don't touch the back of the lens with your finger or you risk leaving a smudge. You may not realize it when taking pictures, but when you get back to your computer, you might find the photos to be blurry and ruined. You should also resist the urge to stick your finger in the camera when the lens is off. You could scratch or smudge the mirror and possibly damage other parts of the camera interior with your finger.

7. **Turn the lens in a clockwise direction until the lens clicks into place.**

   In other words, turn the lens toward the lens release button, as indicated by the red arrow in Figure 1-25.

Always attach (or switch) lenses in as clean an environment as possible to reduce the risk of getting dust, dirt, and other contaminants inside the camera or lens. Changing lenses on a beach on a windy day, for example, isn't a good idea.

Removing a lens

Removing a lens can feel scarier than attaching one — like you're going to drop something. If you need to, practice while sitting on your bed. This will give you the peace of mind you need to concentrate.

When you follow these instructions, the back of the camera should face you. These steps are written from that perspective. If you hold the camera *facing* you, reverse the direction in which you turn the lens and body cap.

Follow these steps to remove a lens:

1. **Make sure that the lens cap is on the front of the lens, and have the rear lens cap (and possibly the camera body cap) handy.**
2. **Get your grip on.**

   In other words, grip the camera and lens using one of the previously suggested methods.

   Until you get the hang of it, removing a lens is a bit nerve-wracking because you don't want to drop it. Get a good grip on things before continuing.
3. **Press in the lens release button fully. (Refer to Figure 1-2.)**

   This unlocks the lens from the camera.
4. **Twist the lens toward you (away from the lens release button) until it stops turning.**

   Use your right hand to twist and support the lens. Really grab it. When it's free, it can drop out of the camera and fall, so don't let go of it.
5. **Pull out the lens and quickly put it somewhere safe.**

   Don't worry about putting the rear lens cap on the lens you just took off. While you stop and fiddle with the lens, the camera is open to the world, which includes dust and other bad things.
6. **Attach the body cap or another lens to the camera by using your right hand.**
7. **Attach the rear lens cap on the lens you removed and put it securely away.**

Zooming in and out

Unless you have a prime lens (a lens that doesn't change focal lengths), you will use the zoom ring to zoom in or out. The Canon 24-105mm f/4L lens has a zoom ring toward the base of the lens, which is shown in Figure 1-26. Turn the zoom ring clockwise (from your perspective behind the camera) to zoom out; turn it counterclockwise to zoom in.

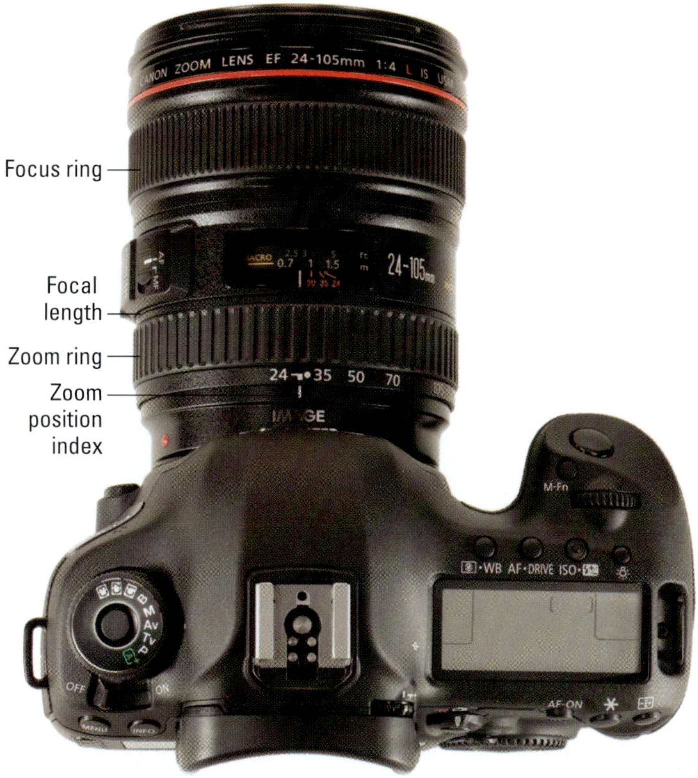

Figure 1-26: Focal lengths help indicate the effective zoom.

Focal lengths are printed on the lens's zoom ring. Read your current focal length by noting the number (extrapolate if you're between printed numbers) lined up with the zoom position index.

I am holding the camera in Figures 1-27 and 1-28 with my left hand on the zoom ring, ready to zoom in or out. This position works well for looking through the viewfinder and using autofocus.

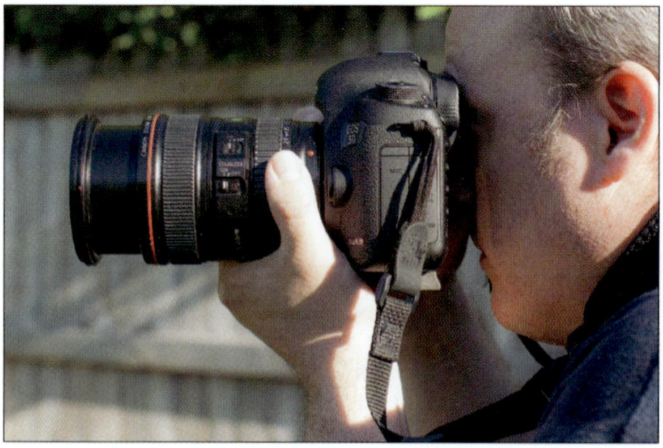

Figure 1-27: Zooming in horizontal hold.

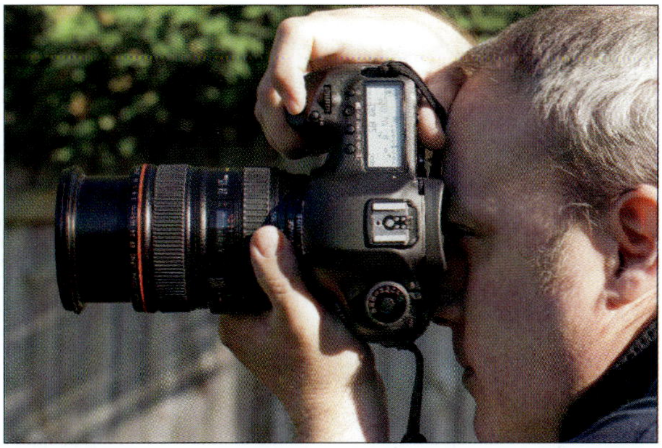

Figure 1-28: Zooming in vertical hold.

If you are manually focusing, zoom in or out first with this grip and then move your hand to the focus ring to manually focus the lens, as shown in the upcoming "Manually focusing" section.

Switching from auto to manual focus

To change to manual focus, simply switch the focus mode switch on your lens to MF, as shown in Figure 1-29.

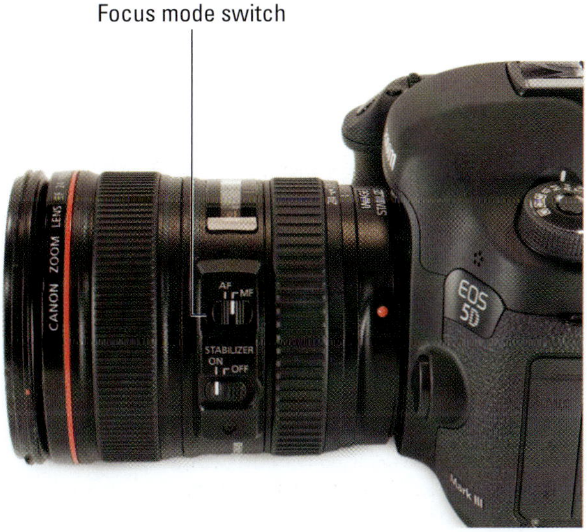

Figure 1-29: Switch to MF to take total focusing control.

Manually focusing

I encourage you to try to work on manually focusing. Nothing distinguishes good from bad photography more than out-of-focus shots, and despite how powerful the AF system is on the 5D Mark III, your own eyeballs, combined with the fantastically large and bright viewfinder on the 5D Mark III (given the right conditions), work better.

- **Close-ups:** When shooting close-ups, especially with wide apertures, nothing can beat your own ability to focus, especially if you're using a tripod. However, with steady hands and a reasonably fast shutter speed, even wiggly things like baby rabbits make a great case study for when manual focus is best. In this case (see Figure 1-30), I found that I needed the precision of manual focus because the depth of field was too small and the camera didn't always focus exactly where I wanted it to. That can sometimes be rectified by selecting a different AF Point Selection mode (and possibly choosing a specific AF point), but in this case, it was easier to switch to MF and handle it myself.

- **Really far-away subjects:** When photographing landscapes and other far-away subjects, set the focus to infinity (or thereabouts) and don't worry about it. Perfect. (This focus works for fireworks and astrophotography as well.)

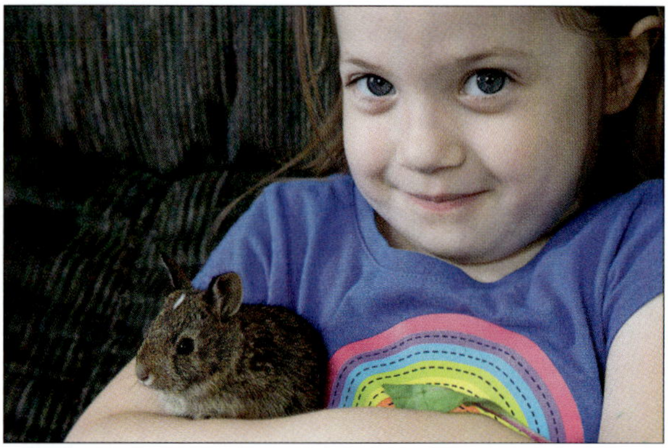

Figure 1-30: Manual focus is very precise for well-lit close-ups.

  There is a sweet spot where things are far enough away for you not to be able to tell whether something is in good focus or not. In those cases, switch to AF.

- **Bright conditions:** Don't bother trying to focus in low-light or dark conditions. You simply can't see well enough to discern the proper focal point. Switch to AF.

Manually focusing will change how you hold and support the camera. Figures 1-31 and 1-32 illustrate this point (compare to Figures 1-27 and 1-28 in which I am using the zoom ring).

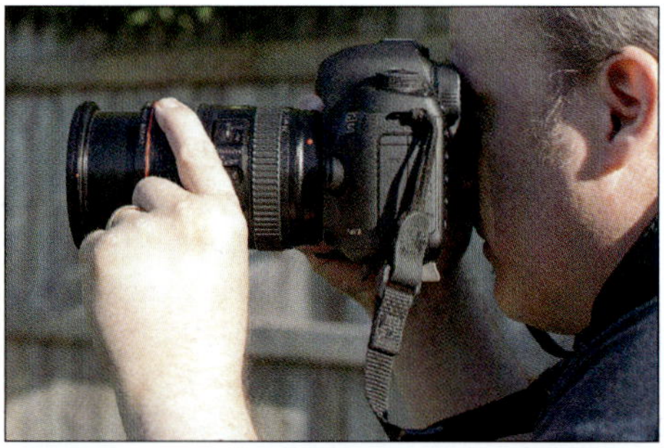

Figure 1-31: Manual focus in horizontal hold.

In Figure 1-31, I am holding the camera horizontally, and my fingers are on the zoom ring. I have finished composing the shot and am ready to focus. Don't be afraid to grab the focus ring and use your left hand to steady the camera as you focus, but let your right hand support most of the camera's weight. Figure 1-32 shows the same principle when holding the camera vertically. In that case, stiffen the fingers on your right hand as you hook them around the front of the grip. The camera can almost hang off them, which helps keep your hand from tiring too quickly.

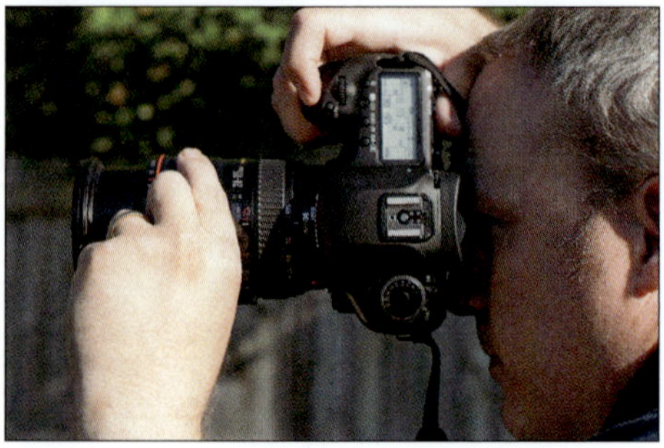

Figure 1-32: Manual focus in vertical hold.

Activating the Image Stabilizer (IS)

Turning on the Image Stabilizer is easy. Set the Stabilizer switch on your lens (see Figure 1-33) to On.

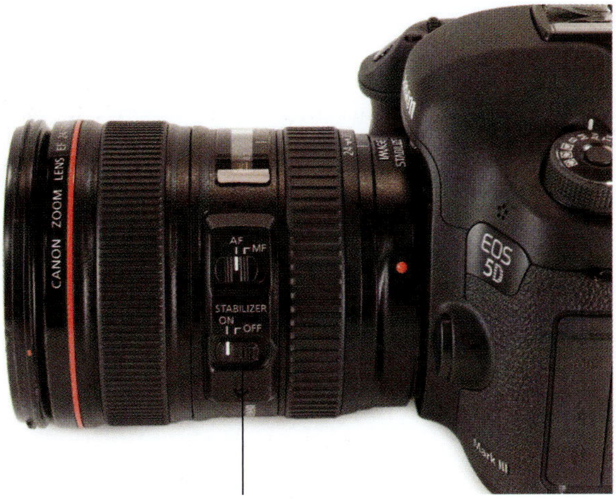

Figure 1-33: Engage the stabilizer!

For a variety of reasons (cost, necessity, and others), not all lenses have IS. Always look for IS in the lens name when shopping.

If you're used to other brands of cameras where the control is on the camera body (due to IS being within the camera as opposed to being part of the lens) or menu system, you will need to get used to using the switch on the lens.

Adjusting the Viewfinder Focus

Perched on the top-right edge of the viewfinder is a tiny black knob, labeled in Figure 1-10 and shown in close-up in Figure 1-12. This knob is officially known as a *Dioptric Adjustment control,* and you use it to adjust the magnification of the viewfinder to accommodate your eyesight.

Adjusting the viewfinder to your eyesight is critical: If you don't, scenes that appear out of focus through the viewfinder may actually be sharply focused through the lens, and vice versa.

Follow these steps to adjust your viewfinder:

1. **Turn the camera on.**
2. **Set the camera up.**

   Set the lens to AF and the Mode dial to Av, point the camera at something light (so that you can see better), and press the Shutter button halfway to initiate metering and autofocus.

You can use whatever mode you want; I like Av. This step is just meant to get the camera to display things in the viewfinder.

3. **Look through the viewfinder.**

   Concentrate on the various viewfinder elements. You can look at whatever you want. Some suggest using AF points or other elements that appear on the focusing screen, such as the spot metering circle, grid (if on), or AF area frame. I think the exposure information at the bottom of the viewfinder works just as well.

   Choose which one gives you the best chance of adjusting the viewfinder and makes you happy.

   If you're paranoid about it, after you adjust the viewfinder, focus on something near and compare how well it appears to you versus something farther away. If they match, you're golden.

4. **Rotate the Dioptric Adjustment knob until the viewfinder elements (not the scene) appear in focus.**

   Don't worry about using the lens to focus on the actual scene now; just pay attention to the sharpness of the viewfinder elements.

If your eyesight is such that you can't get anything in the viewfinder to look sharp by using the Dioptric Adjustment knob, you can buy an additional eyepiece adapter called a Dioptric Adjustment lens. This accessory, which you affix to the eyepiece, enables further adjustment of the viewfinder display. Prices range from about $15–$50, depending on the magnification you need. Look for an Eg-series adapter, which is compatible with the 5D Mark III.

Keep in mind, too, that you can opt to use the LCD monitor instead of the viewfinder to frame and preview your shots. This feature is called *Live View* shooting, which is covered in Chapter 3.

Unfortunately, you can't adjust the focus of the Live View image. However, if you have a good reading prescription (for close objects), glasses or contacts will make the Live View image sharp and clear.

Using Batteries and Memory Cards

The skills for working with batteries and memory cards are mundane but important. Read on for some tips.

The rechargeable lithium-ion batteries that the 5D Mark III uses are potentially dangerous because of their internal chemical composition (lithium). Don't freak out at that. They are durable.

However, you shouldn't crush lithium-ion batteries, overheat them, short-circuit them, hammer with or on them, use a noncompatible power source to charge them, throw them at things (they hurt!), or otherwise do things you shouldn't do with any other battery. Right. Just use common sense.

(***Note:*** This section is written with an eye toward inserting and removing a single LP-E6 battery from the camera. If you have the BG-E11 Battery Grip, you will insert and remove batteries a little differently. Please refer to the manual that comes with the BG-E11 for precise instructions.)

When working with memory cards, the most important issue is protecting your data. If you treat them with a reasonable amount of care, they will last for as long as you have your camera. If you have protective cases for your cards, use them.

You should, however, avoid bending them, setting them on the dash of your car in the summer, or messing with the data contacts. Memory cards aren't susceptible to magnetic damage, but you don't want to leave them in your pocket if you go in for an MRI. Make sure to use the locking tab to keep from accidentally erasing photos.

Inserting the battery

The key to putting the battery in your camera is to push the cream-colored lock lever out of the way as you slide in the battery. If something catches (it shouldn't), take a look so that you don't break anything. Here's how to insert the battery:

1. **Make sure the camera is off.**
2. **Slide the battery compartment cover lever toward the center of the camera.**

   The spring-loaded cover should pop open, as shown in Figure 1-34.

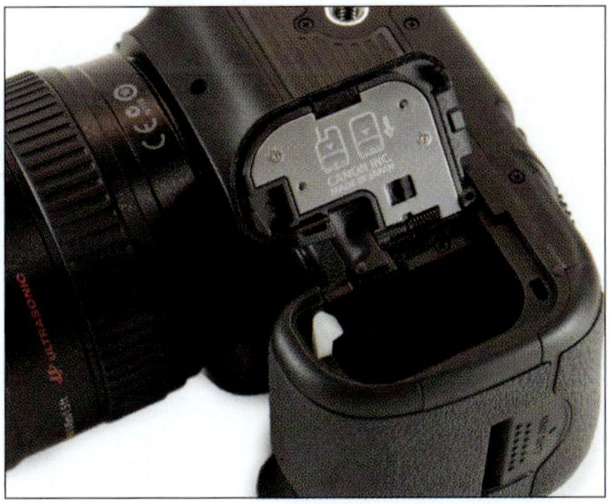

Figure 1-34: When you get enough practice, you won't even need to look.

3. **Put the battery in the camera.**

   The battery goes in contacts first with the flat side facing the center of the camera. You can put the battery in straight, but I like to gently angle in the side of the battery closest to the lock lever so that it shoves the lever out of the way.

4. **Press the battery in until the lever pops out over the battery and it locks in place. See Figure 1-35.**

   If the battery doesn't go all the way down, you may have it in incorrectly. Pull it out and double-check the orientation of the contacts.

5. **Close the battery compartment cover.**

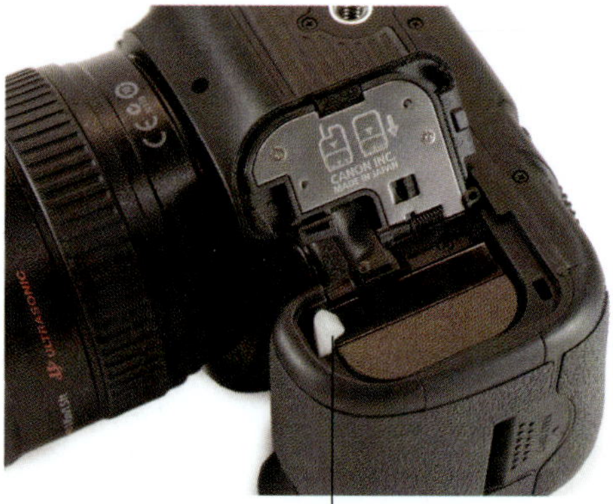

Figure 1-35: The lever holds the battery in place.

Removing the battery

The key to removing a battery is pressing the lock lever with your thumb or finger. If you look at the battery compartment when it's empty, you can see the spring that pushes up on the battery. When it's unlocked, the battery pops right up. Here's how to remove it:

1. **Make sure the camera is off.**
2. **Slide the battery cover lever toward the center of the camera.**

   The cover pops open.

3. **Carefully use your finger to push the lock lever in until the battery pops up.**

   See Figure 1-36.

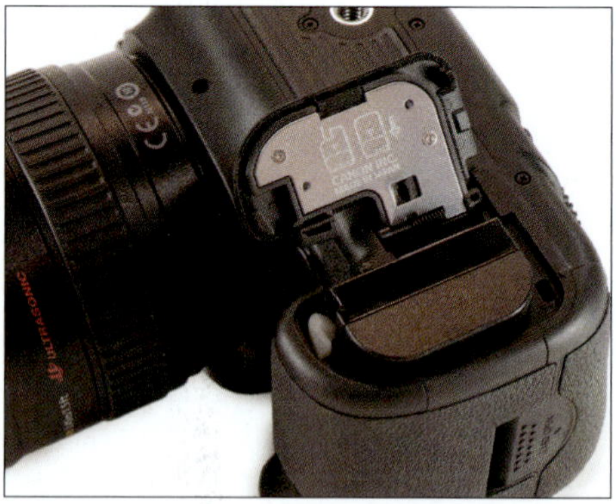

Figure 1-36: The battery pops up when freed from the clutches of the release lever.

4. **Pull the battery out of the camera.**

   If you need to continue shooting, put a fresh battery in and go to Step 5, or just continue to Step 5.

5. **Close the battery compartment cover.**

When you're not using your 5D Mark III, take the battery out and store it in a cool, dry place. It will lose charge over time. That's unavoidable. According to Canon, you should not leave the battery in the camera or plugged in to the recharger, constantly charging. Instead, charge the battery the day before or the day you plan to use it.

Checking battery power

You can find battery status indicators all over the camera. Look for the icon in the following places: the viewfinder; when shooting with Live View (look on the LCD monitor); as part of the shooting information display (seen by pressing the Info button); and when shooting a movie.

You can check the battery level, with a few added informational benefits, by following these steps:

1. **Press the Menu button.**
2. **Navigate to Setup Menu 3.**
3. **Highlight Battery info., as shown in Figure 1-37, and press the Set button.**
4. **Behold, the majesty of Battery Info (see Figure 1-38).**

   As I said, there is a lot of information here:

   - *Battery type:* This shows you whether you're using the standard LP-E6 battery (for the rechargeable lithium-ion batteries), AA batteries, or an external power source (via the AC Adapter Kit ACK-E6).
   - *Remaining capacity:* The total charge left, as a percentage of the original.

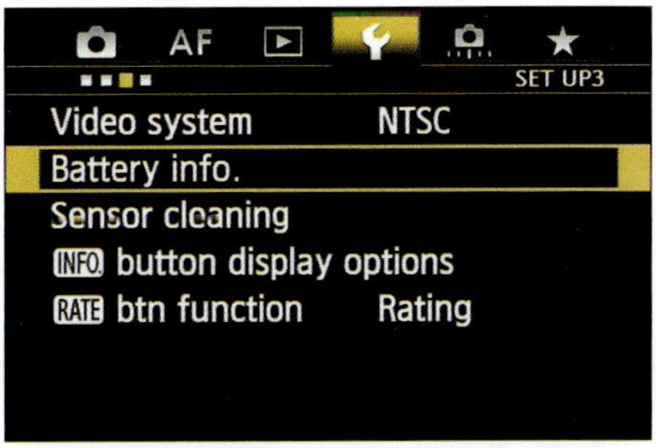

Figure 1-37: Get into the habit of checking battery information.

- *Shutter count:* How many photos you have taken with the battery.
- *Recharge performance:* This display shows you whether the battery is wearing out. Canon recommends buying a new battery when the performance is down to one level.

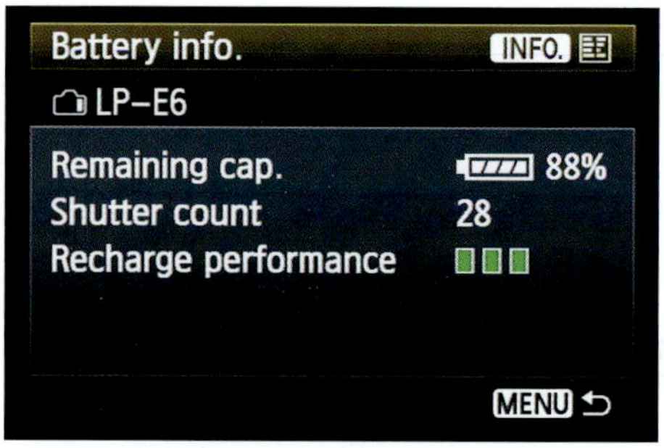

Figure 1-38: The details are very helpful.

5. **If you like, register the battery.**

   If you have more than one battery, registering them (up to six) enables you to tell one from another so that you can track them and try to use them evenly (instead of grabbing the same battery over and over). You can do this because Canon has embedded a microchip in the battery which, among other things, contains an internal serial number.

   Press the Info button on the screen shown in Figure 1-38 to register the battery in the camera's database.

6. **Press Menu to exit.**

Inserting a memory card

WARNING!

Take care when you're inserting the memory card. Make sure that it's facing the right direction and that you slide it into its compartment smoothly and straight. Here's how:

1. **Make sure the memory card access lamp isn't lit.**

   You can turn the camera off if you want, but you don't have to as long as the lamp isn't lit. See Figure 1-39. If the lamp is shining (see Figure 1-39), a card is in the camera and in use.

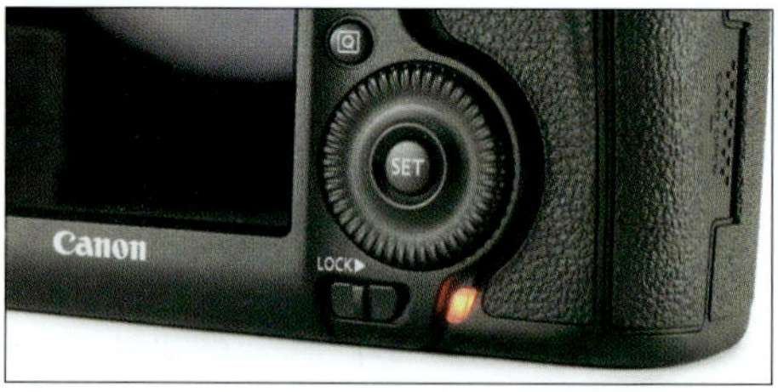

Figure 1-39: The red light indicates card activity.

2. **Slide the memory card cover toward the *back* of the camera (see the top image in Figure 1-40) to open the cover.**

   The spring-loaded cover should pop open (see the bottom image in Figure 1-40).

3. **Insert the memory card into the camera.**

   If a memory card is already in the camera, remove it by following the next sequence of steps (in the upcoming section).

   The data contacts (on Secure Digital, or SD, cards) or pin holes (on Compact Flash, or CF) go in first, and the card labels (both types) should face you. Secure Digital High Capacity (SDHC) cards have a notched corner, which should be oriented as the top corner.

   Try not to drop an SD card into the CF card slot.

4. **Press the card in all the way.**

   CF cards slide in and then resist. You're feeling pushback from the card eject button. Continue pushing (firmly but gently) until the eject button pops all the way up.

   With SD cards, you will feel a spring pushing back. Push until you feel or hear a slight click as the card locks in place. If you don't feel it latch, pull the card out and check to see whether it's oriented correctly.

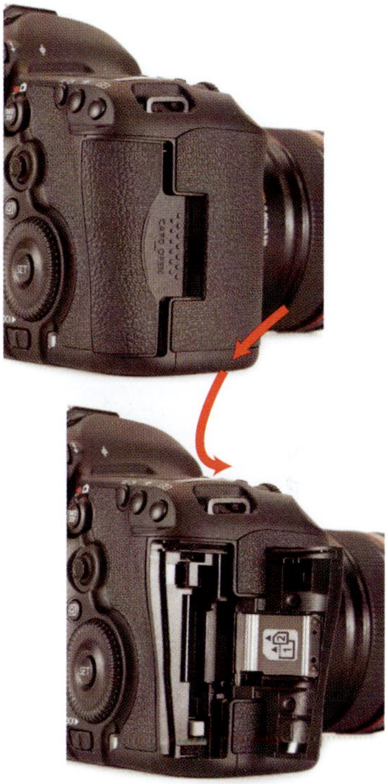

Figure 1-40: The memory card cover slides back and springs open.

5. **Swing the memory card cover closed and push it in to lock it.**

Removing a memory card

Removing your memory card is easier than putting it in because you don't have to line anything up or worry about getting things in upside down and backward. Here's how to go about it:

1. **Make sure that the memory card access lamp is not lit. Refer to Figure 1-39.**

   If it is, wait a moment. You can turn the camera off if you want, but there is no reason to as long as the card isn't being written to.

2. **Slide the memory card cover toward the rear of the camera to open the cover.**

The spring-loaded cover should pop open.

3. **Depending on which card you are removing, follow these steps:**

   a. For CF cards: Firmly push the card eject button. The card should push upward enough for you to grab it. Nothing pops or clicks.

   b. For SD cards: Push down on the memory card and then release. The card will give a bit, which releases the catch (which you can't see) and then springs up so that you can grab it.

4. **Pull out the card.**

   REMEMBER

   At this point, put in a fresh card or leave it empty. When you're done transferring photos, put the card back in the camera. This protects the card, keeps you from spilling something on it, makes it harder to lose, and lets you take photos at a moment's notice.

5. **Swing the memory card cover closed and push it in to lock it.**

Cleaning the Camera Sensor

You've no doubt noticed that your camera displays a "Sensor Cleaning" message every time you turn your camera on or off. This alert tells you that the camera is automatically performing a maintenance step that's designed to shake off dust particles that have made their way into the camera and landed on the sensor (actually, they landed on the low-pass filter that comprises the front layer of the sensor, but that's splitting hairs).

If you don't see these alerts, or you want to configure how the camera is cleaned, follow these steps:

1. **Press the Menu button.**
2. **Navigate to the Setup Menu 3, choose Sensor Cleaning, as shown in Figure 1-41, and then press the Set button.**
3. **Highlight a cleaning option (see Figure 1-42) and press the Set button.**

   The options are

   - *Auto Cleaning:* Choose Enable or Disable (followed by another press of the Set button) to turn auto cleaning on or off.

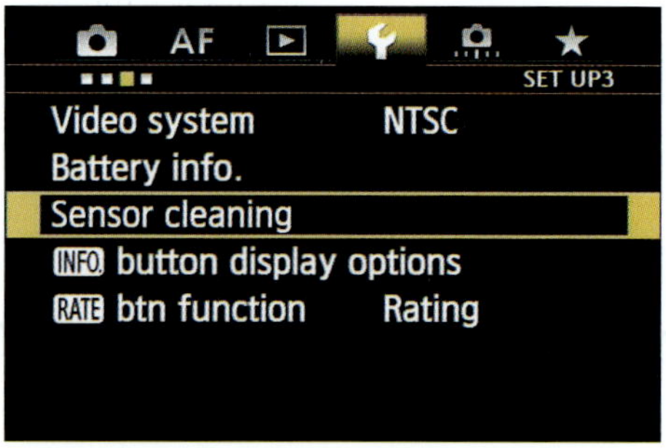

Figure 1-41: When your sensor feels a bit grungy, clean it.

I recommend keeping the Auto cleaning option on Enable. I don't see many good reasons to disable this feature unless you're continually turning the camera on and off, in which case the cleaning delay can be annoying.

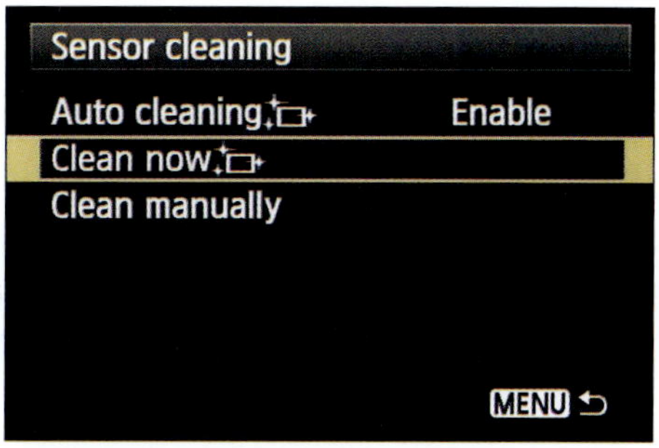

Figure 1-42: Please tip the cleaning staff.

- *Clean Now:* Confirm your decision (highlight OK and press the Set button) to have the camera immediately clean the sensor.

  Don't overdo it. Cleaning more won't necessarily do a better job. If something is stuck on, you should consider taking the camera in to be serviced.

- *Clean Manually:* This is the scary, freaky-deaky option. Do not choose this unless you're sure of yourself and have practiced on something maybe a little less valuable than the 5D Mark III.

  The 5D Mark III is an expensive beast. Even if you are a professional, cleaning the sensor yourself can be nerve wracking, and costly if you make a mistake. If you're in any doubt, take your camera to a good repair shop and have the sensor professionally cleaned.

  If you decide to continue, confirm your decision (highlight OK and then press Set), and wait for the mirror to lock up. Cln will appear on the LCD panel.

  Gently clean the sensor, either with a blower, a brush, or swab — whatever your preferred method is. When you're finished, turn the camera off to reset the mirror. Immediately attach a lens or put the body cover cap on to protect the camera's delicate inner workings.

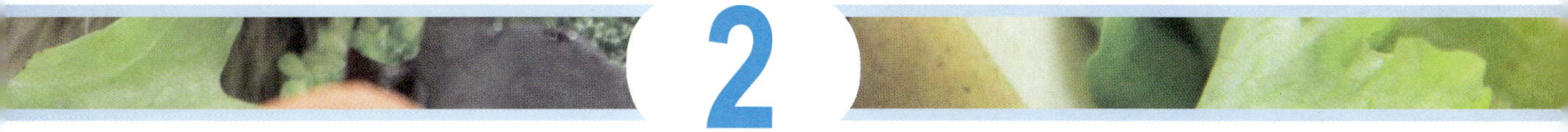

2

Choosing Essential Camera Settings

In This Chapter

- Getting the most out of setting up your camera
- Choosing a shooting mode
- Understanding drive modes
- Setting photo size, quality, and aspect ratio
- Choosing between RAW and JPEG
- Deciding how to decide

You've got your 5D Mark III out of the box. Fannntastic. Don't be afraid to run out and take as many photos as you want without knowing anything more than how to turn your camera on and press the Shutter button. It's all good. That experience will be valuable and set you on the path of knowing what sorts of things bother you and what you might want to change. This chapter is designed to help you make those initial connections between what you want and how the camera comes set up.

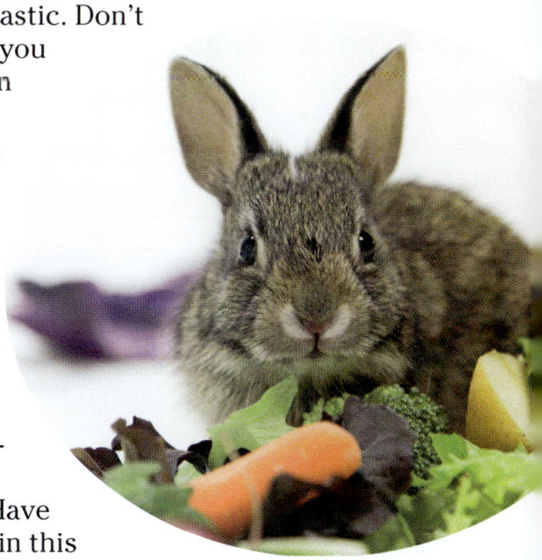

You'll probably be familiar with some of the upcoming information. You might have heard of a few of the shooting modes or understand the general idea of setting photo size and quality. That's good! Each camera is ultimately a unique learning experience, however. Have fun with the options, features, and settings explained in this chapter. There's no test.

Setting Up Your Camera

One of the many advantages of investing in a modern dSLR like the EOS 5D Mark III is that you can customize its performance to suit the way *you* like to shoot. Later chapters explain options related to actual picture taking, such as those that affect flash behavior and autofocusing. The rest of this section details options related to setting up the camera. Some options, such as setting the date and time, you may only perform once. You may conduct other actions, such as formatting a memory card, repeatedly.

This section contains many cross-references. This is intentional. I list every menu in these sections so that you have a thorough reference. Those that I cover in more detail in other parts of the book have a quick description followed by a cross-reference telling you where you can find more information. With this approach, I avoid having to fully cover topics two or three times but can still give you information that isn't missing half the pieces.

Setup Menu 1

At the risk of being conventional, start your camera customization by opening Setup Menu 1, shown in Figure 2-1.

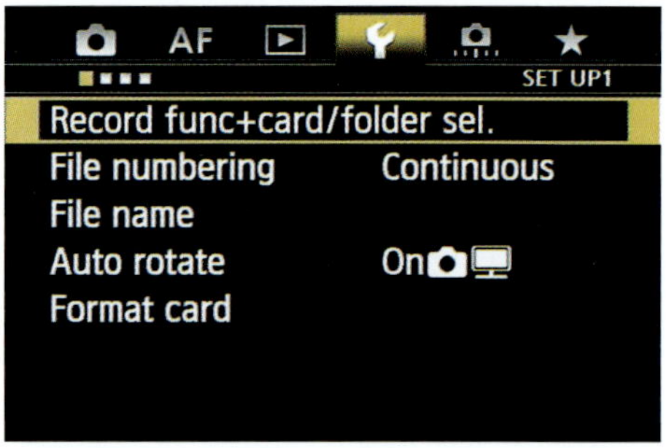

Figure 2-1: Options on Setup Menu 1 deal mainly with photos and the memory card.

Record Function+Card/Folder Selection

Use this option (see Figure 2-2) to create and select folders. Also, use it to choose a memory card to record to or play back from when you have more than one in the camera. You can also set up how the camera uses multiple cards (one at a time; automatically switch; record to both separately; or record to both identically). For more information on creating and using folders, see Chapter 10. For information on using multiple cards, see Chapter 11.

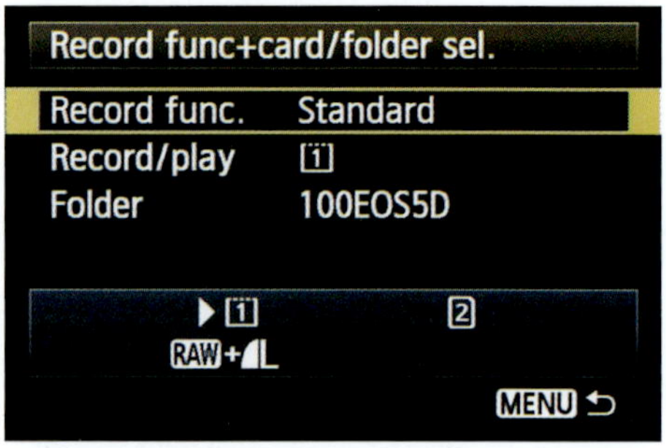

Figure 2-2: This is a dual-purpose screen; use it to work with folders and cards.

File Numbering

This option enables you to configure how files are numbered, which I cover in depth in Chapter 10.

File Name

Use this option to create and choose different filename prefixes (see Figure 2-3). See Chapter 10 for more information.

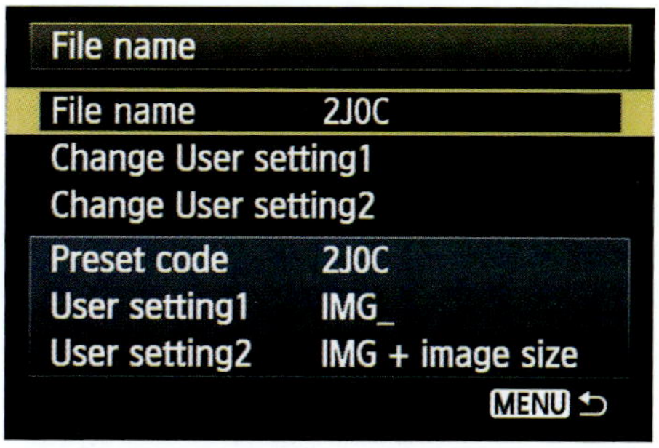

Figure 2-3: Take advantage of the one built-in and two customizable name prefixes.

Auto Rotate

Photos include information that indicates whether the camera was oriented in the vertical or horizontal position when you shot them. Then, when you view the picture on the camera monitor or on your computer, the image is automatically rotated to the correct orientation. (Ideally.)

To automatically rotate images both in the camera monitor and on your computer monitor, stick with the default setting. In the menu, this setting is represented by On followed by a camera icon and a monitor icon. If you want the rotation to occur just on your computer and not on the camera, select the second On setting marked with the computer monitor symbol but not the camera symbol. To disable rotation for both devices, choose Off.

Note, though, that the camera may record the wrong orientation data for pictures that you take with the camera pointing directly up or down. Also, whether your computer can read the rotation data in the picture file depends on the software you use; the programs bundled with the camera can perform the auto rotation.

Format Card

The first time you insert a new memory card into the camera, use this option to format the card. (Formatting is a maintenance function that wipes out any existing data on the card and prepares it for use by the camera.)

When you select the Format Card option and press the Set button, you're shown the Format Card screen (see Figure 2-4).

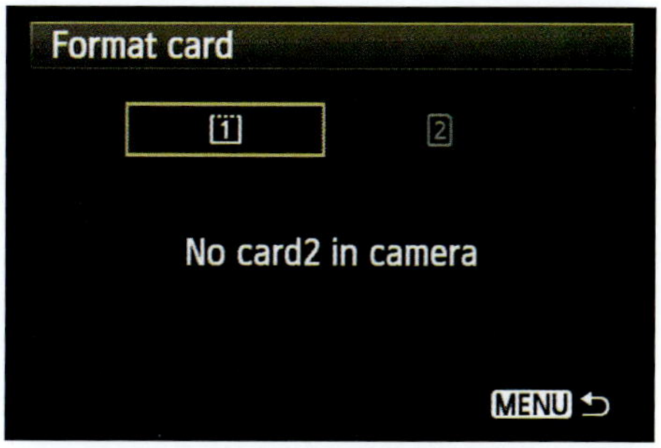

Figure 2-4: If you work with one card, you see this screen.

If you have more than one card in the camera, you need to choose which one to format. Use the Quick Control dial to quickly scroll back and forth between the cards (see Figure 2-5), or use the Multicontroller to select the card you want to format.

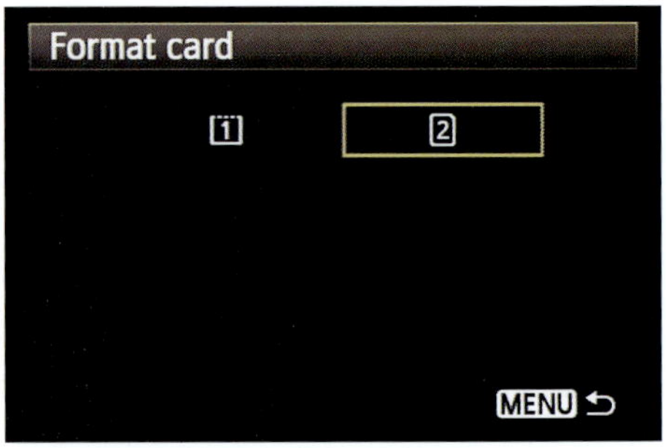

Figure 2-5: If you use two cards, both are selectable.

WARNING!

If you're working with more than one card in the camera at the same time, be absolutely sure to format the right card. If you make a mistake and format a card with data that you haven't saved to a computer yet, you will lose it. Remember, Card 1 refers to the large Compact Flash (CF) memory card. Card 2 refers to the smaller Secure Digital (SD) card.

If you are formatting an SD card, you can opt to perform a normal card formatting process or a *low-level* formatting (see Figure 2-6). The latter gives your memory card a deeper level of cleansing than ordinary formatting and thus takes longer to perform. Normally, a regular formatting will do. Press the Erase button to toggle the low-level format option on and off.

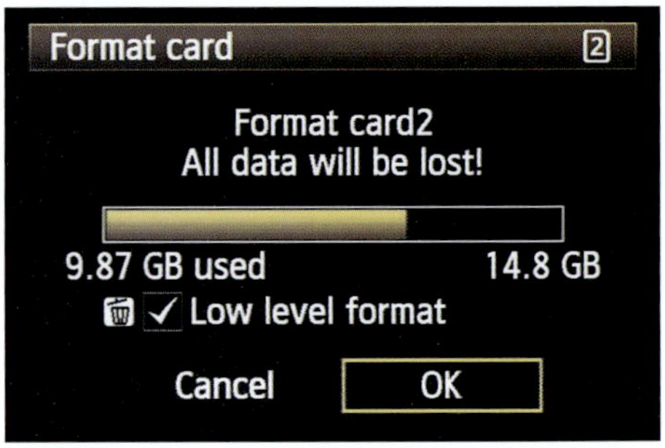

Figure 2-6: You can format SD cards more thoroughly.

In either case, you are shown the card's overall capacity and how much is used.

WARNING!

If you used your card in another device, such as a digital music player, be sure to copy those files to your computer before you format the card. You lose *all* data on the card when you format it, not just picture files.

Eye-Fi Settings

If you have an Eye-Fi card inserted, you see this menu. It enables you to set up your Eye-Fi card on a wireless network. See Chapter 11 for more information on what Eye-Fi is.

Setup Menu 2

Setup Menu 2, as shown in Figure 2-7, offers an additional batch of customization options

Auto Power Off

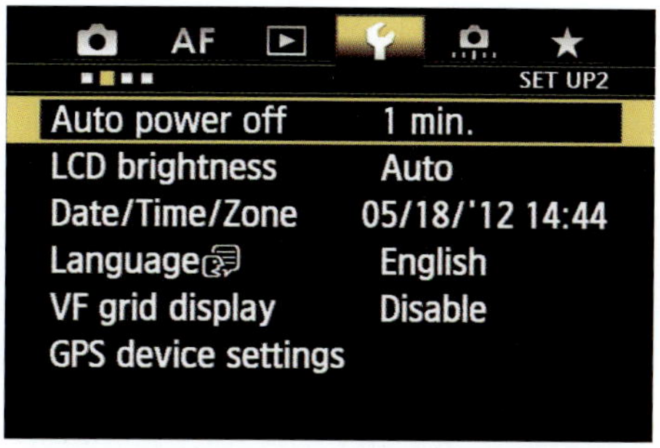

Figure 2-7: Setup Menu 2 offers more ways to customize camera operations.

To help save battery power, your camera automatically powers down after a certain period of inactivity. By default, the shutdown happens after 30 seconds, but you can change the shutdown delay to 1, 2, 4, 8, or 15 minutes. Or you can disable auto shutdown altogether by selecting the Off setting. See Chapter 10 for more information on this option.

LCD Brightness

Use this option to adjust the LCD monitor brighter or darker. Figure 2-8 shows the LCD brightness screen with the control set to Auto. This is the default and should work in most situations.

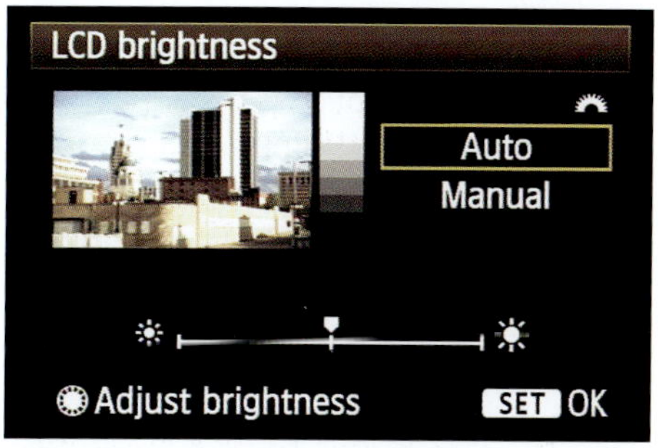

Figure 2-8: The first photo on your memory card (or selected folder) is displayed.

Despite the fact that Auto implies total automatic control, it is possible to adjust the monitor brightness even when set to Auto. Use the Quick Control dial to increase or decrease the brightness by one step.

If you want to take total manual control, highlight Manual by using the Main dial or Multicontroller and press the Set button. Then use the Quick Control dial to adjust the monitor brightness more precisely, as shown in Figure 2-9. Press the Set button to finish the job and return to Setup Menu 2.

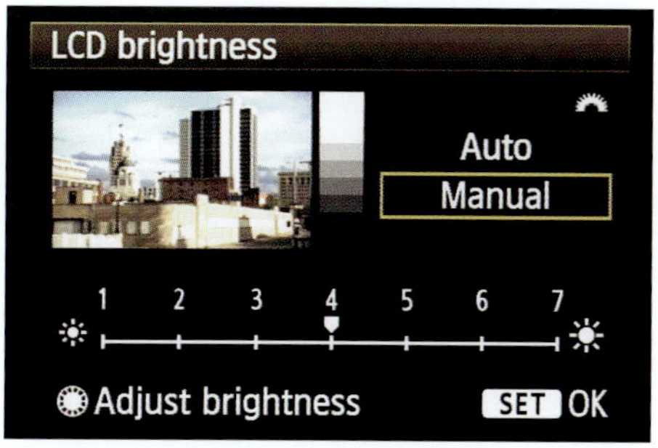

Figure 2-9: Notice the finer degree of control when manually adjusting the brightness.

WARNING!

The camera displays a picture from your memory card to help you adjust the monitor's brightness; if the card is empty, you see a black box instead. The problem is, what you see displayed may not be an accurate rendition of the actual exposure of your image. Crank up the monitor brightness, for example, and an underexposed photo may look just fine.

Keeping the brightness at its default center position is a good idea unless you're shooting in very bright or dark conditions. As an alternative, you can gauge exposure by displaying a histogram tool (explained in Chapter 5) when reviewing your images.

Date/Time/Zone

When you turn on your camera for the very first time, it automatically displays this option and asks you to set the date, time, and time zone.

TIP

Keeping the date/time/time zone accurate is important because that information is recorded as part of each photo file. In your photo browser, you can then see when you shot an image and, equally helpful, search for images by the date they were taken.

To set this data, follow these steps:

1. **Highlight Date/Time/Zone from Setup Menu 2.**
2. **Press the Set button.**

   You are presented with a busy screen (see Figure 2-10), which has the date and time broken up into discrete fields. They are listed in this order by default:

   - **Date:** Day, month, year
   - **Time:** Hours (from 1 to 24), minutes (from 1-60), and seconds (from 1 to 60)

   You can change this order, however. To do so, highlight mm/dd/yy (your order may be different), press the Set button, and then use the Quick Control dial to switch the setting.

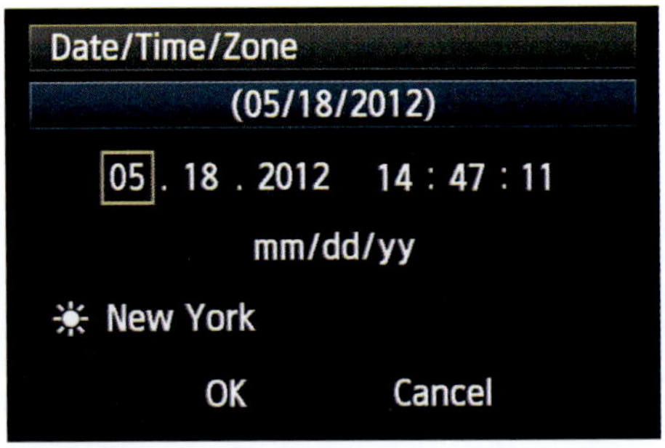

Figure 2-10: Carefully enter each date and time element.

3. **Highlight a field to change and press the Set button.**

   Use the Quick Control dial or Multicontroller to change fields before you press Set.

4. **Use the Quick Control dial or Multicontroller to change the value.**
5. **Press the Set button to lock the change in.**

6. **Rinse and repeat.**

   Return to Step 3 and repeat Steps 3–5 for each data field you want to update until you're done setting the date and time.

7. **To update the time zone, highlight the place name (see Figure 2-11) and press the Set button.**

8. **Use the Quick Control dial to switch locations.**

   The current difference between that time zone and Universal Time (the time at 0 degrees longitude) is shown on the screen.

9. **Press the Set button.**

10. **(Optional) Set daylight saving time.**

    If you are in a time zone that does not observe daylight saving time, highlight the small sun symbol, press the Set button, use the Quick Control dial to change the icon to Off, and then press Set.

11. **Highlight OK and press the Set button to return to the main menu.**

    Or, if you like, highlight Cancel and press the Set button. Doing so aborts any changes.

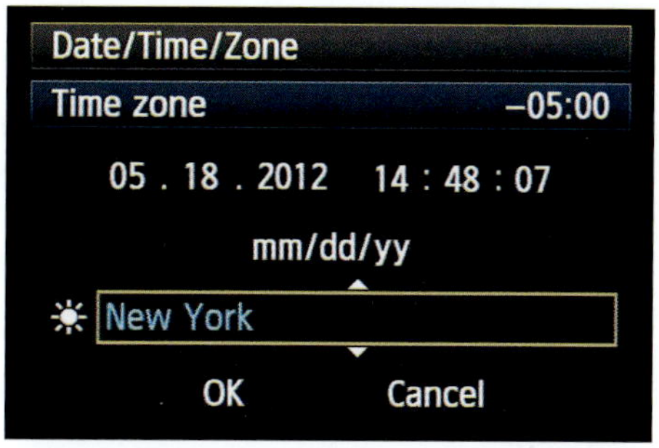

Figure 2-11: Choose a city in the same time zone that you're in.

Language

Highlight the language of your choice and press the Set button to set the camera's interface language (see Figure 2-12).

If you change your language (intentionally or by accident) to something freaky, you'll appreciate the little speech bubble icon next to the Language setting for those times when you can't read the word for *Language*.

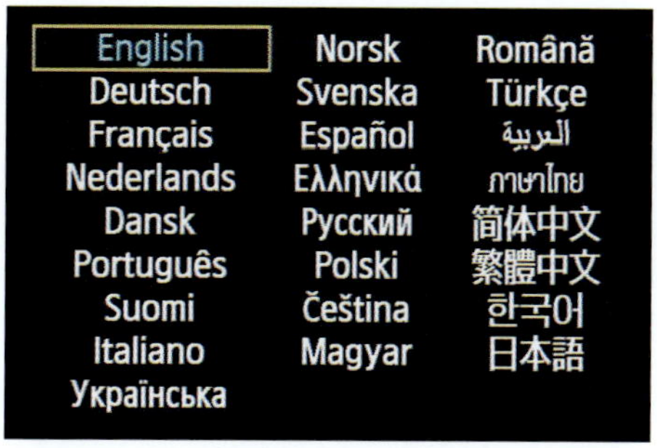

Figure 2-12: Choose the one you can read.

VF Grid Display

This option turns the viewfinder grid on or off. This option has two settings: Enable and Disable. When enabled, an alignment grid appears in the viewfinder, as shown in Figure 2-13. Use it to help you position objects in the frame. This grid can also help you keep the camera level with respect to objects in the scene (such as the horizon).

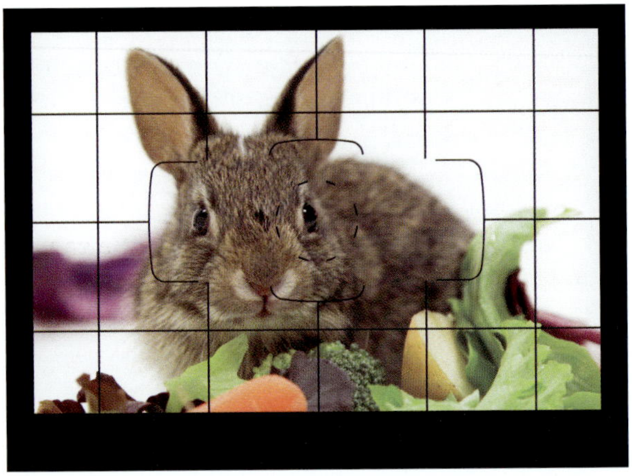

Figure 2-13: The viewfinder grid is a great tool to use.

GPS Device Settings

Set up an external GPD receiver (the Canon GP-E2), to receive Global Positioning System (GPS) information and attach it to a photo. See Chapter 11 for more information about using GPS with photos.

This menu item does not appear unless you have the proper external hardware connected to your camera.

Setup Menu 3

Setup Menu 3, shown in Figure 2-14, contains the following options.

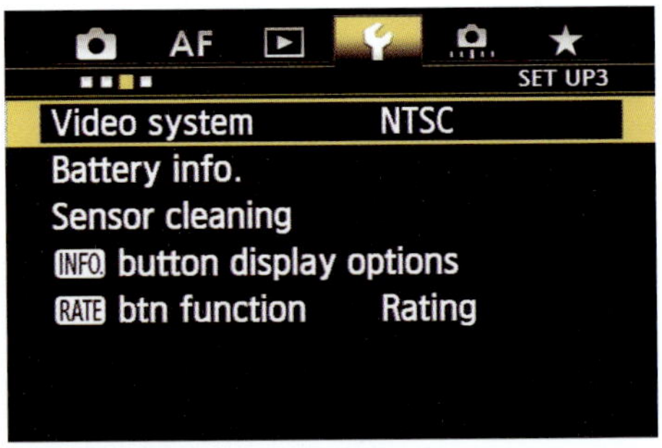

Figure 2-14: Yet another Setup menu (third time's the charm).

Video System

This option is related to viewing your images and movies on a television or other device using the provided Stereo AV Cable (USB on the end that connects to the camera; video and audio RCA connectors go to the TV). Select NTSC if you live in North America or other countries that adhere to the National Television System Committee (NTSC) video standard; select PAL for playback in areas that use Phase Alternating Line encoding.

If you connect your 5D Mark III using a High-Definition Multimedia Interface (HDMI) cable, this setting has no effect. I just stepped into my living room, asked my son to pause his Wii game, and tested it.

Battery Information

Select this option to scope out the battery's current charge, shutter count since last change, and recharge performance. You can also register your batteries to the camera (see Chapter 1 for how to register your batteries).

Sensor Cleaning

This option controls when the camera cleans the sensor. You can clean it automatically anytime, and if the camera is not in Scene Intelligent Auto mode, you can clean the sensor manually. For more information, please turn to Chapter 1.

Info Button Display Options

To control which displays are shown when you press the Info button, select this option. For more information, see Chapter 10.

RATE Button Function

This option toggles the behavior of the Rate button between rating a photo and protecting it. Rating and protecting photos are covered in Chapter 5.

Communication Settings

This menu appears if you have the Canon WFT-E7 Wireless File Transmitter attached to your camera. This unit provides a pretty powerful and attractive Canon-branded alternative to Eye-Fi. It connects to the USB port on the left side of the 5D Mark III and is attached underneath via the tripod socket.

Setup Menu 4

Setup Menu 4, shown in Figure 2-15, contains the following options.

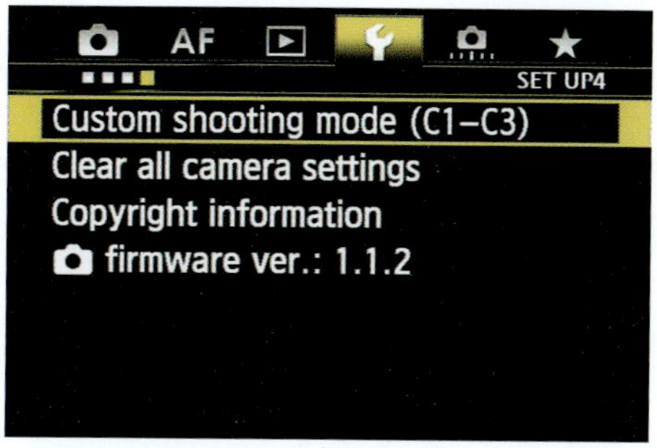

Figure 2-15: The final Setup menu has some advanced features.

Custom Shooting Mode (C1-C3)

Register (Canon's fancy term for save) up to three unique Custom Shooting modes in the camera that you can recall by selecting C1, C2, or C3 from the Mode dial. This feature enables you to set up the camera for different situations. For example, you can create a landscape, portrait, and macro mode, or action, stills, and general photography modes. The sky's the limit. See Chapter 10 for details on how to set up custom modes.

Clear All Camera Settings

Select this option to clear all camera settings. That sounds easy. However, keep in mind that the following settings remain *unchanged*:

- **Flash Function Settings:** In Shooting Menu 1; use Clear Flash Settings or Clear All Speedlite Custom Functions to clear the flash.
- **Date/Time/Zone:** In Setup Menu 2; cannot be cleared unless you go in and reset each data field to something nonsensical.
- **Language:** In Setup Menu 2; cannot be cleared.
- **Video System:** In Setup Menu 3; remains unchanged.
- **Custom Shooting Modes:** In Setup Menu 4; to clear, select the Clear Settings command from the Custom Shooting Mode option. See Chapter 11.
- **Copyright Information:** Also in Setup Menu 4. Clearing the camera doesn't delete this information. You must use the Delete Copyright Information command. See Chapter 11 for more details about entering copyright information.
- **Custom Functions:** In the Custom Functions menu; use the Clear All Custom Functions command to clear all Custom Functions except Custom Controls (which must be separately cleared). See Chapter 10 for more information on Custom Functions.
- **My Menu:** In My Menu; select the Delete All Items command to clear My Menu, or Delete item/items to delete specific items. See Chapter 10 for more information on My Menu.
- **Time code:** In Shooting Menu 4 (Movie); time code settings are not cleared when the camera is reset.

Copyright Information

Enter the appropriate copyright information by using this option. This information is embedded in each photo you take. You can enter a name and other important details. See Chapter 10 for more information on entering copyright information.

Firmware Version

This menu item tells you the version number of the camera firmware (internal operating software). As I write this sentence, the 5D Mark III's current firmware version is 1.1.2 (see Figure 2-15). Camera manufacturers often change the firmware to solve problems, fix bugs, and sometimes add new features.

With a memory card properly prepared, press the Set button with Firmware Version highlighted to begin the update process.

Keeping your camera firmware up-to-date is important, so visit the Canon website (`www.canon.com`) regularly to find out whether your camera sports the latest version. Follow the instructions given on the website to download and install updated firmware if needed.

More customization options

Shooting Menu 1 offers two more basic setup options:

- **Beep:** By default, your camera beeps after certain operations, such as after it sets focus when you use autofocusing. If you're doing top-secret surveillance and need the camera to hush up, set this option to Off.
- **Release Shutter without Card:** Setting this option to Disable prevents shutter-button release when no memory card is in the camera. If you turn on the option, you can take a picture and then review the results for a few seconds in the camera monitor. The image isn't stored anywhere, however; it's only temporary.

  In case you're wondering about the point of this option, it's designed for use in camera stores, enabling salespeople to demonstrate cameras without having to keep a memory card in every model. Unless that feature somehow suits your purposes, keep this option set to Disable.

Adding a final level of customization choices, the My Menu feature does just what its name implies: You can create a personalized menu that contains up to six functions from the existing menus. Then, instead of hunting through all the other menus to find settings that you use frequently, you can access the settings quickly just by displaying My Menu. Chapter 10 shows you how to take advantage of this terrific feature that eliminates burrowing down through menus to find options and change settings.

Selecting a Shooting Mode

The very first picture-taking setting to consider is the shooting mode (sometimes called the exposure mode), which you select via the Mode dial. Your choice determines how much control you have over two critical exposure settings — aperture and shutter speed — as well as many other options, including those related to color and flash photography. To change the mode, press down on the Mode dial lock-release button while turning the dial.

The shooting modes are

- **A+ (Scene Intelligent Auto):** Scene Intelligent Auto is the 5D Mark III's fully automatic shooting mode. Use it to turn control over to the camera. See Chapter 3 for more information.
- **P (Program AE):** Think of Program AE (AE stands for auto exposure) mode as a bridge between Scene Intelligent Auto and the more manual shooting modes. Although the camera determines the exposure settings, you have much more control over different functions, such as the AF mode, metering, and so forth. You can also shift the program by changing which combination of aperture and shutter speed the camera uses in a given situation.

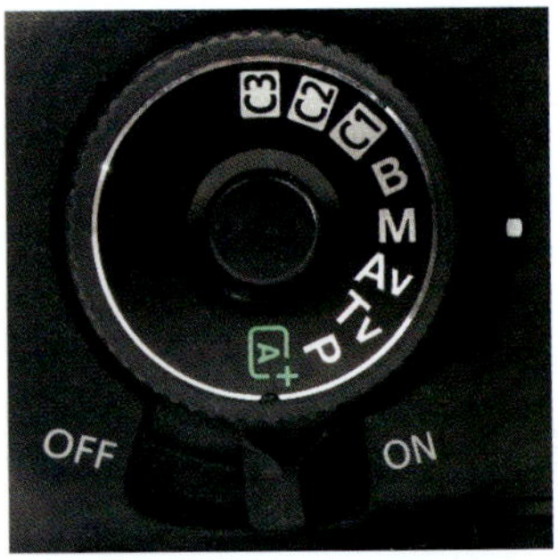

Figure 2-16: Select a shooting mode from the Mode dial.

- **Tv (Shutter-Priority AE):** In Shutter-priority AE mode, you set the shutter speed, and the camera works around that to get the right exposure. In all other aspects, the camera is under your full control.
- **Av (Aperture-Priority AE):** Aperture-priority AE is similar to the Tv Shooting mode, only you set the aperture.
- **M (Manual):** In the manual exposure shooting mode, you are responsible for all exposure settings.
- **B (Bulb):** This special shooting mode opens the shutter for as long as you hold the Shutter button down.
- **C1, C2, and C3:** These are Custom Shooting modes. They enable you to save camera settings in any of the three dial positions for recall later. See Chapter 10 for more information.

You may notice that there isn't a movie mode. To shoot movies, you must first set the Live View Shooting/Movie Shooting switch to Movie. You can be in any shooting mode.

Here's one very important and often misunderstood aspect of the exposure modes: Although your access to exposure and color controls, as well as to some other advanced camera features, depends on the setting of the Mode dial, it has *no* bearing on your *focusing* choices. You can choose manual focusing or autofocusing in any mode, assuming that your lens offers autofocusing. (Chapter 1 shows you how to set the lens to manual or autofocusing.)

All shooting modes are found on the Mode dial. Change modes by depressing and holding down the center of the Mode dial to unlock it while turning the knob to the mode of your choice. You have *no other way* to change shooting modes.

Choosing a Drive Mode

The 5D Mark III has different drive modes that control what happens when you press the shutter button. You can record a single photo or a series of continuous shots, take a picture after a short delay, use a remote, and engage in silent shooting.

The term *drive mode* harkens back to the days of film, when, if you wanted something faster than a single-frame shooting, you had to install a fancy motorized *drive* to speed the film through the camera. Now, of course, motorized drives and film have nothing to do with how fast you can take photos. Instead, your frame rate has to do with the number of pixels the camera sensor has and the rate at which data can be read, processed, and stored from them.

All drive modes explained in the following sections are available in all shooting modes on the 5D Mark III.

Single Shooting

This setting, which is the default in all shooting modes, records a single image each time you press the Shutter button.

This setting's main strength is that you can press the Shutter button without worrying about firing off ten shots. The setting's weaknesses fall into two categories. First, you must press the Shutter button repeatedly if you want to take a string of photos. Second, it's hard to capture fleeting moments if all you're doing is taking one plodding photo at a time.

Continuous Shooting

Continuous Shooting (sometimes known as *burst mode*) is where the action is. Literally. This mode records a continuous series of images as long as you hold down the Shutter button. You can choose from two continuous settings:

- **High-Speed Continuous**: At this setting, the camera can capture a maximum of about six shots per second, also known as frames per second (fps).
- **Low-Speed Continuous:** This setting drops the maximum capture rate to about three fps.

Why would you want to capture fewer than the maximum number of shots? Well, frankly, unless you're shooting something that's moving at a really, really fast pace, not too much will change between frames when you shoot at six-plus fps. So when you set the continuous rate that high, you typically just wind up with lots of shots that show the exact same thing, wasting space on your memory card.

A couple of other Continuous mode pointers:

- Image quality is an important factor in determining frame rate. If you are recording large RAW and JPEGs, you will have a far slower rate than if you are only storing small JPEGs.
- Some other functions can slow down the continuous capture rate. For example, when you use flash or enable the High ISO Noise Reduction feature (explained in Chapter 6), you typically can't achieve the highest burst rate. The speed of your memory card also plays a role in how fast the camera can capture images. In other words, consider six shots per second a best-case scenario.
- The actual number of frames you can record per second depends in part on your shutter speed. At a slow shutter speed, the camera may not be able to reach the maximum frame rate. The maximum frame rate is attained with a shutter speed of 1/500 second or faster.
- Aperture matters, too. If the camera continually has to stop down to take the photo (compared to being wide open when you frame and meter), the action slows.

Silent Shooting

Need to shoot quietly? Try Silent Shooting. Although you might think it a gimmick, I guarantee you it's quieter than normal. The price you pay? You have a bit more of a delay between pressing the Shutter button and taking the photo. If you're taking action shots, that might be a killer. But if you're trying to be quiet and can anticipate, a quieter camera is nicer. You have two types of Silent Shooting modes to choose between:

- **Silent Single Shooting:** The same as Single Shooting, only quieter.
- **Silent Continuous Shooting:** Choose this mode if you want to speed things up. You won't be able to match "noisy" Continuous Shooting, though. In this case, the maximum is about three shots per second.

Self-timer/remote control

The self-timer comes in two flavors, both of which delay the shutter after you press the Shutter button fully.

The remote control part of these modes is meant to apply to wireless remotes such as the Remote Controller RC-6, not wired remote switches or controllers. Because wired controllers have a physical connection to the camera, the remotes need no additional setup unless specifically mentioned or suggested in the product manual. This feature makes them compatible with the delays. However, the camera has to be told to "watch" for a wireless remote. In that case, you set the drive mode to one of these two modes to enable the wireless remote:

- **10-sec. self-timer/remote control:** Want to put yourself in the picture? Select this mode, depress the Shutter button, and run into the frame. You have about 10 seconds to get yourself in place and pose before the image is recorded. Figure 2-17 is a family portrait. I set the camera up on a tripod, composed the shot, set the drive to the 10-second timer, pressed the Shutter button, ran to get into position, and smiled. We took this to commemorate releasing the rabbits we rescued back into the wild.

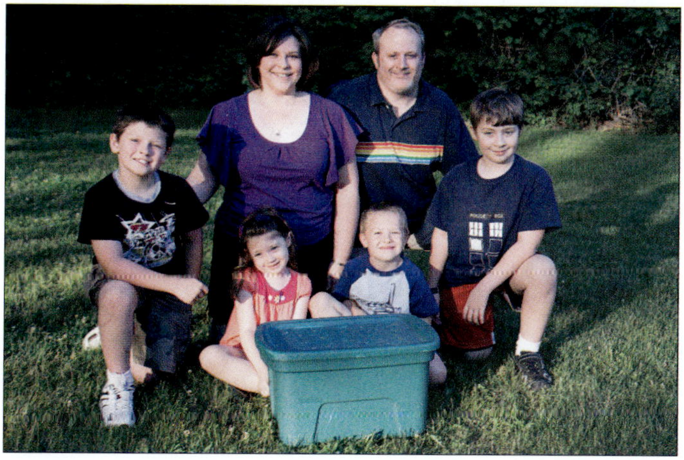

Figure 2-17: Say goodbye to George!

- **2-sec. self-timer/remote control:** This mode works just like the 10-sec. self-timer/remote control mode, but the capture happens just two seconds after you fully press the Shutter button.

  TIP: You can't run far and pose in two seconds, so don't use this mode to take self-portraits. Rather, use it to reduce camera shake by giving the camera a moment to stabilize after you've pressed the Shutter button. A 2-second delay works great for close-ups or macro work, in which camera shake is magnified. In fact, anything that magnifies the subject also magnifies camera shake, including telephoto lenses.

Combine a remote with the 2-sec. self-timer (don't forget about using Mirror Lockup) for the ultimate in hands-free, shake-proof photography.

Choosing a memory card

Choosing a memory card size that's right for you depends on how often you shoot, how much, the image quality you have set, and how often you transfer photos. The following table shows you how many photos you can fit on an 8GB and 16GB memory card. Clearly, the size and quality of the photos you choose to record determine how many will fit on the cards, and the 16GB card has roughly twice the capacity of the 8GB card.

To figure out what size card you need, determine the highest-quality photos you will take, on average, and figure out how long you need to go without transferring them. If you like shooting Raw + JPEG and shoot a few hundred photos a day, you will have to transfer once or twice if you use an 8GB card. If that doesn't sound too burdensome, you're fine. You can buy more cards and swap them out to reduce the transfers, but you would still have to swap cards. If you get too large a card, it will remain largely empty — or, if filled with days of untransferred photos, would only make disasters more disastrous. Would you rather lose 835 photos or 167?

If you shoot high definition (HD) movies, all bets are off. You should buy the largest, fastest card you can afford.

File	***Size/Quality***	***Size***	***8GB***	***16GB***
RAW	Large	21.7 MB	211	414
	Medium	19.1 MB	295	578
	Small	15.1 MB	373	729
JPEG	Large, Fine	7.0 MB	822	1607
	Large, Normal	3.7 MB	1521	2970
	Medium, Fine	3.8 MB	1584	3093
	Medium, Normal	2.0 MB	3232	6308
	S1, Fine	2.5 MB	2552	4981
	S1, Normal	1.3 MB	5186	9999*
	S2	1.4 MB	4978	9716
	S3	0.3 MB	9999*	9999*
RAW + JPEG	Large, Fine JPEG	34.1 MB	167	328
M-RAW + JPEG	Large, Fine JPEG	26.1 MB	216	424
S-RAW + JPEG	Large, Fine JPEG	22.1 MB	255	501

1. 9999 photos represents the most you can have in a folder, not the card. The number is so ridiculously large, however, I chose not to try and figure out how many you could actually store.
2. The RAW+JPEG lines use Large, Fine JPEGs. You can save smaller JPEGs, which increases the total number of photos you can store on card.
3. There is a minor difference between Compact Flash and Secure Digital card capacities. For those I tested, it was only a single photo or so.

Rustling up a Photo Size, Quality, and Aspect Ratio

You've got a modern-day marvel in your hands. The 5D Mark III can take magnificently clear, compelling photos. And let me tell you something more: You can achieve such photos in several sizes, aspect ratios, and qualities.

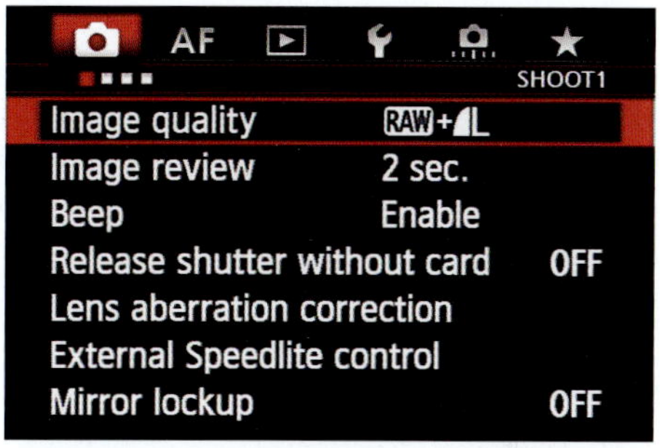

Figure 2-18: Note that the current setting is shown in this menu.

REMEMBER The thing is, the 5D Mark III has no *bad* setting. It has good ones and better ones. Which one you should use depends on your situation. In general, if you plan on printing large copies of your photos, select the highest-quality photo possible. If you expect to use them on a computer screen, for digital photo frames, or for small prints, even the smaller, lower-quality settings are fantastic.

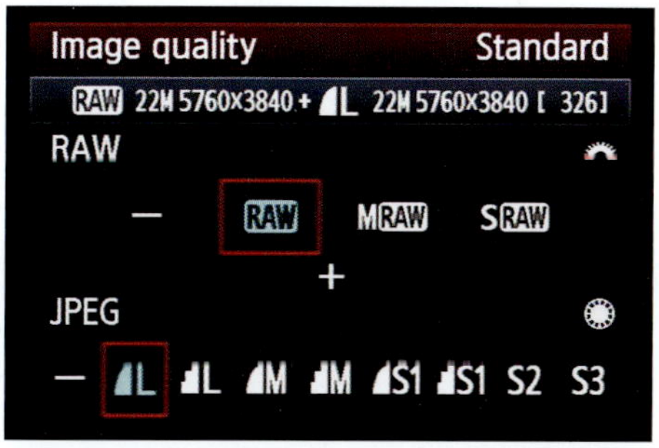

Figure 2-19: Don't press Set prematurely; enter settings for both file types first.

There are at least two ways to set image quality: from the menu or from the Quick Control screen.

- **Shooting Menu 1:** Press the Menu button and then display Shooting Menu 1, as shown in Figure 2-18.

  Highlight Image Quality and press the Set button to display the screen you see in Figure 2-19. Set the Image Quality for RAW photos with the Main dial; use the Quick Control dial to set Image Quality for JPEGs.

  If you have two cards inserted and the Recording Function is set to Record Separately, you see the screen shown in Figure 2-20 when you enter the Image Quality screen.

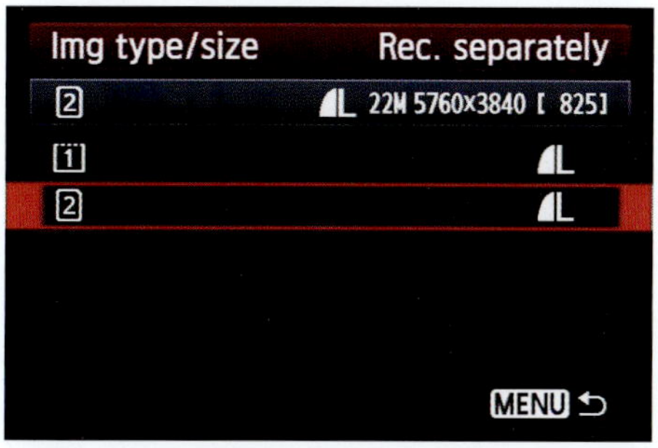

Figure 2-20: Choose each card separately.

Select a card using the Quick Control dial or the Multicontroller; then press the Set button. The screen changes to that shown in Figure 2-21.

Use the Multicontroller or Quick Control dial to highlight a single type of file, with its associated size and quality, for the card in question. Notice that your options are limited. You cannot record JPEG and RAW images to the same card when using Record Separately. Press the Set button to make the changes.

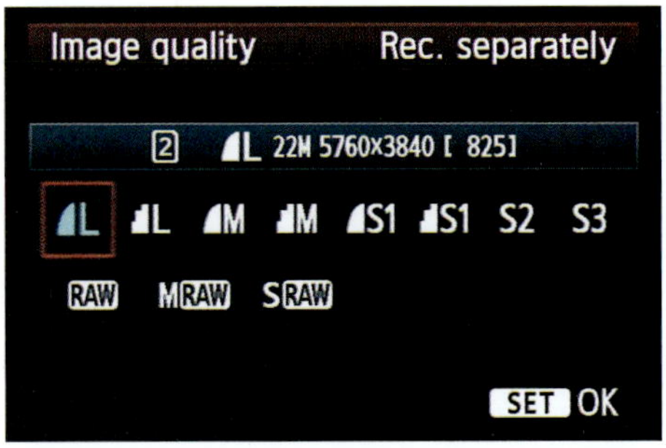

Figure 2-21: Choose a single file type and quality.

- **Quick Control screen:** Press the Quick Control button and use the Multicontroller to highlight the Image Quality option, as shown in Figure 2-22.

  You can then rotate the Main dial or Quick Control dial to cycle through the available Quality settings. Or, if you prefer, press the Set button to display the screen shown in Figure 2-23, which contains all the possible Quality options. Use the Main dial to change RAW settings and the Quick Control dial to highlight the JPEG setting you want to use. Press Set to finish.

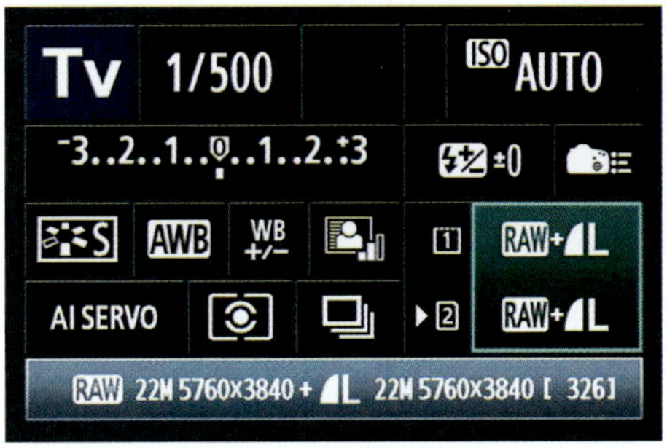

Figure 2-22: Set image quality in Quick Control mode.

Setting the aspect ratio

Quirkily enough, you can set the aspect ratio only for photos shot in Live View (Live View is explained in Chapter 3). When you visit the Shooting 4 (Live View) menu, Aspect Ratio is there, pretty as you please.

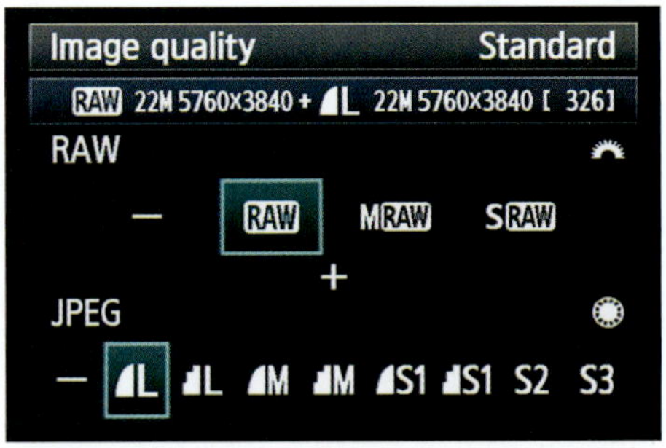

Figure 2-23: Pressing Set reveals this alternative method of changing image quality.

When you highlight it and press Set, you can choose from four different aspect ratios:

- **3:2:** This is the standard photo ratio. It represents the same aspect ratio of a 35mm frame of film.
- **4:3:** This aspect ratio is the same as older, standard-definition vacuum-tube televisions and computer monitors.
- **16:9:** This ratio is the same as widescreen movies (we used to call them Letterbox editions) and HDTVs.
- **1:1:** Square. Use this aspect ratio when you want to take square photos, much like Polaroids.

Aspect ratio, unlike size or quality, has more to do with your artistic goals than quality. Figure 2-24 compares the four in the preceding list.

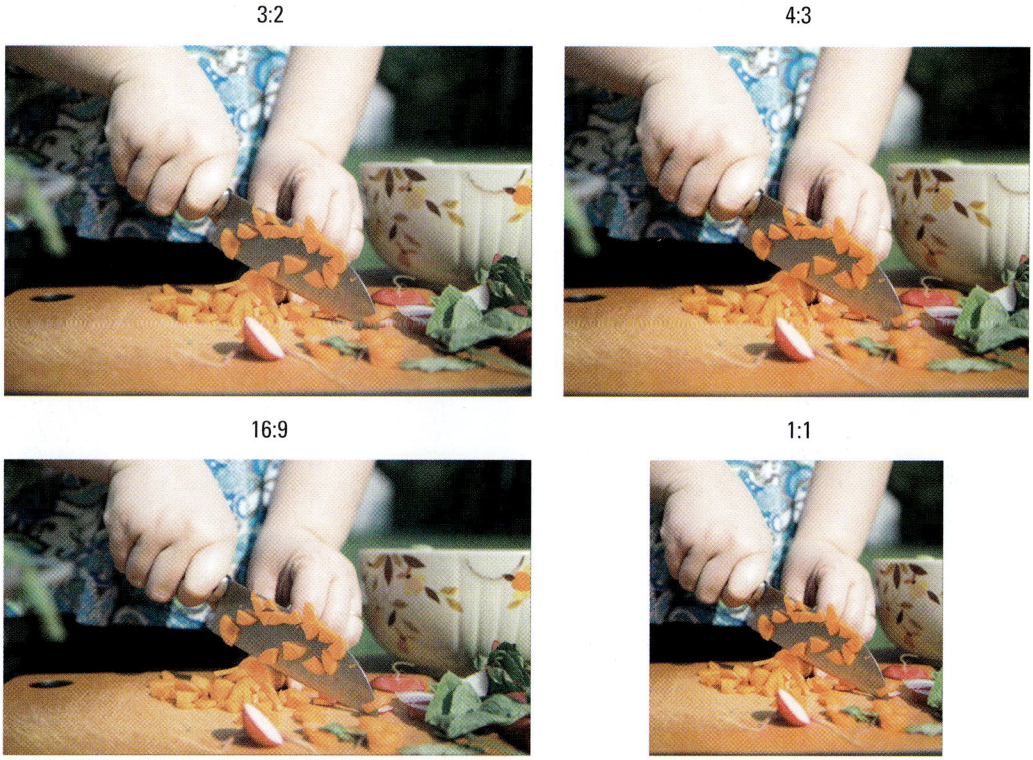

Figure 2-24: Different aspect ratios emphasize different aspects of a photo.

Making the transfer

Transferring (also known as *downloading*) photos and movies to your computer can be a very simple process. You have several methods to choose from, however. Each uses a different approach to hook things up and may require hardware that you don't have. They are

- **Direct USB connection:** Setting up a direct connection between your camera and computer is the most straightforward and easiest method. *Pros:* The only thing you need, besides your camera, is the USB cable that was provided. *Cons:* Your camera has to be on and near the computer (which can be dangerous if you trip over the cord). If your battery is low and you have no backup, recharge the battery a bit so that your camera won't turn off in the middle of a transfer.
- **External USB card reader:** External USB card readers take the camera out of the transfer equation. The reader plugs into your computer. You feed a memory card into the reader and it handles the transfer. *Pros:* You don't have to use your camera's battery and you don't have to worry about running out of power in the middle of the transfer. You aren't endangering your camera. Also, if the card reader goes bad or you break it, you can replace it quickly and cheaply. *Cons:* You need a card reader for each type of memory card you have or buy one that supports multiple card types.
- **Built-in card reader:** Some computers and printers have built-in card readers. New iMac desktop computers, MacBook Air, and MacBook Pro notebooks have built-in SD card readers. If you own a Windows computer, check to see whether it came with an internal card reader (our HP laptop has a convenient SD card reader in front). If not, you can install an internal card reader. *Pros:* They aren't as slippery as portable card readers and can't fall off your desk. You also won't forget to take it with you (should you be using a laptop). *Cons:* Internal card readers aren't portable (unless you're using a portable computer). They aren't as easy to upgrade or repair as the type you plug in.
- **Wireless memory card technology:** Wireless transfer methods (Canon or Eye-Fi) transfer photos and movies from your camera to your computer via thin air. *Pros:* It's portable, doesn't tie you down, is cool, and effectively gives you an unlimited amount of storage while you shoot. *Cons:* This method uses your camera's battery to transfer, may be slower than the other methods, and requires that you be in a wireless network for everything to operate, not to mention the hassle of extra gear, software installation, setup, and configuration.

REMEMBER

Different aspect ratios will not be applied to shots you take unless you use Live View. So there you go.

If you want to set an aspect ratio for photos shot with the viewfinder, you have to set an aspect ratio using the Custom Function, Add cropping information. You have seven options: Off, 6:6, 3:4, 4:5, 6:7, 5:6, and 5:7. See Chapter 10 for more information on how to add cropping information.

Deciding Between RAW and JPEG

Choosing the *file format* (which simply refers to the type of image) of the photos you want to record is just as important as choosing their size. The 5D Mark III offers two file formats, JPEG and RAW (sometimes written as Raw or raw). The next sections explain the pros and cons of each.

JPEG: The imaging (and web) standard

This format is the default setting on your camera, as it is for most digital cameras. JPEG is popular for two main reasons:

- **Immediate usability:** JPEG is a longtime standard format for digital photos. All web browsers and e-mail programs can display JPEG files, so you can share them online immediately after you shoot them. You also can get JPEG photos printed at any retail outlet, whether it's an online or a local printer. Additionally, any program that has photo capabilities, from photo editing programs to word processing programs, can handle your files.
- **Small files:** JPEG files are smaller than RAW files. And smaller files mean that your pictures consume less room on your camera's memory card and on your computer's hard drive.

The downside — you knew there had to be one — is that JPEG creates smaller files by applying *lossy compression.* This process actually throws away some image data. Too much compression leads to defects known as JPEG artifacts.

On your camera, the amount of compression that's applied depends on whether you choose a Quality setting that carries the label Fine or Normal. The difference between the two breaks down as follows:

- **Fine:** At this setting, represented by the symbol you see in the margin, very little compression is applied, so you shouldn't see many compression artifacts, if any.

- **Normal:** Switch to Normal, and the compression amount rises, as does the chance of seeing some artifacting. Notice the jaggedy-ness of the Normal icon, as shown in the margin? That's your reminder that all may not be "smooth" sailing when you choose a Normal setting.

If you keep your image print or display size small, you aren't likely to notice a great deal of quality difference between the Fine and Normal compression levels. The differences become apparent only when you greatly enlarge a photo.

Given that the differences between Fine and Normal aren't all that easy to spot until you really enlarge the photo, is it okay to shift to Normal and enjoy the benefits of smaller files? Well, only you can decide what level of quality your pictures demand. For most photographers, the added file sizes produced by the Fine setting aren't a huge concern, given that the prices of memory cards fall all the time. Long-term storage is more of an issue; the larger your files, the faster you fill your computer's hard drive and the more DVDs or CDs you need for archiving purposes. But in the end, it's usually good practice to take the storage hit in exchange for the lower compression level of the Fine setting. You never know when a casual snapshot is going to be so great that you want to print or display it large enough that even minor quality loss becomes a concern. And of all the defects that you can correct in a photo editor, artifacting is one of the hardest to remove. So stick with Fine when shooting in the JPEG format.

To make the best decision, do your own test shots, carefully inspect the results in your photo editor, and make your own judgment about what level of artifacting you can accept. If you don't want *any* risk of artifacting, bypass JPEG altogether and change the file type to RAW (CR2). Or consider your other option, which is to record two versions of each file, one RAW and one JPEG.

WARNING!

Whichever format you select, be aware of one more important rule for preserving the original image quality: If you retouch pictures in your photo software, don't save the altered images in the JPEG format. Every time you alter and save an image in the JPEG format, you apply another round of lossy compression (simply opening and closing the file does no harm.)

Always save your edited photos in a nondestructive format. TIFF is a good choice and is a file-saving option available in most photo editing programs. Should you want to share the edited image online, create a JPEG copy of the TIFF file when you finish making all your changes. That way, you always retain one copy of the photo at the original quality captured by the camera.

Despite what it sounds like, you do have some control over how the camera processes RAW data and converts it into a JPEG. This control takes the form of Picture Styles (see Chapter 8). For example, when you select Neutral Picture Style, you're telling the camera that you want a more subdued photo with natural colors. It converts the RAW data with that in mind.

RAW: The purist's choice

The other picture-file type that you can create on your 5D Mark III is *Camera Raw,* or just *RAW* (as in, uncooked) for short.

Each manufacturer has its own flavor of RAW files; Canon's are CR2 files (or, on some older cameras, CRW). You'll see that three-letter designation at the end of your photo filenames on your computer.

RAW is popular with advanced photographers, for two reasons:

- **Greater creative control:** With JPEG, internal camera software tweaks your images, adjusting color, exposure, and sharpness as needed to produce the results that Canon believes its customers prefer (or according to settings you chose). With RAW, the camera simply records the original, unprocessed image data. The photographer then copies the image file to the computer and uses special software known as a *raw converter* to produce the actual image, making decisions about color, exposure, and so on at that point. The upshot is that "shooting RAW" enables you, not the camera, to have the final say on the visual characteristics of your image.
- **Higher bit depth:** *Bit depth* is a measure of how many distinct color values an image file can contain. JPEG files restrict you to 8 bits each for the red, blue, and green color components, or *channels,* that make up a digital image, for a total of 24 bits. That translates to roughly 16.7 million possible colors. On the 5D Mark III, a RAW file delivers a higher bit count, collecting 14 bits per channel.

  Although jumping from 8 to 14 bits sounds like a huge difference, you may not really ever notice any difference in your photos; that 8-bit palette of 16.7 million values is more than enough for superb images. Where having the extra bits can come in handy is if you really need to adjust exposure, contrast, or color after the shot in your photo-editing program. In cases in which you apply extreme adjustments, having the extra original bits sometimes helps avoid a problem known as *banding* or *posterization,* which creates abrupt color breaks where you should see smooth, seamless transitions. (A higher bit depth doesn't always prevent the problem, however, so don't expect miracles.)
- **Best picture quality:** Because RAW doesn't apply the destructive compression associated with JPEG, you don't run the risk of the artifacting that can occur with JPEG.

But of course, as with most things in life, RAW isn't without its disadvantages. To wit:

- **You can't do much with your pictures until you process them in a RAW converter.** You can't share them online, for example, or put them into a text document or multimedia presentation. You can print them immediately if you use the Canon-provided software, but most other photo programs require you to convert the RAW files to a standard format first. Ditto for retail photo printing. So when you shoot RAW, you add to the time you must spend in front of the computer instead of behind the camera lens.

- **RAW files are larger than comparable JPEGs.** Unlike JPEGs, RAW doesn't apply lossy compression to shrink files. (A hallmark of the JPEG is its ability to shrink file size dramatically, but that comes at the expense of quality.) This means that RAW files are significantly larger than JPEGs, so they take up more room on your memory card and on your computer's hard drive or other picture-storage devices. Thankfully, the 5D Mark III has three sizes of RAW files for you to choose from. That enables you to shrink the file size down by reducing the photo's dimensions, but not at the expense of overall quality.

Choosing the right photo software

Programs for downloading, archiving, and editing digital photos abound, ranging from entry-level software designed for beginners to high-end options geared to professionals. Canon includes two that come with your camera:

- **ImageBrowser EX (Mac/Win):** This program (which goes by different names depending on whether you use a Windows-based or Macintosh computer), provides a simple photo organizer and viewer. It also offers a few basic photo editing features, including red-eye removal, a cropping tool, and exposure and color adjustment filters.
- **Canon Digital Photo Professional (Mac/Win):** Designed for more advanced users, this Canon product offers a higher level of control over certain photo functions. But its most important difference from ImageBrowser is that it offers the tools you need to convert photos that you shoot in the RAW (CR2) format into a standard format (JPEG or TIFF).

The most popular third-party professional-level software options are the following:

- **Apple Aperture (Mac only):** Aperture is geared more to shooters who need to organize and process lots of images but typically do only light retouching work — wedding photographers and school portrait photographers, for example. It's got powerful RAW-processing abilities.
- **Adobe Photoshop Lightroom (Mac/Win):** Lightroom is the Adobe counterpart to Aperture. It offers top-notch processing and retouching tools. Many pro photographers rely on this program for all their photo organizing and RAW-processing work.
- **Adobe Photoshop (Mac/Win):** Although Aperture and Lightroom are used primarily for organizing and processing photos (including RAW), Photoshop is the industry's most powerful image editor. It has sophisticated retouching tools that make use of image adjustments, layers, masks, and filters, which enable you to perfect your most important photos. It also includes tools for producing high dynamic range (HDR) and 3D images. Photoshop ships with Adobe Camera Raw, which enables you to process RAW images before you edit them.

Whether the upside of RAW outweighs the down is a decision that you need to ponder based on your photographic needs, schedule, and computer-comfort level.

You can abandon JPEGs entirely and store photos in RAW file format. The problem is, you don't have a JPEG and you will have to do all the work of photo processing yourself. If you want a RAW photo, this option is slightly quicker than RAW + JPEG because you're saving only the one file.

RAW + JPEG

You can set the 5D Mark III to save both file types at the same time.

Doing so enables you to store a high-quality RAW file that you can process at your discretion, and capture a finished JPEG that you can immediately use. The JPEG is nice to have if you want to browse through the photos and send some off to clients or friends before you do the intense RAW processing. The downsides to saving both files are space (two files are larger than one) and time (it takes longer for the camera to process and save them).

Selecting a Photo Size

The 5D Mark III has three photo sizes: Large, Medium, and Small. The sizes have different meanings, depending on whether you're referring to RAW or JPEG file types, as well as the different Live View aspect ratios (3:2, 4:3, 16:9, and 1:1).

Table 2-1 shows the standard 3:2 photo sizes. To put the pixel dimensions (Dimensions) of each photo size in perspective, take a look at how large a print would be at a resolution of 300 dpi, which is a high-quality printout (Print@300dpi). For viewing on a computer monitor, anything over the smallest size is overkill and will be scaled to fit. Larger sizes do allow more room for cropping, however, whether you plan to use them on a computer or as a printout.

(***Note:*** The camera manual suggests appropriate print sizes using A-series paper sizes and a resolution of approximately 200dpi. I am going a bit higher on resolution and giving you the straight dimensions in inches.)

TIP

When you choose a photo size, consider the resolution and overall size of the media you intend to publish it in. Small photos look good when published to the web, and you don't have to resize them. However, large photos are necessary if you plan on using them in high-quality prints, especially large ones.

WARNING!

Beware. All the RAW sizes and the Large and Medium JPEG sizes will look pretty close to the same when you look at them on most computer monitors because the monitor (or software you're using) scales them to fit.

Table 2-1 Image Size (3:2 Aspect Ratio)

Option	*Size*	*Dimensions*	*Megapixels*	*Print@300dpi*
RAW	Large	5,760 x 3,840	22.1	19.2 x 12.8 in
M-RAW	Medium	3,960 x 2,640	10.45	13.2 x 8.8 in
S-RAW	Small	2,880 x 1,920	5.5	9.6 x 6.4 in
L JPEG	Large	5,760 x 3,840	22.1	19.2 x 12.8 in
M JPEG	Medium	3,840 x 2,560	9.8	12.8 x 8.5 in
S1 JPEG	Small 1	2,880 x 1,920	5.5	9.6 x 6.4 in
S2 JPEG	Small 2	1,920 x 1,280	2.5	6.4 x 4.3 in
S3 JPEG	Small 3	720 x 480	0.35	2.4 x 1.6 in

Figure 2-25 illustrates RAW sizes and JPEG photo sizes in action. I took these photos of a single subject (in this case, of a funny fish we gave my mom for her kitchen some years back) under controlled conditions. Each size is shown. The aspect ratio was set to 3:2. At this magnification, you can tell a size difference, but not a quality difference. You would have to print relatively large copies or view them at extreme magnification to discern those types of differences.

Of course, if you choose a different aspect ratio, the sizes will all change. That information is presented in Table 2-2.

Table 2-2 Comparing Large Photo Sizes for Aspect Ratios

Aspect Ratio	*Dimensions*	*Megapixels*
3:2	5,760 x 3,840	22.1
4:3	5,120 x 3,840	19.7
16:9	5,760 x 3,240	18.7
1:1	3,840 x 3,840	14.7

Table 2-3 shows the sizes (in megapixels) of the main aspect ratios for each photo quality.

Table 2-3 Image Sizes in MP for Each Aspect Ratio

Quality	*3:2*	*4:3*	*16:9*	*1:1*
RAW	22.1	19.7	18.7	14.7
M-RAW	10.45	9.3	8.8	7.0
S-RAW	5.5	4.9	4.7	3.7
L JPEG	22.1	19.7	18.7	14.7
M JPEG	9.8	8.7	8.3	6.6
S1 JPEG	5.5	4.9	4.7	3.7
S2 JPEG	2.5	2.2	2.1	1.6
S3 JPEG	0.35	0.31	0.29	0.23

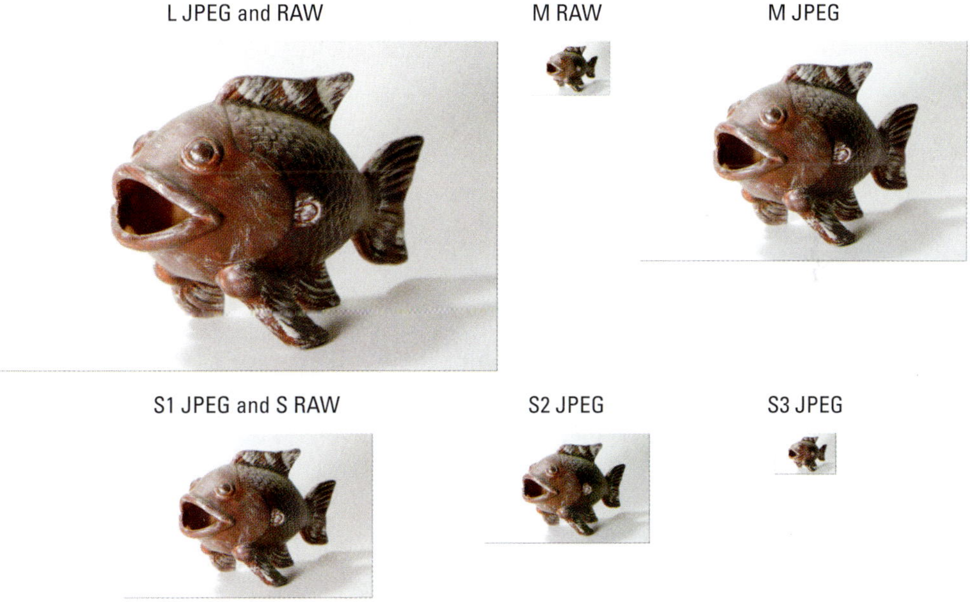

Figure 2-25: 5D Mark III photo sizes from Large to S3.

In the end, don't let all the numbers scare you away from choosing the right image size for you. Here is what I recommend:

- **Be better safe than sorry:** Choose the largest photo of whatever type you happen to be shooting. Choosing the largest photo size preserves your option to print high-quality photos at 300dpi regardless of your intention when you took them. Large photos also give you room to crop without losing too much detail or print resolution.

- **Know when to compromise:** If space or speed is more important than ultimate print resolution, choose Medium for each type. You can still view and print high-quality photos. What you lose is being able to print them at larger sizes and, to some degree, visual detail when viewing them magnified.

You *can't* go in the opposite direction, adding pixels to a low-resolution original in your photo editor to create a good, large print. Even with the very best software, adding pixels doesn't improve the print quality of a low-resolution image.

Putting Your Best Photo Forward

Knowing the Image Quality options available to you and making the decision about which one(s) to use are two different propositions. Use this section to help you figure out which combination of file type, size, and quality is best for you.

When choosing a file type, consider these things:

- **Choose JPEG** if you want a final product coming out of the camera and you don't want to mess with processing the RAW file yourself. You don't need the ultimate in quality and are happy with what the camera produces. You're happy using JPEGs on your computer or putting them online. (You can't upload RAW files to Flickr, Facebook, your blog, or your web page. Don't even think of tweeting them.)
- **Choose RAW** if you want creative control over your photos and don't mind doing the processing yourself. You want the flexibility of making multiple edits throughout the process. For you, saving storage space and speeding up transfer rates aren't as important as quality.

Use these guidelines when choosing an image size:

- **Choose Large if you expect to print or crop the photo**. You can always create a low-resolution copy of the image in your photo editor for use online.
- **Choose Medium for everyday images.** The Large setting is overkill for most casual shooting, which means that you're creating huge files for no good reason.
- **Reduce size to Small (S1, S2, or S3) if shooting speed is paramount.** If you're shooting action and the shot-to-shot capture time is slower than you'd like — that is, the camera takes too long after you take one shot before it lets you take another — continuing to dial down the size may help.

When trying to decide on a JPEG quality, keep the following points in mind:

- **Choose JPEG Fine** if great photo quality is good enough for you, you don't have wads of spare time, or you aren't that comfortable with the computer. Stick with one of the Fine JPEG settings (Large/Fine, Medium/Fine, or Small/Fine).
- **Choose JPEG Normal** if you aren't shooting pictures that demand the highest-quality level and you aren't printing or displaying the photos at large sizes. The smaller file size also makes JPEG Normal the way to go if you're running seriously low on memory card space during a shoot.

Finally, if you are shooting in Live View mode, you can choose an aspect ratio:

- **Choose 3:2 for almost all occasions.** You get the most photo and can crop later if you want.
- **Choose another aspect ratio if you want the photo cropped immediately.** If you save a RAW version of the file, you can change your mind later if using Canon Digital Photo Professional software. RAW photos are saved in a 3:2 aspect ratio, regardless of the actual aspect ratio setting. The aspect ratio is instead saved in the file's metadata. Only JPEGs are actually cropped with a 4:3, 16:9, or 1:1 aspect ratio.

Now, for one final test. At normal magnifications, the photos come pretty close to looking the same (with the possible exceptions of S2 and S3). Figure 2-26 is a shot of the inside of my old Marshall 9001 Stereo Valve Pre-amp. I used the RAW photo to create this figure.

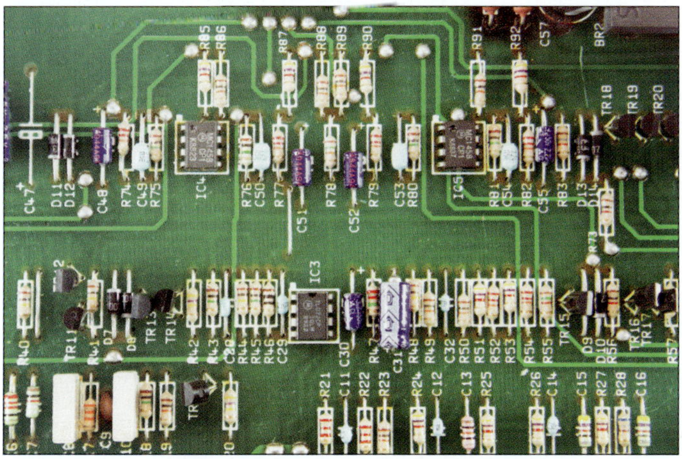

Figure 2-26: This circuit board makes beautiful music.

Figure 2-27 shows a small portion of the photo under extreme magnification. Even when you zoom in, though, it's hard to tell the difference between photos, regardless of the quality settings. The only clear stinker is S3, which is not that apparent when viewed at normal magnification. S2 is a bit soft, but not as bad as you might think. Bear in mind that the blue capacitor in the center of this close-up is only 3mm wide!

In the end, then, one of the most important factors in determining overall photo quality is how much you have to blow it up.

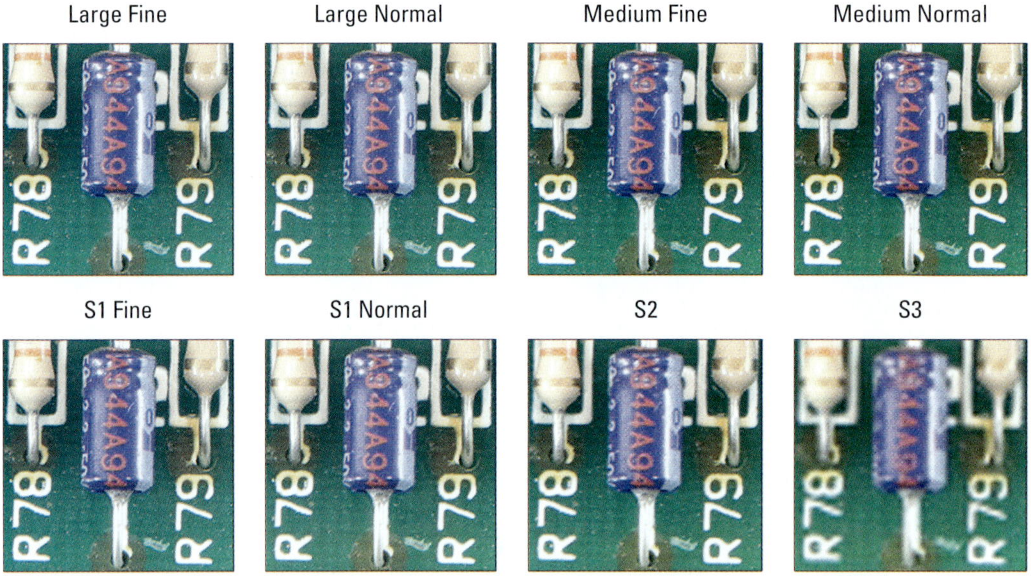

Figure 2-27: At what point can you tell a difference between quality settings?

Part II
Fast Track to Super Shots

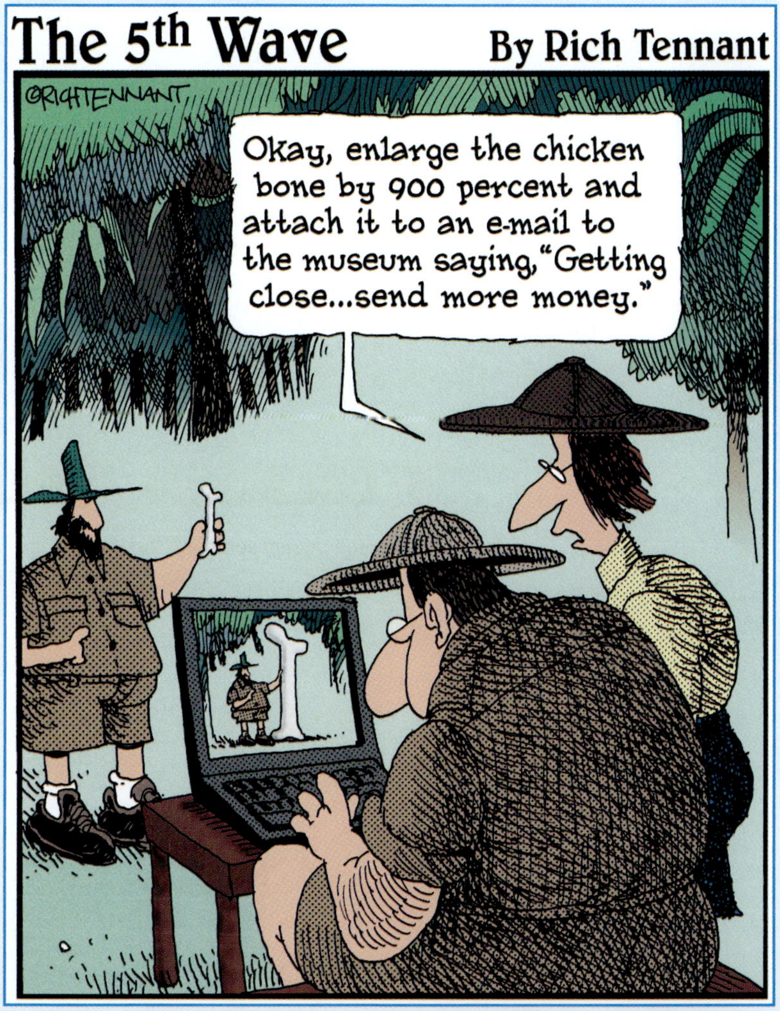

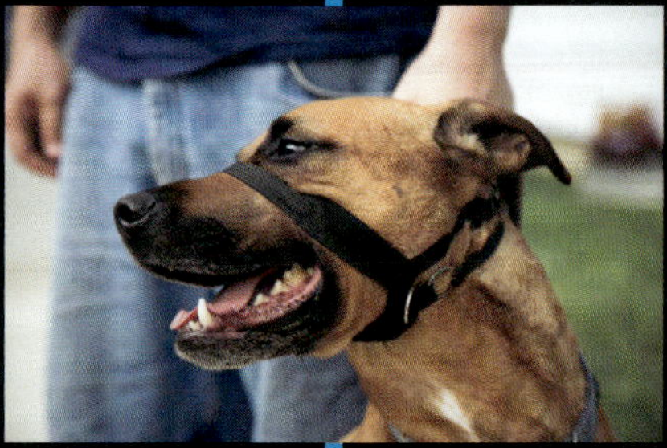

This part shows you how to take best advantage of the 5D Mark III's Scene Intelligent Auto shooting mode. By using this "point-and-shoot" automatic mode, you can capture terrific images with very little effort. All you do is compose the scene; the camera takes care of almost everything else.

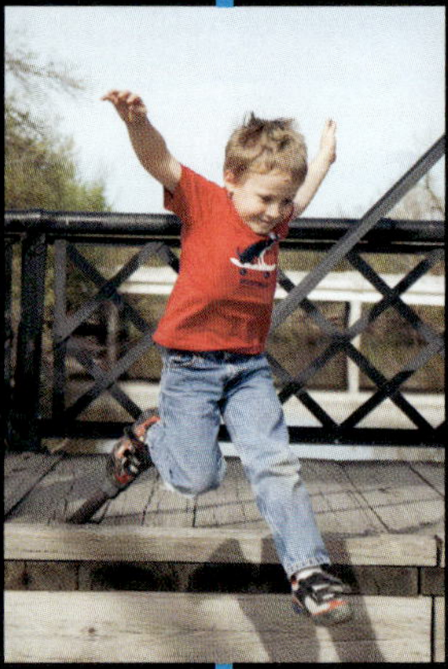

In this part, you also learn how to shoot using your camera's Live View feature, as well as how to shoot movies in Full HD.

After that, it's on to image playback. Digital photography enables you to immediately confirm that the composition, focus, exposure, and color of the photos you take are what you want them to be. You also find out how to review, rate, protect, or delete a picture from your memory card. And then some!

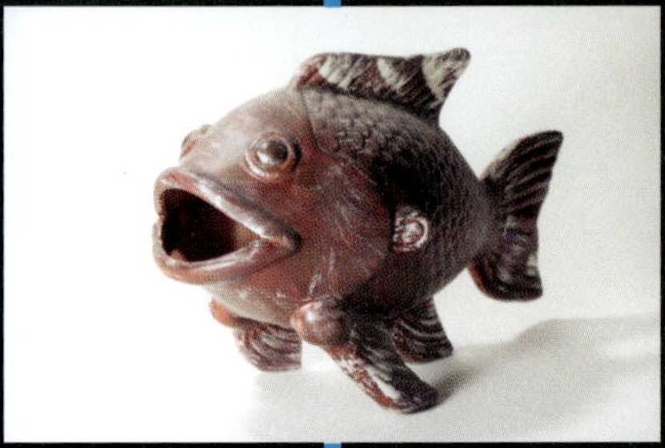

3

Using Scene Intelligent Auto and Live View

In This Chapter

- Reviewing how to hold the camera
- Using Scene Intelligent Auto
- Solving problems in Scene Intelligent Auto mode
- Getting acquainted with Live View mode
- Customizing the Live View display
- Exploring Live View autofocusing options

This chapter is devoted to two completely unrelated features on the Canon 5D Mark III: Scene Intelligent Auto and Live View shooting modes. I have placed them together because they are different from everything else. They share one important aspect, however: They are special-purpose features that you may use at times to great effect, but probably won't use 24/7.

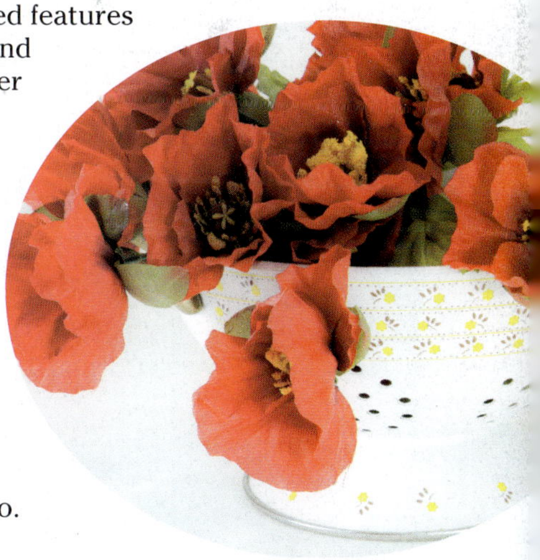

This is a tale of two intros:

Although the Canon EOS 5D Mark III has more power than you can shake a stick at, it also has an outstanding point-and-shoot mode called Scene Intelligent Auto. That's right, your $3,400 camera (not counting lenses and accessories) can be operated as simply as a $100 compact digital camera. Gloriously so.

Live View shooting, in which you view the scene on the LCD monitor prior to shooting (it's literally a *live view* of the scene), is a great alternative to using the viewfinder to frame and focus your shots. It's different enough from using the standard viewfinder, however (how you set it up and use it), that you will benefit from the material in this chapter.

Whether you're a novice who needs a helping hand to get started using these features, or you're pretty darn good and want a quick reference to remind you of some of the details, this chapter is for you.

Reviewing the best way to hold a digital SLR camera is a great way to start this chapter.

Holding on Tight

Handling your camera is one of the most important skills you can master as a photographer. If you don't provide a stable platform, you'll be plagued with poorly composed, often blurry shots. Even though many Canon lenses have a de-shake-ifier built in (called Image Stabilizer), excess movement makes it hard to frame the scene and capture the image without blurring. I call that the "hope and pray" method.

If you're upgrading from a lighter dSLR, it is apparent that the 5D Mark III is noticeably heavier. To me, it's a good kind of heavier. It speaks of quality and ruggedness. However, the extra weight may pose a challenge for you if you are a younger photographer or have small hands. If you add a heavy lens, it gets even, well, heavier.

Becoming one with the camera

In Figure 3-1 I'm holding the camera in a traditional pose, looking through the viewfinder. Try this stance if you're just starting, and modify your stance to suit your style as you get more experience.

Whether you're shooting vertically or horizontally, keep your knees bent a bit and almost hunch into the camera. It feels like you position it first and then bring your body up to meet it. Stand with your feet apart, as if you're bracing yourself, but don't lock your knees. Keep them a bit springy.

Hold your head close to the camera, pressing your eye into the eyepiece cup (the soft rubber piece surrounding the viewfinder). Don't be afraid to use the space just below your eyebrow to help support the camera. Stick the eyepiece cup right in there. However, if that's not comfortable, simply float your eye behind the viewfinder and try to stay still.

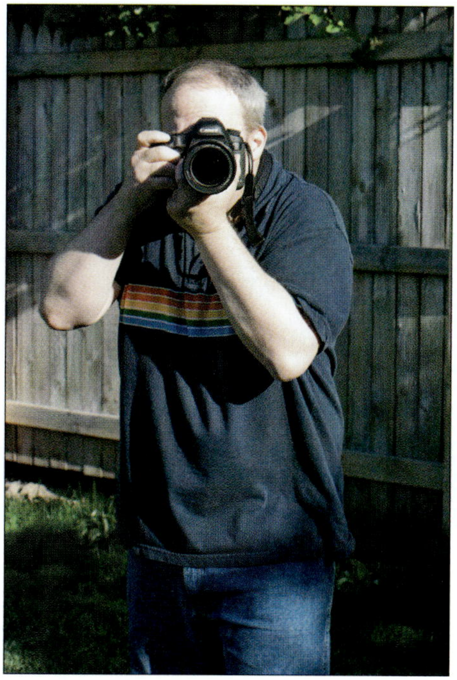
Figure 3-1: Hold your camera steady.

Your right hand should be on the grip with your index finger on the Shutter button. Curl the lower fingers of your right hand around the grip and use them, in part, to hold on to the camera. That leaves your right thumb and index finger free to work controls on the front, top, or back of the camera.

Your left hand does most of the work of supporting the camera. Notice that I have it under the lens near the body of the camera, with my thumb and index finger on the lens's zoom ring. This hold is optimized for autofocus. If you want to manually focus, your left thumb and index finger should move to the front of the lens and support it by the focus ring (see Chapter 1 for tips on holding the camera while manually focusing). Your elbows should be reasonably close to your body, with your left elbow almost propped against you. Keeping your arms firm and close will stabilize you quite a bit more. The camera strap is there in case of an emergency. When you hold the camera like this, the strap bears no weight.

In Figure 3-2, I'm shooting vertically. The only thing that changes from Figure 3-1 is my right elbow, which I extend upward so that my right hand can hold the camera. If you have a vertical grip accessory, you can hold the camera vertically almost as you would horizontally.

Keeping your distance

Maybe you'll be more comfortable shooting with Live View (looking at the LCD monitor on the back of the camera, conveniently covered in this chapter). You can see me checking my composition in Figure 3-3.

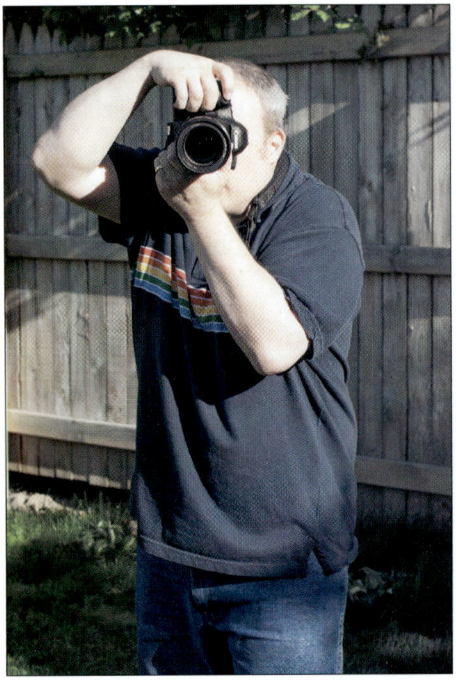

Figure 3-2: Adjust your arms to reposition the camera.

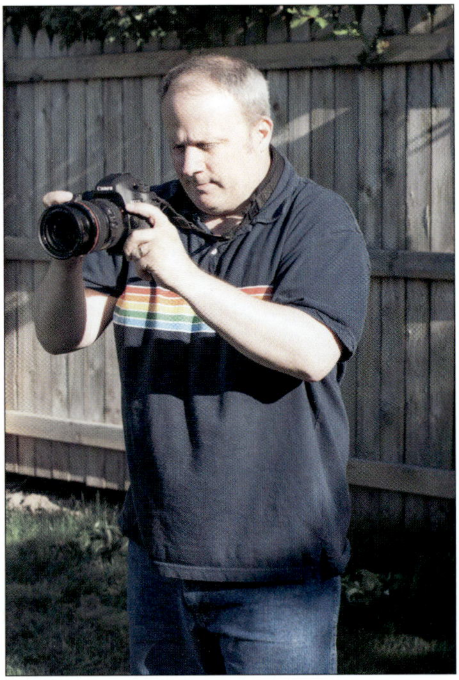

Figure 3-3: Shooting hand-held using Live View.

Hold the camera away from your face so that you can see the LCD monitor. When zooming or focusing, move your left hand back to the lens to operate these controls. Your right hand doesn't change at all.

TIP

Shooting in Live View from the LCD monitor is a much more casual setup, with benefits. Aside from providing comfort, this position lets you keep track of what's going on around you better, whether the activity is kids playing football in your yard or cars going by. You're also able to talk and interact with your subjects better without having your face grafted onto the camera. However, the style has drawbacks. This position is much harder to stabilize than when you hold the camera up against your body.

Kneeling down

Figures 3-1 through 3-3, shown previously, were taken with me standing up. If you are kneeling (and I encourage you to mix things up vertically to make your photos look more interesting), hold the camera the same way as if you were standing. If anything, it's easier to lock your elbows into your body, which makes your platform even more stable. The hard parts are getting used to holding it while you kneel down and try not to fall over, and getting sore knees.

Shooting with Scene Intelligent Auto

It's tempting for more experienced photographers to ignore easy shooting modes in general and the Canon 5D Mark III's Scene Intelligent Auto in particular. For someone who wants, needs, and demands a great degree of control over the process, giving any of it back doesn't always seem like a good bargain. However, automatic modes provide several benefits. They enable you to

- **Concentrate:** You can focus on composition and not worry about everything else.
- **Learn:** Having the ability to afford an expensive camera doesn't always guarantee that you have the skill to use it, or use all of it. Canon doesn't make you take a test (thankfully!) to prove that you know what you're doing before you buy the 5D Mark III. Even if you do know a bit, you may be new to this specific model.

  Having an auto mode like Scene Intelligent Auto gives everyone a chance to take it slow and yet still take good photos.
- **Relax and have fun:** It's nice to be able to simply point the camera and take a photo sometimes. In fact, for those of you on the professional side of the spectrum, it can be a nice change of pace and might even help break you out of the doldrums. Creativity can be hard to muster up on demand. Switch to Scene Intelligent Auto and let yourself go. If you like what you see, you can always design the perfect shot using a different shooting mode in which you control more of the camera. (Yes, it's overkill with the 5D Mark III. But use your camera; use every little bit of it.)

You should, however, be aware that shooting in Scene Intelligent Auto has some drawbacks. Some of them are

- **Limited ability to solve exposure problems:** If the exposure is off, you're sort of stuck. In the more advanced modes, you can adjust settings, add or subtract exposure compensation, adjust your metering mode, and more.
- **Limited creative discretion:** You can't purposefully shoot with a small or large aperture, fast or slow shutter speed, low or high ISO speed (sensor sensitivity to light); also, you can't change other settings that affect what your photo will look like.
- **No ability to control autofocus:** That's right. The camera is set to AI Focus AF and decides on its own what to focus on and how. That's why it's called point-and-shoot.

Taking the photos

My editor notes with irony that I have created an extensive 13-step list to illustrate something that's supposed to be as simple as "point and shoot." So true! I should explain myself a bit. In this section, I give you some pointers in case you're a relative newcomer to photography. Even if you're not, you still have a lot to think about and do, even in this, the most auto of the shooting modes. That's the nature of the 5D Mark III. Some of these steps are optional. This information is meant to help you get the most out of your camera. Some steps are critical. They represent the minimum you need to know.

Follow these steps, then, to get starting shooting with the Scene Intelligent Auto mode:

1. **Get ready.**

   Make sure that you have the battery and at least one memory card inserted correctly into the camera. If necessary, attach or change lenses. Turn the camera on; take the lens cap off. See Chapter 1 if you need help.

   If this is the first time you've used the camera, see Chapter 2. It has important information that will help you get the camera set up correctly. At a minimum, you should have set the date, time, your location, and image quality and size.

2. **Turn the Mode dial to the green A+ symbol to set the shooting mode to Scene Intelligent Auto, as shown in Figure 3-4.**

3. **Set the focus mode as desired.**

Use the focus mode switch on the lens to set the focus to manual (MF) or auto (AF).

If you truly want a point-and-shoot experience, choose AF, as shown in Figure 3-5.

If you are dealing with a tricky subject and want to handle focusing yourself, choose MF.

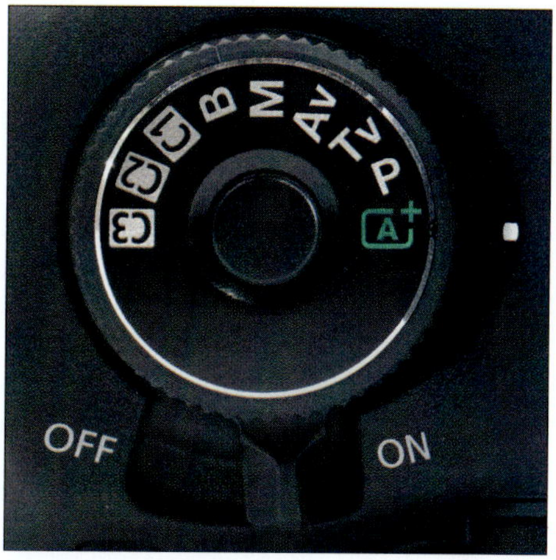

Figure 3-4: Think green for Scene Intelligent Auto.

4. **Enable image stabilization, if desired.**

   Think of this as a quality-control check. Make sure that the Stabilizer switch is set to On (see Figure 3-5) unless you specifically want it off or are in bulb mode (which you aren't). This enables the Image Stabilizer, which helps reduce camera shake when shooting without a tripod.

5. **(Optional) Press the Info button to configure the LCD monitor.**

   If nothing happens, press the Shutter button halfway to wake the camera up. Then press Info and cycle through the displays. You can view the electronic level (see Chapter 12), the Camera settings display (see Chapter 1), or the Shooting settings display (also covered in Chapter 1).

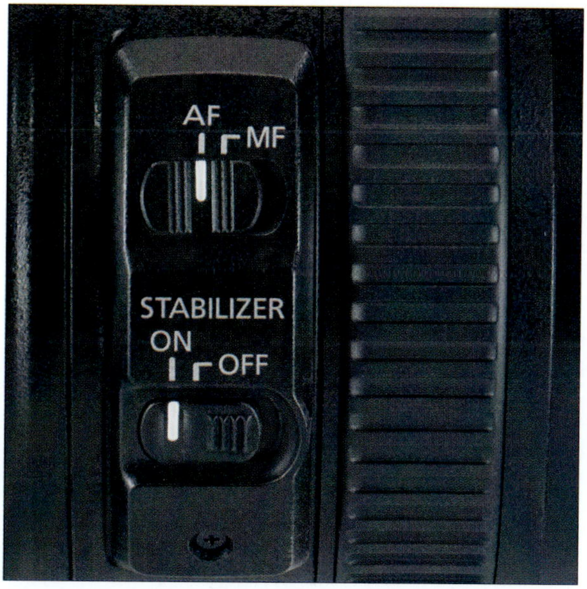

Figure 3-5: Engaging autofocus and image stabilization.

The Shooting settings display (see Figure 3-6) shows several bits of information that are beyond your control. These items are displayed in dark gray. Those in white (aside from the battery level and shots remaining) can be changed if you press the Quick Control button or the Drive button on top of the camera.

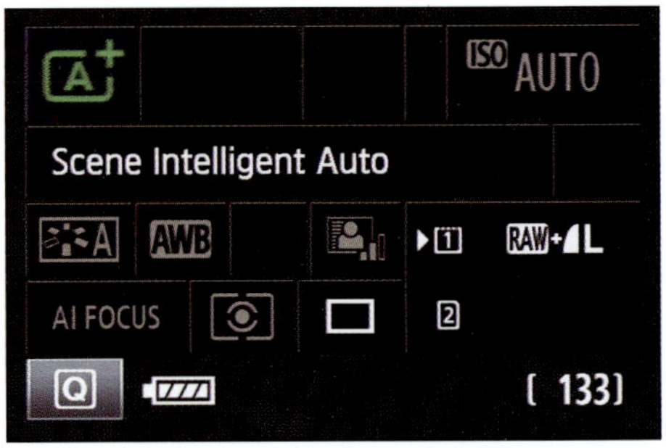

Figure 3-6: Use this display to inspect shooting settings.

6. **(Optional) Press the Drive button to change the drive mode.**

   In Scene Intelligent Auto, you can press the Drive button and change the drive mode as shown in Figure 3-7.

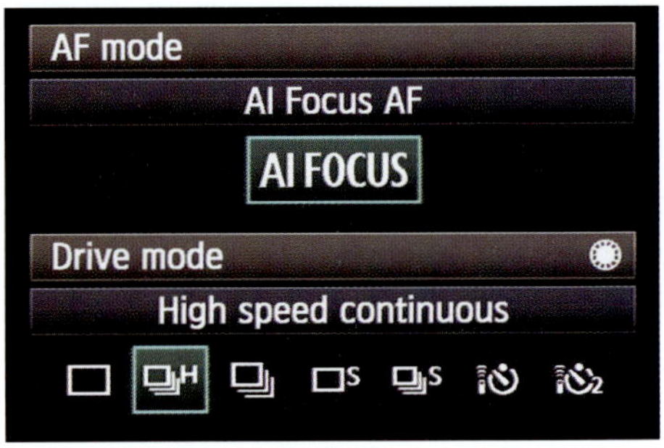

Figure 3-7: Notice that you can change only the drive mode; use the Quick Control dial to change settings.

7. **(Optional) Press the Quick Control button to change the settings.**

   Your shooting options are limited to deciding on a drive mode (see Chapter 2), Image Quality, and, if you have more than one memory card inserted into the camera, which one you want to record to (see Chapter 11).

   Use the Multicontroller to highlight an option, as shown in Figure 3-8, where I have selected Image Quality (there are two readouts because the camera has two memory cards inserted).

   Spin the Quick Control dial to change the highlighted option's settings.

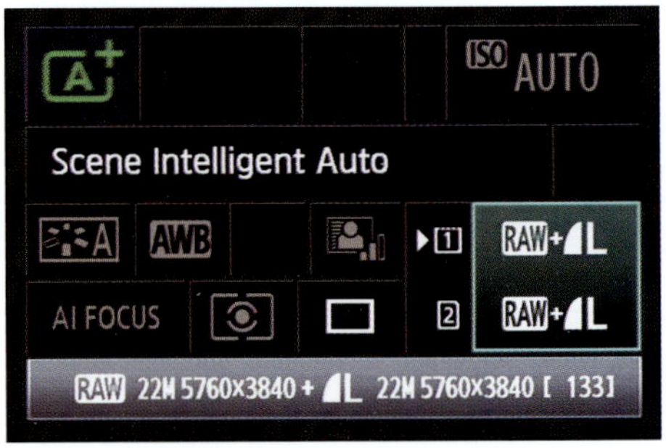

Figure 3-8: Changing Image Quality in Quick Control mode.

8. **(Optional) Press the Start/Stop button to enter Live View shooting mode and configure.**

See Chapter 4 for more information on using Live View. Because there are some quirky aspects of using Live View (namely, focusing), the rest of these steps are written as if you were using the viewfinder.

9. **Point your camera at the subject.**

10. **Compose the scene, zooming in or out, as desired.**

    In other words, decide what's in the photo and where it sits within the frame. Those are important decisions.

    The viewfinder should look like Figure 3-9. It is very bare, provided that you haven't pressed the Shutter button halfway.

    (For you dog lovers out there, the dog's name is Toby. He is wearing a Halti-brand head halter, not a muzzle. No dogs were harmed or otherwise abused in the making of this book.)

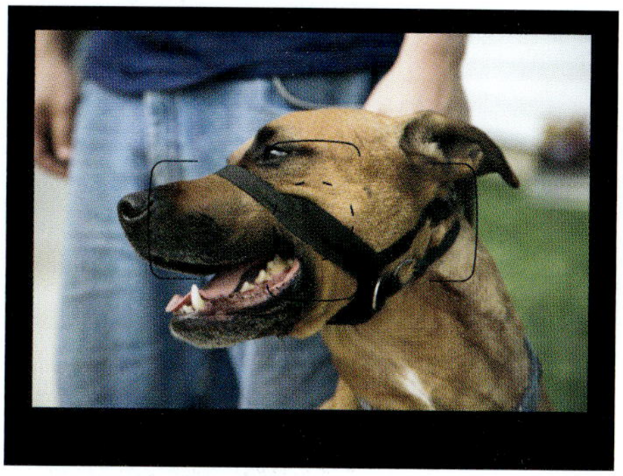

Figure 3-9: Frame first.

11. **Press and hold the Shutter button halfway to focus and meter.**

    If manually focusing, focus using the focus ring on the lens. You'll hear the camera beep when it considers you to be in focus. You can trust this feature or ignore it

    If you use autofocus, the camera initially shows you the AF status indicator (the little green triangles) to let you know that autofocusing is in progress. When autofocus is achieved, the camera beeps (unless you've turned that feature off) and displays those AF points that the camera will use to focus, as shown in Figure 3-10. The focus indicator, a small green circle on the right side of the information shown at the bottom of the viewfinder, lights up.

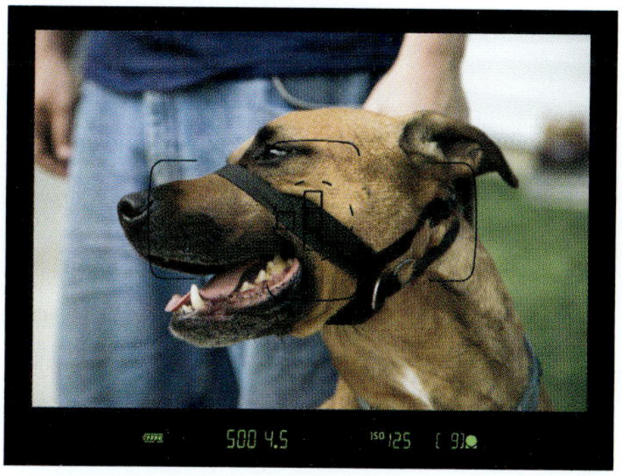

Figure 3-10: Focus and shoot.

If you are shooting in low light, the focusing screen flashes red briefly and then returns to normal.

12. **When you're ready to take the shot, press the Shutter button fully.**

    Figure 3-11 shows the resulting photo.

13. **Review and repeat.**

    Review the photo to make sure that the composition is what you want, the exposure is good, and the focus is sharp (you may have to zoom in to check this). Erase if necessary. (See Chapter 5 for photo review and playback options.)

    Correct problems if necessary and shoot again.

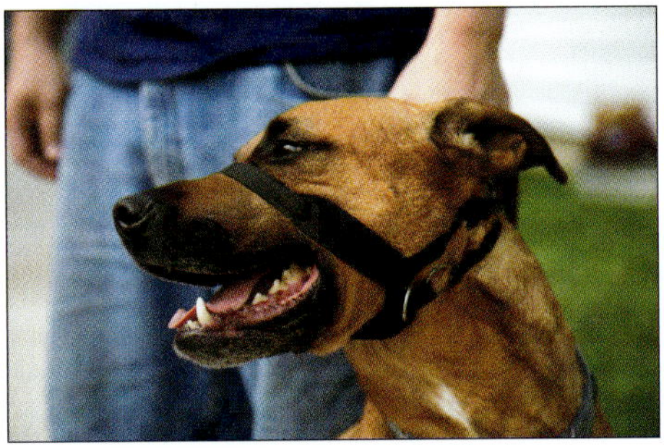

Figure 3-11: The finished product.

Fine-tuning your technique

Use the techniques in this section to help improve how you manage Scene Intelligent Auto mode and for times when your shots don't turn out as you hoped.

Improving your composition skills with focus lock

Although many subjects lend themselves to being centered in the viewfinder, it's often more pleasing to shift the main subject to the side. Doing so makes room for you to showcase the background a bit, and the photo will look more natural.

The 5D Mark III has such a wide spread of AF points, it's often possible to offset a subject and have no trouble getting it in focus. It becomes more of a problem, however, when intervening objects are in the immediate foreground and the camera wants to focus on them.

Either way, you can intentionally focus on a subject off to the side (provided that you don't want to switch to manual focus) by following these steps:

1. **Center the subject.**

   This works best with still subjects. If the subject is moving, the autofocus mode switches to AI Servo AF (see Chapter 8) and tries to track and lock onto the movement. See the next section.

2. **Press and hold the Shutter button halfway to meter and focus.**

   By centering the subject, you're giving it top priority. If the camera focuses properly, you're ready for the next step. If you can't get the right subject focused, no matter how you initially compose the shot, you'll have to switch to a more advanced shooting mode (in which you have more control over autofocus) or focus manually.

3. **Recompose the shot to take the subject off-center.**

   Remember to keep holding the Shutter button halfway.

4. **Fully press the Shutter button to take the photo.**

   Figure 3-12 illustrates how I used focus lock to place my primary subject to the right of the frame but still have her in focus. I wanted the lights and other performers to be featured prominently, yet not take center stage in this shot.

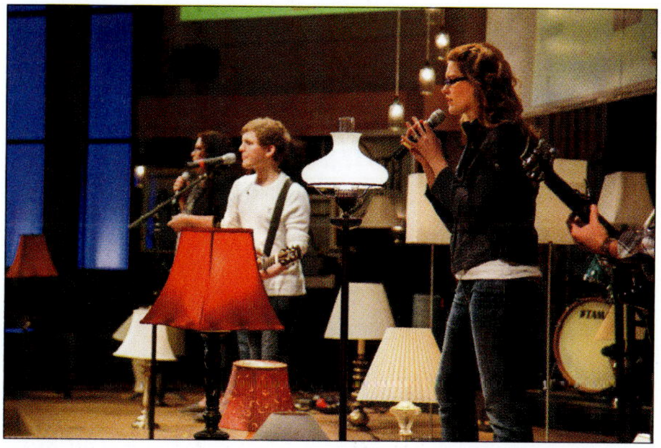

Figure 3-12: Focus lock gives you the flexibility to place your subjects off-center.

Taking action shots

You shouldn't have to do anything special to take action shots when in Scene Intelligent Auto mode. The 5D Mark III switches to AI Servo AF mode (see Chapter 8), in which it continually focuses on a subject even when it is in focus (as opposed to focusing once, beeping, and then quitting). The subject therefore can be moving toward (as shown in Figure 3-13) or away from you and the camera will continue to keep it in focus.

That sounds all well and good. However, there are so many types of action that you might want to shoot — and some with distracting objects — that focusing on the right moving object can be very hard when you leave it all up to the camera. That's why the 5D Mark III has so many AI Servo AF modes.

If Scene Intelligent Auto isn't working, you should switch to a different mode. You'll more than likely find Tv, Shutter-Priority AE, the best for your needs, unless you want to go full manual (M). In these modes, you can manage the shutter speed yourself, plus take more control over different AF modes and AI Servo AF cases. See Chapter 8 for more information.

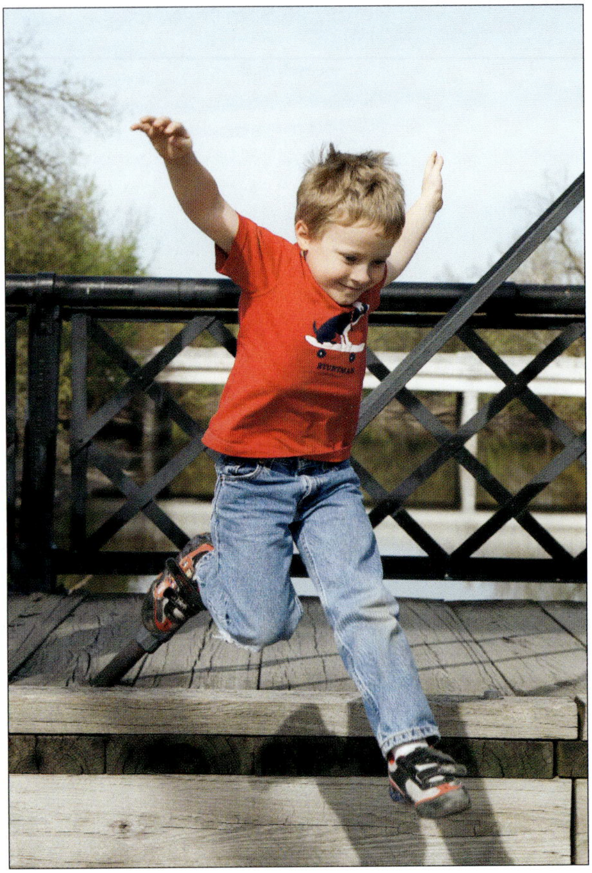

Figure 3-13: Super Sam!

Oh, and there's always manual focus. Give it a try!

Handling backlighting

When you photograph something in front of a bright light source, most often a window or when looking up into the sky, you run the risk of underexposing the subject (see Figure 3-14). The camera's light meter works overtime to try to keep the bright light source from turning completely white, which is known as *blowing out*. When that happens, you'll see an ugly featureless patch in your photo that may be hard to rescue. It's best to keep this from happening!

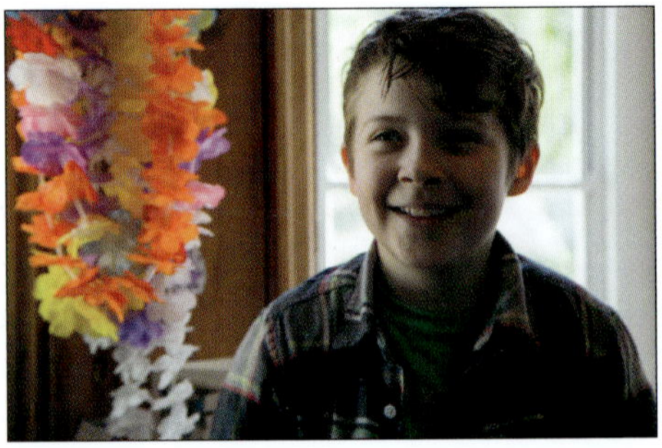

Figure 3-14: Bright background without a flash equals an underexposed subject.

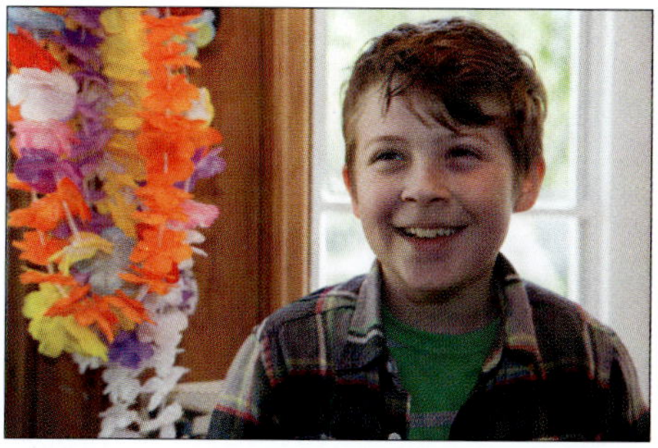

Figure 3-15: Using a fill flash fixes the problem.

One way to handle backlighting is to use *fill flash* (using a flash to brighten a dark subject, often backlit, even if the scene has enough light to take the photo without the flash). Because the 5D Mark III doesn't have a built-in flash, you have to be prepared beforehand. If possible, carry a Speedlite in your bag. Simply mount it on your 5D Mark III's hot shoe and turn it on. For fully auto shooting, you shouldn't have to do anything else. The problems shown in Figure 3-14 are corrected in Figure 3-15.

You cannot take control of the flash when in Scene Intelligent Auto mode. Your Speedlite should automatically set itself to ETTL (Evaluative-Through The Lens) or TTL (Through The Lens) flash mode. If the flash looks too bright, you will have to bounce it or shoot through a modifier (an umbrella or soft box) to soften it, because you cannot use flash exposure compensation.

You may also use other light sources, whether continuous (always on) or stroboscopic (a flash), to handle back lighting, and work them independently of the camera.

If you don't have a flash or other light source, try recomposing the shot to avoid the backlighting issue entirely.

Working in low light

Dim lighting, unless part of a creative effect, is almost always problematic. Here are some things to look out for:

- **Shutter speed:** Low light pushes shutter speeds slower and slower. At some point, you won't be able to hold the camera steady enough, even with a still subject. When the shutter speed display in the viewfinder blinks, the camera is warning you that you may be in for a blurry photo. If possible, support the camera on a tripod or add lighting.
- **Focus:** Autofocus is harder to achieve in low light. The problem is, because of the dim light, manual focus can be even harder. You might be able to switch to Live View shooting. More on this using Live View in "Live View: Using the LCD Monitor as a Viewfinder," later in this chapter.
- **Lens:** Depending on your lens, you may not have great low-light capability. The kit lens, which opens to f/4.0, is not the best performer.

  Don't get me wrong: The EF 24-105mm f/4L IS USM is still a great lens with outstanding optical characteristics. But it won't outperform the EF 85mm f/1.2L II USM when it comes to letting in more light. The kit lens is helped, however, by the 5D's incredible full-frame, high ISO performance and image stabilization.

If you find yourself working in low-light conditions a lot, consider investing in a lens with the widest possible aperture. Even if you don't open it all the way, you should be able to get a few stops more light than f/4.0.

TIP

Play back your photos (see Chapter 5) and review what settings the camera is using when in Scene Intelligent Auto. If the camera isn't using all your aperture, you may want to switch to Av mode (Aperture-Priority AE) and set it yourself (see Chapter 6 for more about using the Aperture-Priority AE shooting mode).

Overcoming autofocus problems

At times, even the best autofocus system can be overwhelmed or underfed to the point where it can't achieve focus. If the focus confirmation light blinks and autofocus is never achieved, consider the following possible problems and potential solutions:

- **Low contrast:** Any AF system will have trouble when trying to focus on a scene with limited contrast. Imagine trying to take a picture of a polar bear on the ice in a snow storm with clouds and fog swirling around. If possible, add some contrast to the scene (change subjects), add lighting (light produces shadows, which adds contrast), change your position (you might find more contrast when coming to the scene from a different angle), wait for another day, or switch to Manual focus and try yourself.
- **Low light:** The camera needs light to be able to focus.
- **Extreme backlight:** When you shoot into extreme backlighting, the camera may have trouble focusing. It's just too bright. Try recomposing the scene or switching to Manual focus.
- **Movement:** If you or your subject are moving too fast, you might have trouble locking onto your target. The 5D III's AI Servo AF mode is very capable, but not foolproof. Consider switching to another shooting mode so that you can configure the system to better match the circumstances (see Chapter 8) or switch to manual focus.
- **Distance:** If you are too close to the subject, the lens cannot physically focus. The minimum focus distance for the kit lens (EF 24-105mm f/4L IS USM) is 45cm, or about 18 inches, which is about how far away I was from my basketball, shown in Figure 3-16. This is not as close as a good wide-angle or macro lens. The closest focusing distance of the EF 17-40mm f/4L USM lens is 28cm, or 11 inches; the 100mm f/2.8L Macro IS USM can be as close as 30cm, which is just under 12 inches. Check your distance and, if necessary, stand back a bit.

TIP

In any situation in which you can mount the camera on a tripod, consider using Live View shooting with the image magnifier and manual focus to really zoom in and check your focus.

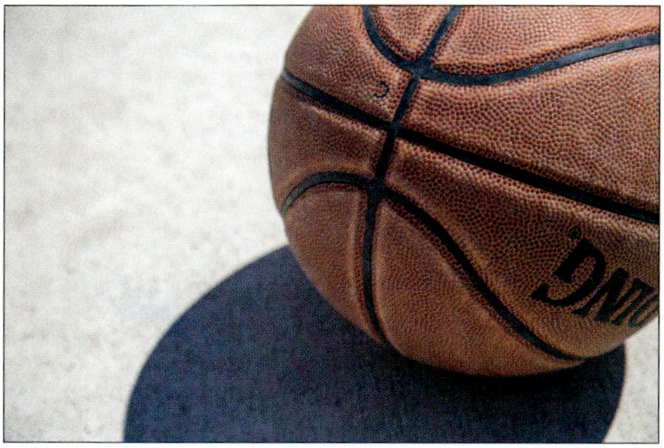

Figure 3-16: Look at your lens's manual to find its minimum focus distance.

Available menus in Scene Intelligent Auto

This section is devoted to providing an easy reference for what menu options are available when you're in Scene Intelligent Auto shooting mode. Tables 3-1 through 3-3 are organized by main menu sections:

- **Shooting menus:** Table 3-1 reveals the Shooting options.
- **Playback menus:** Table 3-2 lists Playback options.
- **Setup menus:** Table 3-3 shows you the setup options available when you're in Scene Intelligent Auto.

Note that these menus are completely absent: Autofocus, Custom Functions, and My Menu.

Table 3-1 Shooting Options in Scene Intelligent Auto

Shooting Menu 1	*Shooting Menu 2 (Live View)*	*Shooting Menu 2 (Movie)*	*Shooting Menu 3 (Movie)*
Image Quality	Live View Shooting	AF Mode	Time Code
Image Review	AF Mode	Grid Display	Silent Control
Beep	Grid Display	Movie Recording Size	
Release Shutter Without Card			
Lens Aberration Correction			

When compared to what's available at other times, the Shooting menus are pared down to the bare minimum.

The Playback menus (see Table 3-2) are largely unchanged.

Table 3-2 Playback Options in Scene Intelligent Auto

Playback Menu 1	*Playback Menu 2*	*Playback Menu 3*
Protect Images	Resize	Highlight Alert
Rotate Images	Rating	AF Point Display
Erase Images	Slide Show	Playback Grid
Print Order	Image Transfer	Histogram Display
Image Copy	Image Jump with Main Dial	Movie Play Count
		Magnification (approximate)
		Control over HDMI

Most Setup menus (see Table 3-3) are the same. However, Custom Shooting modes are not available, nor are the other options available in Setup Menu 4.

Table 3-3 Setup Options in Scene Intelligent Auto

Setup Menu 1	*Setup Menu 2*	*Setup Menu 3*
Record Function+Card/Folder Select	Auto Power Off	Video System
File Numbering	LCD Brightness	Sensor Cleaning
File Name	Date/Time/Zone	Info Button Display Options
Auto Rotate	Language	Rate Button Function
Format Card	VF Grid Display	

Live View: Using the LCD Monitor as a Viewfinder

Live View is the now-standard name given to the camera feature with which you frame images via its LCD monitor rather than the viewfinder (as shown in Figure 3-17), just as you may have done when using a point-and-shoot digital camera. On the 5D Mark III, you can opt for Live View shooting for still photography. For movie recording, it's your *only* option because you can't use the viewfinder when making movies. (Shooting movies is covered in Chapter 4.)

Whatever you're shooting, be aware of the following monitor-related tips and warnings anytime you take advantage of Live View:

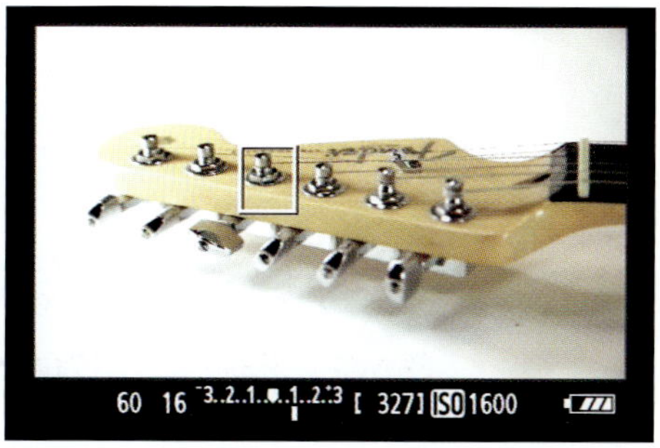

Figure 3-17: Using Live View on the 5D Mark III.

- **Consider your focusing methods.** In addition to manual focus, you have a choice of three autofocusing methods, described in "Focusing in Live View," later in this chapter. These autofocusing options are different from those available during regular still photography, which are covered in Chapter 8.

WARNING!

- **Using Live View for an extended period can reduce picture quality and harm your camera.** When you work in Live View mode, the camera's innards heat up more than usual, and that extra heat can create the right electronic conditions for *noise,* a defect that gives pictures a speckled look. Perhaps more critically, the increased temperatures can damage the camera.

  If the yellow symbol shown in the margin appears on the monitor, the camera is warning you that it's getting too hot. If you continue shooting and the temperature continues to increase, the camera will display a blinking red icon (the second symbol). The camera is warning you that it will soon automatically shut off to prevent damage. Don't let the situation progress to that point, though. Your pictures will probably be noisy, and you risk permanently harming the camera. So when you see this yellow symbol, quickly wrap up your Live View shooting to give the monitor a rest. Also, seriously consider turning off the camera so that the temperature can stabilize and start to fall.

  Keep in mind that in extremely warm environments, you may not be able to use Live View mode for long before the system shuts down.

- **Aiming the lens at the sun or other bright lights also can damage the camera.** Of course, you can cause problems doing this even during normal shooting, but the potential risk increases when you use Live View.

- **Anytime you use the camera monitor, whether composing a shot or reviewing images, you put extra strain on the battery.** Keep an eye on the battery level icon to avoid running out of juice at a critical moment.

- **The monitor display can wash out in bright sunlight.** You may find it difficult to compose outdoor shots in Live View mode although the 5D Mark III has improved the appearance of the LCD in sunlight.
- **It's not a panacea.** Although using the monitor as a viewfinder frees your head from being permanently attached to the camera, it doesn't solve all your composition problems. The main reason is that the monitor on the 5D Mark III is not articulated. As a result, you can't lower the camera down to the floor or raise it up high or shoot around corners the way you can with other, more consumer-oriented dSLRs (the Canon EOS 60D and the Canon EOS Rebel T3i/600D come to mind).

Entering Live View shooting mode

Before you dig in, be aware of the following caveats about Live View photography:

- **Some photography features are disabled or limited in Live View mode.** Here's the list of affected features:
    - *Flash:* Flash Exposure Lock (covered in Chapter 6) is disabled. Additionally, non-Canon flash units won't work when Silent LV Shooting is set to Mode 1 or Mode 2. Disable it in Shooting Menu 4. Here's yet one more quirk: When you take a flash shot in Live View mode, the camera's shutter sound leads you to believe that two shots have been recorded; in reality, though, only one photo is captured.
    - *Continuous Shooting:* You can shoot continuously (covered in Chapter 2), but the camera uses the exposure settings chosen for the first frame for all images. Also, as with flash shots, you hear two shutter sounds for the first frame in the continuous sequence.
    - *Metering mode:* You cannot use partial, spot, or center-weighted average exposure metering; the camera always uses evaluative metering in Live View mode. Chapter 6 explains metering modes.
    - *Mirror Lockup:* You can't enable Mirror Lockup (see Chapter 11) in Live View mode because the mirror is already locked up.
- **You must be extra careful to keep the camera steady.** When you use the monitor to frame the image, you must hold the camera away from your body (see Figure 3-3), a shooting posture that increases the likelihood of blurry images caused by camera shake. When you use the viewfinder, you can brace the camera against your face, creating a much steadier shooting stance. Also, if you use a *long lens* (a telephoto or zoom lens that extends to a long focal length), the potential for camera shake is compounded. So, for best results, mount the camera on a tripod when

you use Live View, or choose an ISO that enables you to use higher shutter speeds. (Chapter 6 goes more fully into the topics of ISO and shutter speed.)

- **Cover the viewfinder to prevent light from seeping into the camera and affecting exposure.** The camera ships with a cover designed just for this purpose.

This laundry list of warnings doesn't mean that you shouldn't use Live View, however — just that you shouldn't envision it as a full-time alternative to using your viewfinder. Rather, think of Live View as a special-purpose tool that can help in shooting situations in which framing with the viewfinder is cumbersome.

TIP

Live View is helpful when doing still-life studio or tabletop photography, for example, especially in cases that require a lot of careful arrangement of the scene. Often, you want to place your camera at a low or high position to compose the subject with the drama and perspective you desire. Scrunching down or climbing on tippy toes to get your eye to the viewfinder can be a real hassle. With Live View, you can alleviate much of that bothersome routine (and pain) because you can see how objects look in the monitor no matter the camera position. You can also zoom in to check focus.

With that lengthy preamble out of the way, enabling Live View is pretty easy. Here's how:

1. **Decide whether you want to use auto or manual focusing; set the lens to the appropriate position.**

   For manual focusing, set the lens switch to MF; for autofocusing, set it to AF. If the switch on your lens is labeled differently, consult the lens manual for specifics.

2. **If the camera is mounted on a tripod, turn off the Image Stabilizer feature.**

   Image stabilization (IS) isn't necessary when you shoot with a tripod. Also, because IS consumes extra battery power, turning it off is a good idea for Live View tripod shooting with most lenses. However, check your lens manual just to be sure: Some lens manufacturers vary in their recommendations on this issue.

3. **Make sure that the Live View shooting/ Movie shooting switch is set to Live View (see Figure 3-18).**

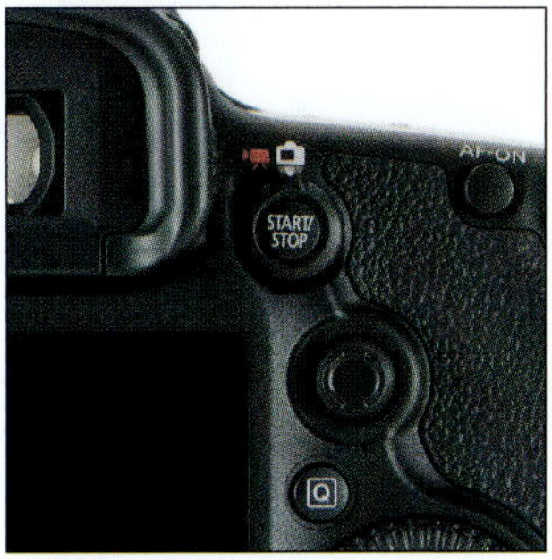

Figure 3-18: The switch goes up for Live View; the button in the center activates it.

For Live View shooting, the switch should point straight up.

4. **Press the Start/Stop button (see Figure 3-18) to display the Live View image on the LCD monitor.**

   Five display options, shown in Figure 3-19, are available during Live View shooting. Press the Info button to cycle through the display modes. The next section explains them and how to interpret everything you see.

   REMEMBER

   If nothing appears on your monitor, you may have accidentally disabled Live View shooting from the menu. Press the Menu button, navigate to Shooting Menu 4, and make sure that Live View Shooting is set to Enable. If not, highlight Live View Shooting, press the Set button, and choose Enable.

5. **Focus, meter, change shooting functions, take the shot, and review it.**

   These aspects of Live View shooting (except for playback and review) are covered more in depth as this chapter continues.

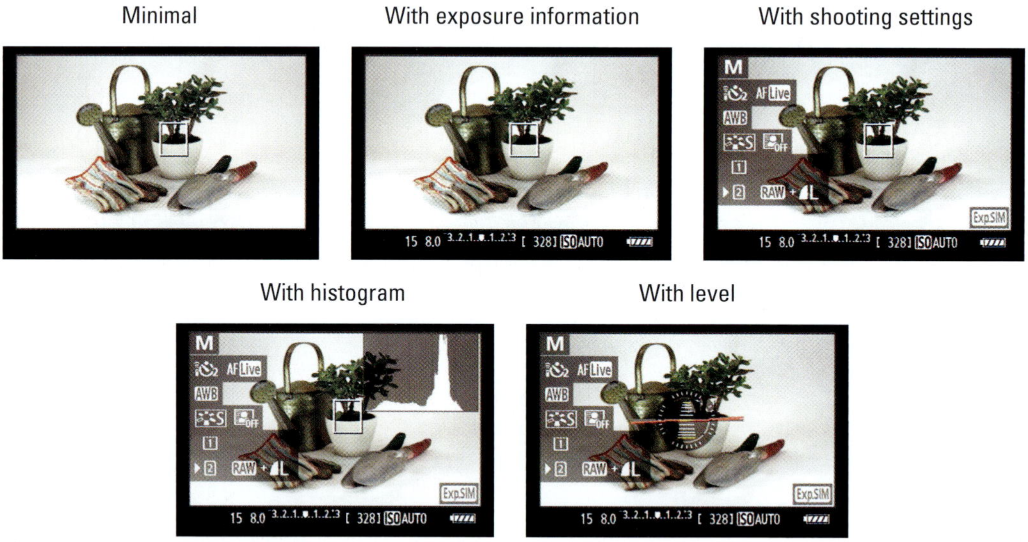

Figure 3-19: Cycling through Live View display options.

Decoding the information display

When you first use Live View mode, you see your subject and the focusing frame. You can press Info to add basic shooting information (the exposure index, ISO, and battery indicator, to name a few) to the bottom of the display. A second press reveals an assortment of settings along the left side (White Balance, AF mode, and so forth). A third press of the button adds Brightness Histogram into the mix, and a fourth removes the histogram and adds the electronic level. Press Info again to cycle back to the default display.

Figure 3-20 serves as your road map to the maxed-out data display; the following list gives you the guided tour:

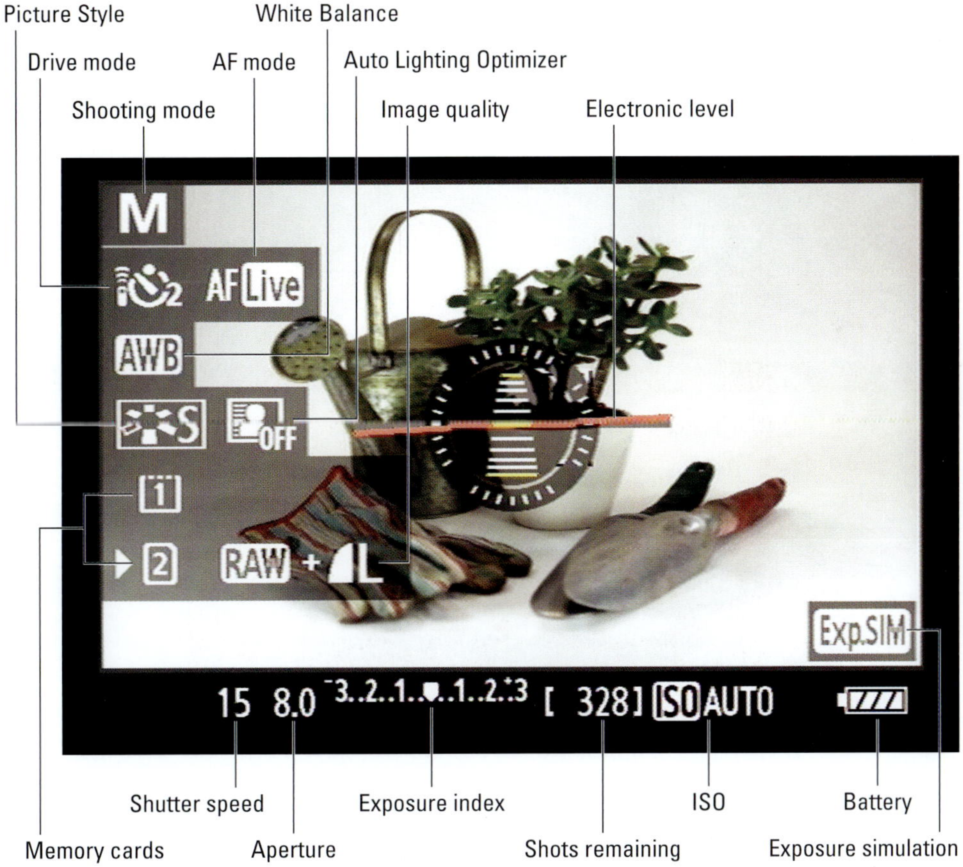

Figure 3-20: You can choose to display all this shooting data in the Live View frame.

- **Data along the bottom of the screen is similar to data you normally see in the viewfinder display.** With the exception of the shots-remaining value and the battery level status, these settings relate to exposure issues (which you can explore in Chapter 6). Additional Flash Compensation and Highlight Tone Priority symbols (not shown in Figure 3-20) appear only if you enable those features from menus.
- **The autofocus mode symbol appears regardless of whether you set your lens to manual or autofocus.** The symbol tells you which of the three possible autofocus options is selected.
- **Some other symbols on the left side of the screen are the same as when you view shooting information in Playback mode.** Playback is discussed in Chapter 5; here's a quick preview:
  - *Picture Style:* Chapter 8 details Picture Styles, which affect picture color, contrast, and sharpness. The symbol you see in Figure 3-20 represents the Standard style.
  - *White Balance:* The initials AWB, shown in Figure 3-20, represent Auto White Balance. To see what icons for other settings look like and find out what white balance does in the first place, visit Chapter 8.
  - *Drive mode:* The icon you see in the figure represents Single Drive mode, in which you capture one image for each press of the Shutter button. See the end of Chapter 2 for information about other drive modes.
  - *Card indicators:* These icons tell you which memory cards you have inserted into the camera and which one (or it can be both) is set to record to.
  - *Quality:* This icon tells you the selected Quality setting, which Chapter 2 explains. The symbol shown in the figure represents the Large/Fine Quality setting.
  - *AE (Autoexposure) Lock* and *Flash Status* are two more symbols you might see on your screen. Neither symbol appears if you don't use these features (they weren't used for Figure 3-20). Both of these features are covered in Chapter 6.
- **Symbols you might see in the lower-right corner indicate the following:**
  - *AEB:* This symbol appears when you enable Automatic Exposure Bracketing (AEB), an exposure tool covered in Chapter 6. If you see an *FEB* indication (for Flash Exposure Bracketing), be aware that that function is possible only when you shoot with a compatible Canon Speedlite external flash. See the flash unit's manual for help with this option.

- *Exp.SIM:* This symbol, which stands for Exposure Simulation, indicates whether the image brightness you see on the monitor is simulating the actual exposure you will record. If the symbol blinks or is dimmed, the camera can't provide an accurate exposure preview, which can occur if the ambient light is either very bright or very dim. Exposure Simulation is also disabled when you use a flash in Live View mode.

- **The Brightness histogram is another tool you can use to gauge whether your current settings will produce a good exposure.** See the discussion on interpreting a Brightness histogram in Chapter 5 to find out how to make sense of what you see. When you use a flash, however, the histogram is dimmed; what you can see isn't accurate because it doesn't reflect the exposure as it will be when the flash is used.

Customizing Live View

Shooting still photos in Live View mode involves a few options that differ from those you encounter for regular photography with the 5D Mark III. In fact, there's even a separate Live View menu that contains options available only when the camera is in Live View mode. Shooting Menu 4 contains the Live View settings, which are described in the following list and shown in Figure 3-21.

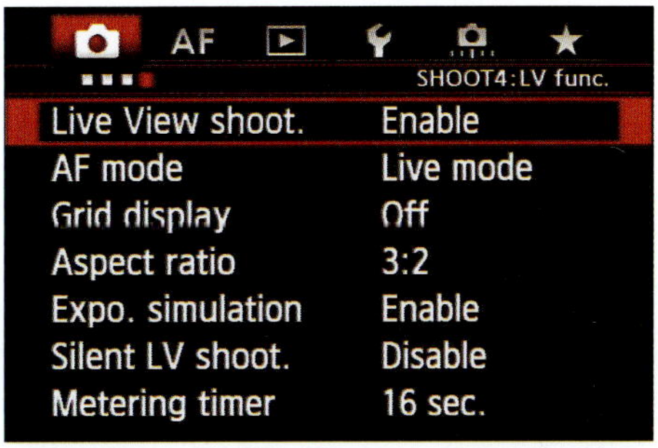

Figure 3-21: Shooting Menu 4 houses Live View settings.

- **Live View Shooting:** Enable or disable Live View. When disabled, pressing the Live View button does nothing.
- **AF Mode:** Choose a Live View AF mode from this menu. Options are:
  - *Live mode:* This is the standard AF mode in Live View. It's slower than standard autofocus and requires that you move a focus rectangle over the subject.
  - *Face Detection Live mode:* This AF mode can detect faces, which is great when you're photographing people or animals and the camera can reliably see their faces. In fact, it's ideal when shooting standard portraits and casual shots of your friends and family. The camera may not always be able to make out faces, however, in low light or when the subject is moving about or not looking directly at you.

  - *Quick mode:* This mode uses the AF sensor that the camera uses when you are in viewfinder mode. The downside to Quick mode is that it blanks out the Live View monitor when focusing.

  I provide more info on each AF mode in the next section.

- **Grid Display:** When you're doing the kind of work for which Live View is best suited, such as taking product shots or capturing other still-life subjects, you often have the ability to place objects in the frame very precisely. To assist with this careful composition, the camera can display a grid on the monitor. You can choose from three types of grids (shown in Figure 3-22):

  - *3 by 3:* Grid lines that divide the screen horizontally and vertically into thirds. This makes composing according to the Rule of Thirds much easier.
  - *6 by 4:* This display adds more grid lines to the screen. There are twice as many horizontal lines, which subdivide the screen into six equal parts. The vertical space is divided into quarters instead of thirds.
  - *3 by 3 Plus Diagonals:* Start with a 3 by 3 grid and then add diagonal lines that connect each corner to its opposite (the diagonals look like a large X). This combination gives you a feeling of perspective if you make the center of the screen the vanishing point.

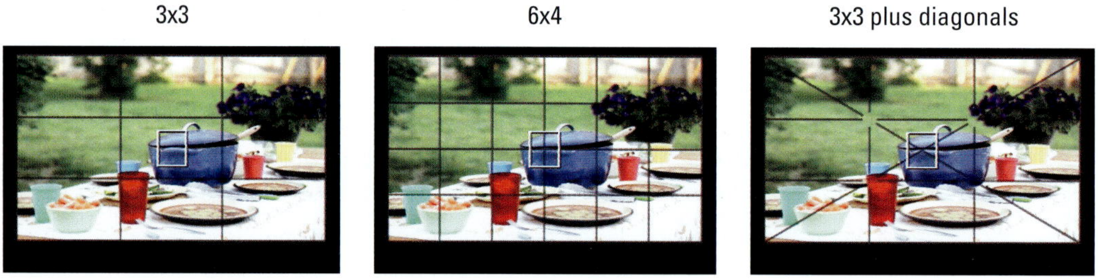

Figure 3-22: The grid helps you align objects in the scene.

- **Aspect Ratio:** The 5D Mark III takes photos with a traditional 3:2 *aspect ratio* (the relationship of a photo's width to its height) by default, but this isn't the only option. You can set the following aspect ratios when shooting in Live View mode:
  - *3:2:* The standard aspect ratio, derived from the aspect ratio of the sensor, which is the same as 35mm film
  - *4:3:* The same aspect ratio as older televisions
  - *16:9:* Creates photos with a widescreen appearance
  - *1:1:* Square photos

  See Chapter 2 to translate these aspect ratios into pixel measurements based on the image quality you've set.

  When you select an aspect ratio, the JPEGs produced are cropped, and the original data cannot be recovered. RAW photos, although they appear cropped, contain all the original data, which means that you can change your mind about the aspect ratio later (when using Digital Photo Professional).
- **Exposure Simulation:** When enabled, the monitor displays the photo as it would look given the current exposure settings. In other words, if you're underexposing the scene, the preview will be too dark. This is a great way to visualize exposure before you commit by taking the photo.

  When disabled, you see a preview that is exposed so that you can see it on the monitor better. It may bear little resemblance to the actual photo.

  If you're having trouble seeing to focus, disable Exposure Simulation so that the screen looks brighter.

  If you want the best of both worlds, select During Depth-of-Field Preview. This option disables Exposure Simulation unless you press the depth-of-field preview button.
- **Silent LV Shooting:** Silent LV shooting changes how the camera sounds. You can disable it or choose between two modes that sound and behave differently:

- *Mode 1:* This mode is quieter than normal but does not prohibit continuous or high-speed continuous shooting.
- *Mode 2:* Shooting noise is minimized at the expense of shooting speed. Taking a photo and holding down the Shutter button prevents you from taking another photo. You have to release the Shutter button halfway to be able to take another photo. Clearly, only single shots are possible in this mode.
- *Disabled:* Turns off Silent Shooting; you hear more clunks and knocks (normal camera noise) as the mirror flips back and forth in the camera body.

- **Metering Timer:** Controls how long the camera displays exposure information after you press the Shutter button halfway and the camera meters the scene. The default is 16 seconds, but other values range from 4 seconds to 30 minutes.

If you are in Scene Intelligent Auto shooting mode, your Live View menu is more limited. As Figure 3-23 reveals, there are only three options: Live View Shooting, AF Mode, and Grid Display.

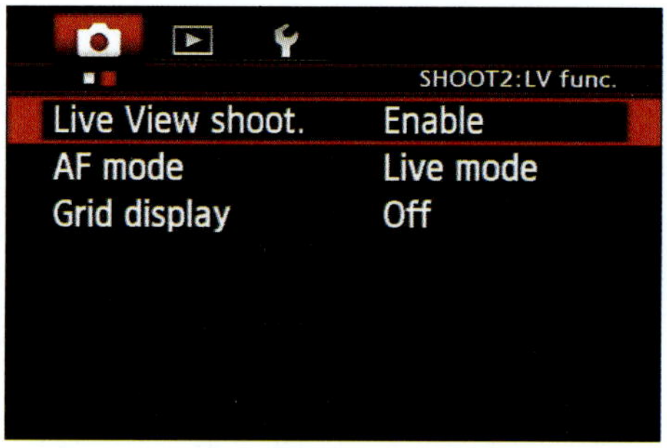

Figure 3-23: The Live View menu is more limited when in Scene Intelligent Auto mode.

Managing the Camera in Live View

Okay, so after you're in Live View mode, how do you change things such as the aperture, shutter speed, or ISO? The answer is, by pressing the associated button directly (for example, ISO) or by entering a limited Quick Control mode. Both methods are explained in this section.

Changing shooting functions

After you have entered Live View mode and are viewing the scene on the monitor, press any of the following buttons to bring up an associated settings screens; then use the appropriate control to change the setting:

- **White Balance Selection button:** Spin the Quick Control dial to change white balance (see Figure 3-24). Note that you cannot change the metering mode in Live View.
- **AF Mode Selection/Drive Mode Selection button:** Change the Live View AF mode with the Main dial, or change the drive mode with the Quick Control dial. See Figure 3-25.
- **ISO Speed Setting/Flash Exposure Compensation button:** Change ISO speed with the Main dial and Flash Exposure Compensation with the Quick Control dial (as in Figure 3-26).
- **AF Point Selection button:** When the Live View AF mode is set to Quick, pressing the AF Point Selection button enables you to change the AF Selection mode, as shown in Figure 3-27.

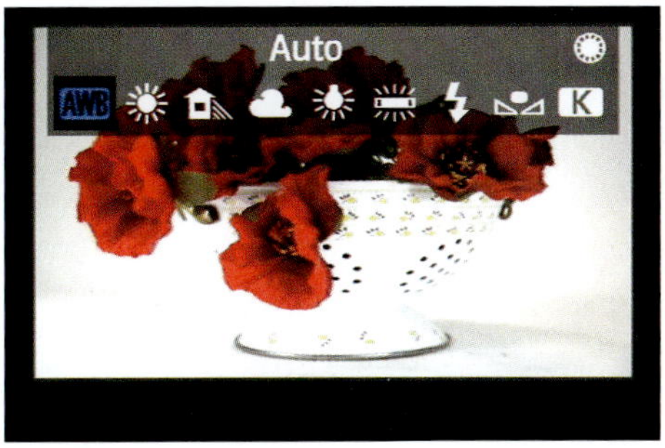

Figure 3-24: Changing white balance in Live View.

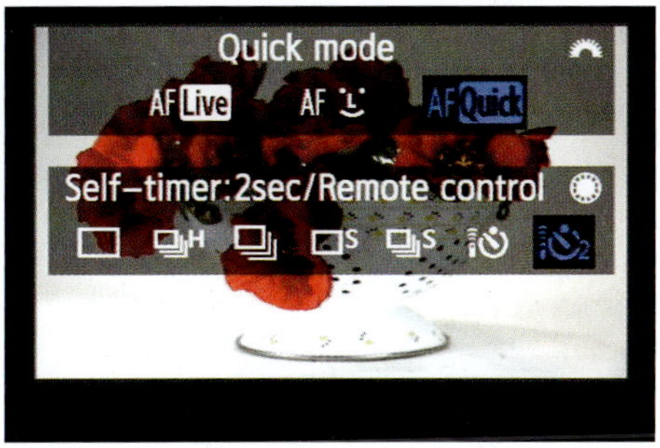

Figure 3-25: This is a double-whammy: AF mode or drive mode.

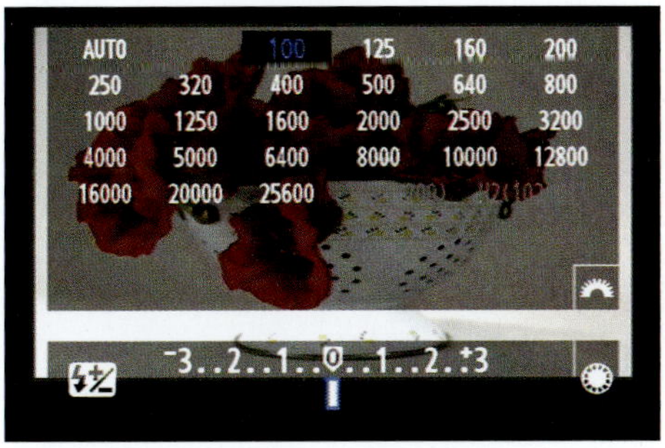

Figure 3-26: Notice that the top control is governed by the Main dial and the bottom by the Quick Control dial.

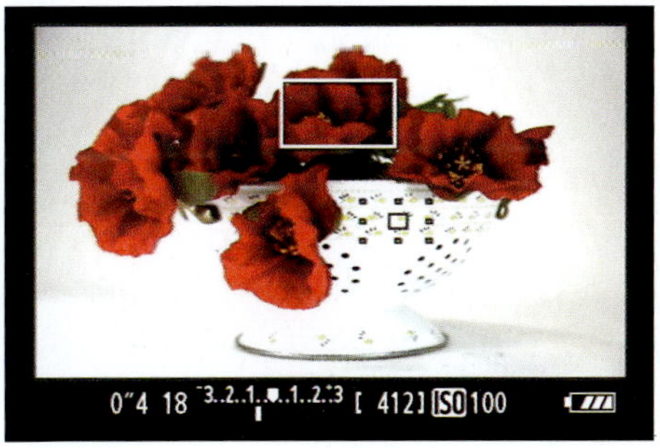

Figure 3-27: Select AF points in Quick mode.

Switch modes by pressing the M-Fn button. After the mode is selected, use the controller of your choice to change AF points or zones.

- **Creative Photo button:** Press this button to choose a new Picture Style (Chapter 8), shoot with multiple exposures (Chapter 11), or shoot using HDR Mode (Chapter 6). See Figure 3-28.

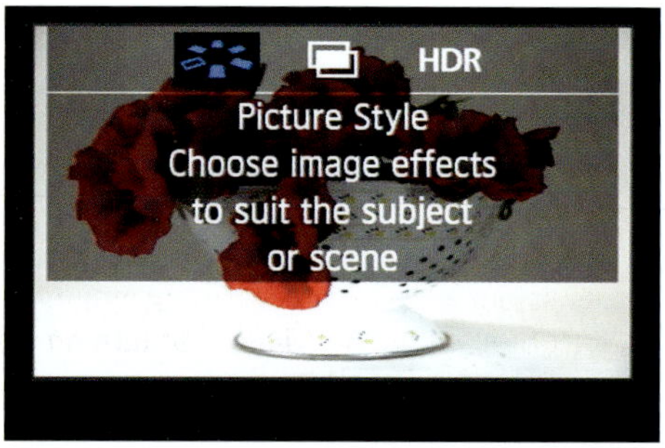

Figure 3-28: You can even access creative modes in Live View.

Using Quick Control

Chapter 1 explains how you can use the Quick Control screen to adjust certain camera settings. In Live View mode, you can use the Quick Control method to adjust the Auto Lighting Optimizer, card selection, recording function (see Chapter 11), and image quality.

That's it. Quick Control mode is much less capable in Live View mode than it is when you're shooting with the viewfinder.

To use this feature, press the Quick Control button to activate the strip of icons on the left side of the screen. Then use the Multicontroller to highlight the option you want to adjust. Text appears at the bottom of the screen to show you the current setting. For example, in Figure 3-29, the Auto Lighting Optimizer option is highlighted; the text label shows that the Standard setting is active.

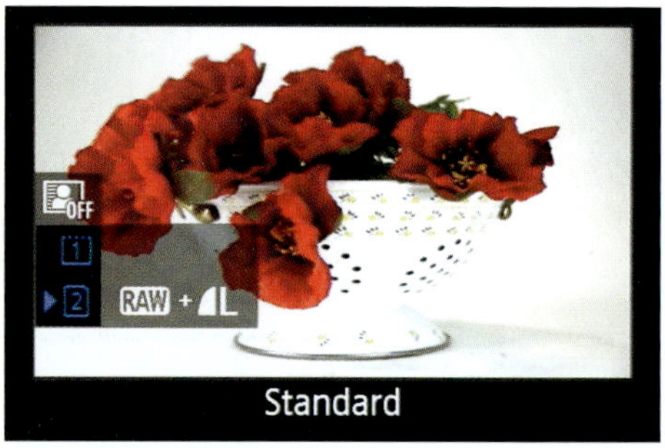

Figure 3-29: Press the Quick Control button to use the Live View version of the Quick Control screen.

After you highlight an icon on the left side of the screen, rotate the Main dial to cycle through the available settings. Press the Quick Control button again (or half-press the shutter release) to return to the normal Live View display and take the picture.

Live View and HDTV

If you want to blow your mind, get an HDMI cable and run it from your camera's HDMI terminal to a high-def TV. Turn the camera on and select it from your TV's input options. Press Start/Stop on the 5D Mark III to turn on the live preview; then watch in stunned amazement as the camera uses the TV (the bigger, the better) in place of the monitor on the back.

This shot illustrates the point.

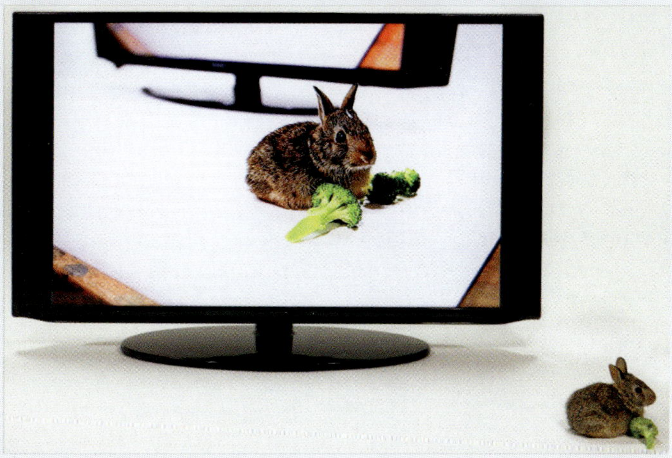

I unplugged our 40-inch HDTV and carried it from our living room to my studio; then I hooked it to the 5D Mark III via an extra HDMI input terminal on the TV. I got my wife to help wrangle with the rabbit while I set up a close-up using Live View and manual focus. I then stepped back and took this photo with another camera while the 5D Mark III continued to channel Live View video out to the TV. Awesome!

Focusing in Live View

Live View mode offers three distinctly different autofocus modes, which I explain in the preceding section. This section shows you the basics of each mode. As you continue to read how to take photos in Live View mode later in the chapter, return here for detailed information on using autofocus modes.

Focusing with the Live View autofocus modes

When in Live View mode, you can choose any of the three focus modes: Live, Face Detection Live, and Quick mode. Each one differs from the others, and the rationale for choosing to use each one differs as well. You may also use manual focus when in Live View mode, although focus harder to achieve unless you increase the magnification (covered later in this chapter, in "Precision focusing in manual focus mode") or use a large HDTV or widescreen computer monitor as your Live View monitor.

Live mode

Live mode autofocus is best suited for shooting static subjects, such as landscapes, portraits, or still lifes. If you're shooting someone who is running all over the place, you'll have an impossible time focusing and getting a good shot using Live mode.

To use Live mode, follow these steps:

1. **Set AF mode to Live mode:**

   a. *Press Menu, navigate to Shooting Menu 4, highlight AF Mode (see the left image of Figure 3-30), and then press Set.*

   b. *Highlight Live mode (see the right image of Figure 3-30) and then press Set again to lock in your choice.*

2. **Press the Live View button.**

   You see a white rectangle in the middle of the screen. This is the Live View AF point, which is the area the camera will "lock on" to when it focuses.

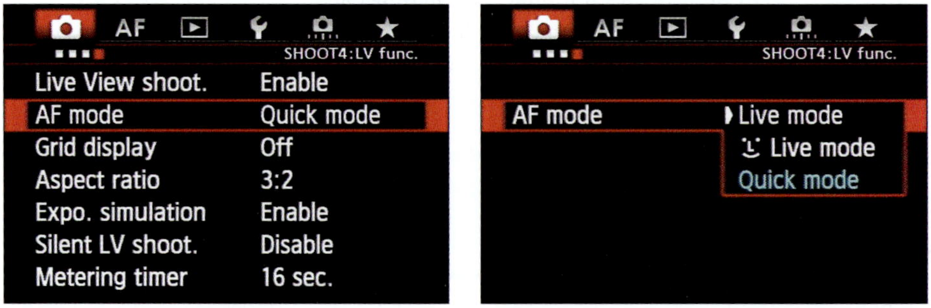

Figure 3-30: Selecting an AF mode.

3. Move the AF point around the screen with the Multicontroller.

The rectangle isn't always where you need it. You therefore have to be ready to move it around, which, as you will quickly realize, is a far cry from how fast autofocus works when you're using the viewfinder.

This procedure takes some skill — and patience — with your fingers while you wait for the box to move around.

If you want to reset the box to the center of the screen, press the Set button.

4. Initiate autofocus by pressing the Shutter button halfway or by pressing AF-ON.

The camera will attempt to achieve focus. When successful, it beeps and the white box turns green (see Figure 3-31). As long as you continue to hold the Shutter button halfway down (or press the AF-ON button), autofocus is locked. If you release the button before taking the photo, autofocus is lost.

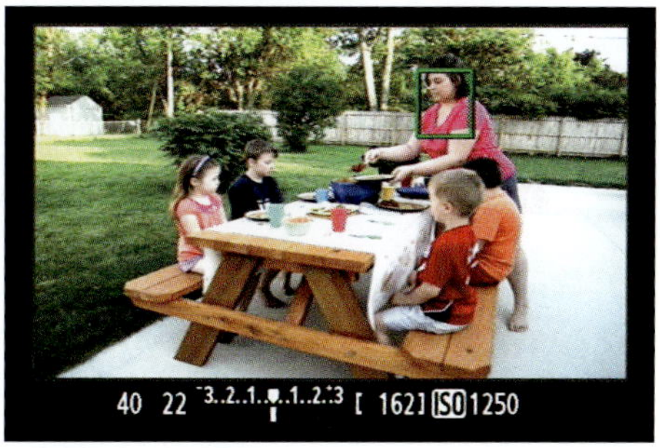

Figure 3-31: When the box turns green, you're in focus.

5. Take the photo.

If you're satisfied with the focus, composition, and exposure, go ahead and press the Shutter button all the way down to take the photo.

Face Detection Live mode

Face Detection Live mode is best suited for taking portraits and casual shots of people and animals. The camera attempts to detect faces, automatically moves the AF point over faces, and then focuses. One big difference between this mode and the normal Live mode is that you don't have to move the focus box around the screen. The camera tries to automatically detect and frame faces with an autofocus frame. That's right, *faces*. The 5D Mark III can detect multiple faces in the scene, which can cause confusion over which face to focus on. (You use the Multicontroller to move the target over a different face.)

Face detection works best when people or animals are looking directly at the camera, and the most prominent features that make up their face (their eyes and mouth) aren't obscured by hair or other objects. Face detection becomes more problematic when your subject is in profile or turned mostly away from the camera.

This mode isn't foolproof, but it's faster than normal Live mode and may enable you to shoot Live View shots of casual get-togethers and parties without becoming so frustrated that you blow a gasket.

To use Face Detection Live mode, follow these steps:

1. **Set AF mode to Face Detection Live mode:**

   a. *Press Menu, navigate to Shooting Menu 4, highlight AF mode, and press Set.*

   b. *Highlight Face Detection Live mode and then press Set again to lock in your choice.*

2. **Press the Live View button.**

   The camera analyzes the scene and tries to find faces. If it finds one, it places a frame around it. If it finds more than one, it places a frame with arrows on one (see Figure 3-32). To switch to a different face, use the Multicontroller. Face detection will follow a person around the screen. You don't need to do anything.

   If the camera can't detect a face in the scene, the normal AF rectangle is shown in the center.

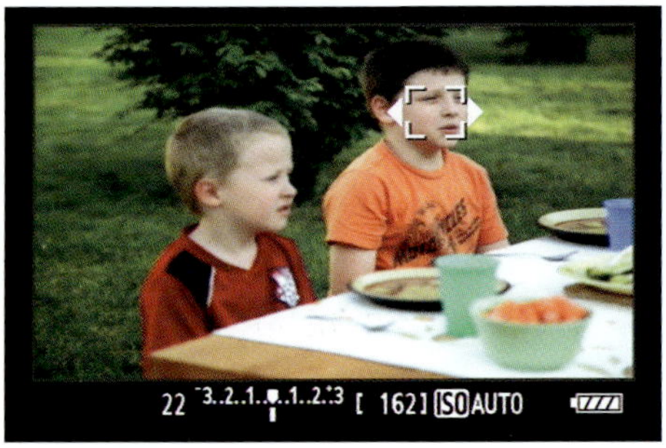

Figure 3-32: Detecting faces.

3. **Focus.**

   Detecting faces isn't the same thing as focusing. You still have to initiate autofocus by pressing the Shutter button halfway or pressing AF-ON. When focus is achieved, the white focus box turns green (see Figure 3-33), and you hear a beep.

4. **Press the Shutter button all the way down to take the photo.**

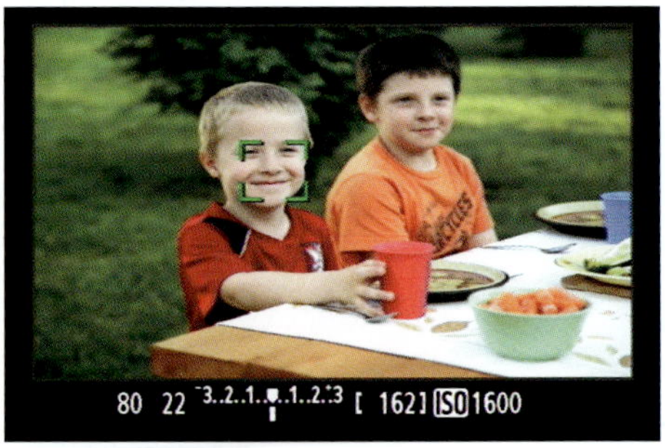

Figure 3-33: Locked on and in focus.

Quick mode

Quick mode sounds great, and it certainly sounds quicker than other modes, but it has some quirks that you have to get used to:

- The monitor is blacked out when the camera is focusing. You can't see what's in the frame during this time. This black-out can be disconcerting.
- You have to select an AF Area Selection mode and then choose an AF point or zone (provided that 61-Point Automatic Selection AF isn't the option). This process can take more effort than the other Live View AF modes. It feels less like point-and-shoot.

To use Quick mode, follow these steps:

1. **Set the AF mode to Quick mode:**

   a. *Press Menu, navigate to Shooting Menu 4, highlight AF Mode, and press Set.*

   b. *Highlight Quick mode and then press Set again to lock in your choice.*

2. **Press the Live View button.**

   If the AF mode is set to Quick mode (as in Step 1), you see the familiar white AF box appear on the LCD monitor, only it's not an AF box anymore. It's a magnifying frame that you can move.

   Also present are the AF points that match your mode. They are dark gray and seemingly don't do anything. At the moment, they don't.

3. **Focus by using one of two methods:**

   61-Point Automatic Selection AF: This is the "Take what the camera gives you" method, which is probably where the term *Quick mode* comes from. It's pretty fast, but the camera doesn't always focus on what you want. This path requires nothing more from you than this:

   a. *Press the Shutter button halfway (or AF-ON) to initiate autofocus and meter.*

   The camera makes a lot more noise than normal as the mirror clunks in and out of the way as the camera autofocuses.

   As you press the Shutter button halfway, the LCD screen goes black as the camera autofocuses. Try to stay motionless. When the picture comes back (see Figure 3-34), you're ready to take the shot.

Don't be fooled. The camera sounds like it's taking a photo, but it's not.

Manual AF Point Selection: The second path requires more work from you, but you get to control the focus points. Here's how:

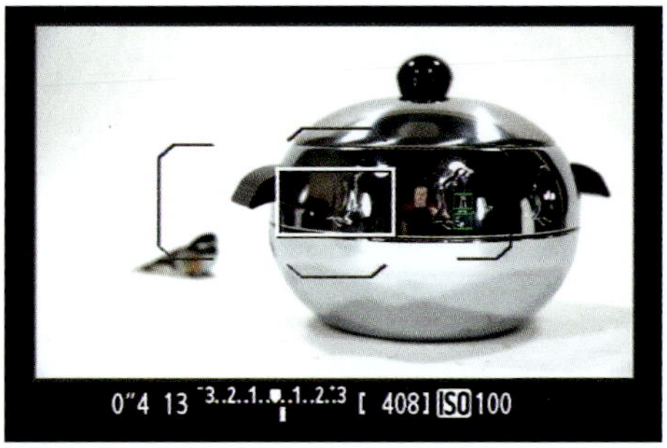

Figure 3-34: 61-Point Automatic Selection AF in action using Quick mode in Live View.

a. Press the AF Area Selection button.

b. Switch AF Area Selection modes by pressing the M-Fn button.

Look at the monitor to see the modes as they are shown (see the left image in Figure 3-35).

c. Select an AF point or zone by using the Main dial, Quick Control dial, or Multicontroller (see the right image in Figure 3-35).

d. If necessary, put the AF point or zone over the subject and press the Shutter button halfway (or press AF-ON).

4. Press the Shutter button completely to take the photo.

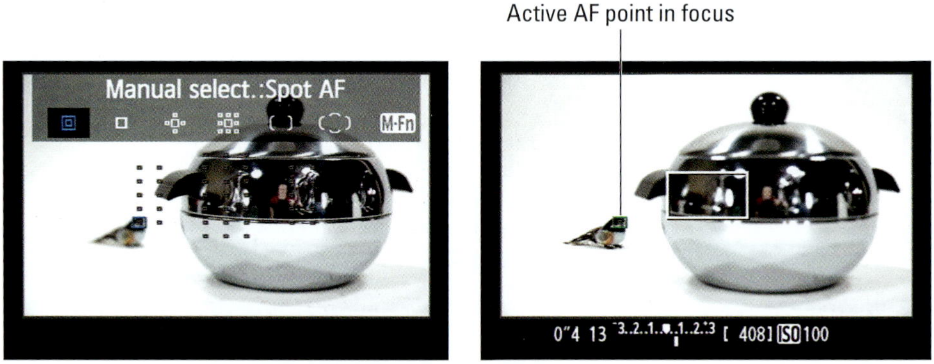

Figure 3-35: Manually selecting a new AF point to move the focus back.

Precision focusing in manual focus mode

When in manual focus mode, you can zoom in and focus with amazing precision when shooting in Live View mode (you should use a tripod to stabilize the camera while you zoom in and focus).

Here's how to magnify the view when in Live View mode:

1. **Switch the lens to MF.**

   See Chapter 1 for information on how to switch the focus mode on the lens.

2. **Make sure that you are in Live View mode (as opposed to Movie shooting) and press the Start/Stop button.**

   The focusing frame is replaced by a magnifying frame (see Figure 3-36).

3. **Use the Multicontroller to adjust the magnifying frame's position.**

   Put it on whatever you want to use as a focal point, as shown in Figure 3-37.

4. **Press the Zoom button to zoom in.**

   Each time you press it, you step up in zoom, from normal to five times the magnification (see Figure 3-38), and then 10 times, and then back to normal.

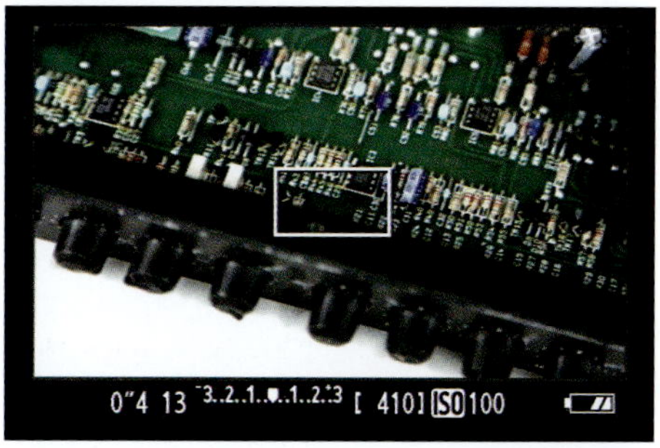

Figure 3-36: The initial frame is in the center of the screen. (Or if it's not, press the Set button.)

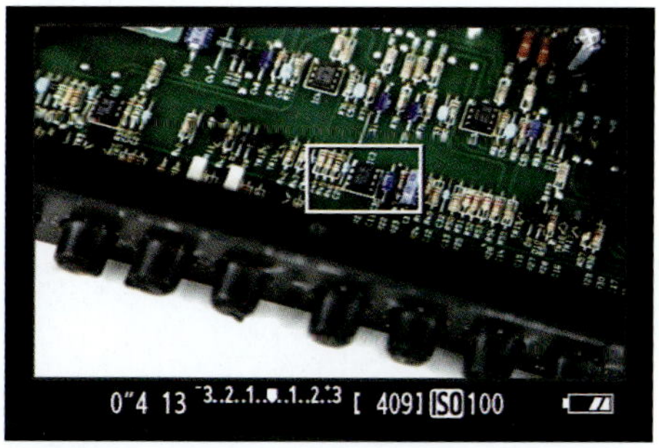

Figure 3-37: Move the frame where you want to zoom.

In the lower-right corner of the monitor is a label showing the current magnification level. Underneath that label, the box inside the small rectangle indicates the portion of the overall frame that's visible. If you need to, you can reposition the focusing frame to check another part of the image by using the Multicontroller. Figure 3-39 shows the highest magnification.

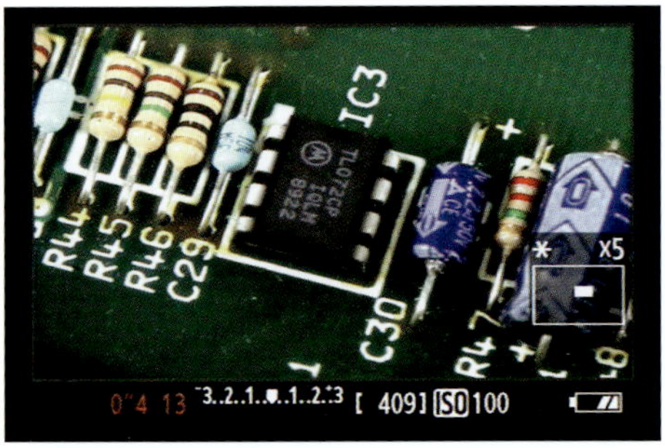

Figure 3-38: The initial zoom is five times the magnification.

If you want to see additional information on the screen, press the Info button at any time.

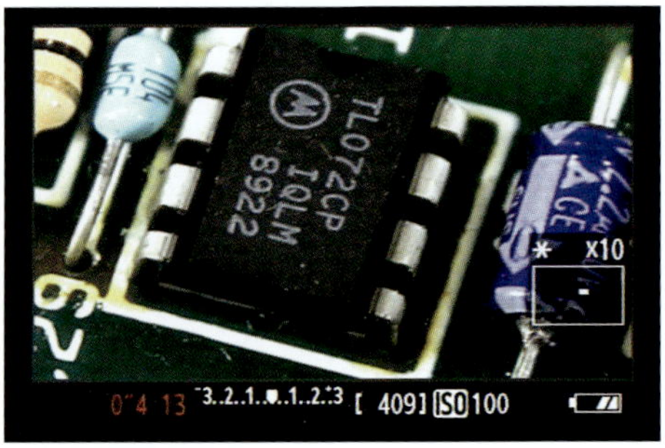

Figure 3-39: x10 is the closest you get.

5. **Twist the Focus ring on the lens to focus.**
6. **(Optional) If you like, press the Zoom button to cycle back to the normal view.**
7. **Take the shot.**

   Bask in the glow of a job well done (see Figure 3-40).

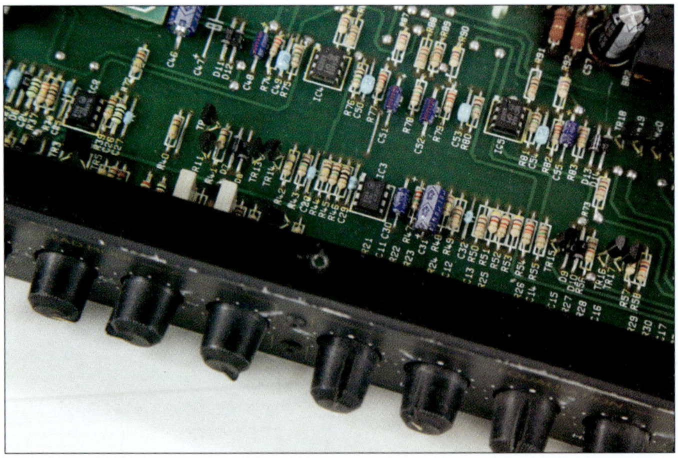

Figure 3-40: Magnifying gives you a lot of precision when manually focusing.

4

Making Movie Magic

In This Chapter

- Making the transition to "movie think"
- Configuring your camera to take movies
- Setting an exposure mode
- Reviewing movie information
- Shooting movies
- Playing back and editing movies in-camera
- Bringing your A game

The 5D Mark II was heralded as a breakthrough in shooting movies with a dSLR. It provided a relatively inexpensive avenue into film and television for independent filmmakers who wanted to shoot full HD. Not content to be an indie-only phenomenon, the 5D Mark II made it to the big time. The Mark II was used for several point-of-view action shots on the blockbuster movie *The Avengers* (2012) because of its small size and minimal operator footprint.

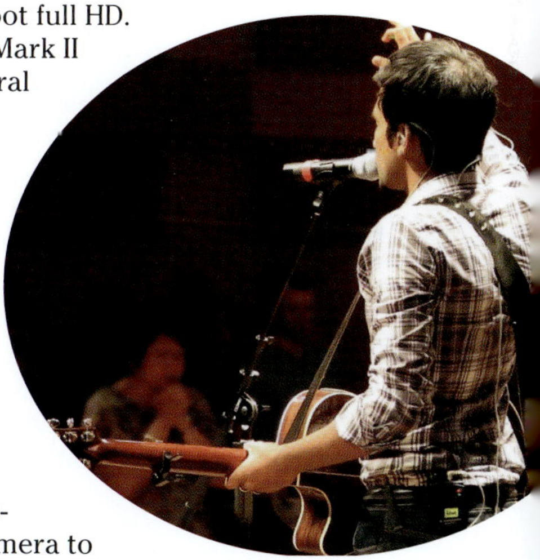

Enter the Mark III. It's newer, faster, has a new sensor and processor, adds an SD card slot, has an expanded ISO range, a slightly larger LCD monitor, better metering, and more.

In every way, the Mark III is just as good as or better than the Mark II. It will enable you to shoot outstanding movies, whether you're shooting them for your school, business, church, for yourself, or you're a filmmaker. In this chapter, you learn how to set up the camera to shoot movies, change exposure settings, shoot movies (with and without sound), play back movies, and trim movies in the camera.

Yelling, "Action!" versus Saying "Cheese"

Although it might sound obvious, shooting movies is a fundamentally different task than taking still photos. There are three differences you're going to have to wrap your mind around to make the transition with a reasonable chance of success:

- **Movies last longer than 1/60 second:** If you shoot a lot of still photos, you're used to thinking of time in terms of fractions of a second. These small segments are sometimes unbelievably short — as short as 1/8000 second with the 5D Mark III.

  Movies last unbelievably longer than this! If you shoot a 10-minute movie that has a maximum playback rate of 60 frames per second, you've shot the equivalent of 36,000 1/60 second photos.

  And guess what? You have to be still and quiet, keep the camera in focus, and have everything work for as many frames of video as you can. If you mess up five minutes in, you should have some sort of plan for how to use what you've shot to be able to create a finished product.

  It helps tremendously if you're part of a team using multiple cameras. You can cut back and forth among cameras and use the best footage from each one. It also helps if you're acting as the director and can shoot more than one take of an event.

  I don't mean to scare you away; I just want to get you thinking. Everything lasts longer, and you have to be "on" the entire time.

- **Steady as she goes:** You can't run around with the camera and act like a high-def Steadicam operator. The camera would shake, rattle, and roll to the point where you induce motion sickness in your audience.

  Use a tripod whenever possible, especially when shooting reasonably still subjects. If your subject is moving, though, you may need to shoot while holding the camera by hand.

- **You can record sound:** Unlike still photos, movies can include sound. The 5D Mark III has a built-in internal microphone. Being able to record sound is a blessing but also a major challenge. You have to be careful not to make noise when shooting and consider the overall aural environment where you are. Are large trucks driving by? Are they making a terrible racket? Your microphone (internal or external) may pick that audio up.

- **Autofocus is a major hassle:** Although the 5D Mark III uses tremendous and effective autofocus technology when shooting still photos, here are three reasons that you shouldn't use it while shooting movies:

  - *It messes with the exposure:* If you try to refocus when shooting, and press the AF-ON button, the exposure changes while the camera focuses. This exposure change ruins what you're shooting.

- *It's not infallible:* You may find yourself in a situation in which the camera chases focus. It may go in, out, and back in before it settles. This is clearly a problem.
- *It makes noise:* If you're recording audio, the motor in the lens will make noise, which you will likely record.

✓ **Hot blooded:** Unless you're using Live View a lot, you probably don't even think about your camera heating up so much that it shuts down. When shooting movies, you should be aware anytime the camera's yellow internal temperature warning indicator comes on. If you keep shooting and the temperature continues to increase, the camera displays a blinking red icon (the second symbol). The camera is warning you that it will soon automatically shut off to prevent damage.

Configuring the 5D Mark III for Movies

Before you run out and record movies, you should configure the 5D Mark III to record the movies *you* want. Most of the settings you'll want to look at and possibly change reside in two movie menus.

To access these menus, you must first set the Live View Shooting/Movie Shooting switch to Movie. Then press the Menu button and navigate to Shooting Menu 4 and Shooting Menu 5 to follow along with the upcoming sections.

Shooting Menu 4 (Movie)

Shooting Menu 4 (Movie) is shown in Figure 4-1.

This menu has several important options, as well as options that are similar to setting the camera up for Live View shooting, which I cover in Chapter 3.

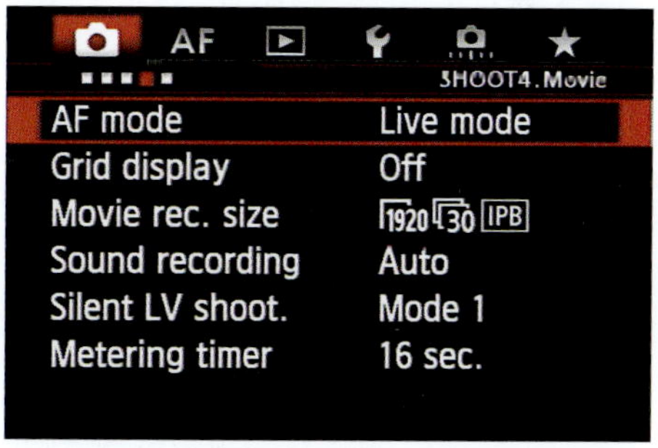

Figure 4-1: You must switch to movie shooting to see this menu.

AF Mode

If you decide to try autofocusing (I advise against it), you can choose from the three Live View autofocus methods: Live mode, Face Detection, and Quick mode. I cover the details of these three methods in Chapter 3.

If you must use AF, try to establish the initial focus on your subject before you begin recording. If you are in the process of recording and press the

AF-ON button (*not* the Shutter button), the focus mechanism tends to "hunt" for the focus point, going in and out of focus until it locks onto something. To boot, if you're using the internal microphone, you'll probably record the sound of the lens as it focuses, which is not an especially pleasant addition to your movies. So unless you're recording a static subject — say, a guitar player sitting on a stool or a speaker at a lectern — opt for manual focusing. You can then adjust focus manually any time during the recording.

TIP

If you plan to zoom in and out, practice before the big event. It's a bit of a challenge to zoom and focus at the same time, especially while holding the camera in front of you so that you can see the monitor. (Using a tripod makes the maneuver slightly easier.)

Grid Display

As with Live View shooting, you can display three different styles of grids to help keep your shots aligned properly. Choose 3x3 for a "Rule of Thirds" grid, choose 6x4 for a more tightly spaced grid, and choose 3x3+diagonals to add diagonal lines to the standard 3x3 grid. Chapter 3 has more information on the different grids.

Movie Recording Size

You can record seven different movie recording sizes, as illustrated in Figure 4-2. In this case, *Recording Size* encapsulates three different attributes: image size (pixel dimensions), frame rate, and compression method. Table 4-1 summarizes each setting.

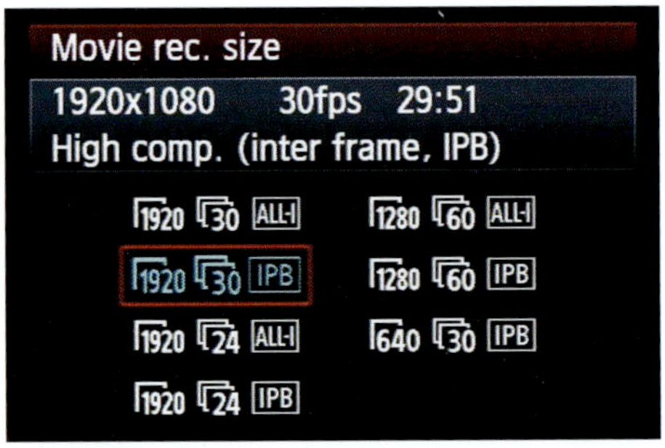

Figure 4-2: The recording size sets a number of movie parameters.

- **Image size:** The setting you choose determines the frame size and aspect ratio of the movie:
  - *Full High-Definition (Full HD):* 1920 x 1080
  - *High Definition (HD):* 1280 x 720
  - *Standard definition:* 640 x 480

  The two HD settings produce movies that have a 16:9 aspect ratio, which is used on new HDTV sets and computer monitors. The 640 x 480 setting delivers a 4:3 format, used by CRT monitors and TVs.

- **Frame rate:** The frame rate setting determines how many frames are recorded and played back per second. You have three options:
  - *60/50 (NTSC/PAL):* This frame rate is available only in HD, not Full HD. Use it when you want smooth action.
  - *30/25 (NTSC/PAL):* You have to use this setting (or 24 fps) when shooting Full HD.
  - *24:* The motion picture industry uses 24 frames per second. Use this setting if you want to replicate the feel of watching a movie on the large screen. Most people see no noticeable difference between 30 and 24 fps unless your movies include a lot of motion or you *pan* (move the camera across the scene) during your recording.

  The frame rates you see are determined by the Video system setting you have chosen in Setup Menu 3. Choose a setting that matches your location or target audience. The NTSC format (60 and 30 fps) includes North America, Japan, Korea, Mexico, and others, including many countries in Central and South America and the Caribbean. PAL frame rates (50 and 25fps) are standard in Europe, Russia, China, Australia, and many other areas of the world. The worldwide default for film is 24 fps.
- **Compression Method:** There are two compression methods:
  - *ALL-I:* This compression method treats each frame independently when compressed and recorded. It's a lot like compressing a long line of still photos, one at a time. The goal is to preserve each frame's quality at the expense of size. Pay attention to how many minutes you can fit on a 16GB card, as listed in Table 4-1.

    Because each frame is compressed alone, movies shot in this format are easier to edit; the computer doesn't need to fudge (or interpolate) data between frames. All the computer needs to render each frame is contained in that frame.
  - *IPB:* This compression method compares neighboring frames to find the regions that stay the same and those that change, and then uses that information to more efficiently compress the movie. These movies are much smaller than those that use the ALL-I method.

    Editing takes more computer power, because the computer must load and analyze more than one frame of movie to be able to show one frame.

Table 4-1 Movie Recording Size Options

Image Size	*Frames per Second (NTSC/PAL)*	*Compression*	*Minutes per 16GB Card*	*Record Rate (MB/min.)*
1920 x 1080	30/25	ALL-I	22 min	685 MB/min.
1920 x 1080	30/25	IPB	64 min	235 MB/min.
1920 x 1080	24	ALL-I	22 min	685 MB/min.
1920 x 1080	24	IPB	64 min	235 MB/min.
1280 x 720	60/50	ALL-I	25min	610 MB/min.
1280 x 720	60/50	APB	74 min	205 MB/min.
640 x 480	30/25	IPB	194 min	78 MB/min.

The compression method you choose has the most effect on file size, and hence on how much space you need to store the movie. At the highest setting (ALL-I), you can fit about 22 minutes of Full HD movie on a 16GB memory card; drop the compression setting to IPB and you can virtually triple the length of the movie.

You have several limits to how large your movies can be and how long, regardless of what size your memory card is. They are as follows:

- **Maximum file size:** The maximum file size for a movie is 4GB, regardless of the capacity of your memory card. When a movie is close to the 4GB limit (about 30 seconds prior to hitting it), the elapsed time or time code readout on the monitor starts blinking. This blinking light lets you know that something is about to happen. If you keep shooting, the camera automatically creates a new file so that you don't miss a beat. Your intervention is not required. Note, however, that you will have at least two files to work with instead of one. Use your favorite movie-editing program to join them later.
- **Maximum length:** At 29 minutes and 59 seconds (29:59), the camera automatically stops recording. If you want to continue, you must press the Start/Stop button again and hope that you don't lose too much in between.

  Your best course of action is to control the situation and not let it reach this point.

Use larger memory cards for longer movies. Because a 16GB card doesn't hold a full 16GB of data, you can't record a 16GB movie on a 16GB card. If you want to get the full 29:59 recording time into a single video clip, you have to use a larger card.

And no, at the current time, you cannot effectively record a movie using the 5D Mark III with an external device. This is because the camera does not have what's called *clean HDMI output*. In other words, movie data that is sent out the HDMI terminal has distracting Live View overlays. Look for possible firmware updates to change this in the future.

WARNING!

For the best movie recording and playback performance, use the fastest memory cards you can afford to buy. At a minimum, you should look for cards with these write/read speeds:

- **CF:** For IPB, look for 10 MB/seconds or faster. If using ALL-I, look for 30 MB/seconds or faster.
- **SD:** If using IPB, use a card with 6MB/second or faster write/read speed. If using ALL-I compression, your card will need to have 20 MB/second speed rating.

Keep an eye on the five-level recording indicator that appears onscreen during recording. The indicator shows you how much movie data the camera has in its *buffer* — a temporary data storage tank — awaiting transfer to the memory card. If the indicator level reaches the top, the camera stops recording new data so that it can finish sending existing data to the card. You can also try reducing the movie size setting to improve the transfer speed. If the recording progress indicator keeps hitting the limit, buy a faster memory card.

Sound Recording

You can record sound or shoot a silent movie. If you enable sound, note the position of the microphone: It's the little five-hole area on the front of the camera, just above the EOS label, as shown in Figure 4-3. Don't inadvertently cover the microphone with your finger! And keep in mind that anything *you* say is picked up by the mic along with any other audio present in the scene. For better sound quality in your movies, use an optional microphone with the new External Microphone IN terminal (right above the remote control terminal on the camera's left side). This terminal lets you record in stereo (see Figure 4-4; also note the headphones terminal) if you attach a stereo microphone.

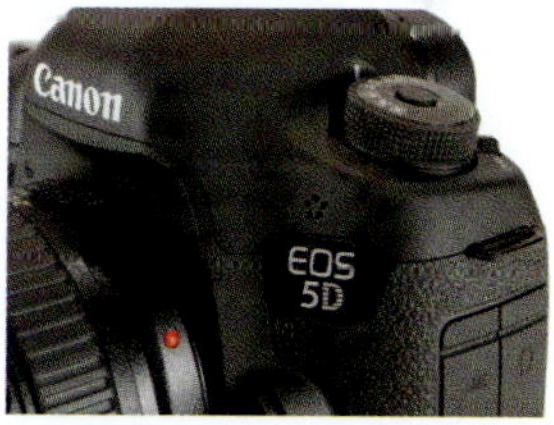

Figure 4-3: These tiny holes lead to the camera's internal microphone.

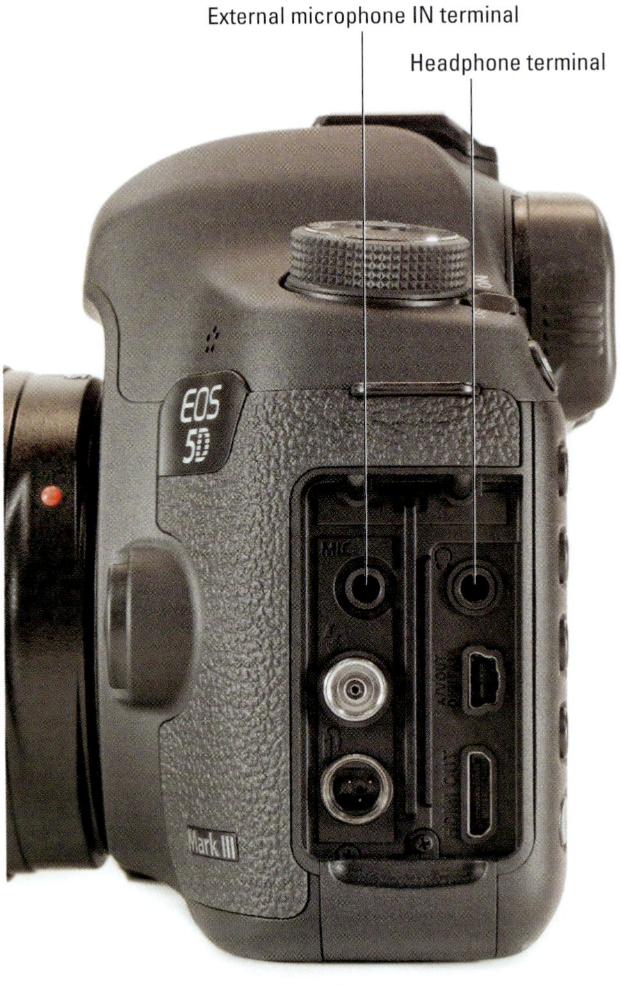

Figure 4-4: Attach an external microphone for better sound quality.

To configure audio, choose the appropriate menu setting:

- *Disable:* Turn off sound recording.
- *Auto:* You want the camera to record sound with either the built-in microphone or an optional external stereo mic, and you don't want to mess with any settings. See Figure 4-5.

- *Manual:* You want to set the recording level (microphone sensitivity) yourself. More on this shortly.
- Enable the wind filter to have the camera minimize the effects of wind noise as if the microphone were protected by a wind barrier. This option may subtly change the tone of the sound you record, however, so do not turn it on unless you really need it.

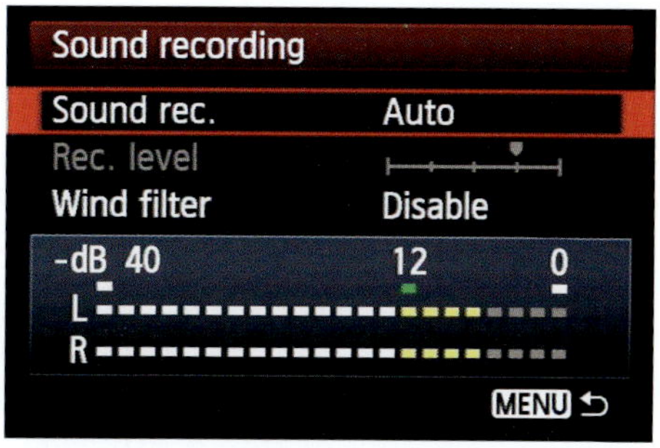

Figure 4-5: When in Auto mode, the camera sets the level based on the sound.

If you have chosen Auto or Manual, the bottom of the screen displays an audio meter. This meter shows you the strength of the audio signal being monitored by the microphone. Audio levels are measured in decibels (dB), and the scale runs from –40 (very, very soft) to 0 (as much as can be measured digitally without running out of room).

The camera takes care of turning the sound up or down if you chose Auto. If you choose to manually set the audio levels, you have to do a bit more work. Follow these steps to manually set the audio levels:

1. **Press the Menu button.**

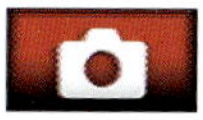

2. **Navigate to Shooting Menu 4 (Movie).**
3. **Highlight Sound Recording, as shown in Figure 4-6, and press Set.**
4. **Highlight Sound Recording and press the Set button.**

   Highlighting the first instance of Sound Recording and pressing Set gets you here. Highlighting the second instance of Sound Recording (on the following screen) and pressing Set enables you to change the settings.

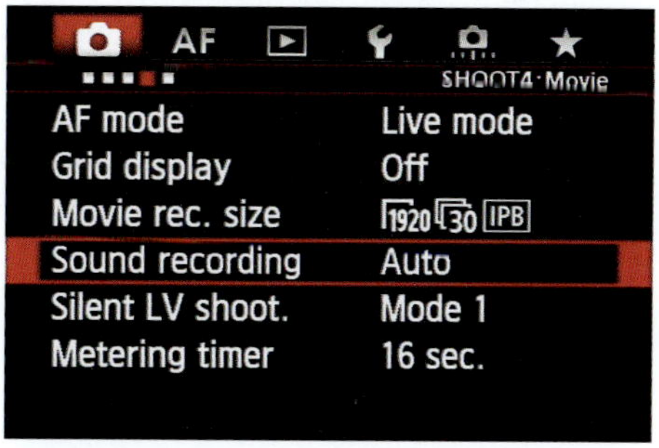

Figure 4-6: Enter the recording studio here.

5. **Select Manual (see Figure 4-7) and press the Set button.**

6. **Highlight Recording Level, as shown in Figure 4-8, and press the Set button.**
7. **Use the Quick Control dial or Multicontroller to adjust the recording level up or down.**

   To get a good setting, you must listen to the source of the sound and watch the meter as you adjust the level. You want the sound to peak consistently in the –12 range (as in Figure 4-9). The indicators on the meter turn yellow at this point, which is good. You want to have a strong signal. However, you don't want it to be too strong. The extra space to the right of the current sound level, called *headroom,* should be large enough to give you a comfortable margin of error. If sounds get louder, you won't immediately clip or distort. This happens when the meter reads 0 and appears red (see Figure 4-10). You should avoid pegging the meter! The audio will stink.
8. **Press the Set button to finish.**

   Press the Menu button to cancel the changes.

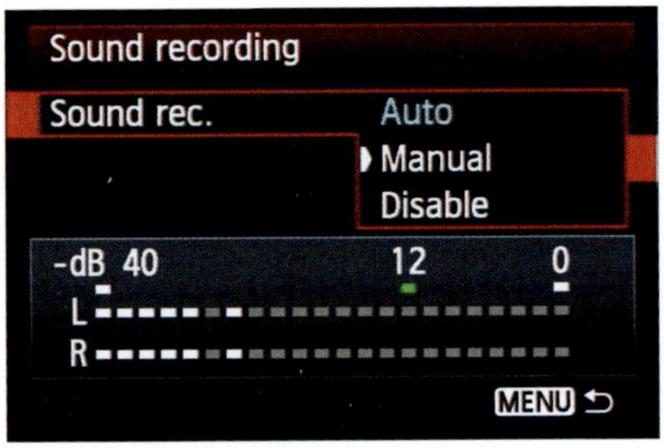

Figure 4-7: Choose Manual to take control of sound levels.

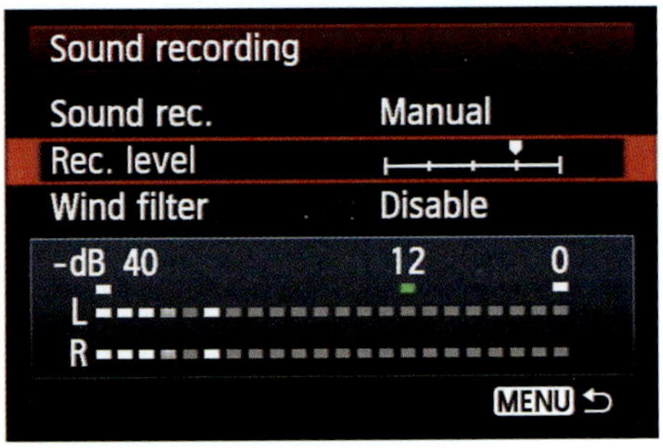

Figure 4-8: To set sound levels, select Recording level and press Set.

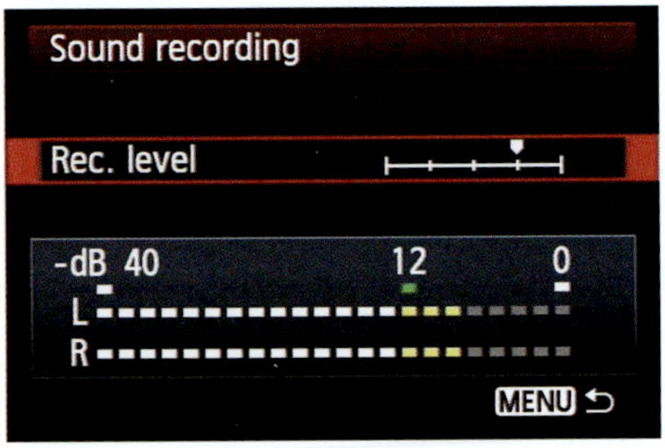

Figure 4-9: This is good.

Silent LV Shooting

These are the same options as I cover in the Live View portion of Chapter 3: Mode 1 (quiet), Mode 2 (quieter), and Disabled.

Metering Timer

This option works exactly as it does for regular Live View shooting. To recap: When you press the Shutter button halfway, the exposure meter comes to life and the camera then establishes the autoexposure settings needed to produce a good exposure. To save battery power, the meter goes to sleep after 16 seconds, but you can request a shorter or longer delay by changing the settings.

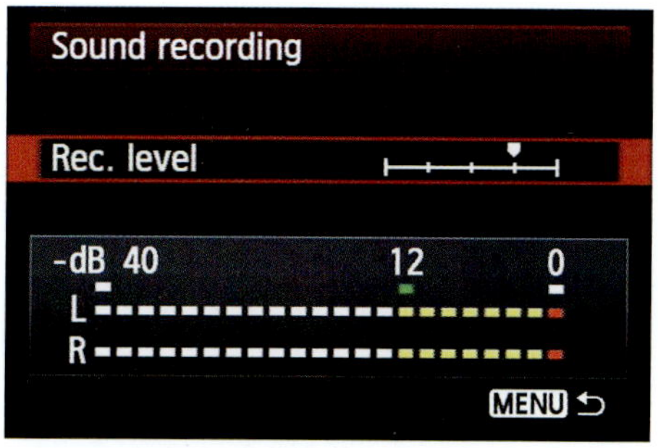

Figure 4-10: This is bad.

Shooting Menu 5 (Movie)

Shooting Menu 5 is shown in Figure 4-11. It has only three settings.

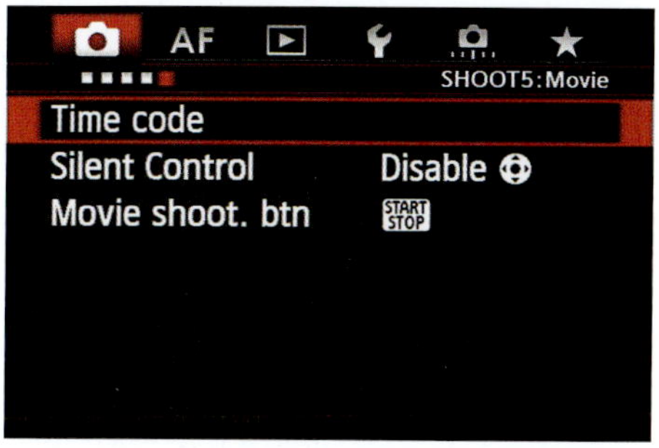

Figure 4-11: Shooting Menu 5 (Movie) is more sparse.

Time Code

Time Code is about knowing where you are in a movie. Fundamentally, the reason Time code exists is that simple time references (hours, minutes, and seconds) are not precise enough to determine the exact location in a movie. For the exact location, you need something that references specific frames, which is exactly what Time Code does.

Just because the 5D Mark III *can* record the Time Code doesn't mean that you *need* to. You don't if you are conducting very simple edits using one or more clips taken with a single camera and you aren't messing with the audio, adding closed captioning, and so forth.

However, if you need to be able to sync specific frames of video, whether from one or more cameras, are adding closed captioning, and are doing more serious audio editing, you will benefit greatly by enabling Time Code.

Several Time Code options are available (displayed in the menu shown in Figure 4-12):

- **Count Up:** Set to Recording Run to have the Time Code count up when shooting a movie only. Set to Free Run to have the Time Code keep count regardless of whether you're recording.

- **Start Time Setting:** Set to Manual Input Setting to set the hour, minute, second, and frame yourself. Select Rest to reset the Time Code to 00:00:00:00. Choose Set to Camera Time to set the time part of the Time code to match the camera's internal clock. The frame will be 00.

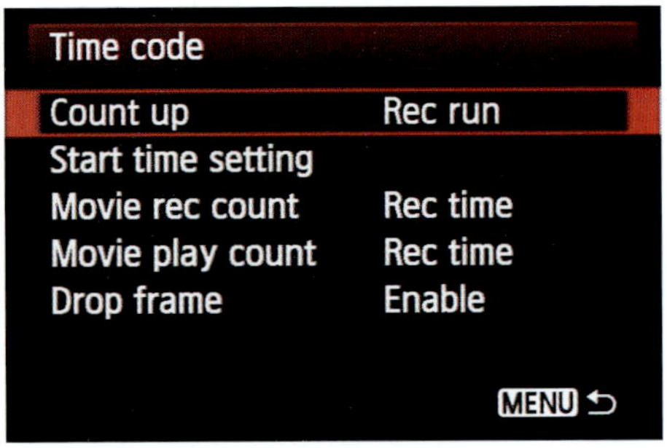

Figure 4-12: Set Time Code options here.

- **Movie Recording Count:** This setting determines what's displayed on the movie-shooting screen (when you're not actually recording). Set to Recording Time to display the elapsed time. Set to Time Code to show the Time Code.
- **Movie Playback Count:** In contrast to the previous setting, this setting controls what is displayed during movie playback (but not when actually playing back). Set to Recording Time to display the elapsed time during playback, and Time Code to display the Time Code when you're paused or are advancing frames.
- **Drop Frame:** When enabled, the discrepancy between the Time Code and actual frame count (caused by the difference between the advertised frame rates of 30/25 or 60/50 fps and actual frame rate of 29.97 or 59.94 fps) is corrected by dropping (also called skipping) Time Code frame numbers. This does not apply when the frame rate is set to 24 fps (23.976 fps actual).

Silent Control

When enabled, Silent Control gives you a quieter way to change a limited number of shooting settings as you shoot your movie. The Quick Control dial turns into a touch pad (as mentioned in Chapter 1.)

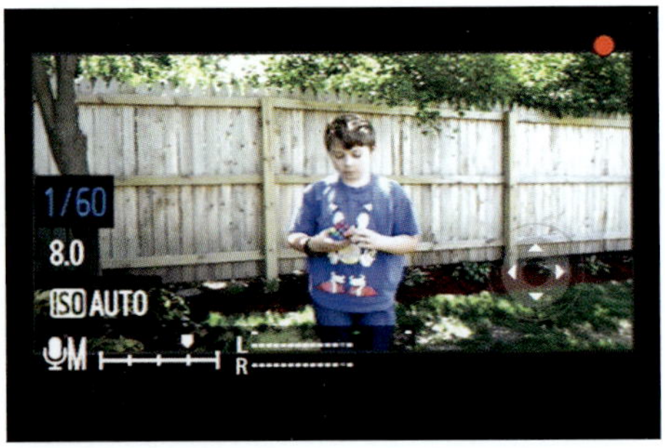

Figure 4-13: When in Silent Control, you can change settings with a touch on the Quick Control dial.

To use it, follow these steps:

1. **During shooting, press the Quick Control button.**

   Try to press this button silently. The display changes to Quick Control mode with a graphical reminder that you have Silent Control on (see Figure 4-13).

2. **Highlight the setting you want to change by gently touching up or down on the face of the Quick Control dial.**
3. **Change the setting by gently touching the left or right side of the control dial.**
4. **Press the Quick Control button to get back to the normal display.**

As you'll see in the upcoming section on using the Quick Control screen, Silent Control differs from Quick Control only in that it turns the Quick Control dial into a silent touch pad.

Movie Shooting Button

This setting controls which button starts and stops recording. The options are

- **Start/Stop:** The default setup. Press the Start/Stop button to start and stop recording.
- **Shutter/Start/Stop:** This setting adds the Shutter button into the mix. In other words, you can press either the Start/Stop button or the Shutter button to start and stop recording. This setup effectively makes it possible to shoot movies with a remote controller. The downside is that by doing so, you eliminate the option of taking still photos while shooting a movie.

Using the Quick Control screen

TIP

You can adjust several settings from the Quick Control screen, which is faster than using the Movie menu. Follow these steps to do so:

1. **Press the Quick Control button to enter Quick Control mode.**

   You see a column of control icons running down the left side of the screen. One of the icons is highlighted, as shown in Figure 4-14, and the bottom of the screen tells you the current setting for that option. In Figure 4-14, the Auto Lighting Optimizer setting is highlighted, for example, and it is disabled.

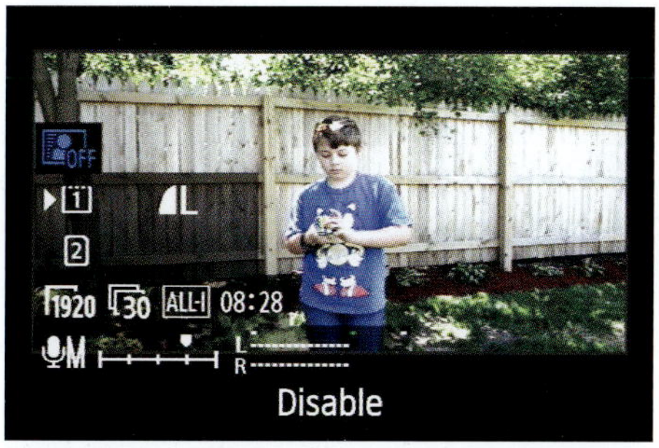

Figure 4-14: Press the Quick Control button to shift to Quick Control mode and then use the Main dial to adjust the highlighted option.

2. **Press up or down using the Multicontroller to highlight the icon that represents the option you want to change.**

As a reminder, from top to bottom, the icons enable you to adjust these settings:

- Auto Lighting Optimizer
- Recording/Playback
- Still Picture Quality
- Movie Size
- Sound Recording: If set to Manual, you can control the level.
    - Autofocus Mode
    - Still Photo Drive
    - White Balance
    - Picture Style
    - Auto Lighting Optimizer
    - Still Picture Quality
    - Movie Size

3. **Rotate the Main or Quick Control dial to change the setting.**

   Alternatively, press Set to see the full list of options onscreen.

4. **Press the Quick Control button again (or press the shutter release halfway) to exit Quick Control mode and return to the normal display.**

Note: These steps are the same as those you would take to enter Quick Control mode *during* recording. When recording, though, the number of settings you can change is very limited. The display is very similar to Silent Control, which is shown in Figure 4-13, but without the graphic of the Quick Control dial.

Even more movie options

Although the primary movie options reside in the two Movie menus, some other options that are spread out in the menu system will affect your movies. Don't forget about them:

- **White Balance:** You can set the White Balance option for movies. Press the Metering Mode Selection/White Balance Selection button on top of the camera to quickly call up the White Balance settings. Use the Quick Control dial to switch. Press the button again or press Set to get back to the Shooting Information screen. Check out Chapter 8 for more info on white balance.

- **Autofocus mode:** Press the AF Mode Selection/Drive Mode Selection button on top of the camera. Change the autofocus mode using the Main dial. See Chapter 3 for more information on Live View (and hence movie) autofocus modes.
- **ISO:** When you're in manual shooting mode (M), press the ISO Speed Setting/Flash Exposure Compensation button on top of the camera. Set the ISO with the Quick Control dial. See Chapter 6 for more information on ISO.
- **Picture Style:** Likewise, you can assign a Picture Style (explained in Chapter 8) to movies. Press the Creative Photo button on the back of the camera to access Picture Styles.
- **Exposure Compensation:** You can apply exposure compensation for movies just as you can for still photos. Use the Quick Control dial. You have a total of five stops to work with. See Chapter 6 for more information on exposure.
- **Auto Lighting Optimizer:** This works just like still photos, as explained in Chapter 6. Set in Quick Control mode.

Making Exposure Decisions

You can shoot movies in any of three exposure conditions:

- **Autoexposure:** When in Scene Intelligent Auto, Program AE, or Bulb modes, the camera handles the exposure without your input.

  ISO is set automatically from 100–12800, unless you're in P or B shooting mode and have expanded the maximum ISO speed range to 25600/H. In addition, if Highlight tone priority is enabled and you are in P or B modes, the ISO range is limited to 200–12800.

  You can dial in exposure correction before and during shooting with the Quick Control dial.
- **Autoexposure-Priority:** There are two Autoexposure-Priority modes:
  - *Tv:* When in Shutter-Priority AE mode, you control the camera's shutter speed. Before recording, switch the camera's Mode dial to Tv shooting mode; then, when in Movie shooting mode, set the shutter speed with the Main dial.

    When shooting movies at 30/25 or 24 frames per second, you can set the shutter speed from 1/4000 second to 1/30 second.

    When the frame rate is set to 60/50 fps, you can choose from 1/4000 second to 1/60 second.

Solid advice to start with is to set your shutter speed at twice the frame rate. If shooting at 30/25 fps, go for 1/60 or 1/50 second. If shooting at 24 fps, use 1/50 second shutter speed (the closest thing to 1/48 second). Shooting faster will result in action that looks artificial.

- *Av:* When in Aperture-Priority AE mode, you control the camera's aperture. Set the Mode dial to Av and dial in your favorite aperture with the Main dial.

  As with still photos, larger apertures produce shallow depths of field. Smaller apertures produce larger depths of field. Use a shallow depth of field carefully, because keeping your subject in focus when shooting a video is harder than taking a still photo.

ISO is set automatically between 100 and 12800 unless you have changed the maximum ISO to 25600/H. If Highlight Tone Priority is enabled, the ISO range is limited to 200–12800.

- **Manual exposure:** In manual mode (the Mode dial is set to M), you control the exposure. Set the aperture and shutter speed yourself using the Main and Quick Control dials.

  The same restrictions and rationale apply to choosing an appropriate shutter speed and aperture in manual mode as were discussed in Tv and Av modes.

  You can set the ISO speed directly when shooting in M mode.

Changing the Information Display

After you set the Live View Shooting/Movie Shooting switch to Movie, the viewfinder turns off and you see your scene on the monitor. If you don't, press the Shutter button halfway to wake the camera up.

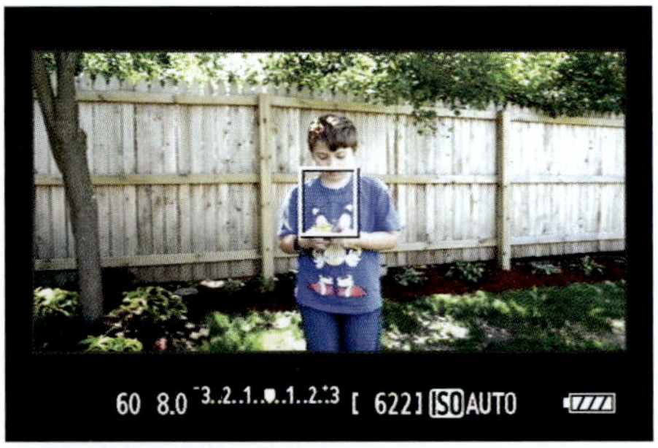

Figure 4-15: The default Movie display contains only a few pieces of shooting data plus the focusing frame.

Initially, the screen looks like the one you see in Figure 4-15. The same focusing frame you get in Live View mode appears, and the bottom of the screen shows the aperture and shutter speed (depending on the Shooting mode you are in, either or both aperture and shutter speed values may apply only to still photos taken when shooting movies), the exposure level indicator, and so forth.

As with Live View mode, you can press the Info button to change the display mode. You have five display options: to show nothing but the focusing frame; view the exposure settings and battery level; display shooting information; add the histogram (see Figure 4-16); and use the electronic level.

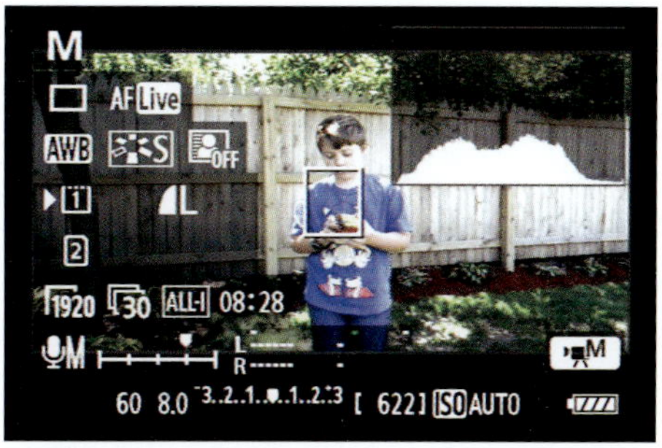

Figure 4-16: Press Info to reveal these additional shooting options.

Don't get fixated by having all this information at your fingertips. Review this screen and then turn most of it off or ignore it.

You don't want to get too distracted looking at all the symbols and forget to pan or lose focus. Set the camera up and then trust your decisions. The main points you should worry about when recording are the Recording Movie dot (know when you're recording!), focus (as in, keep), exposure (not too bright, not too dark), elapsed time (so that you don't hit the limits of the camera or card), temperature warnings, and battery level.

Shooting Movies

You have a lot to remember when shooting movies, so don't expect to get it all right the first time. Keep learning, practicing, and growing. Follow these steps to shoot your movies:

1. **Set the scene.**

   Sometimes setting the scene takes a lot of work. Sometimes it just means showing up (see Figure 4-17).

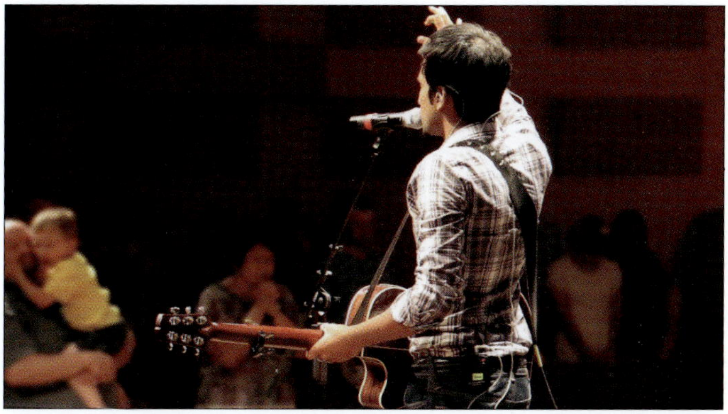
Figure 4-17: Standing behind the artist and shooting outward required little setup.

TIP

Keep these tips in mind when shooting movies:

- *Tripod or other support:* Use a tripod whenever possible when shooting movies that are stationary. If your subject is moving, you may need to shoot hand-held or get a nice pan/tilt tripod head that you can use to smoothly follow the action. Consider purchasing a support (such as a handgrip, offset rig, or dSLR cinema rig) specifically designed to hold dSLRs when shooting movies.
- *Lighting:* Creative license notwithstanding, movies where you are giving a review, telling a story, or explaining something benefit from good lighting. Turn on lamps and overheads, bring in extra lights, or open the curtains (see Figure 4-18).

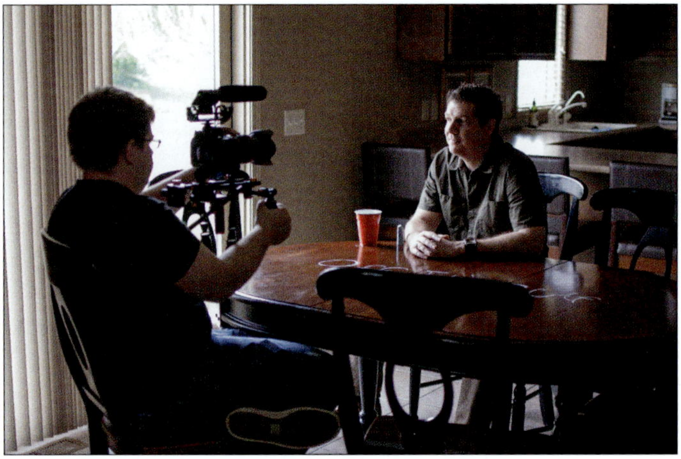

Figure 4-18: Use natural lighting whenever possible.

REMEMBER

If outdoors, shoot with the sun behind or to the side of you. It should shine toward or across your subject.

- *Background:* This may be the most challenging aspect of filming a movie of a stationary subject. Set your camera up to show off a pleasing area of your home, a nicely decorated wall, window (although that can mess with the exposure), or somewhere outside that looks like a good movie backdrop. Figure 4-19 shows a well-kept kitchen in the background. The subject sat at his dining room table for the video.

You may be able to point the camera down at something. If so, a nice table or cloth will work. It doesn't have to be perfect. Keep it natural, but you may need to clean and position things in or out of frame to remove distractions or add interest.

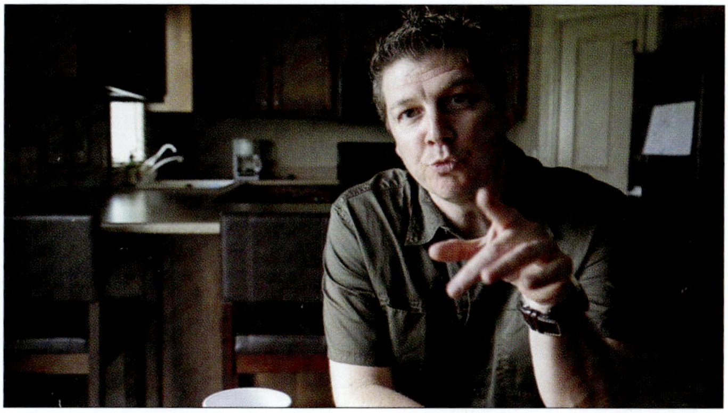

Figure 4-19: Good backgrounds might be right behind you.

- *Wide-angle:* When shooting general home movies inside, wide-angle lenses work well. They keep you from feeling claustrophobic and capture more action. If you are filming a single person, use a normal or zoomed-in focal length.
- *Short clips:* Shoot short clips instead of long takes. Delete the bad ones. Keep the good ones. Later, trim to specific scenes and combine into larger videos later.
- *Rerecord audio:* Record a scratch track while you're shooting the movie, but replace it with rerecorded audio in editing. Yes, that's a bit more complicated than normal, but it's possible with today's sophisticated editing programs and a little elbow grease. Unfortunately, I can't tell you exactly how to do this given the space constraints of this book.
- *Bloopers:* Everyone loves bloopers. Keep them and use them as DVD extras.
- *No audio:* Sometimes no audio is better. Do you want people to hear you yelling at your kids as they fight over presents they just opened? Even if you record it, you may be better off using a music track.

- *Family get-togethers or trips:* Use your camera to film family members talking about their lives or when on trips. In Figure 4-20, my father-in-law talks about his family at the gravesite of his great-great grandfather and grandmother (see Figure 4-21). You can combine video and still photos into memorable family genealogies.

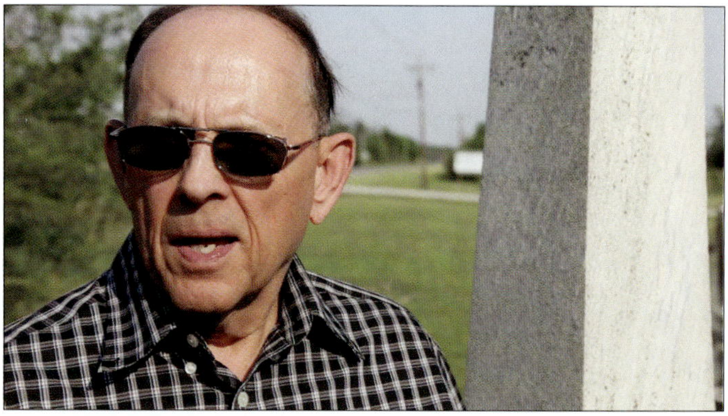

Figure 4-20: Movies are great at capturing memories.

2. **Set the Live View Shooting/Movie Shooting switch to Movie shooting (see Figure 4-22).**

   As soon as you select Movie Shooting, the scene appears on your monitor. You also see various bits of recording data on the screen; remember that you can press the Info button to cycle through the different data display modes if you want more or less screen clutter.

3. **Press the Info button to set the display to your liking.**

   Don't be afraid to call up all the information at this stage. After all, you're configuring the camera. When you're done, press the Info button to cycle through the displays to find a clean one you like. Balance the information you will need when shooting against the chance of distraction. Too much on the display will make it harder to see what's happening on the monitor.

4. **Configure the camera.**

   Set general movie settings:

   - *AF mode:* Set autofocus mode or switch camera to manual focus.

     Manual focusing is the best way to go, for all the reasons covered earlier in this chapter. So set the lens switch to MF and twist the focusing ring on the lens to bring your subject into focus.

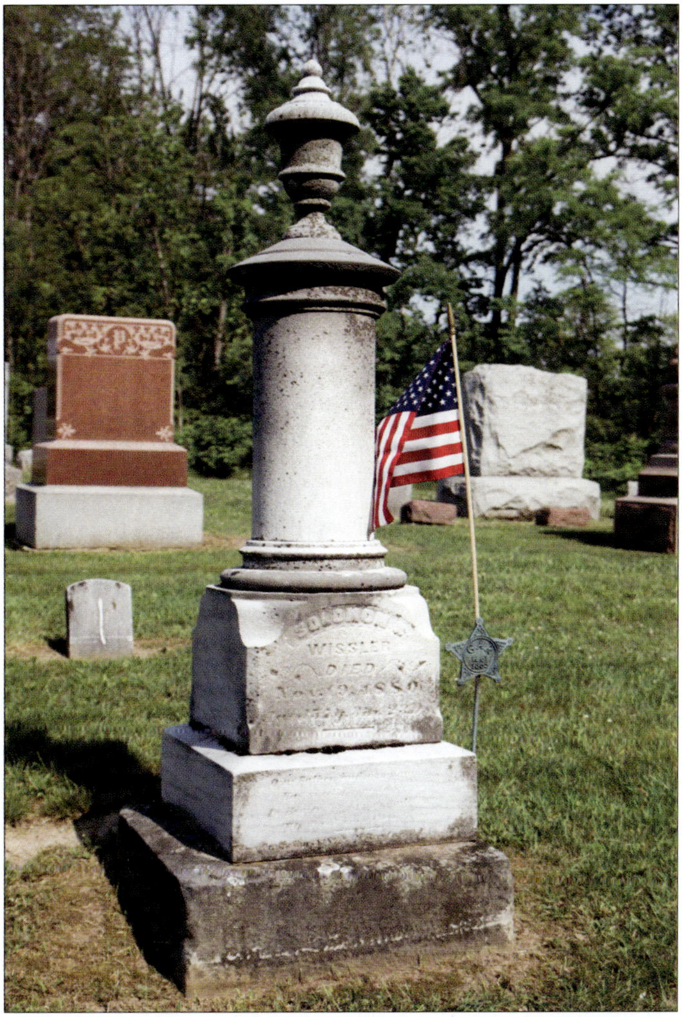

Figure 4-21: Take some still photos, too.

To double-check focus, you can use the same techniques as when you're in Live View mode: Use the Multicontroller to move the focusing frame over the area you want to inspect. Then press the Enlarge button once to zoom to 5X magnification; press again to zoom to 10X magnification. Press the button once more to return to normal magnification. To return the focusing frame to the center of the screen, press the Set button.

- *Grid Display:* Turn on or off.
- *Movie Recording Size:* Determine movie size and frame rate.
- *Sound Recording:* Enable or disable. Check levels.
- *Silent LV Shooting:* Choose mode or disable.
- *Metering Timer:* Change, if desired.
- *Time Code:* Enable, if desired. Configure.
- *Silent Control:* Enable, if desired.

5. **Set the camera's shooting mode.**

   If you want to shoot an autoexposure movie, choose Scene Intelligent Auto, Program AE, or B.

   If you want to control shutter speed, choose Tv.

   If you want to control the aperture, choose Av.

   If you want complete manual control over exposure, including ISO, set the Mode dial to M.

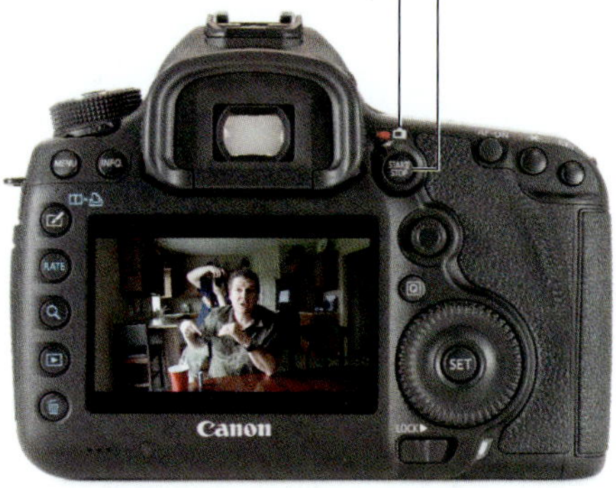

Figure 4-22: That's me in the background.

6. **Set shutter speed, aperture, and ISO, if possible.**
7. **Set other options.**

   These include:

   - *White Balance*
   - *Drive mode for still photos*
   - *Picture Style*

     One of the more powerful Picture Styles is monochrome, as shown in Figure 4-23. I love shooting in black and white.
   - *Auto Lighting Optimizer*
8. **Focus.**

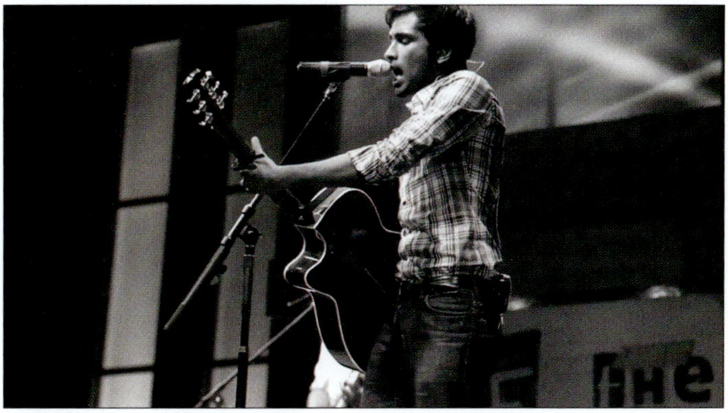

Figure 4-23: Black and white movies are simply gorgeous.

9. **Press the Shutter button halfway to meter.**
10. **Use AE Lock, as desired.**

    Normally, the camera adjusts exposure during the recording as needed. If you prefer to lock in the exposure settings, you can do so by using AE (autoexposure) Lock. Just as you do when shooting stills, press the AE Lock button if you want to lock exposure during movie recording. To cancel AE Lock, press the AF Point Selection button. Of course, you can *lock* exposure by using manual exposure mode when shooting movies, too. It boils down to your preference as to which method you choose to lock exposure during movie recording.

11. **Change exposure settings, if necessary.**
12. **Dial in Exposure Compensation, if necessary.**

    To apply this exposure shift, rotate the Quick Control dial and look at the exposure meter at the bottom of the screen (it will appear automatically, if hidden). Move the bar under the meter to the right for a brighter picture; move the indicator left for a darker picture.

    If in Manual mode, you can't use Exposure Compensation. In your case, change an exposure setting: ISO, aperture, or shutter speed.

13. **Press the Start/Stop button (see Figure 4-22) to begin recording.**

    This is it! You're recording. Keep quiet, try to maintain a steady camera, and keep things in focus.

    A red recording symbol appears in the top-right region of the monitor, as shown in Figure 4-24.

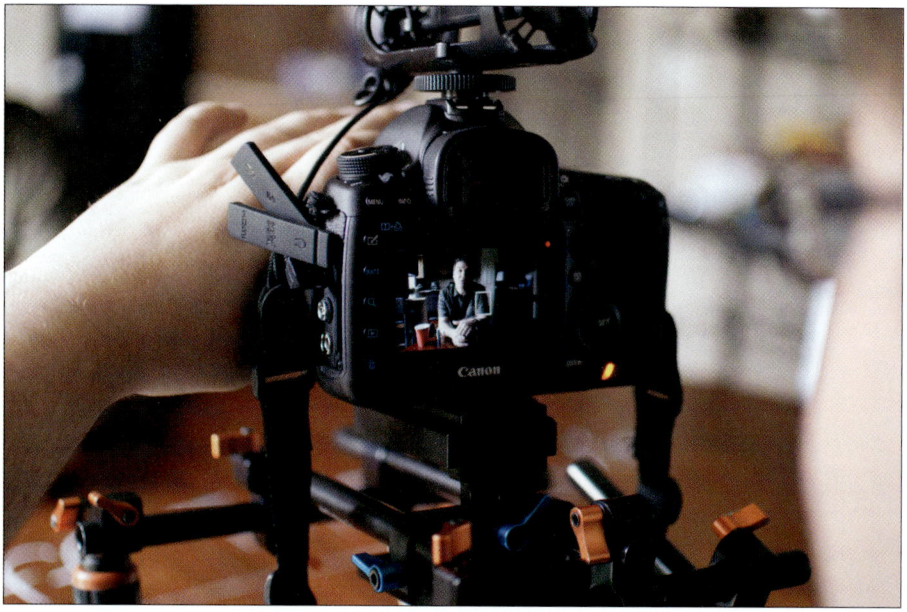

Figure 4-24: The red dot indicates that you're recording.

In the full-data display mode — the one in which all the setting icons appear on the left side of the screen — all icons except the movie recording Quality symbol disappear.

Keep a lookout for any temperature warnings.

14. **Change settings during recording, if necessary.**

    Press the Quick Control button to access functions you can change.

15. **If desired, take still photos when shooting.**

    You can interrupt your recording to take a still photo without exiting Movie mode. Just press the Shutter button as usual to take the shot. The camera records the still photo as a regular image file, using the same Picture Style and White Balance setting you set for your movie. The Still Quality setting determines the picture resolution and file format.

    Here are a few drawbacks to capturing a still photo in Movie recording mode:

    - If you're shooting a movie at one of the Full HD or HD settings, which capture movies with a 16:9 aspect ratio, the still photo will share the aspect ratio of the movie and be at 16:9.

      If the movie size is set to 640 x 480, the still photo will have a normal, 3:2 aspect ratio.

- You can't use flash. Although your video might look okay, the light level may not be adequate for a good-looking still photo. You may be shooting in a situation where you want to use fill flash to light someone's face. You won't be able use fill flash if you take a still photo when shooting a movie.
- Perhaps most important, your movie will contain a still *moment* at the point you take the photo; the moment lasts about one second. Ouch. If you're savvy with a video editor, you can edit each still photo out of the video, but if you shoot 50 stills in five minutes of video, editing will take a while.

16. **Press the Start/Stop button to stop shooting.**
17. **Review the movie, if desired.**

Enjoying the Show: Movie Playback

To play back movies (whether on the camera monitor or an external television), follow these steps:

1. **Press the Playback button and then locate the movie file.**

   When reviewing pictures in full-frame view, you can spot a movie file by looking for the little movie camera icon in the upper-left corner of the screen, as shown in Figure 4-25.

   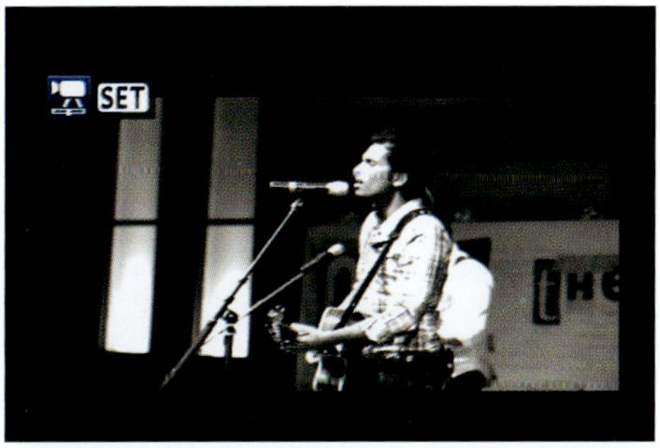

   Figure 4-25: The movie camera symbol indicates that you're looking at a movie file.

   If this isn't the movie you want to see, use the Quick Control dial to scroll through files available for playback until you find the one you want, or use the Multicontroller to jump ahead. (These tasks are covered in Chapter 5.)

   If the index is displayed, movie files are identified by sprocket holes along the left edge of the thumbnail. Highlight the movie you want to play by using the Quick Control dial or Multicontroller; then press the Set button.

   At this point, the movie you want to play should be on the monitor at full size, paused.

2. **Press the Set button.**

   A strip of playback controls appears at the bottom of the screen, as shown in Figure 4-26. This is known as the movie playback panel. Use these controls to control playback, as shown in Step 3.

3. **To adjust the volume, rotate the Main dial.**

   The movie playback panel must be visible. If it's not, press the Set button.

   Note the little white wheel in the volume display area of the screen when the movie playback panel is displayed. That icon reminds you to use the Main dial to adjust a setting. Rotating the dial controls only the camera speaker's volume; if you connect the camera to a TV, control the volume from the TV instead. The volume is shown as a series of green bars. More bars equals louder playback.

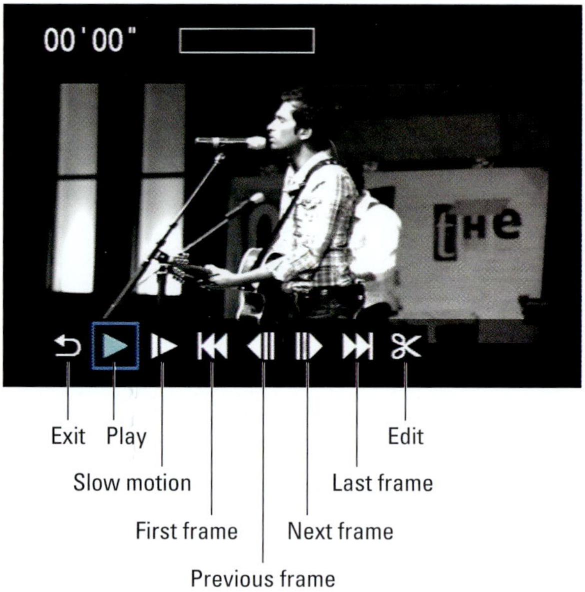

Figure 4-26: Handy playback controls.

4. **Use the Quick Control dial or Multicontroller to highlight a playback control; then press Set.**

   Here's what the controls do:

   - **Exit:** Closes the movie playback panel. Does *not* exit playback.
   - **Play:** Plays the movie. The movie playback panel disappears, and your movie begins playing. If the movie is playing, choosing Play pauses it.
   - **Slow Motion:** Plays the clip in slow motion. You can control the playback speed with the Quick Control dial. Note the scale that appears in the top-right corner of the screen. This scale shows you the current speed.
   - **First Frame:** Rewinds the movie and displays the first frame.
   - **Previous Frame:** Rewinds one frame.
   - **Next Frame:** Advances one frame.
   - **Last Frame:** Skips to the end.
   - **Edit:** Opens the Editing screen, where you can remove unwanted sections from the beginning or end of the movie. More on this next.

During playback, you can pause the movie and redisplay the movie playback panel at any time by pressing Set.

5. **When done, press the Playback button to exit.**

   You can also press the Shutter button halfway or the AF-ON button.

Editing Movies In-Camera

Although never intended as a substitute for computer-based video editing software, the 5D Mark III Edit feature lets you easily remove unwanted parts from the beginning or end of a movie — right on the camera. To perform more complicated edits, including cutting out something from the middle of your movie, you'll have to use a computer and dedicated video-editing software. This onboard editing is handy but basic, so don't expect miracles.

Here are the simple steps for trimming the start or finish of a movie:

1. **Highlight the Edit control (it looks like a pair of scissors; see Figure 4-27) and press Set to enter the Editing screen.**

   If you don't see it, you should have the movie in question called up for playback. Press the Set button to reveal the movie playback panel.

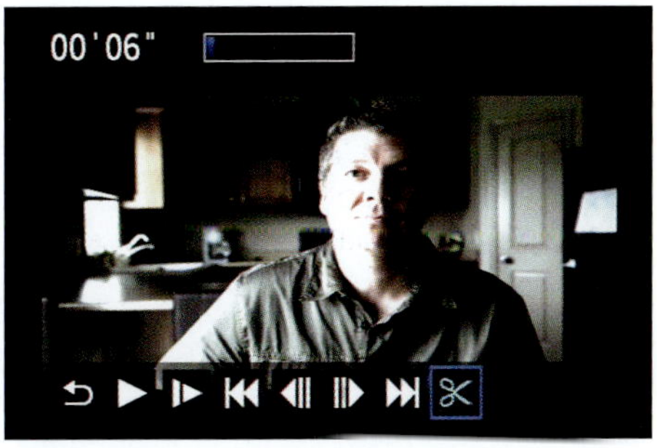

Figure 4-27: Highlight the Edit control and press Set to open the Editing screen.

2. **Select the Cut Beginning control or the Cut End control and then press Set to begin the editing process.**

   In this example, I want to cut some wasted space in the first part of the movie, so I pressed Cut Beginning, which is annotated in Figure 4-28, and then Set.

3. **Use the Multicontroller or Quick Control dial to advance frame by frame. (See Figure 4-28.)**

   If you hold down the Multicontroller, you fast-forward (or fast-backward) in your movie. Do this until you find the last point at which you want to cut the movie. Press the Set button to remove that beginning or ending portion. The blue portion of the bar at the top of your screen shows what will be saved.

4. **Highlight the Save Edited Movie control and press Set to commit your edit.**

   When you highlight Save and press Set, you're asked whether you want to save your edited movie as a new file or overwrite the original (see Figure 4-29). It's *much* safer to save the edited version as a new file. That way, if you ever decide that you did a lousy job (you edited out the candle blowing at your son's birthday, for instance), you'll have your original movie on the memory card to save the day.

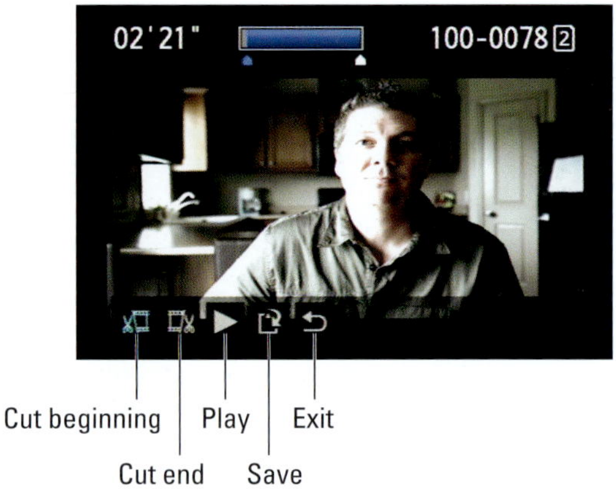

Figure 4-28: Camera editing controls to cut the beginning or end of a movie.

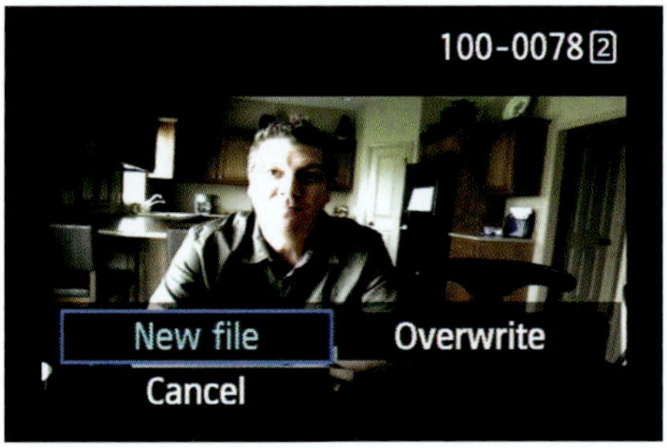

Figure 4-29: Saving the edited movie as a new file on the memory card.

Stepping Up Your Game

Technically speaking, the 5D Mark III has everything you need to shoot movies, but another aspect of its attractiveness is its compatibility with many professional-level video accessories. Each one can solve a problem or augment your capability.

For example, manually focusing can be hard. Considering how pervasive and powerful autofocus is in still photography, focus rings on lenses aren't getting any larger. Until you can buy a "video" version of your favorite lens that sports a massive focus ring, using a focus follower will help you tremendously.

Here is a short list of some gear you should consider to make your setup more professional and your videos more polished:

- **5D Mark III:** 'Nuff said.
- **Your favorite L-series lens:** Don't skimp. Don't even think about skimping. This is what makes the video look good. The camera is a lens platform, when you think about it.
- **Shoulder rig:** Also known as a handset, offset rig, handheld support, or dSLR cinema rig, a shoulder rig transforms your 5D Mark III from a hand-held still camera to a shoulder-mounted video camera. Shoulder

rigs come in numerous styles, but they all allow you to more comfortably hold your camera for extended periods of time in a position suitable for viewing the LCD monitor. They are, simply put, necessary if you want to shoot steady handheld video without your arms falling off (see Figure 4-30).

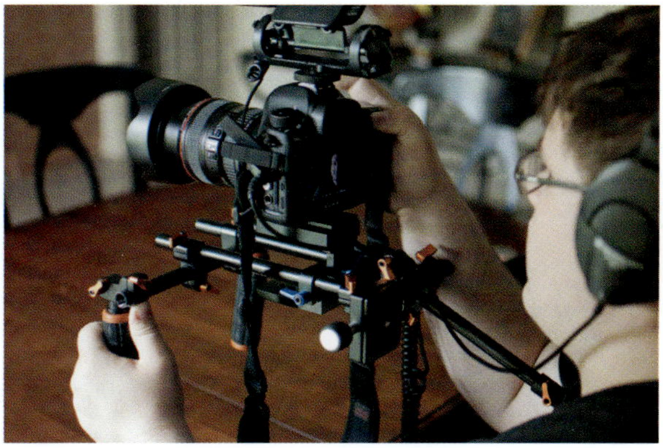

Figure 4-30: Rigs like these are arm savers.

- **LCD Loupe:** These gizmos fit on the back of the camera. They magnify and shield the LCD and turn it into a quasi-viewfinder. LCD Loupes enable you to shoot video using the LCD monitor on the back of the camera in bright lighting. Other benefits are increased magnification and the fact that you concentrate better when all you see is the scene. LCD loupes turn the LCD monitor into a 3.2-inch viewfinder.
- **Focus follower:** Focus followers attach to the lens to improve manual focus action. They are very nice if you want to be able to manually focus while shooting. The action is really smooth, doesn't make noise, and keeps you from bumping or jiggling the camera or lens.
- **Matte box:** You can get away with using the lens hood to keep light from hitting the front of the lens, but the best solution for video is a full-fledged matte box. It makes your dSLR look like an old-school movie camera. Matte boxes offer better protection from stray light than lens hoods and enable you to drop in filters.

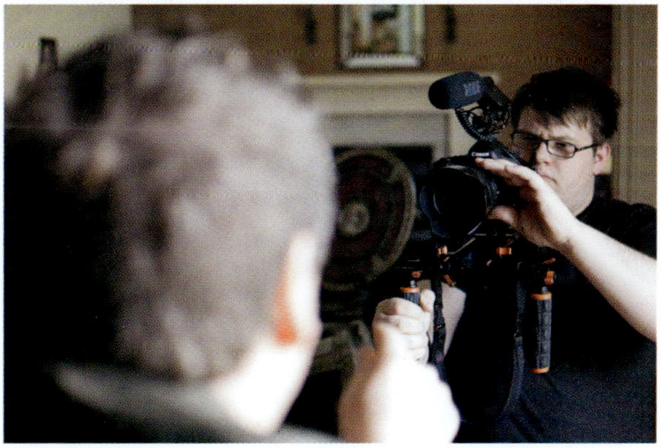

Figure 4-31: This microphone can be mounted on the camera's hot shoe.

- **External stereo microphone:** If you want to shoot serious video, record some serious audio. That means stepping up from mono to stereo and, most often, mounting the microphone on top of the camera, as shown in Figure 4-31.

- **Headphones:** Use them to monitor the sound and keep your head in the game and away from distractions. In Figure 4-32, Dustin is seriously concentrating on his job with the help of his headphones.

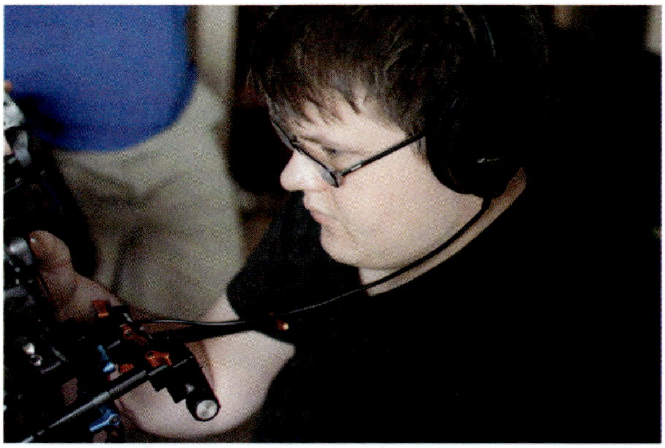

Figure 4-32: Headphones let you hear the sound clearly and concentrate better.

- **External audio recorder (optional):** You may benefit from an external boom mic and audio recorder (see Figure 4-33). This moves sound completely off the camera and eliminates the possibility of stray camera noise (unless you drop the camera and make a loud crash or something.)

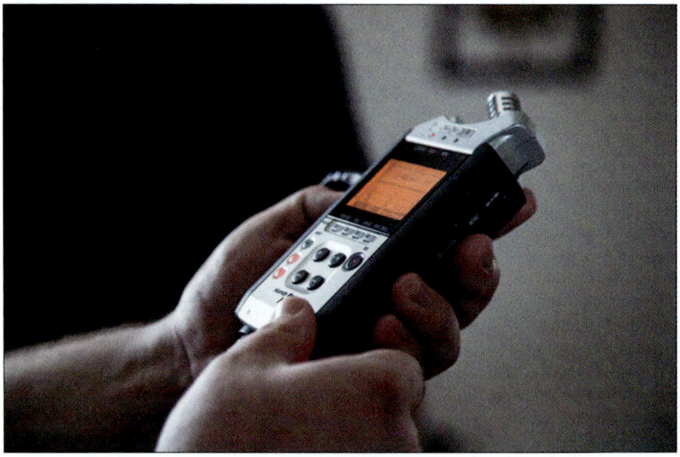

Figure 4-33: We used this external recorder for additional audio.

- **Other lighting gear (optional):** Spots, floods, LCD lighting as required.
- **A crew:** Shooting by yourself can be hard. Don't be afraid to ask for help. Figure 4-34 shows the team: Nate is on boom mic, recording audio separately from the camera, while Dustin operates the 5D Mark III. Mike is the talent. Although you could pull this off yourself, it's always fun to work with good people.

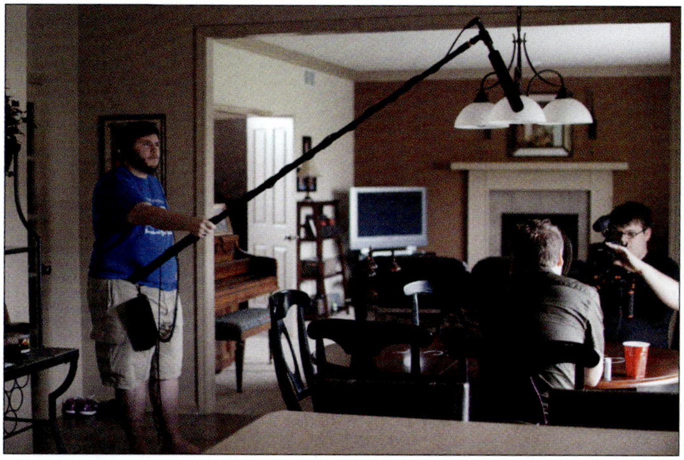

Figure 4-34: Shooting as a team helps ease your workload.

What's next?

Shooting movies is phase 1. If you want to do more than the basic in-camera editing functions allow, you should purchase dedicated video-editing software. You'll be able to edit audio; add text overlays; create special effects; use filters; rerecord audio; create and manage movie projects with multiple source files; create DVDs or Blu-Rays; convert your movies to other sizes and formats; and perform other tasks. (You can upload videos to YouTube and Facebook with the ImageBrowser EX, but not much more.)

This is a very small list of some popular video-editing software. Some of these programs are professional-level applications and downright expensive. Some are suited only for beginners with limited needs. Shop around. Compare applications with the features you need. The best way to save money is to avoid paying for things you don't need. Within a general category, price isn't always the best gauge of quality.

- **Adobe Premier Elements** (Macintosh and Windows) is Adobe's entry-level video-editing software. Visit `www.adobe.com`.
- **Adobe Premier Pro** (Macintosh and Windows) is Adobe's pro-level video-editing software. Visit `www.adobe.com`.
- **Apple iMovie** (Macintosh only) comes standard on most Macintosh computers. iMovie (with iDVD) is an entry-level video-editing application.. Visit `www.apple.com`.
- **Corel VideoStudio** (Windows only) has several inexpensive video-editing applications. Visit `www.corel.com`.
- **Pinnacle** (Windows only), a division of Avid, offers reasonably priced HD video-editing solutions. Studio HD is the entry-level product. Visit `www.pinnaclesys.com`.
- **Avid** (many Windows and Mac) has a range of pro-level audio and video-editing suites that range from software-only solutions to full-fledged, Avid-certified workstations. Visit `www.avid.com`.

5

Getting More from Picture Playback

In This Chapter

- Dealing with folders, cards, and movies
- Tweaking instant photo review
- Understanding picture data
- Deleting and protecting files
- Copying, resizing, and processing images
- Configuring slide shows and using a TV

Use this chapter to help you take advantage of one of digital photography's greatest advantages over film: review and playback. Continually review your photos and movies to make sure they are in focus, the colors are right, things are well framed, and they aren't too dark or too bright.

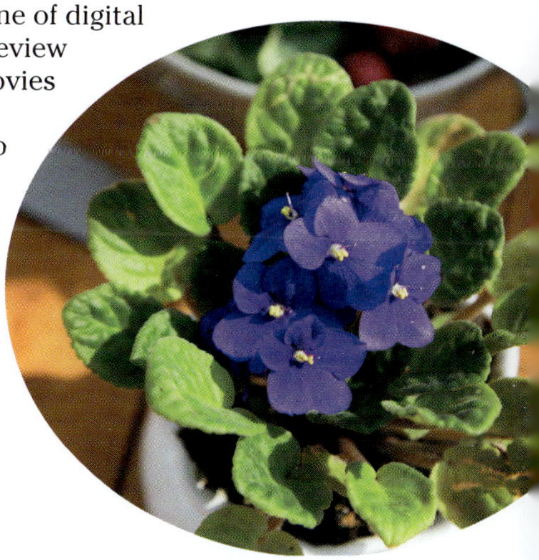

This chapter also tells you how to rotate photos, protect or delete pictures and movies, set photos to automatically print (using a DPOF-compatible printer), and check each photo's histogram. The playback features of the 5D Mark III give you access to these powerful features.

Folders, Cards, and Movies

First, a housekeeping note. There are three things about the 5D Mark III that make discussing photo and movie playback a bit cumbersome. It's not that these features are technically difficult to understand. Rather, it's a nuisance to keep mentioning them over and over. Therefore, I want to tell you about these particulars once, at the outset of the chapter:

- **Folders:** Folders are mostly ignored during playback. You can select a new folder to record into, but that doesn't change where you are in the playback rotation. If you want to know what folder a photo or movie is located in, look at the first number of the folder-file number pair, which is located at the top-right corner of the display when the photo or movie is being played back (I discuss the display later in the chapter, in "Viewing Picture Data").

  Folders are not ignored in terms of the options you have available when setting up the jump and slide show features. You can also protect, copy, and delete photos by folder.

- **Cards:** Playback features don't span memory cards. Therefore, the material in this chapter assumes that, should you have two memory cards in the camera, you have chosen the card you want to work with first. If you're playing back photos or movies and can't find the one you're looking for, it might be on the other card. The card number that the photo or movie is on is located in the top-right corner of the display, next to the folder and file number.

  Change cards by activating the Setup Menu 3 or from the Quick Control screen. See Chapter 11 for more information on working with two cards.

- **Movies:** During playback, movies are included in the mix with still photos. When you come across a movie, you will see its thumbnail. It doesn't start playing automatically. You must press the Set button to display its movie playback panel first. See Chapter 4 to find out more about playing movies.

  You cannot process, magnify, resize, or rotate movies, nor can you set their print order.

  You can include movies in slide shows and protect, copy, and erase them.

Adjusting Image Review

After you take a picture, it automatically appears briefly on the camera monitor. By default, the review period lasts just two seconds. You can customize this behavior via the Image Review option on Shooting Menu 1. Highlight Image Review and then press Set. You can select among the following:

- **A specific review period:** Pick 2, 4, or 8 seconds.
- **Off:** Disable automatic instant review. Turning off the monitor saves battery power, so keep this option in mind if the battery is running low. You can still view pictures by pressing the Playback button.
- **Hold:** Display the current image indefinitely, or at least until the camera automatically shuts off to save power. See the Chapter 2 section about Setup Menu 2 to find out about the Auto Power Off feature.

Viewing Images in Playback Mode

To switch your camera to playback mode and view the images on your memory cards, take these steps:

1. **Press the Playback button, shown in Figure 5-1.**

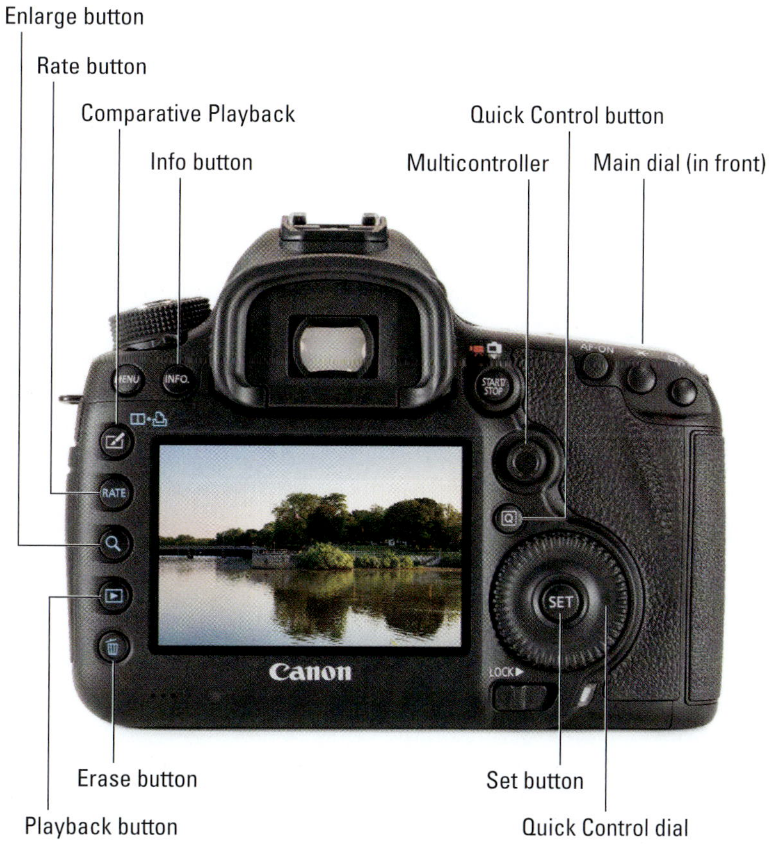

Figure 5-1: These are your primary playback controls.

This action initiates playback.

2. **Inspect photos or movies.**

   At the default settings, the camera displays a single picture at a time, with no other information. Not even a shred, as shown in Figure 5-2 (yes, that's a cabbage). Press the Info button to change the display (I cover changing the display later, in "Viewing Picture Data") to add more information.

   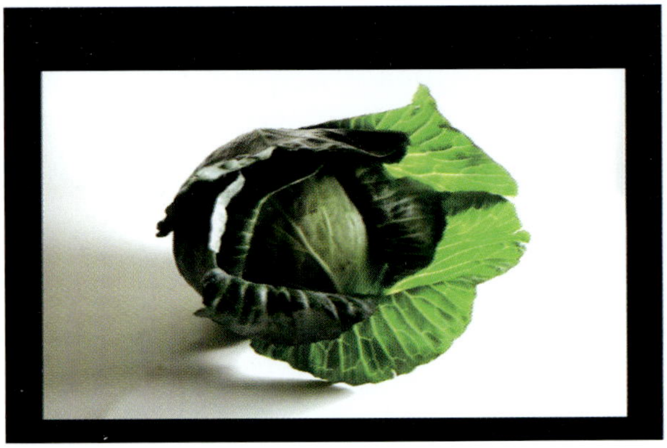

   Figure 5-2: The default playback mode displays one picture at a time, with no picture data.

   You can display multiple images at a time. That's called an *index*, which is covered later in the chapter, in "Zooming out to show the index display."

3. **Rotate the Quick Control dial right or left to scroll through your pictures.**

   - *Right:* View images in the order they were taken.
   - *Left:* View images in the reverse order, starting with the most recent picture.

   Each click of the dial scrolls to the next photo. Keep rotating to browse through them all.

4. **Exit playback when desired.**

   You can press a number of different buttons to go on to another task. Press the Playback button, the Shutter button halfway, or AF-ON to exit playback mode and get back to shooting. Press the Menu button to open the camera's menu.

Isn't that simple? It is.

Jumping through images

If your memory card contains scads of images, here's a trick you'll love: Rotate the Main dial to leapfrog through pictures rather than continually dialing right or left with the Quick Control dial or pressing the Multicontroller right or left a gazillion times to get to the picture you want to see. You also can search for the first image shot on a specific date or tell the camera to display only movies or only still shots.

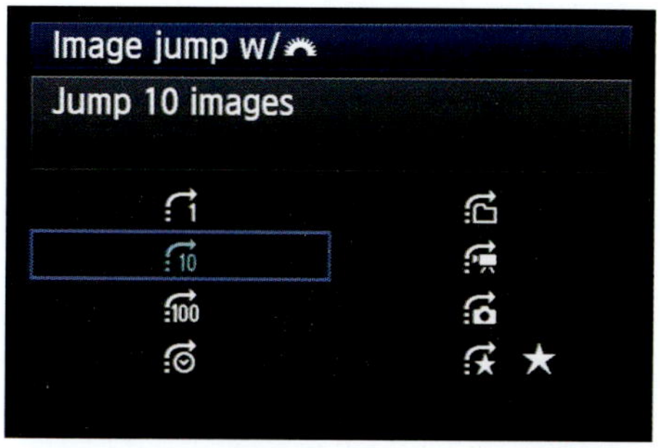

Figure 5-3: Jumping is a fast way of skipping around.

By default, Image Jump is set to jump 10 images at a time when you rotate the Main dial during image playback. Change Image Jump options by displaying Playback Menu 2 and highlighting Image Jump with Main Dial. Press Set to display the screen in Figure 5-3, where you can adjust the settings:

- **1 Image:** This setting, in effect, disables jumping, restricting you to browsing pictures one at a time. So what's the point? You can use this setting to scroll pictures by using the Main dial instead of the Quick Control dial if you prefer.
- **10 Images:** Advance 10 images at a time.
- **100 Images:** Advance 100 images at a time.
- **Date:** If your card contains images shot on different dates, you can jump between dates with this setting. For example, if you're looking at the first of 30 pictures taken on June 1, you can jump past all others from that day to the first image taken on, say, June 5.
- **Folder:** This setting jumps you to the first photo in a different folder on the memory card. Pretty snazzy!
- **Movies Only:** Say that your memory card contains still photos and movies. If you want to view only the movie files, choose this setting. Then you can rotate the Main dial to jump from one movie to the next without seeing any still photos.
- **Stills Only:** This is the opposite of the Movies setting. Your movie files are hidden from view when you use the Main dial to scroll photos. You scroll one picture at a time, just as when you use the 1 Image setting.
- **Image Rating:** If you've set ratings for one or more photos on the memory card, you can view only those, or only the photos with a specific rating. The section "Rating Photos," later in this chapter, explains how to assign a rating to pictures.

For any setting except Image Rating, highlight the setting name and then press Set. If you select Image Rating, use the Main dial to select a rating before you press Set. Then take the following steps to jump through your photos:

1. **Press the Playback button to put the camera into playback mode.**
2. **If necessary, set the camera to display a single photo.**

   To leave the image index, press the Set button. See "Zooming in for a closer view" or "Zooming out to show the index display" for information about changing the magnification to display an index versus a single photo.

   REMEMBER: The Main dial turns the page when you're viewing the four- or nine-image index; it does not jump ahead according to the criteria you've chosen.
3. **Rotate the Main dial.**

   The camera jumps to the next image. The number of images you advance, and whether you see movies as well as still photos, depends on the setting you selected earlier.

   If you select any setting but 1 Image, a jump bar appears at the bottom of the monitor, as shown in Figure 5-4, indicating the current setting.

   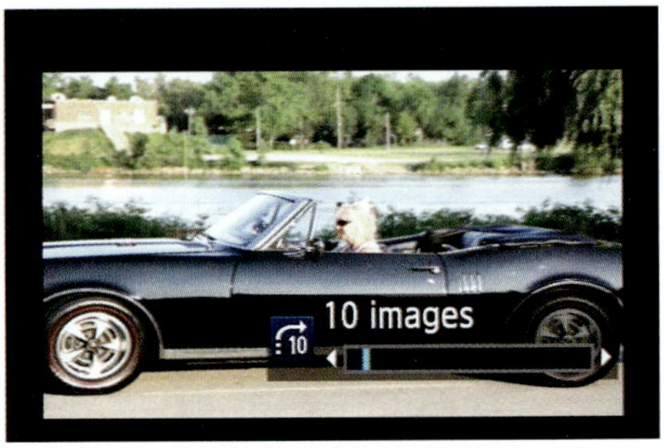

   Figure 5-4: The jump bar is a reminder that you're jumping to and fro.

   TIP: You can change the setting without having to return to Playback Menu 2. Press the Quick Control button while in playback (that part is important) to enter Quick Control mode, select the Image Jump option at the bottom of the screen, and choose a new setting.
4. **Continue as desired.**

   To keep jumping, continue rotating the Main dial. When you stop and view a photo, the jump bar disappears in a moment. To get back to jumping, rotate the Main dial while still in playback. You can also use the Quick Control dial at any time to revert to single-image advance.

Rotating pictures

Normally, the 5D Mark III records the image orientation with each photo you take. Image orientation refers to whether you held the camera horizontally or on its side to shoot vertically. This bit of data is simply added into the picture file. Then when you view the picture, the camera reads the data and rotates the image so that it appears upright in the monitor. (See Chapter 2 for more information on how to control this behavior from Setup Menu 1.) The image is also rotated automatically when you view it in the photo software that shipped with your camera.

Regardless of how you have Auto Rotate configured, you can still rotate images during playback. Here's how:

1. **Press the Menu button and navigate to Playback Menu 1.**
2. **Highlight Rotate Image and press the Set button.**

   An image appears on the monitor.
3. **Navigate to the photo you want to rotate.**

   Spin the Quick Control dial right or left to scroll to the photo that needs to be rotated.
4. **Press the Set button to rotate the image.**

   Press once to rotate the image 90 degrees clockwise; press again to rotate 90 degrees counterclockwise; press once more to return to where you started.
5. **Press Menu to exit rotate mode and return to the menu.**

REMEMBER

These steps apply only to still photos; you can't rotate movies during playback. You can also rotate photos during playback by entering Quick Control mode.

Zooming in for a closer view

To more closely inspect a portion of a photo, zoom in by using the Enlarge button. This feature is especially handy for checking small details, such as whether anyone's eyes are closed in a group portrait. As with image rotating, zooming works only for still images.

Use the following techniques to adjust the image magnification:

- **Zoom in and out.** Press the Enlarge button once. Now you can use the Main dial to zoom in. Rotate it clockwise until you're at the level you desire (see Figure 5-5). You can magnify the photo up to approximately ten times its normal display size on the monitor.

  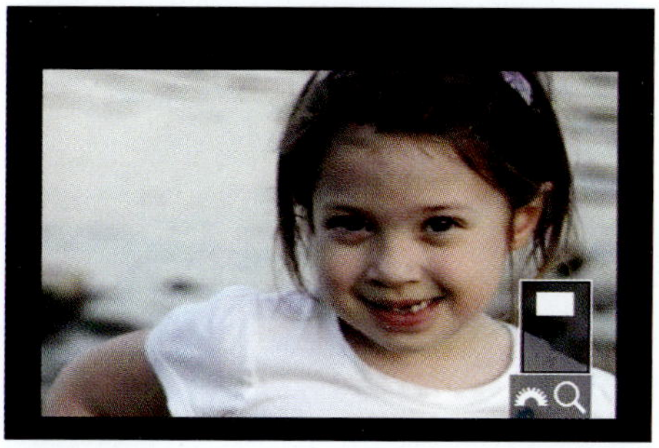

  Figure 5-5: Checking for open eyes and focus.

  Zoom out by rotating the Main dial counterclockwise.

  The magnified area is shown in the lower-right portion of the screen, accompanied by a reminder to use the Main dial. If the white box disappears but the Main dial and Enlarge symbols are still present, you are at the normal display magnification but can still zoom in or out. If you continue to zoom out, you will display the index instead of a single photo.

If you rotate the Quick Control dial, you will change the image that is displayed but continue to view at the same magnification and area.

- **Move around the photo.** When the image is magnified, a small thumbnail representing the entire image appears in the lower-right corner of the monitor. The white box indicates the area of the image that's visible.

  Use the Multicontroller to pan the display to a different position.

- **View more images at the same magnification.** Here's a cool trick: While the display is zoomed, rotate the Quick Control dial to view the same area of the next photo at the same magnification. This is helpful for checking focus across similar photos or for looking at people's faces in portraits.

- **Return to normal view (whether full-screen or index).** When you're ready to exit the magnified view and return the camera to normal (this doesn't work when viewing the index), press the Playback button. Bam.

Zooming out to show the index display

If you like, you can zoom out and view the four- or nine-image (see Figure 5-6) index display.

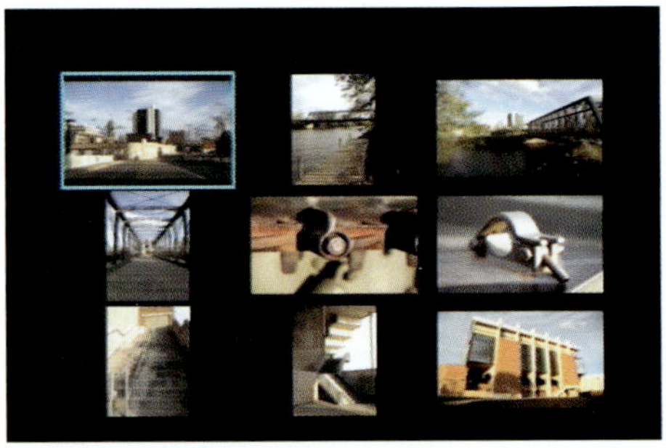

Figure 5-6: Quickly scan photos with an index; the top-left photo is selected.

Getting there is very similar to zooming in. Press the Playback button and then press the Enlarge button. Rotate the Main dial counterclockwise until the display transforms into the four- or nine-image index. When you have reached the index you want to display, press the Enlarge button again (you can also press Playback). The Main dial and Enlarge button reminders disappear from the screen and the index display is locked in as the default playback view, enabling you to zoom into other photos and return to the index.

Remember these factoids about navigating and viewing your photo collection in index display mode:

- **A blue-highlighted box surrounds the selected image.** Refer to Figure 5-6.
- **Use the Quick Control dial or Multicontroller to select a different image.** Turn the dial clockwise to scroll through photos to the right and counterclockwise to go left. Or, press up using the Multicontroller to shift the selection box up, press right to move it right, and so on.
- **Rotate the Main dial to page through screens of thumbnails.** Rotate right to shift to the next screen; rotate left to go back one screen.
- **Press Info to toggle the minimal information displayed for the selected photo on and off.**
- **Press the Set button to view the selected image full screen.** This action cancels the image index.

Entering Quick Control during playback

You can enter Quick Control during playback and set several image properties. Follow these steps and it's a snap:

1. **During playback, press the Quick Control button.**
2. **Press the Multicontroller up or down to select a function from the left side of the screen (see Figure 5-7).**

   Don't use the Quick Control dial, which changes settings. Use the Multicontroller to change functions.

   You don't need to press Set to activate the function. After the function is highlighted, it is automatically active.

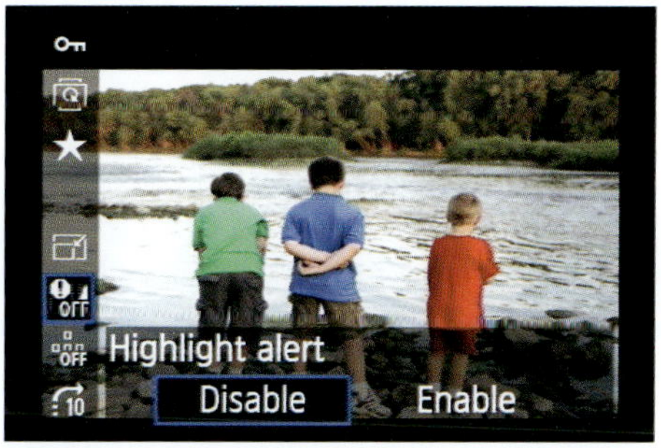

Figure 5-7: After being highlighted, a function displays its options.

   Look for a blue box that surrounds the function symbol on the left side of the screen. Its name and possible settings are displayed at the bottom of the screen.

   You can choose from the following list of functions (starting with the icon in the upper-left corner):

   - *Protect Images:* Prevent photos from being accidentally deleted.

     WARNING!

     Keep in mind that formatting the memory card wipes out even protected photos.

- *Rotate Image:* Rotate the current photo.
- *Rating:* Rate photos from zero to five stars.
- *RAW Image Processing:* Enables you to use the current shot settings or open the custom RAW processing screen to process the RAW photo in-camera. I cover this in more depth in "Processing RAW photos," later in this chapter.
- *Resize:* Resize the current photo. I cover resizing in more detail in "Resizing JPEG photos," later in the chapter.
- *Highlight Alert:* If enabled, shows areas of the photo that have lost their detail and are too bright. These areas, quite often the sky, lights, or bright reflections, slowly blink, no matter what playback display mode you're in. (See the discussion in "Histogram display," later in this chapter, on histograms and what it means to blow highlights.)
- *AF Point Display:* Shows or hides autofocus points when reviewing photos.
- *Image Jump:* Sets the jump behavior when using the Main dial during playback.

You can read more about rotating, rating, protecting, and jumping through images in other sections of this chapter.

3. **Use the Quick Control dial to switch settings.**

   You can also press the Multicontroller left or right.

4. **Press the Quick Control button to exit Quick Control and return to normal playback.**

   No need to press Set. The settings are locked in.

Viewing Picture Data

When you review still photos, you can press the Info button to change the type and amount of shooting data that appear with the photo in the monitor. The next several sections offer a guide to the data-display options, starting with the most basic and advancing through the other playback display screens. See Chapter 4 to find out about the information displayed during movie playback.

Changing the image playback display

Displaying photo information and changing the amount to display is a pretty simple matter:

1. **Press the Playback button to enter playback.**

2. **Press Info (refer to Figure 5-1) to change display formats.**

   The four displays (each of which are covered in the following sections) are

   - *No Information:* Displays the image only.
   - *Basic Information:* Shows only the most basic info.
   - *Shooting Information:* Shows a much more comprehensive list of information, including a Brightness histogram.
   - *Histogram:* Replaces some shooting information with an RGB histogram.

   If the AF point display option is enabled in the Playback Menu 4 (or through the Quick Control screen), autofocus points show up as red rectangles corresponding to their location in the viewfinder in all displays.

   If the photo was taken in Live View and used Live mode or Face Detection Live mode autofocusing methods (see Chapter 3 to decode all these terms), you see a focus rectangle instead of individual autofocus points. If you used Quick mode, which uses the camera's normal autofocus points, you see them displayed.

   When you zoom in or are displaying an image index, only the first two display modes are available. The other data disappears.

3. **Continue pressing Info to cycle through the different display formats.**

   When you find the one you want, stop pressing the Info button. When you return to playback, you'll be in the same display format because the display mode carries over between playback sessions.

   The displays look the same whether you took the photo in Scene Intelligent Auto shooting mode or some other advanced mode.

No Information display (image only)

In the first display mode, officially called No Information display, your LCD appears as shown in Figure 5-8.

As you might guess, No Information mode includes, well, no information (except for the autofocus points, as explained in the previous section).

You see a large, uncluttered view of your image. It's perfect for checking composition, color, and general exposure. Pressing the Info button advances you to the next viewing mode.

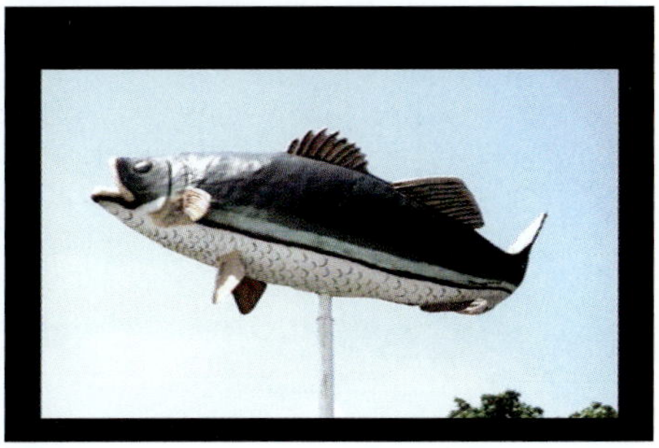

Figure 5-8: The simplest playback mode showcases the image.

Basic Information display

Basic Information mode, shown in Figure 5-9, adds enough information about your photo for you to know its name and the basic exposure details.

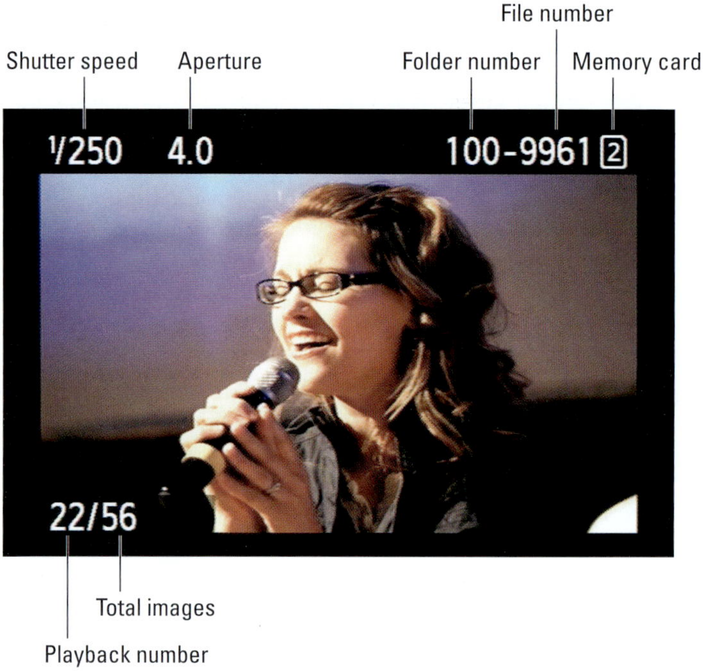

Figure 5-9: This display mode includes basic exposure and file information.

Along the top of the screen are the following bits of information (labeled in Figure 5-9):

- **Shutter speed and aperture:** Chapter 6 explains these two exposure settings.
- **Exposure compensation:** If you used exposure compensation for your shot, that value is noted at the top edge of the display (not shown in Figure 5-9). See Chapter 6 for info on exposure compensation.
- **Protection:** If you protected the image, a little key icon appears. You can find out how to protect your images later in this chapter; see "Protecting Photos."

- **Rating:** If you rated the photo, the rating is shown right by the folder and file number. See the section "Rating Photos" for details about image ratings.
- **Folder number and last four digits of file number:** See Chapter 10 for information about how the camera assigns folder and file numbers.
- **Memory card:** The number of the memory card the photo is stored on.

In the bottom-left corner of the LCD are two numbers separated by a slash (/): image number/total images. This pair of values shows you the current image number and the total number of images on the memory card. For example, in Figure 5-9, you see picture 22 out of 56. (Don't confuse the image number with the file number; again, the last four digits of the file number appear in the top-right corner of the display, along with the folder number.)

All information presented in Basic Information mode is also included in the last two comprehensive modes, too. It's a more-info-as-you-go approach, with a twist.

From Basic Information mode, press the Info button again to shift to Shooting Information display mode. There, you hit the mother lode of information, which I discuss next.

Shooting Information display

In Shooting Information display mode, the camera presents a thumbnail of your image along with scads of shooting data (see Figure 5-10). To open this screen, make sure that the display is now showing a four- or nine-image index. Next, press the Info button until you see the one shown in the figure.

The graph on the top-right side of the screen is an exposure-evaluation tool known as a *Brightness histogram*, which I explain in the upcoming section "Histogram display."

If you're a fan of RGB histograms, you may be interested in another possibility: You can swap the standard Brightness histogram that appears in the Shooting Information display with an RGB histogram. Visit Playback Menu 3, highlight the Histogram display option, and press the Set button. Select RGB instead of Brightness and press the Set button again.

To sort out the maze of other data, it helps to break the display into five rows of information: the row along the top of the screen and the four rows that appear under the image thumbnail and histogram. One note about the next few figures, which detail what you see in each row: The figures include all possible symbols, values, and other shooting data only for the purpose of illustration. If a data item doesn't appear on your monitor, it simply means that the feature wasn't enabled when you captured the photo.

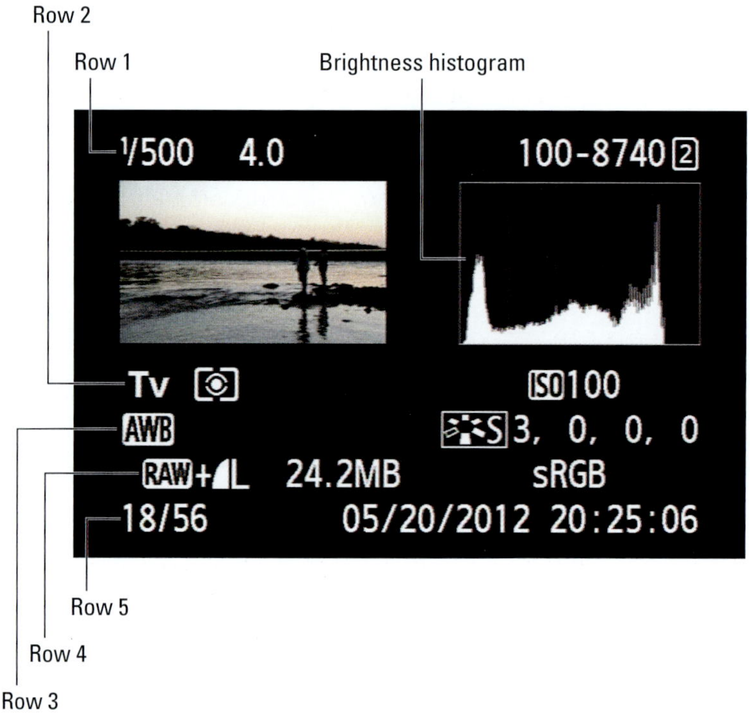

Figure 5-10: The Shooting Information display adds much more data.

Here is what appears in the five rows:

- **Row 1 data:** You see the same data that appears in the Basic Information display at the top of the screen.
- **Row 2 data:** Shift your attention to the row of symbols just underneath the thumbnail and histogram:
  - *Shooting mode:* This symbol indicates which of the camera's shooting modes you used. The symbols mirror what you see on the camera Mode dial.
  - *Metering mode:* This symbol represents the metering mode, which determines which part of the frame the camera uses when calculating exposure. Chapter 6 explains how the different metering modes work.

- *Flash/flash exposure compensation amount:* See whether the flash fired — and if so, how much you adjusted the flash power using the Flash Exposure Compensation feature (detailed in Chapter 6), if any.
- *AF Microadjustment amount:* Displays how much, if any, you have corrected the autofocus distance using AF Microadjustment. This is explained in Chapter 11.
- *ISO speed:* Chapter 6 also explains this option, which controls the light sensitivity of the camera's image sensor.
- *Highlight Tone Priority:* If you enabled this exposure feature for the shot, you see the little D+ symbol. See Chapter 6 to find out how Highlight Tone Priority affects photos.

- **Row 3 data:** Information on this row of the display relates mostly to color settings. Here's the scoop:
  - *White Balance setting:* Chapter 8 has details on this option, which helps ensure accurate photo colors. The setting shown in the figure, AWB, stands for Auto White Balance. When a custom color temperature is used, you see it displayed as a number. See Chapter 8 for a look at the symbols representing other White Balance settings.
  - *White Balance correction:* This collection of data tells you whether you applied an adjustment to the White Balance setting you used. Chapter 8 explains this advanced color option.
  - *Picture Style:* Shows you the Picture Style. Pay attention to the letter, which tells you at a glance what picture style you used for the photo. The *S* in Figure 5-10 represents the Standard Picture Style, for example. The values to the right relate to four characteristics that you can adjust for each Picture Style. Chapter 8 explains how each Picture Style affects an image.
- **Row 4 data:** This row tells you the following tidbits of information:
  - *Image recording quality and file size:* Shows the Image recording quality; also, file size is shown in megabytes (MB). For details on the setting and its effect on file size and picture quality, see Chapter 2.
  - *Color space:* Displays the photo's color space: sRGB or Adobe RGB. Chapter 8 has details about the two options.
- **Row 5 data:** Wrapping up the smorgasbord of shooting data, the bottom row of the Shooting Information Display holds three more pieces of data:
  - *Image number/total images recorded:* Again, this pair of numbers indicates the current image number with respect to the total number of images on the current memory card.
  - *Eye-Fi card transmission status:* If you use an Eye-Fi memory card (see Chapter 11 for more information on wireless file transfer using

Eye-Fi cards), a small icon depicting a wireless connection appears on pictures that you downloaded to your computer wirelessly. That icon is not shown here. See Chapter 11 for more information on Eye-Fi. You can also visit `www.eye.fi` for details about Eye-Fi memory cards.

- *Date and time:* These values show you the exact moment that the image was recorded. Of course, you must first set the camera date and time, as Chapter 2 explains.

Histogram display

The Histogram display shows the data you see in Figure 5-11. The image thumbnail remains the same as in the last display, but some of the shooting data is removed to make room for another histogram. The histogram on the top-right is called an RGB histogram. The Brightness histogram on the bottom is held over from the Shooting Information display.

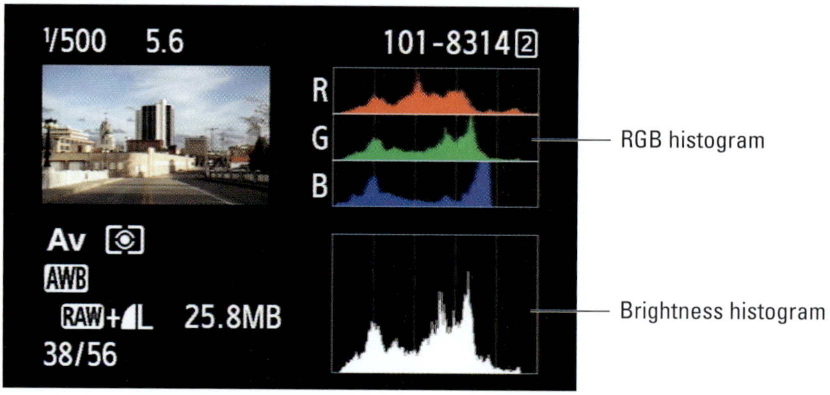

Figure 5-11: The Histogram display contains two histograms: Brightness and RGB.

As with the Shooting Information display, this display is available only when you're viewing photos or movies one at a time. If your monitor is showing four or nine thumbnails, you must zoom out to show a single photo or movie.

One of the more difficult things to get about histograms is that they can't tell you whether a photo is good or bad. They exist to give you details *about the exposure*. These details can relate to overall brightness, as in the case of Brightness histograms, or color channel, which is where RGB histograms come in. Although playback histograms are created after the photo is taken, you can display a real-time Brightness histogram on the 5D Mark III in Live View mode.

Using the Brightness histogram

A Brightness histogram shows you the distribution of brightness in an image by charting two pieces of data along two axes. The horizontal axis of the graph represents the possible brightness values, from the darkest shadows on the left to the brightest highlights on the right. The vertical axis shows you how many pixels fall at a particular brightness value. A spike indicates a heavy concentration of pixels at that brightness.

Use the Brightness histogram to help you evaluate overall exposure and protect against *blown,* or *clipped,* highlights, one of the more difficult problems to correct if you have large areas of the photo that are too bright (small amounts of clipping can be acceptable).

In plain English, blown or clipped mean that *highlights* — the brightest areas of the image — are so overexposed that areas that should include a variety of light shades are instead totally white.

Areas that fall into this category blink in the image thumbnail in all display modes if you have enabled Highlight alert in Playback Menu 3. This warning is a helpful feature because viewing the image on the camera monitor isn't always a reliable way to gauge exposure.

Keep in mind that there is no single "perfect" histogram that you should try to duplicate. Instead, you need to interpret the histogram with respect to the amount of shadows, highlights, and midtones that make up your subject and your artistic goals.

Using the RGB histogram

Everything that was said of Brightness histograms applies to RGB histograms, except that RGB histograms chart color saturation by color channel instead of using a composite brightness value.

To make sense of an RGB histogram, you first need to know that digital images are known as *RGB images* because they're created from three primary colors of light: red, green, and blue. Whereas the Brightness histogram reflects the brightness of all three color channels rolled into one, RGB histograms let you view the values for each individual channel.

When you look at the brightness data for a single channel, though, you evaluate color *saturation.* We don't have space in this book to provide a full lesson on RGB color theory, but the short story is that when you mix red, green, and blue light, and each component is at maximum brightness, you create white. Zero brightness in all three channels creates black. If you have maximum red and no blue or green, though, you have fully saturated red. If you mix two channels at maximum brightness, you also create full saturation. For example, maximum red and blue produce fully saturated magenta. And, wherever colors are fully saturated, you can lose picture detail. For example, a rose petal that should have a range of tones from medium to dark red may instead be a flat blob of dark red.

The upshot is that if all the pixels for one or two channels are slammed to the right end of the histogram, you may be losing picture detail because of overly saturated colors. If all three channels show a heavy pixel population at the right end of the histograms, you may have clipped highlights — again, because the maximum levels of red, green, and blue create white. Either way, you may want to adjust the exposure settings and try again.

A savvy RGB histogram reader can also spot color balance issues by looking at the pixel values. But frankly, color balance problems are fairly easy to notice just by looking at the image on the camera monitor.

Exploring some samples

Okay, enough histogram theory. I want to show you several examples of what histograms show and how to use them to interpret a scene.

Figures 5-12 through 5-21 are captures of the Histogram display. To save space, I have chosen not to show you the full-sized photo. The point is to quickly compare the histograms with the photo thumbnail, as you would on the back of your camera, and to be able to discern at a glance what is going on. You don't need to zoom in to 1,000 percent when evaluating exposure with histograms.

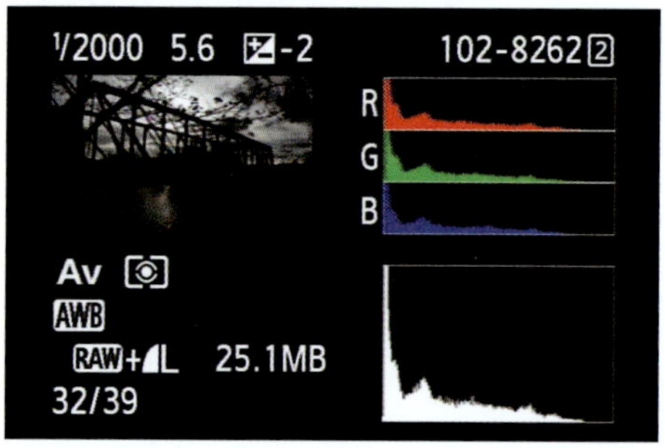

Figure 5-12: Notice that details are lost off the left edge of the histogram.

- **Underexposed:** Figure 5-12 is a shot taken from a riverbank, looking up toward a nice old bridge and into the sky beyond. As you can tell from the heavy concentration to the far left side of both histograms, this photo is underexposed (although it still has a nice quality to it).
- **Low key:** Although Figure 5-13 is dark, it's not underexposed. The histograms do not extend off the left edge. This means that shadowy detail is present, but dark.

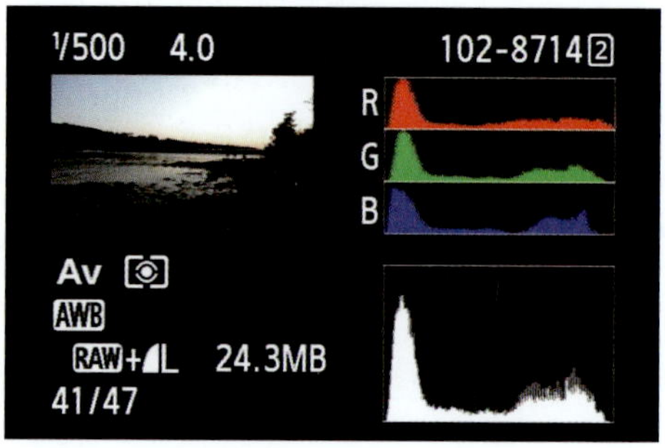

Figure 5-13: Dark, but no loss of details.

- **High key:** The flowers and colander in Figure 5-14 are presented very brightly. Notice that the histograms do not go off the far right edge. This means that I haven't lost any data, even though everything looks white.
- **Overexposed:** In Figure 5-15, I'm shooting into the sun. Two people are sitting on benches inside a gazebo. The sun overpowers the bright side of the histogram, resulting in clipped highlights.
- **Low contrast (mid-tone heavy):** Figure 5-16 is a photo of a rough concrete path. It's almost perfectly gray. The large hump in the middle of both histograms, combined with little extremely bright or dark areas, indicates low contrast.
- **Even contrast using full histogram:** A woman is making a salad on a picnic table in Figure 5-17. The scene has a nice mixture of reds, greens, and blues, as well as brightness values. The histograms are wide and the photo shows good, but not overpowering, contrast.
- **High contrast:** Figure 5-18 introduces more contrast. Notice the lack of mid-tones in the center of the histograms. Most of the data in this picture is on one end or the other, without being clipped. The fact that the data has not been lost is key to preserving detail, and typical of a well-executed, high-contrast photo.

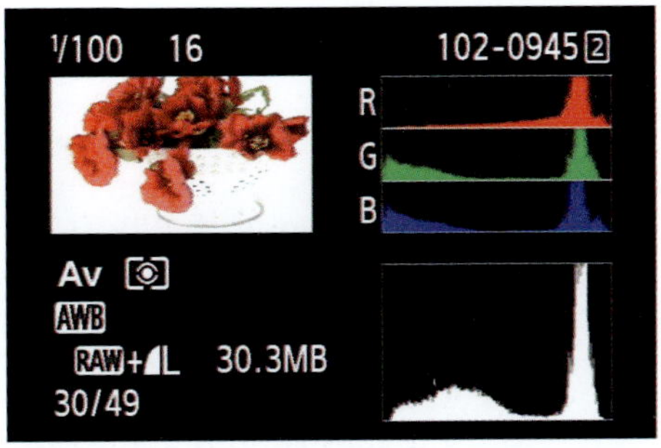

Figure 5-14: Bright, but everything is here.

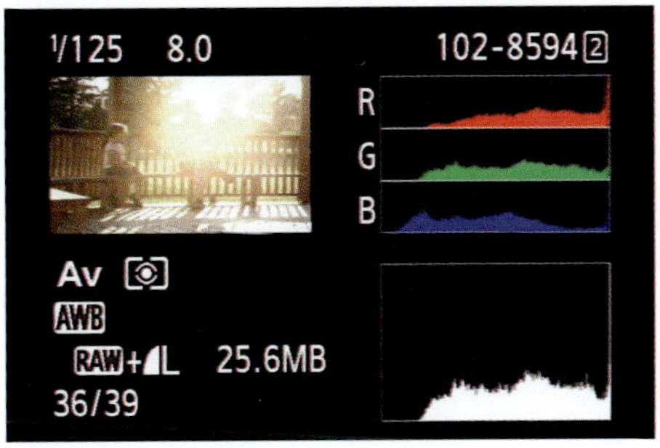

Figure 5-15: This photo is overexposed because of the bright sun.

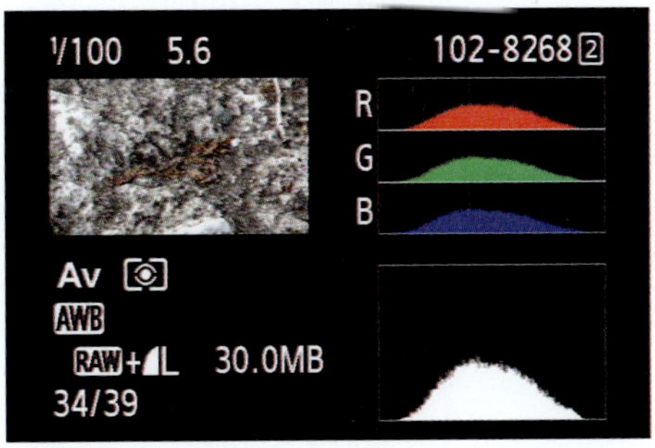

Figure 5-16: The histogram indicates low contrast with plenty of gray.

- **Extreme contrast with loss of detail:** I shot Figure 5-19 from the inside of a garage. I had to enter manual shooting mode and set the aperture and shutter speed to maximize contrast. I was able, despite the impressive dynamic range of the 5D Mark III, to blow out details in the window and push the dark areas of the photo off the left side of the histogram.
- **Good color:** Figure 5-20 shows a nice range of color and brightness. The main reason I include it is to compare with the next photo and prove that histograms can display similar properties while the photos are very different.
- **Color imbalance:** In Figure 5-21, two children are having fun bowling. Although the pins in the distance appear white, the overall color balance of the photo is skewed toward an ugly yellow. One look at the RGB histogram confirms that the photo has too few blues. Although Figure 5-20's blues are primarily dark, they extend throughout the brightness range. In this photo, they drop out early.

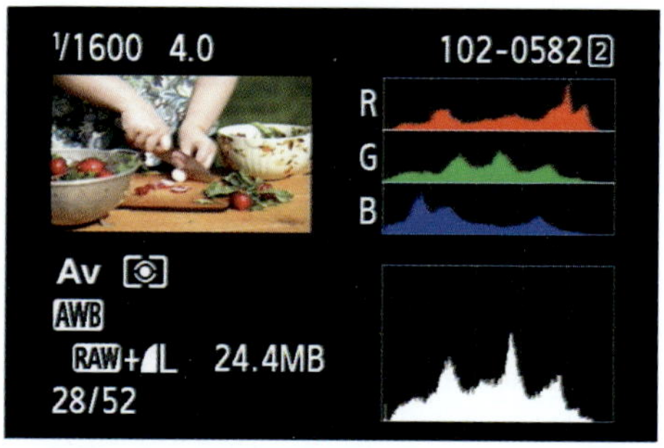

Figure 5-17: Cutting red radishes with green leaves in a blue shirt.

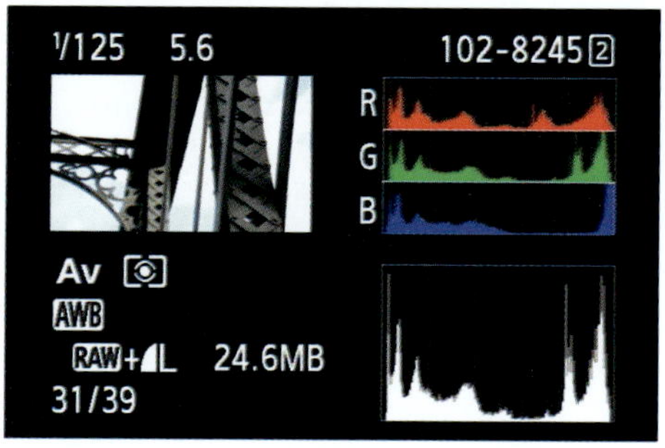

Figure 5-18: This scene has a wide dynamic range without losing details because of clipping.

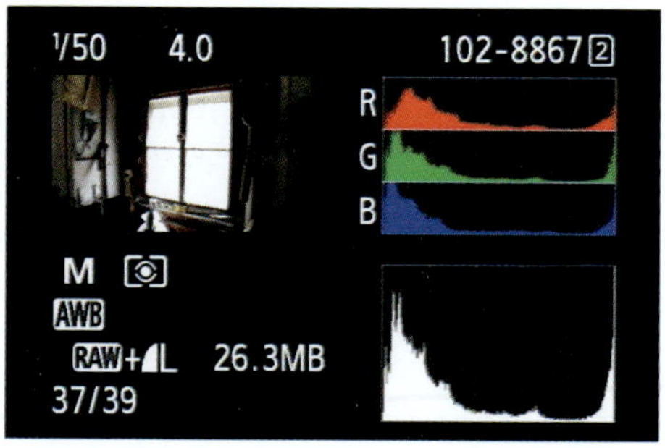

Figure 5-19: Losing data on both ends of the spectrum.

Deleting Files

When you spot a clunker during your picture review, you can erase it from your memory card in a few ways, as outlined in the next few sections.

Erasing single images

This one's pretty simple: Press the Erase button when playing back a photo. If you just took the shot and it's still being displayed, press the Erase button to delete it.

Either way, you will need to confirm your decision. Highlight Erase and press the Set button. Your picture is zapped into digital oblivion.

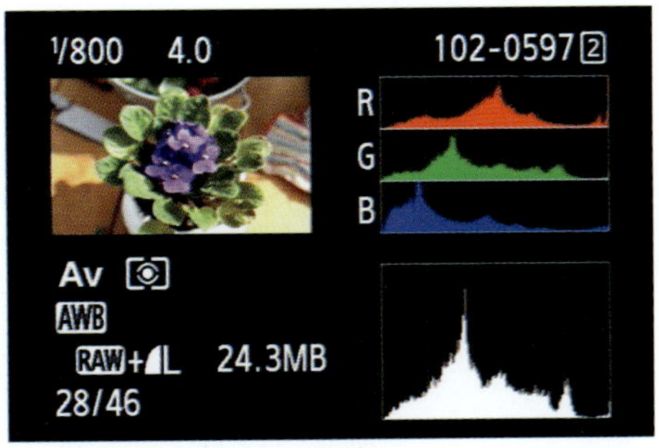

Figure 5-20: The colors are nicely distributed in this photo.

TIP: If you accidentally erase a picture, don't panic. You *may* be able to restore it by using data-restoration software. Lexar (`www.lexar.com`) and SanDisk (`www.sandisk.com`) are two popular memory card companies that either sell or recommend recovery software to help you in case a card becomes corrupted or you accidentally delete images. To have a chance at recovering deleted data, you must *not* take any more pictures or perform any other operations on your camera while the current memory card is in it. If you do, you may overwrite the erased picture data for good and eliminate the possibility of recovering the image.

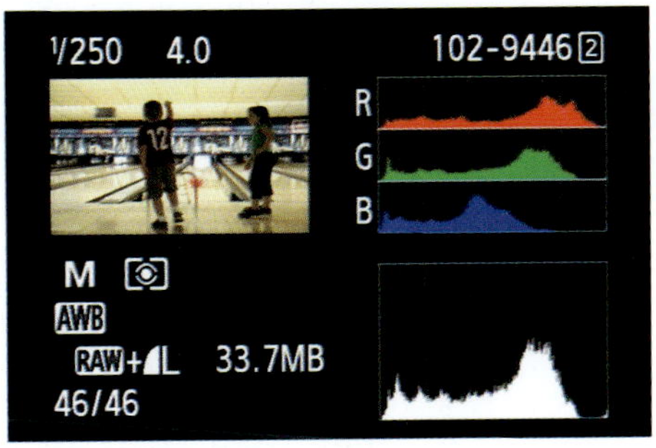

Figure 5-21: This photo is too yellow.

Erasing tons of stuff

You can, of course, delete more than one file at a time. You can choose files individually for mass deletion, erase them by folder, or delete all unprotected photos from either memory card.

Here's how:

1. **Press the Menu button and navigate to Playback Menu 1.**
2. **Highlight Erase Images, as shown in Figure 5-22, and press the Set button.**
3. **Choose the setting you want (see Figure 5-23) to use and press the Set button.**

   There are three possible settings:

   - *Select and Erase Images:* Enables you to select and mark files for deletion. They aren't deleted until you commit.

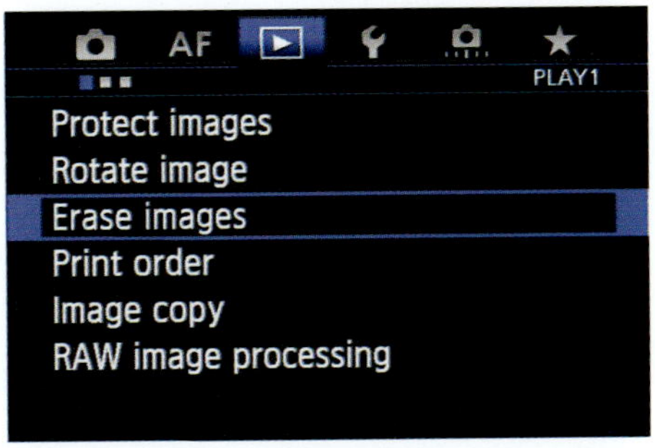

Figure 5-22: When not playing back, you can erase files using the menu.

Play back photos one at a time or zoom out to show a three-image index. Select each file you want to delete by pressing the Set button. Deselect it by pressing the Set button if you change your mind. When finished selecting, press the Erase button and confirm.

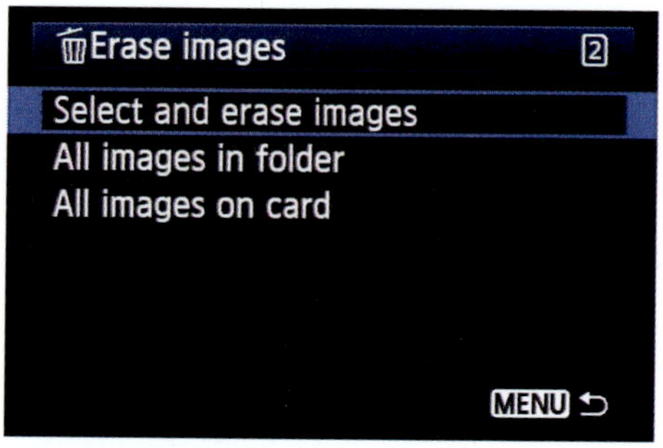

Figure 5-23: Choose a criteria that will determine how you choose files.

- *All Images in Folder:* Enables you to choose a folder and delete everything within. No need to identify or choose individual images.

  Select the folder, press Set, and then confirm.

- *All Images on Card:* This option deletes every photo on the currently selected memory card that has not been protected (see the upcoming section "Protecting Photos" for more information on how to protect and unprotect photos). Highlight OK and press the Set button.

4. **Press Menu to return to Playback Menu 1.**

   Or press the Shutter button halfway to return to shooting pictures.

Deleting versus formatting: What's the diff?

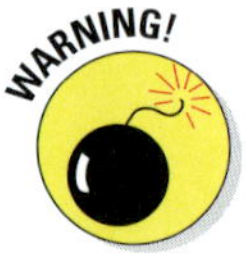

Although using the Protect feature (explained next) prevents the Erase function from erasing a picture, formatting erases all pictures, protected or not. Formatting also deletes any other information from the card (maybe you're using it to hold some MP3s or something). Formatting also ensures that the card is properly prepared to store any new images you may take.

Protecting Photos

You can protect pictures from accidental erasure by giving them protected status. After you take this step, the camera doesn't allow you to delete a picture from your memory card, regardless of whether you press the Erase button or use the Erase images option on Playback Menu 1.

As an additional bonus, protected photos show up as read-only files when you transfer them to a computer. Although they can be deleted, they can't be easily altered.

WARNING!

Formatting your memory card, however, *does* erase even protected pictures. For more about formatting, see the preceding discussion on deleting versus formatting.

Take these steps to protect photos:

1. **Display Playback Menu 1 and highlight Protect Images.**
2. **Press Set.**

   From the Protect Images submenu, you may choose (see Figure 5-24):

   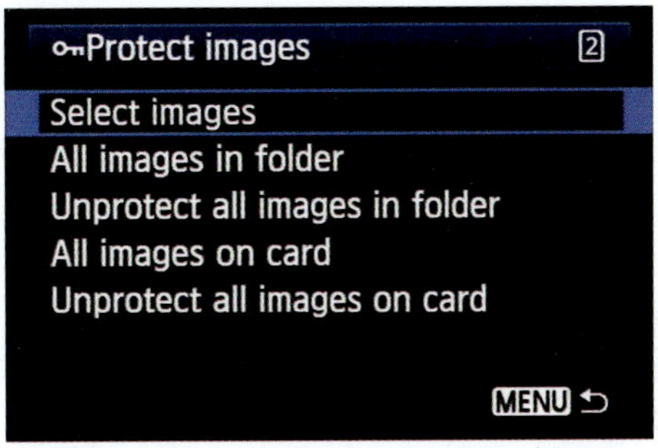

   Figure 5-24: The selection criteria make choosing which files to protect easier.

   - *Select Images:* Choose the photos you want to protect.
   - *All Images in Folder:* Protects all the photos in the current folder.
   - *Unprotect All Images in Folder:* This option does the opposite of the previous one in this list, in case you downloaded those images and no longer need them protected.
   - *All Images on Card:* This is a handy option for protecting all photos on the card. Note that it protects only *existing* photos; any photos you take after selecting this option are unprotected.
   - *Unprotect All Images on Card:* The opposite of protecting all the photos on the card. This option provides a handy way to clear everything so that you don't have to hunt for individual photos to unprotect.

3. **To select photos to protect, highlight Select Images and then press Set.**

   An image appears on the monitor, along with a small key icon in the upper-left corner of the screen, beneath the top information line. This icon indicates that you are in Protect mode. The Set button is displayed beside the key, reminding you to press Set to toggle the protection on or off.

4. **Navigate to the picture you want to protect.**

   Use your finely honed playback skills.

   If you are looking through a lot of photos, press the Enlarge button and zoom in (use the Main dial) to display the four- or nine-image index. Select photos with the Quick Control dial.

5. **Press Set to lock the picture.**

   A key icon appears with the data at the top of the screen, as shown in Figure 5-25.

6. **Press the Menu button to exit the protection process.**

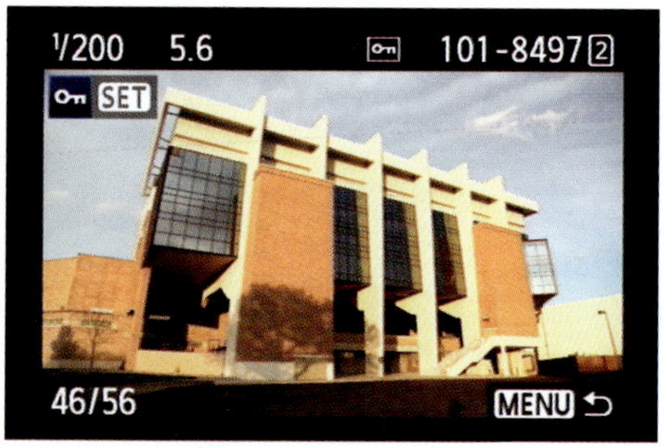

Figure 5-25: The key icon indicates that the picture is protected.

TIP: To remove picture protection from individual photos while the card is still in the camera, follow these same steps. When you display the locked picture, press Set to turn off the protection. The key icon disappears from the top line of the information display to let you know that the picture is no longer protected.

You can also protect photos in Quick Control during playback.

You can also protect photos with the Rate button during normal photo playback if you have changed the function of Rate to Protect (look in Setup Menu 3).

Rating Photos

You have three ways to rate photos. The easiest way is to press the Playback button, display the photo you want to rate, and then press the Rate button to cycle through the star-based rating system (which ranges from no stars to five).

The harder way to rate photos is to go into Playback Menu 2, highlight Rating, press the Set button, and then choose and rate each photo. Use the Quick Control dial to scroll one photo at a time in either direction, or use the Main dial to jump by screens. Press the Set button to rate the selected photo. A rating box becomes active. Use the Quick Control dial or Multicontroller to scroll through the different ratings you can apply. Each rating you

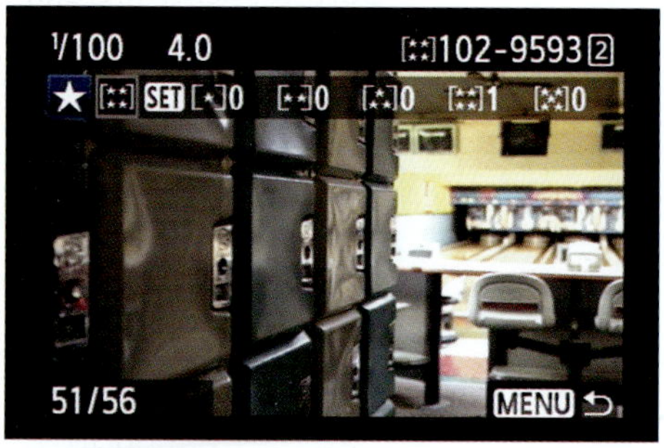

Figure 5-26: This photo was rated at four stars and is the only one so far.

apply is tallied with the others and displayed above the rating box (see Figure 5-26). When finished, press Menu.

Press the Enlarge button and rotate the Main dial counterclockwise to see three thumbnails at a time, as shown in Figure 5-27.

You can rate photos when in Quick Control mode during playback.

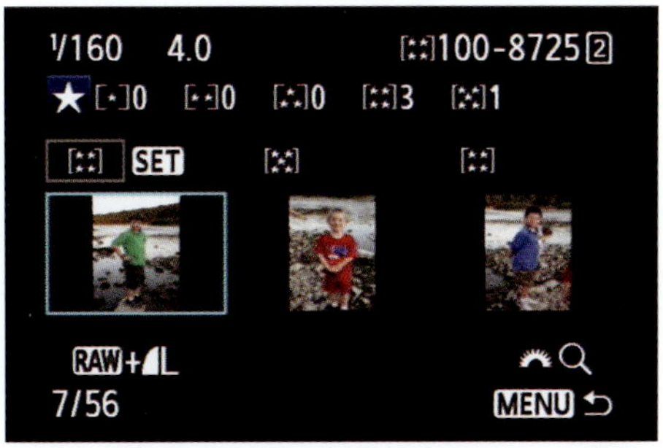

Figure 5-27: Use the index to select files faster.

Enjoying Side-by-Side Photo Playback

One of the cooler playback tools the 5D Mark III has to offer is side-by-side photo playback. (That's right; it won't show movies.) Use it to compare two photos and choose the best one. Check focus by zooming in. You can display a minimal amount of photo information, including a histogram. Rate the photos appropriately or delete the worse one. Your call.

(Psst. Connect your 5D Mark III to a large-screen HDTV and compare photos if you want your socks blown off. I tell you how to hook things up in "Connecting Your Camera to a TV," later in this chapter.)

Follow these steps to display photos side by side:

1. **Press the Playback button.**

   Resist pushing the Two-Image Display button first. Although using that button seems logical, the button serves as the Creative Photo button prior to entering playback.

2. **Press the Two-Image Display button.**

   Refer to Figure 5-1. It's the top button of the series of four on the left side of the rear of the camera.

3. **Bask in side-by-side playback.**

   Figure 5-28 shows how the display immediately changes to feature side-by-side playback.

   The selected photo is surrounded by a blue frame. Remember that.

   You can use many features from here. You can magnify, jump, rate, protect, and delete photos. You can also change how much information the screen displays, including the photo's histogram. For the most part, the display works the same as normal playback. Here are the details:

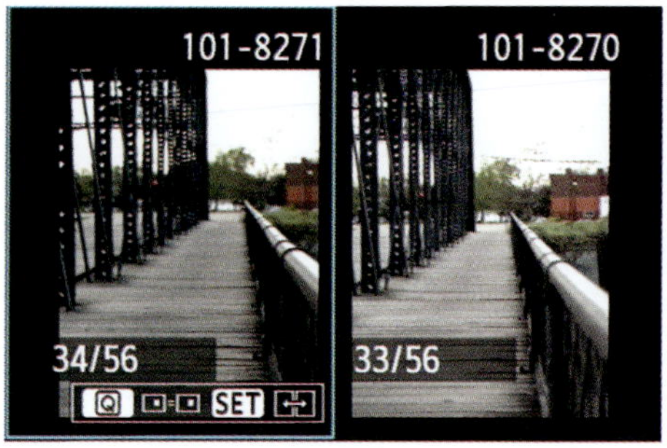

Figure 5-28: This display makes comparing similar photos much easier.

- To select a new image to be displayed in the active frame, turn the Quick Control dial.

  If both images are the same, a small chain link appears in both displays. Because the magnification of each frame works independently, you can see an overview of the photo in one frame and zoom in using the other frame.

- To use Image Jump, turn the Main dial.
- To rate the active image, press the Rate button. If you have changed the Rate button's behavior to protect images, press the Rate button to protect the active photo.
- To switch the blue frame to the other image, press the Set button. Doing so toggles the active frame from one side to the other.
- To magnify the active image, press the Enlarge button.
- To copy the magnification level and frame location from one frame to the other, press the Quick Control button.
- To display the active image full screen, press and hold the Playback button. When you release the button, both images return to the display.
- To erase the active image, press the Erase button.
- To change the amount of shooting information displayed, press the Info button. You can see several screens, but the level of information available is very limited because of the amount of space that each photo uses. The displays show the following: No information; photo name, its playback number, and the total number of photos; the photo name, White Balance, and Picture Style settings; exposure information (aperture, shutter speed, and ISO); name and histogram.
- Press the Menu button to toggle to a full-screen display with all the regular information onscreen. While there, you can press the Info button to change the display. To return to the two-image display, press the Two-Image Display button. (This is undocumented behavior, so I can't guarantee that it will last.)

4. To exit the dual-image display, press the Two-Image Display button.

Copying Photos and Movies

This just in: You can copy photos *and* movies from one memory card to the other on the 5D Mark III. Sounds like fun if you're waiting in line to get your driver's license updated and don't have your phone with you. Seriously, though, having the ability to copy files from one card to another without taking them out of the camera might just save your day.

Here's how to copy images or movies from one memory card to another:

1. **Press the Menu button.**

2. **Navigate to Playback Menu 1 and highlight Image Copy, as shown in Figure 5-29.**

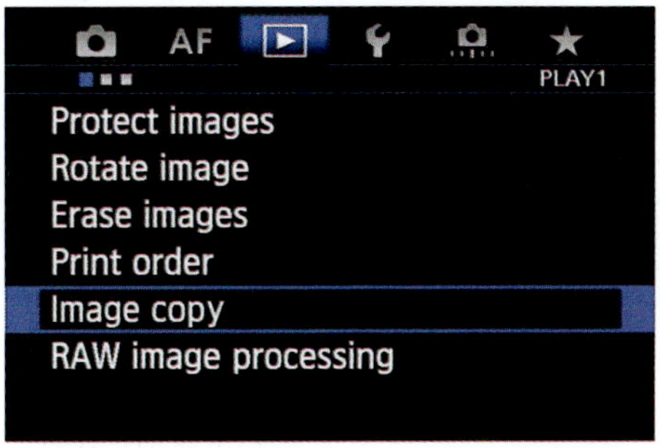

Figure 5-29: Copying files from one card to the other is easy.

3. **Press the Set button.**

   The Image Copy screen is displayed, as shown in Figure 5-30.

   The top part is informational. It shows you the source and destination cards and lists how much free space is available on the latter.

4. **Use the Quick Control dial to highlight Select Image and press the Set button.**

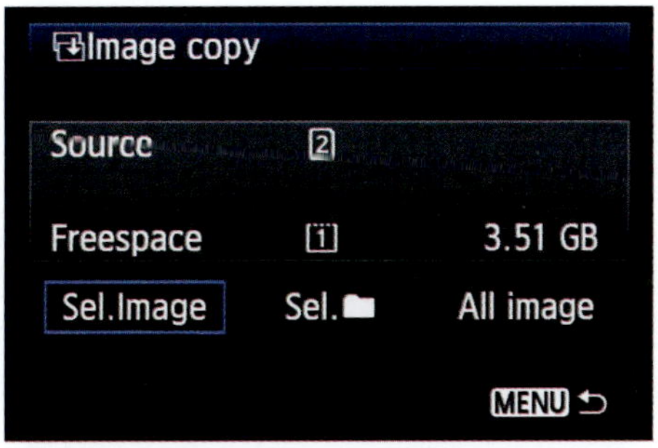

Figure 5-30: You have to select the images before you can copy.

   This starts the process of selecting the files you want to copy.

   If you want to copy the entire card, highlight All Image and press Set. Confirm your choice and then highlight OK from the Image Copy screen you are returned to. Press Set to start copying. You see a summary when finished. Press Set to dismiss and return to the Image Copy screen.

   You don't need to highlight Select Folder because you get the chance to select a folder in the next step, anyway.

5. **Highlight a source folder (see Figure 5-31) and press the Set button.**

   Notice that thumbnails appear on the right side of the screen to remind you visually what files are in the folder you have highlighted.

   Even if you have only one folder on the source card, you still see this step.

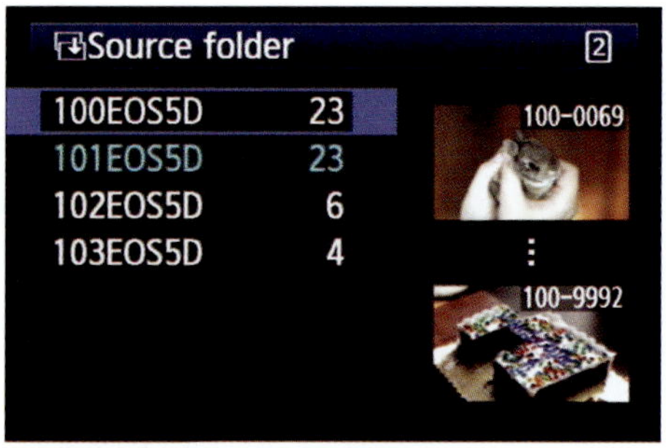

Figure 5-31: Choosing the source folder.

6. **Highlight files you want to copy and press the Set button (see Figure 5-32).**

   Use the Quick Control dial to move from one photo or movie to another. Use the Main dial to jump back and forth.

   When you press Set, the selected image displays a check mark and the total number of check marked photos is updated on the screen.

   To deselect a file, highlight it and press the Set button again.

   To display three thumbnails at a time, press the Enlarge button and rotate the Main dial counterclockwise once.

   Press Menu to return to the previous screen without doing anything.

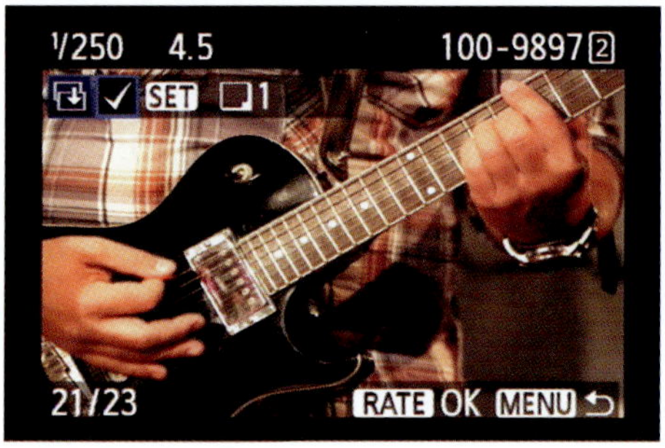

Figure 5-32: This file is selected to copy.

7. **Press the Rate button to continue and then the Set button to confirm.**

8. **Highlight the folder you want to copy the file to on the destination card, as shown in Figure 5-33.**

   If you have only one folder, leave it highlighted.

   Highlight Create Folder and press the Set button to create a new folder to copy the file to.

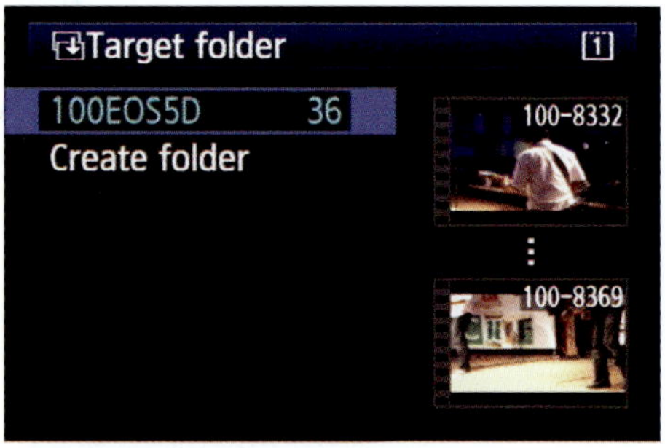

Figure 5-33: The target folder is the destination.

9. **Press the Set button.**

   You return to the Image Copy screen. The Source and Target areas have more information now, including the size of the file you have chosen, its folder, and the target card, folder, and amount of free space available.

10. Highlight OK and press the Set button.

The next screen shows you how many images you copied and how many may have failed to copy, as shown in Figure 5-34.

If the camera detects files with the same name, it will ask whether you want to skip the image and continue copying, replace the existing image with the new one, or cancel the copy operation.

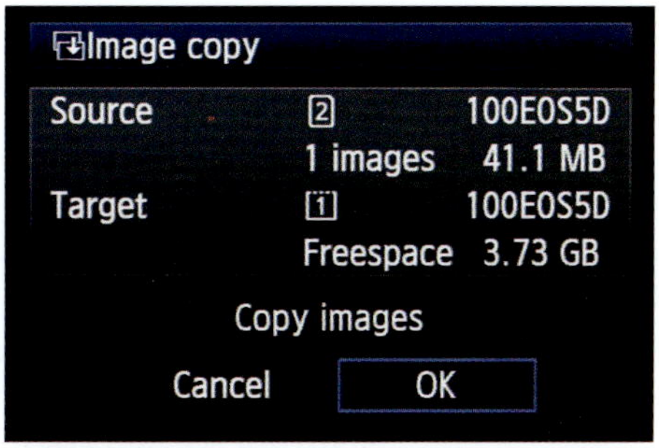

Figure 5-34: Review this screen before continuing.

11. Press Set to return to the Image Copy screen.

From here, you can highlight Select Folder and press the Set button to start again, or highlight Select Image.

Processing Photos In-Camera

You don't have to be content with simply playing back photos on the 5D Mark III. You have the ability to resize JPEGs and process RAW photos (the results are saved as JPEGs) using the camera. No computer required.

Resizing JPEG photos

You can resize all JPEGs except the smallest, known as S3, and RAW images. That means that all Large, Medium, S1, and S2 JPEGs are shown as you flip through photos on your memory card.

If you have photos on more than one card in the camera at the same time, please use the Record Function+Card/Folder Selection option in Setup Menu 1 to select the card you want to work with. It's not necessary to select a folder.

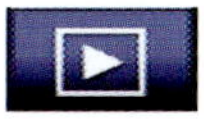

1. **Press the Menu button.**
2. **Navigate to Playback Menu 2.**
3. **Highlight Resize, as shown in Figure 5-35, and press the Set button.**
4. **Use the Quick Control dial to display the photo you want to resize.**

5. **Press the Set button.**
6. **Highlight a target size, as shown in Figure 5-36, and press Set.**

   If you are resizing a photo that you shot using Live View, and the aspect ratio is not 3:2, the target size that is displayed will not match the actual target size. What's more, some target sizes will not match their original aspect ratio. They are just a hair off. (This is true of four cases out of 16, if you're counting: M and S2 target sizes for 4:3 photos; and S1 and S3 target sizes for 16:9 photos.)

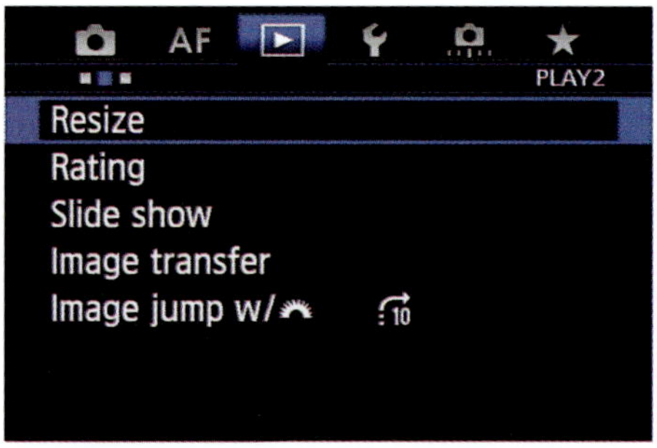

Figure 5-35: Resizing photos is pretty easy.

7. **Confirm by highlighting OK and pressing Set.**

   Take note of the name of the new file. (You'll surely be able to tell which files you resized by inspecting the pixel dimensions later, though.)

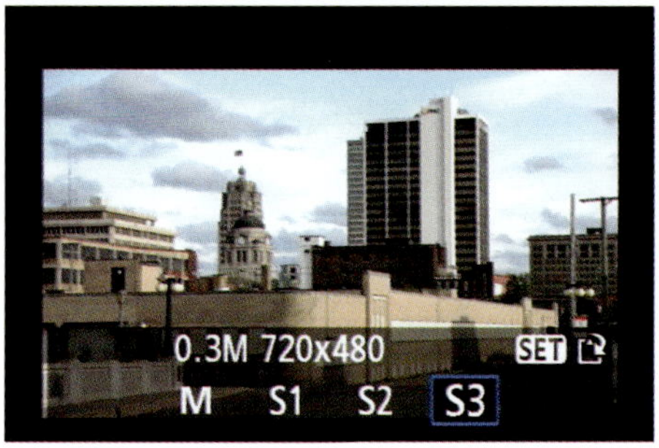

Figure 5-36: Selecting a new size.

8. **Rinse and repeat, if desired, or press the Menu button to exit.**

   Return to Step 4 if you want to resize more than one photo.

You can resize photos in Quick Control during playback.

Processing RAW photos

This feature is simply awesome: Using the 5D Mark III, you can take Large RAW photos and process them according to your creative discretion. The result is saved as a JPEG.

Two caveats. First, you obviously have to shoot RAW photos to be able to process them. Second, you can process only Large RAW photos. Medium and Small need not apply. (Use Digital Photo Professional or another favorite RAW processing application to work with the smaller RAW photos.)

Follow these steps to process a Large RAW photo:

1. **Press the Menu button.**

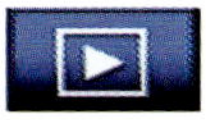

2. **Navigate to Playback Menu 1 and highlight RAW Image Processing, as shown in Figure 5-37.**

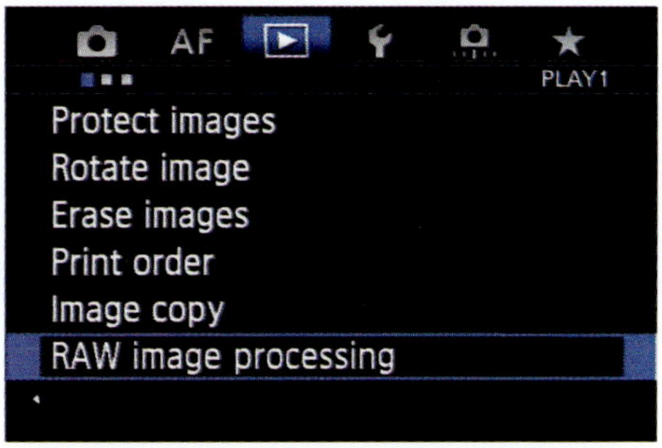

Figure 5-37: This option puts power at your fingertips.

3. **Press the Set button.**
4. **Use the Quick Control dial to display the photo you want to process; then press Set.**

   You should know the drill by now.

   Press the Enlarge button and spin the Main dial counterclockwise to change to a four- or nine-image index display. Turn the Main dial clockwise to return to the single-image display or zoom in.

5. **Use the Multicontroller to highlight the RAW processing option of your choice, as shown in Figure 5-38.**

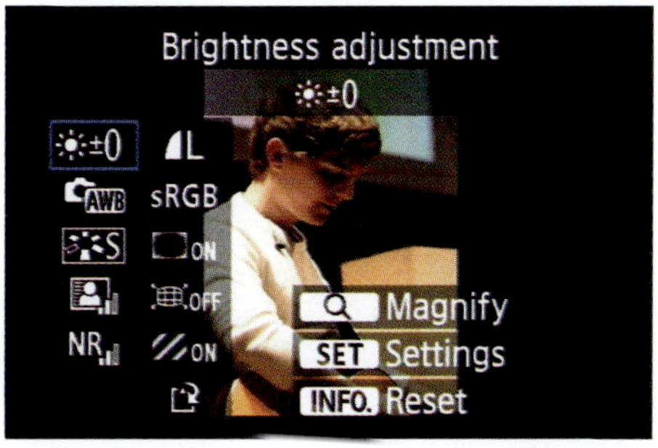

Figure 5-38: Selecting an option to adjust.

   The RAW options are as follows:

   - *Brightness Adjustment:* Darkens or brightens the photo up to +/- 1.0 EV in 1/3-EV steps.
   - *White Balance:* Sets the target photo's white balance.
   - *Picture Style*: Enables you to set the Picture Style (Shot settings, Auto, Standard, Portrait, Landscape, Neutral, Faithful, Monochrome, and User Defined 1-3) and change individual parameters (Sharpness, Contrast, Saturation, Color Tone).
   - *Auto Lighting Optimizer:* Set to Disable, Low, Standard, or High.
   - *High ISO Speed Noise Reduction:* Set to Disable, Low, Standard, or High.
   - *Image Quality:* Set to the desired JPEG size and quality.

- *Color Space:* Set to sRGB or Adobe RGB.
- *Peripheral Illumination Correction:* Corrects vignetting (when the corners appear darker than the center of the photo) caused by the lens. Set to On or Off.
- *Distortion Correction:* Automatically corrects lens distortion (ideally). Set to On or Off.
- *Chromatic Aberration Correction:* Corrects chromatic aberration caused by the lens. Set to On or Off.

Press the Enlarge button to magnify the photo. Use the Multicontroller to pan. Press Enlarge again to return to normal magnification.

Press the Info button to erase your changes and reset the photo.

6. **Change the setting in one of two ways:**
   - Use the Quick Control dial to cycle through the different settings for each option.

     Some roll over. For example, you can spin the Quick Control dial clockwise when changing Image Quality and you will return to where you started if you keep going.

     Some parameters do not roll over. For example, if you are making a Brightness adjustment, turning the Quick Control dial counterclockwise makes the photo darker. It does not roll over to the other end of the scale. For that, turn the other direction.
   - Press the Set button to display the highlighted option's setting screen, as shown in Figure 5-39.

     Use the Quick Control dial to highlight a new setting; then press the Menu button or Set to lock it in and return to the main processing screen.

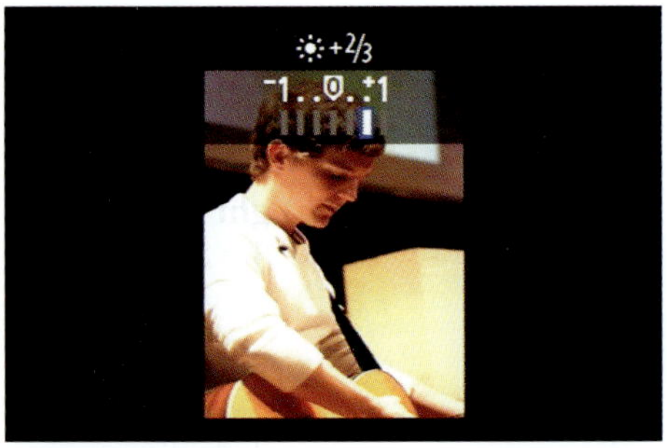

Figure 5-39: This photo was a tad dark.

7. **Highlight Save and press the Set button to save your work.**
8. **Confirm by highlighting OK and pressing Set again.**

You don't get a chance to resize when saving. You have the option of setting the target photo's size and quality in Step 5 of the preceding list.

You can change RAW processing settings in Quick Control during playback.

Presenting a Slide Show

No need for an extensive intro here; you know what a slide show is. The 5D Mark III has a pretty good routine that enables you to identify photos and movies and get them to play back automatically on your camera.

I like slide shows because you don't have to constantly press a button to advance to the next photo or movie. (The 5D Mark III has no provision for adding background sound to photos; that would be too cool.) A slide show is a great finger saver.

To create and run a slide show, follow these steps:

1. **Press the Menu button, navigate to Display Playback Menu 2, and highlight Slide Show, as shown in Figure 5-40.**

2. **Press Set.**

   The Slide Show display appears, as shown in Figure 5-41. The first image to appear in the slide show is prominently displayed on the left side of the screen.

   You also see the total number of images slated for inclusion in the show. On your first trip to this menu screen, all images on the card are selected.

3. **Highlight All Images and then press the Set button.**

   This turns the All Images option into a list that contains the different selection criteria (explained in the next step).

4. **Use the Quick Control dial to scroll through the six playback options and then make your choice:**

   - *All Images*: Choose this setting and then press Set to include all files, regardless of whether they're still photos or movies.

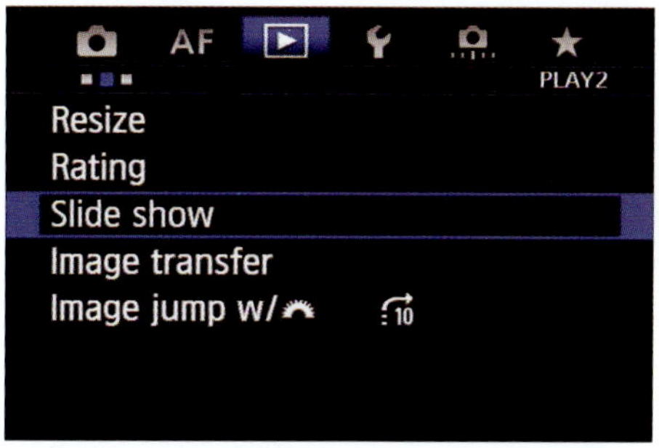

Figure 5-40: Choose Slide Show and then use the options to customize a few aspects of the playback.

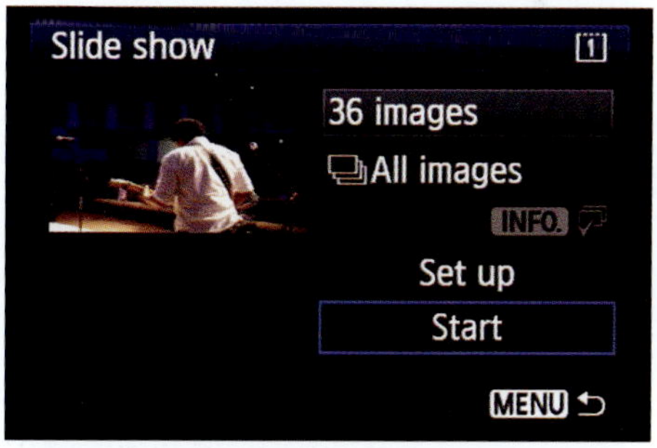

Figure 5-41: Configure slide shows starting here.

- *Date:* With this option, play only pictures or movies taken on a single date. As soon as you select the option, the screen changes to show you the thumbnail of the first photo you took on the most recent shooting day, along with the number of pictures taken on the same day. To select a different date, press the Info button. Select a new date from the next screen and then press Set.
- *Folder*: This option includes still photos and movies in the selected folder in the slide show. To change folders, press Info, select a new folder, and press Set to return.
- *Movies*: Select this option and press Set to include only movies in your show.
- *Stills*: Select this option and press Set to include only still photos in the show.
- *Rating*: This option enables you to select the photos and movies you want to see based on their rating. Press Info to specify the rating.

You can also use the Multicontroller to navigate up and down through the list.

5. **After determining the criteria, highlight Set Up and then press Set.**

   Use this screen to set up the slide show options. You can change two items:

   - *Display Time:* This sets the time that each still photo will be displayed, from 1 to 20 seconds. The default display time for photos is 1 second. Movies just run.

     To change the time, highlight Display time, press Set, highlight a choice from the menu, and press Set again.

   - *Repeat:* Choose whether you want the slide show to loop. To enable Repeat, highlight Repeat, press Set, highlight Enable from the menu, and press Set again. If you are disabling it, highlight Disable instead.

   (In contrast to some other Canon dSLRs, you cannot specify slide show transitions with the 5D Mark III.)

6. **Press Menu to return to the main Slide Show screen.**
7. **Highlight Start and press Set.**

   Your slide show begins playing.

To present your slide show to a roomful of people, connect your camera to a television, as outlined in the following section.

During the show, control the display by

- **Pausing/restarting playback:** Press the Set button. While the show is paused, rotate the Quick Control dial to view the next or previous photo. Press Set again to restart playback.
- **Changing the information display style:** Press the Info button.
- **Adjusting sound volume for movies:** Rotate the Main dial.

  REMEMBER

  This adjustment applies to the volume level for movies that you have shot and are including in the slide show.

Connecting Your Camera to a TV

Your camera is equipped with a playback feature with which you play pictures and movies on a television screen. In fact, you have three playback options:

- **Regular video playback:** Need to connect your 5D Mark III to an older TV set? No worries: You can use the camera to send a regular standard-definition (SD) audio and video signal to the TV. For this option, no added cable investment is necessary because the cable you need is included with the camera. It has a USB plug on the end that connects to the camera. The cable has three plugs (one yellow, one red, and one white) at the other end (the Stereo AV Cable, part number AVC-DC400ST).

  If you're playing back on a normal TV, confirm the camera's Video System settings from Setup Menu 3. Select NTSC or PAL, depending on your location. Users in North America, Japan, Korea, and Mexico should select NTSC. If you're in Europe, Russia, China, or Australia, select PAL. For other locations, consult your television manual to confirm the video specifications.
- **HDTV playback:** If you have a high-definition (HD) television, use the camera for high-def playback. Unfortunately, the necessary HDMI cable is not included.

  Many makes and models of HDMI cable are available. Make sure to get one that has a Mini HDMI jack on the end that will connect to the camera. It isn't the full-sized HDMI terminal that may be on your HDTV. The Canon part number is HDMI Cable HTC-100. (It's a bit pricey; I paid far less for my off-brand cable.)
- **For HDMI CEC TV sets:** If your television is compatible with HDMI CEC, your 5D Mark III enables you to use a TV's remote control to rule your

playback operations. Just put the camera on the coffee table and sit back with your normal remote in hand to entertain family and friends with your genius. To make this operation work, you must enable Ctrl over HDMI via Playback Menu 2.

(I was skeptical about this feature until I tried it. I pulled out the manual of our new HDTV and checked to see whether it was compatible with HDMI CEC. It is, although the feature is called Anynet+. I was able to play back photos using the television's remote control with no trouble at all. Different manufacturers may call HDMI CEC by different names; check with your manufacturer to confirm compatibility.)

To get things running, make sure that your camera's video or HDMI settings are set. Then turn all devices off. Make the proper cable connections to the appropriate terminals on the camera and your TV set. Turn the TV on. Select the video input source on your TV that matches the camera connection. For example, on an older set, you might have to toggle between TV and Video. On an HDTV, you should select the appropriate HDMI port (mine is HDMI 3). Finally, turn the camera on and start playing back photos and videos, shooting in Live View with the TV as your monitor, or set up a slide show.

Part III

Expressing Your Creativity

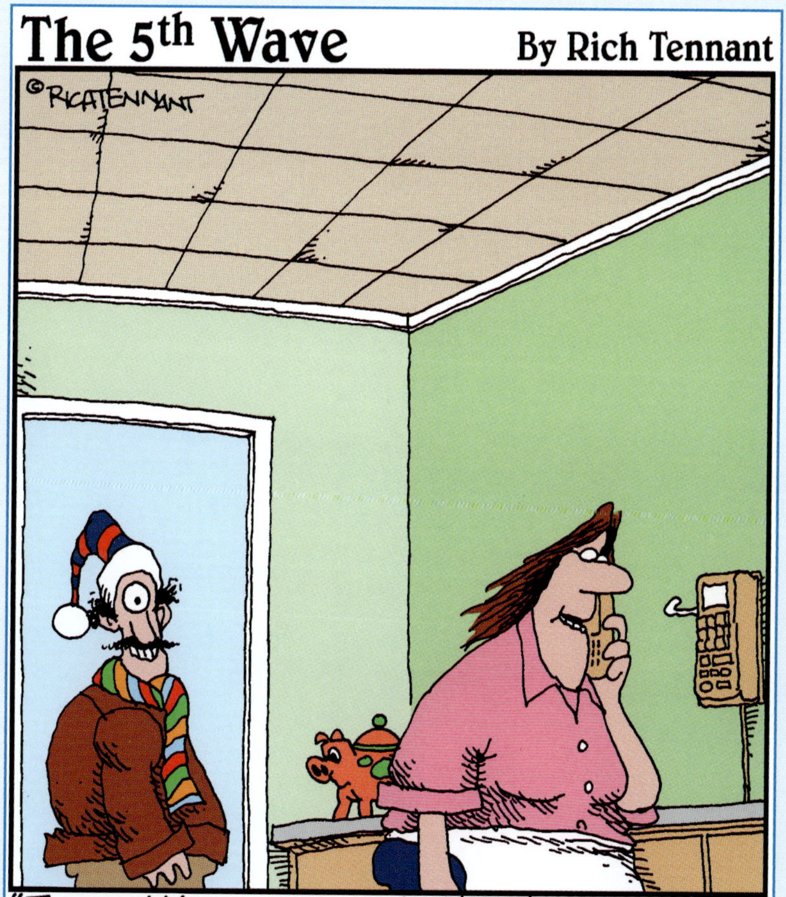

"Try putting a person in the photo with the product you're trying to sell. We generated a lot of interest in our eBay Listing once Leo started modeling my hats and scarves."

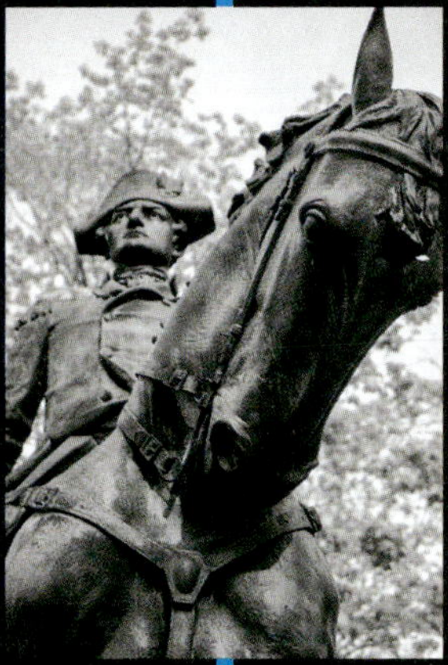

In this part, you discover how to make creative decisions with your 5D Mark III. The first three chapters cover the advanced shooting modes, exposure settings, flash options, focus modes and cases, color, and style. Following that, Chapter 9 helps you draw together all the information presented earlier in this book, summarizing the best camera settings and other tactics to use when capturing portraits, action shots, landscapes, cities, and more.

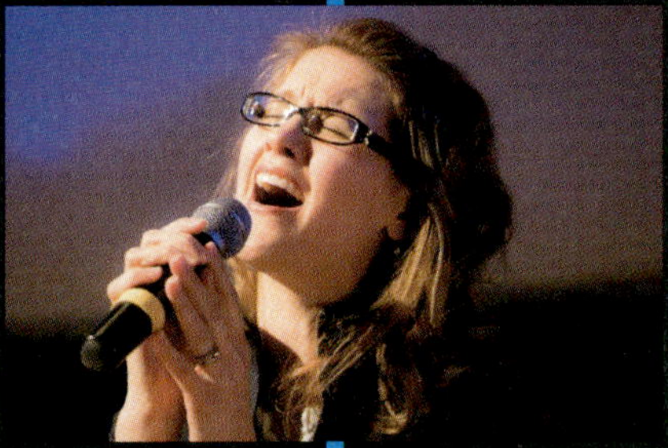

Although this part of the book is intense, don't think that you have to be a genius or spend years to be successful. Adding just a few simple techniques to your photographic repertoire can make a huge difference in how effective you are as a photographer.

This part helps you make sure that you're getting your money's worth out of that 5D Mark III.

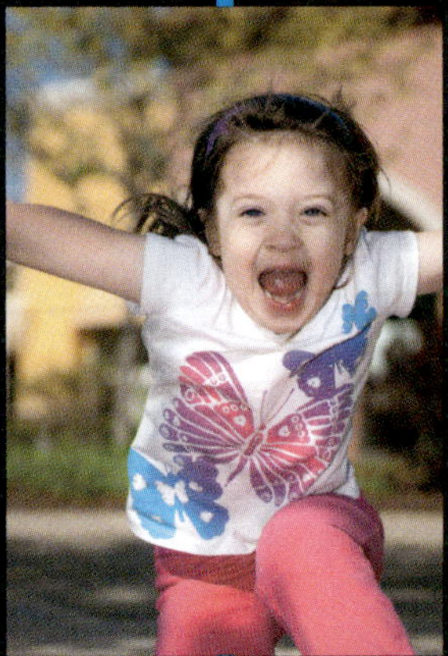

6

Making Exposure and Flash Decisions

In This Chapter

- Getting a grip on shutter speed, aperture, and ISO
- Understanding exposure-setting side-effects
- Making exposure decisions
- Choosing advanced shooting modes
- Metering
- Correcting exposure
- Expanding your dynamic range
- Using an external flash

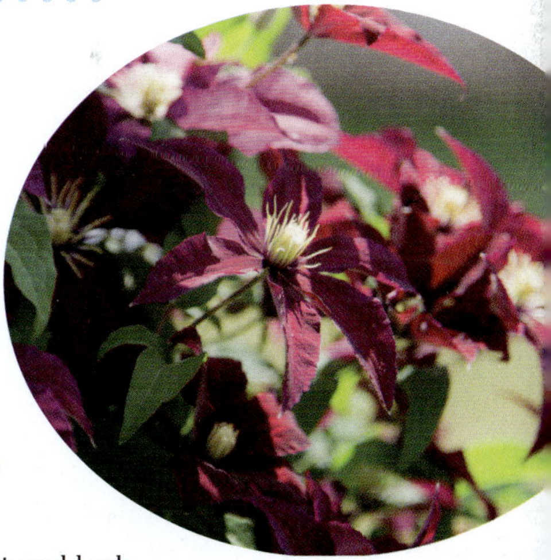

This chapter is meant to give you enough information about the 5D Mark III's shooting modes and exposure settings for you to know how to choose the effects and side effects that work for you. You should be taking the photos *you* want, not merely accepting what the camera gives you.

First, you get an introduction to three critical exposure controls: shutter speed, aperture, and ISO. Adjusting these settings enables you to not only fine-tune image exposure but also determine other aspects of your image, such as *depth of field* (the zone of sharp focus) and motion blur.

You also learn how to change metering modes, correct and lock autoexposure, use tools to protect or enhance a scene's highlights and shadows, expand your dynamic range, and review flash options available to you when you attach an external Speedlite to the camera.

Understanding and Controlling Exposure Settings

When it comes to exposure, your job is to control *how much* light makes it into the camera and *how* you allow it to enter (quickly or slowly, among other things). As you decide the "how" part, you can express a good deal of creativity because each exposure setting has its own effects and side effects.

Introducing shutter speed, aperture, and ISO

Whether you use your camera's exposure controls for "how much" (exposure) or "how" (creativity), you have only three such controls to work with: shutter speed, aperture, and ISO.

Shutter speed

Your camera's *focal plane shutter* is situated in front of the sensor and behind the mirror, as shown in Figure 6-1. Its purpose is to block light and keep the sensor in the dark until you press the Shutter button. When you press the Shutter button, the shutter opens to let light through for a discrete amount of time (unless you are in bulb mode), and then closes. The elapsed time that the shutter is open is called the *shutter speed*. Fast shutter speed is measured in fractions of a second, such as 1/250 second. Longer speeds are measured in whole seconds.

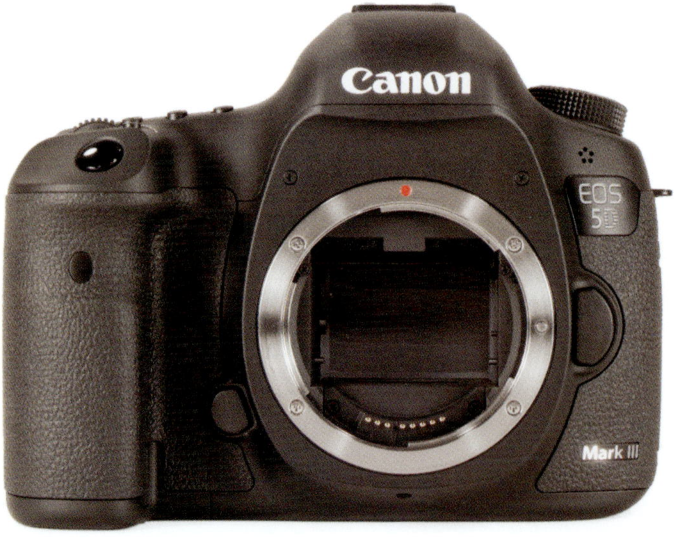

Figure 6-1: The shutter sits behind the mirror (not shown) and in front of the sensor.

- Fast shutter speeds let less light strike the sensor.
- Slow shutter speeds let more light strike the sensor.

The 5D Mark III's fastest shutter speed is 1/8000 second. It's slowest timed shutter speed is 30 seconds, although you can increase this speed in bulb mode.

Aperture

Very generally, an *aperture* is an opening. In photography, an aperture is the adjustable opening in the lens. Light passes through the aperture in the lens (see Figure 6-2) and continues into the camera. Aperture settings are also known as *f-stop numbers, f-stops, or f-numbers*. They are expressed with the letter *f* followed by a number: f/2, f/5.6, f/16, and so on.

- Large apertures allow more light to pass through the lens.
- Small apertures allow less light to pass through the lens.

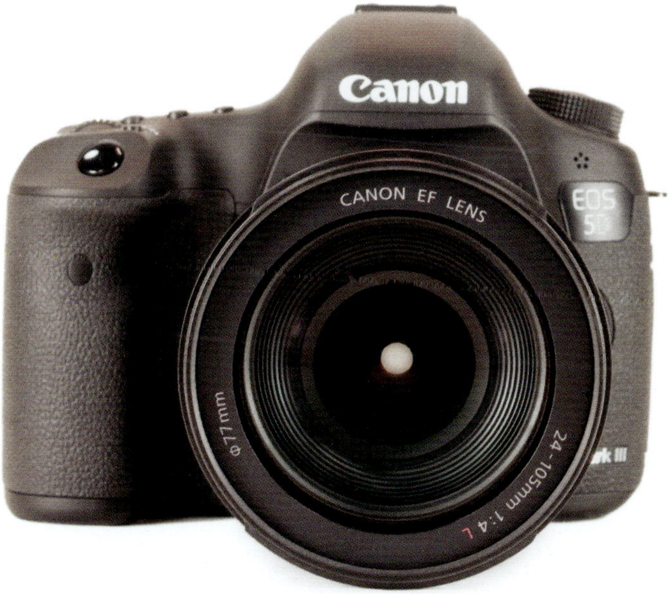

Figure 6-2: The aperture opens and closes to let more or less light through the lens.

The range of possible apertures depends on your lens. The EF 24-105mm f/4L IS USM kit lens has an aperture range from f/4 (large) to f/22 (small). With this lens, all apertures are available at all focal lengths. You may not be able to select the maximum aperture at all focal lengths with other zoom lenses.

ISO Speed

ISO speed (most often simply referred to as ISO) controls the sensor's sensitivity to light. This sensitivity alters how much light you need to gather over a certain amount of time, thus determining the exposure. Quite often, ISO is expressed in unitless multiples of 100 (50 being the exception) that double or halve, depending on whether you are increasing ISO or decreasing it (100, 200, 400, 800, and so forth). The 5D Mark III, however, defaults to ISO increments of 1/3 of a stop (you can change it to full stops if you want). The 5D Mark III's normal ISO range is from 100 to 25600, although this range can be expanded.

- Higher ISOs increase sensitivity.
- Lower ISOs decrease sensitivity.

The term *ISO* is a holdover from film days, when an international standards organization rated film stock according to its light sensitivity: ISO 100, ISO 200, ISO 400, ISO 800, and so on.

Understanding exposure setting side-effects

Distilled to its essence, the image-exposure process is this simple:

- Aperture and shutter speed together determine the quantity of light that strikes the image sensor.
- ISO determines how much the sensor reacts to that light.

The tricky part of the equation is that aperture, shutter speed, and ISO settings affect your pictures in ways that go *beyond* exposure. You need to be aware of these side effects to determine which combination of the three exposure settings will work best for your picture.

The settings you select affect your image beyond exposure, though, as follows:

- **Aperture affects depth of field.** The aperture setting affects *depth of field,* or the distance over which sharp focus is maintained.

  When you reduce the aperture size by choosing a higher f-number, you increase depth of field, as shown in Figure 6-3. Smaller f-numbers increase the aperture size, which decrease the depth of field.

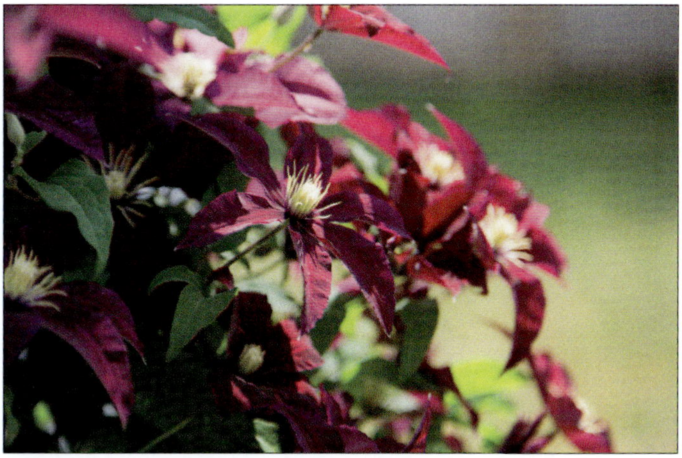

Figure 6-3: The depth of field is about one flower wide at f/4 and this distance.

Shallow depths of field are effective in portraits and other scenes in which you want to separate the subject from the foreground or background. Larger depths of field are effective when shooting landscapes, or any scene for which you want sharp focus from front to back.

Aperture is just one contributor to depth of field. The camera-to-subject distance and the focal length of your lens also play a role in this characteristic of your photos. (Chapter 7 has more information on depth of field.)

- **Shutter speed affects motion blur.** Movement (yours or the subject's) causes motion blur. In Figure 6-4, this bowler's left foot, cockeyed as it is, is in focus and not blurred. Compare that to the rest of his body, arm, and the bowling ball, which are in motion. At 1/80 second, the shutter speed wasn't fast enough to freeze him in mid-bowl. To minimize this type of blur, increase the shutter speed. The shutter speed you need to use depends on the speed of the subject and the relative direction of motion.

  To intentionally blur movement, use a slow shutter speed. How slow can you go? That depends on your physical capabilities and the lens. Camera shake affects your picture more when you shoot with a lens that has a long focal length. For example, you may be able to use a much slower shutter speed when you shoot with a lens that has a maximum focal length of 50mm than if you switch to a 200mm telephoto lens.

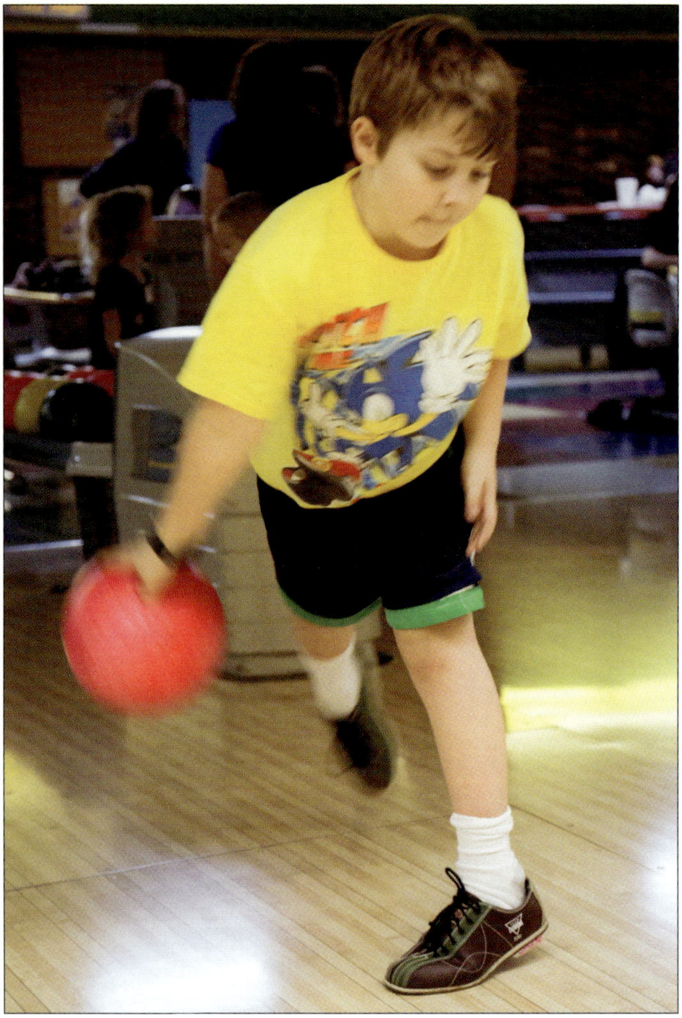

Figure 6-4: To freeze action, speed up shutter speed.

The best idea is to do your own tests to see where your handholding limit lies. Start with a slow shutter speed, in the neighborhood of, say, 1/10 second (the delay is obvious to the ear). Click off several shots, increasing the shutter speed for each picture. If you have a zoom lens, run the test first at the minimum focal length (widest angle) and then zoom to the maximum focal length for another series of shots. Then it's simply a matter of comparing the images on the camera in playback, on a TV, or on your computer to see where the sharpness falls off to unacceptable levels.

Regarding long exposures, I have one caveat that has nothing to do with motion blur: A long exposure will result in a noisier photo than one taken with a shorter time. Your camera offers built-in noise-reduction filters that can compensate for this type of noise as well as ISO noise (see the next bullet).

- **ISO affects image noise.** The relationship between ISO and noise is axiomatic. Regardless of whether it is immediately apparent, selecting a higher ISO makes the image sensor more sensitive to light, which also makes it more sensitive to *noise.* Image noise looks like blotchy pixelation, as shown in Figure 6-5. This photo was taken at ISO 16000. I processed the RAW file in Digital Photo Professional with noise reduction applied. (DPP is pretty good at handling noise in the 5D Mark III's RAW files.) The inset shows a 100 percent crop of the area right behind the boy's ear.

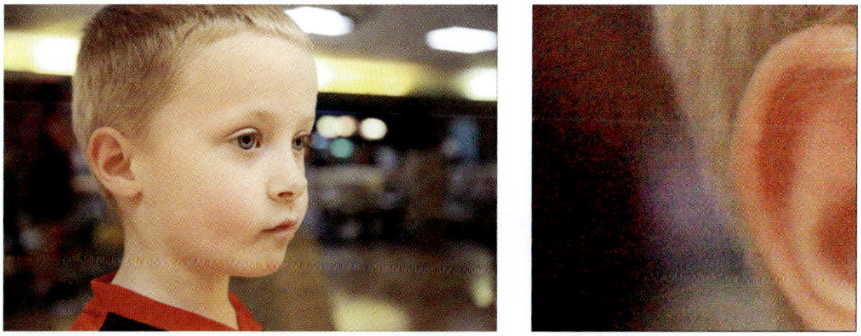

Figure 6-5: Although the 5D Mark III has outstanding high-ISO performance, it's not impossible to coax a noisy photo out of it.

Noise is more apparent in dark areas of photos and ruins smooth textures and color gradation. Enlarging photos makes noise more apparent. Reducing them makes noise less problematic. In fact, you can resize many photos for web use whose noise levels make printing impractical.

Ideally, you would always use the lowest ISO setting on your camera — namely, ISO 100 — to ensure top image quality. Sometimes, though, the lighting conditions simply don't permit you to do so. Fortunately, you won't encounter serious noise with the 5D Mark III until you really crank up the ISO.

Noise control

The 5D Mark III offers two noise-removal filters, one to address each cause of noise: long exposure times and high ISO settings. Both filters are located in Shooting Menu 3.

To control Long Exposure Noise Reduction, select one of these three settings:

- *Off:* No noise reduction is applied. This setting is the default.
- *Auto:* Noise reduction is applied when you use a shutter speed of one second or longer, but only if the camera detects the type of noise that's caused by long exposures.
- *On:* Noise reduction is always applied at exposures of one second or longer. (*Note:* Canon suggests that this setting may result in more noise than either Off or Auto when the ISO setting is 1600 or higher.)

The High ISO Speed Noise Reduction option has four settings:

- *Standard:* The default setting.
- *Low:* Applies a little noise removal.
- *High:* Goes after noise in a more dramatic way.
- *Disable:* Turns off the filter.

As always, your mileage may vary. If you want to control all noise reduction yourself, disable both types on the camera. If you don't mind the camera handling it, with some delay (in the case of Long exposure noise reduction, it doubles your exposure time over a second), then by all means leave High ISO Speed Noise Reduction on. Feel free to give Long Exposure Noise Reduction a chance, but I've found that I'm always too antsy to wait for it to get done (and I know that I can reduce noise in software).

Long story short: Understanding how aperture, shutter speed, and ISO affect an image enables you to have much more creative input over the look of your photographs — and, in the case of ISO, to control the quality of your images.

Making exposure setting decisions

REMEMBER

When you change any of the three exposure settings — shutter speed, aperture, or ISO — one or both of the others must also shift to maintain the same image brightness.

All photographers have their own approaches to finding the right combination. Here are some handy recommendations, however:

- Use the lowest possible ISO setting unless the lighting conditions are so poor that you can't use the aperture and shutter speed you want without raising the ISO.
- If your subject is moving (or might move, such as a squiggly toddler or an excited dog), give shutter speed the next highest priority in your exposure decision. Choose a fast shutter speed to ensure a blur-free

photo or, on the flip side, select a slow shutter speed to intentionally blur that moving object, an effect that can create a heightened sense of motion. When shooting waterfalls, for example, consider using a slow shutter speed to give the water that blurry, romantic look.

- For images of nonmoving subjects, make aperture a priority over shutter speed, setting the aperture according to the depth of field you have in mind. For portraits, for example, try using a wide-open aperture (a low f-stop number) to create a short depth of field and a nice, soft background for your subject.

You can find tips in Chapter 9 for choosing exposure settings for specific types of pictures; keep moving through this chapter for details on how to monitor and adjust shutter speed, aperture, and ISO settings.

Selecting an Advanced Shooting Mode

The advanced shooting modes are summarized in Chapter 2, as are the steps necessary to set the mode of your choice. In this section, I address why you would want to choose one mode over another.

See Chapter 10 for information on how to customize the Main and Quick Control dial.

Program AE (P)

Choose Program AE when you want more camera control than Scene Intelligent Auto provides (you want to be able to set the metering mode, White Balance, Program Style, and so forth) but don't want to select a specific aperture or shutter speed. Program shift enables you to switch between several aperture/shutter speed combinations by rotating the Main dial. The Quick Control dial controls exposure correction.

Shutter-Priority AE (Tv)

Choose Shutter-Priority AE in any situation in which you want to control motion blur. Examples include sports and action, animals, kids, concerts, and when you are in motion. Your goal is to capture a crisp photo. Change shutter speed by rotating the Main dial.

Aperture-Priority AE (Av)

Choose Aperture-Priority AE to control the photo's depth of field. It works great for portraits, close-ups, landscapes, and so forth. Basically, Av works anytime movement (you or the subject) is not an issue. Av is probably the most popular shooting mode. Change the aperture by rotating the main dial.

Manual (M)

Choose manual exposure shooting mode when you want the ability to override the camera's standard exposure without using Exposure Compensation. To override the standard exposure, you must manually set the ISO. If you fail to do so, the 5D Mark III will automatically raise or lower the ISO to set the standard exposure, defeating the purpose. When that happens, you're basically operating in Tv or Av mode. In manual mode, change shutter speed by rotating the Main dial; change the aperture by rotating the Quick Control dial.

Bulb (B)

Use bulb mode when you need an exposure longer than 30 seconds. This situation occurs most often at night or in low light, when shooting fireworks, or while engaging in astrophotography.

Custom Shooting Modes (C1-C3)

Create and use Custom Shooting modes to be able to save and quickly recall your favorite camera settings. Custom modes are based on an advanced shooting mode. Chapter 10 has information on creating and using Custom Shooting modes.

Monitoring Exposure Settings

When you press the Shutter button halfway, the current shutter speed, aperture, and ISO speed can appear in these places:

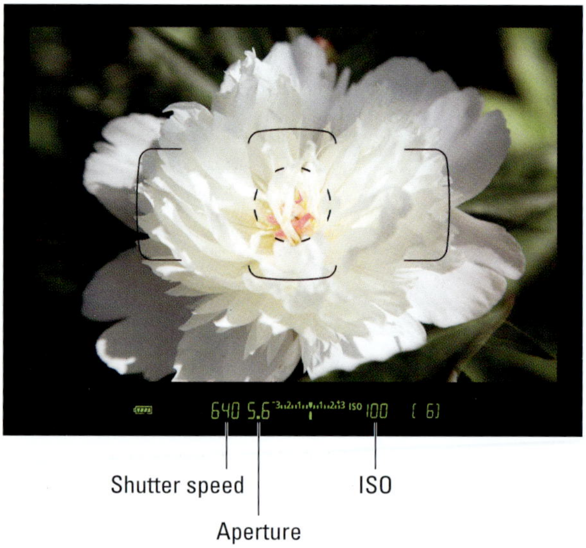

Figure 6-6: The shutter speed, aperture, and ISO speed all appear in the viewfinder.

- **Viewfinder:** The exposure settings appear prominently at the bottom of the viewfinder, as shown in Figure 6-6.
- **LCD monitor:** The exposure settings also appear in the Shooting Information display, as shown in Figure 6-7. They are along the top. When you enter Quick Control mode, the metered autoexposure values disappear, and you are left with the settings you can change. Those depend on the shooting mode you're in.

When in Live View or when shooting movies, the exposure data appears at the bottom of the monitor and takes a form similar to what you see in the viewfinder.

- **LCD panel:** You can also check the exposure settings on the LCD panel (see Figure 6-8), which is located on top of the camera.

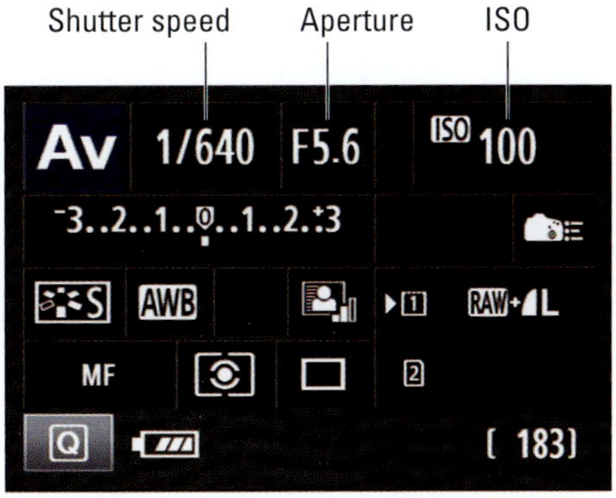

Figure 6-7: You also can view the settings in the Shooting Information display or Quick Control mode.

You'll notice that shutter speed and aperture are grouped together in all displays. ISO is separated vertically or horizontally.

In the viewfinder, on the LCD panel, and on the monitor in Live View mode, shutter speeds are presented as whole numbers, even if the shutter speed is set to a fraction of a second. For example, for a shutter speed of 1/640 second, you should see just the number 640 in the display (refer to Figure 6-8). When the shutter speed slows to one second or more, you see quotation marks after the number in both displays: 1" indicates a shutter speed of 1 second; 4" means 4 seconds; and so on.

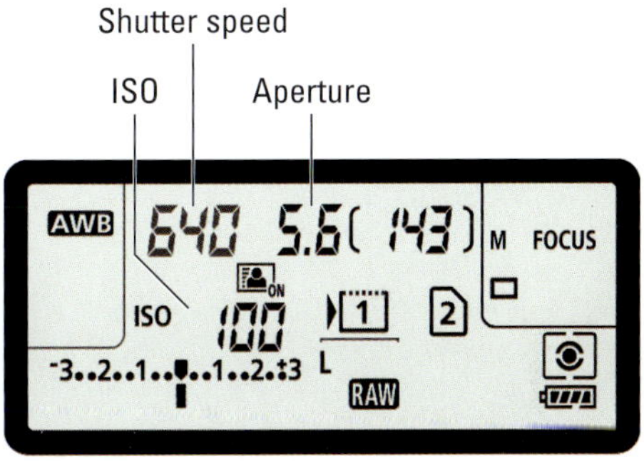

Figure 6-8: Don't forget to look at the LCD panel as well.

All these displays have an *exposure level indicator* scale (often shortened to exposure scale, also called an exposure meter), shown in Figure 6-9.

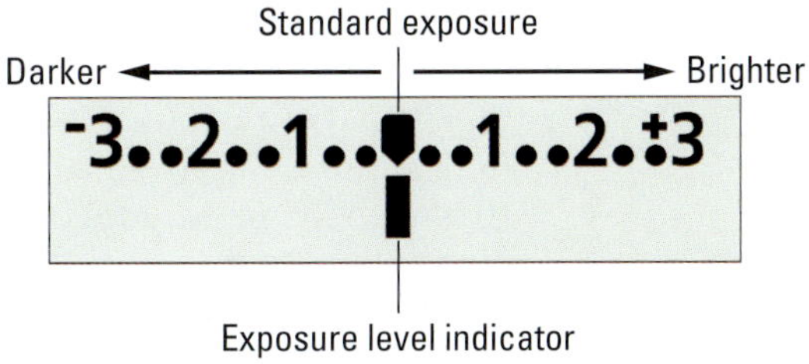

Figure 6-9: The exposure level indicator scale illustrates the exposure.

The exposure scale serves several purposes. In each one, however, the center of the scale (sometimes labeled with a 0 but often not) indicates the *standard exposure*. This is the combined exposure value (with inputs from all the camera's exposure settings) that the camera thinks will produce the best photo. The numbers to the left and right of center tell you how many stops (or levels of exposure value, EV) you are away from center. Negative numbers indicate underexposure. Positive numbers indicate overexposure. The scale goes to +/- 5.0 EV on the LCD monitor but reaches only +/- 3.0 EV in the viewfinder and on the LCD panel.

Normally, the bar under the scale, known as the *exposure level indicator* (also shown in Figure 6-9), predicts the exposure of a photo, relative to the standard exposure, taken with the current meter reading and using the current exposure settings.

In autoexposure modes, the exposure level indicator stays pegged to the standard exposure. After all, that's the point of autoexposure. In manual mode (when the ISO is not set to Auto), the exposure level indicator moves back and forth, depending on the exposure settings you have chosen. After you set the exposure (even if it is the standard exposure), the settings will not change even slightly between shots, even if the meter displays a slightly different light level. This is an excellent way of making sure that your photos consistently use the same exposure settings, which is to your advantage when processing them the same way later.

The indicator can be moved left or right by a process known as Exposure Compensation (described in "Overriding autoexposure results with Exposure Compensation," later in the chapter).

When shooting using the Auto Exposure Bracketing feature (*not* while in HDR mode, *nor* when shooting White Balance brackets), each bracket's exposure is marked relative to the center shot. When Auto Exposure Bracketing (AEB), the camera changes the exposure automatically and shoots more than one photo of the same scene, each with a different exposure. This feature is more fully explained in the "Capturing More Dynamic Range" section, later in this chapter.

Because the scale is designated as an exposure compensation guide when you shoot in P, Tv, and Av modes, the camera uses different exposure-warning alerts in those modes. Here's what happens in each mode if the camera thinks you're headed for a lousy exposure:

- **P:** In Program AE mode, both the aperture and shutter speed values blink if the camera can't select a combination that will properly expose the image. Your only recourse is to adjust the lighting or change the ISO setting.
- **Tv:** The aperture value blinks to warn you that the camera can't set the aperture to expose the image properly at the selected shutter speed. Solution: Change the shutter speed or ISO.
- **Av:** The shutter speed value blinks to let you know that the camera can't select a shutter speed that will produce a good exposure at the aperture you selected. Solution: Choose a different f-stop or adjust the ISO.

Trust but verify

Your 5D Mark III offers instant exposure feedback in the form of photo playback. You can look at the photo, analyze the histogram, and magnify the photo to evaluate every pixel if you want. Although we would all like to get it right the first time, trial and error can play an important role in improving your photos.

To trust your own eyes, you have to be willing to step out from under the protective umbrella of fancy metering modes and autoexposure. That takes time, which I realize may be limited in a given situation.

When possible, trust but verify. Take test shots to evaluate the lighting and exposure settings that the camera suggests. If necessary, change the metering mode, dial in exposure correction, or change the exposure settings to override the standard exposure.

The camera's take on proper exposure may not always be the one you want to follow, and here's why. First, the camera bases its exposure decisions on the current exposure metering mode. You can choose from four different metering modes (covered next), and each calculates exposure on a different area of the frame. Second, you may want to purposely choose exposure settings that leave parts of the image very dark or very light for creative reasons. In other words, the meter and the blinking alerts are guides, not dictators.

Choosing a Metering Mode

The *metering mode* determines which part of the frame the camera analyzes to calculate the standard exposure. The 5D Mark III offers four metering modes:

- **Evaluative metering:** The 5D Mark III divides the frame into 63-zones, analyzes the brightness in each zone (including the AF points), and then sets the exposure that will produce the best balanced photo. Sounds unbeatable. You are restricted to this metering mode when shooting Live View stills or movies. In most cases, Evaluative metering does a good job of calculating exposure, but it can get thrown off when a dark subject is set against a bright background or vice versa.

  Use Evaluative metering unless you have a reason to change it. It's the best mode for general photography.
- **Partial metering:** The camera bases exposure only on the light that falls in the center 6.2 percent of the frame. This mode enables the camera to evaluate the proper exposure for a backlit subject. See Figure 6-10.
- **Spot metering:** This mode works like Partial metering but uses a smaller region of the center of the frame (2.8 percent) to calculate exposure.

The circle in the center of the viewfinder is the Spot metering circle. Use this metering mode (and AE lock so that you can meter and recompose) when you need to measure the exposure of something very precisely and ignore the rest of the frame. Spot is also useful for bright subjects with dark backgrounds such as the moon. Set the camera to Spot metering mode to get the right exposure for the moon, not the night sky. See Figure 6-10.

- **Center-Weighted Average metering:** The camera evaluates the brightness of the entire frame but puts extra emphasis (weight) on the center. This can be a good mode when photographing people or other objects that take up the center of the frame and then some. See Figure 6-10.

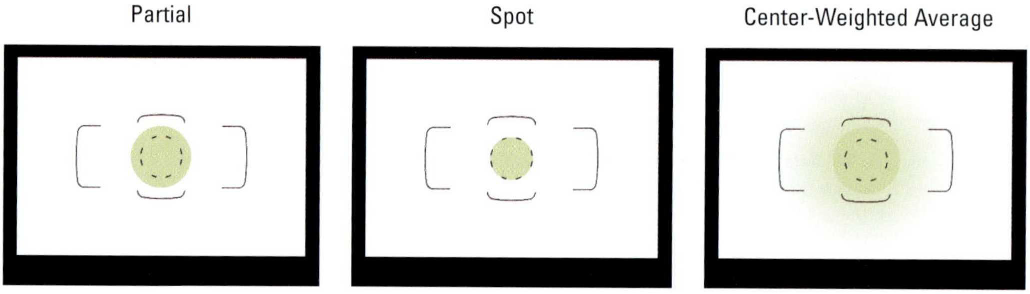

Figure 6-10: Choose a metering mode based on where things fall in the frame.

Use either of these two options to change the metering mode:

- **Quick Control screen:** Press the Quick Control button to shift into Quick Control mode and use the Multicontrollercontroller to highlight the metering mode icon, as shown on the left in Figure 6-11. The selected setting appears in the label at the bottom of the screen. Rotate the Main dial to cycle through the four modes or press Set to display a list of all four modes, as shown on the right in the figure.

  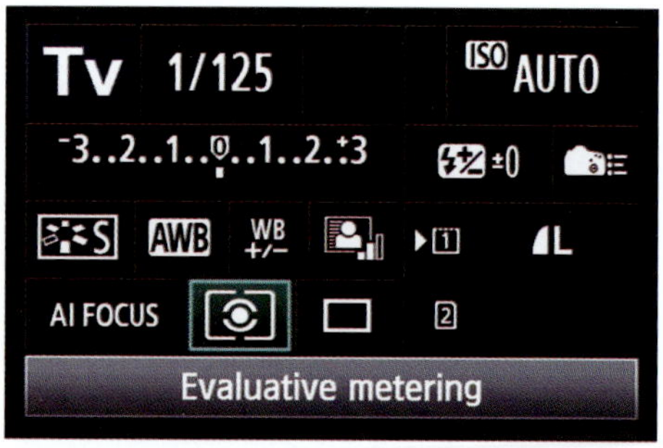

  Figure 6-11: Quickly adjust the Metering mode from the Quick Control screen.

  If you take the second route, use the Multicontroller or the Main dial to highlight the icon for the mode you want to use and then press Set to lock in your decision.

- **Metering mode selection button:** When the Shooting Information display is visible, press the Metering Mode Selection/White Balance Selection button. You then see the screen shown in Figure 6-12. Highlight your choice and press Set again to return to the menu.

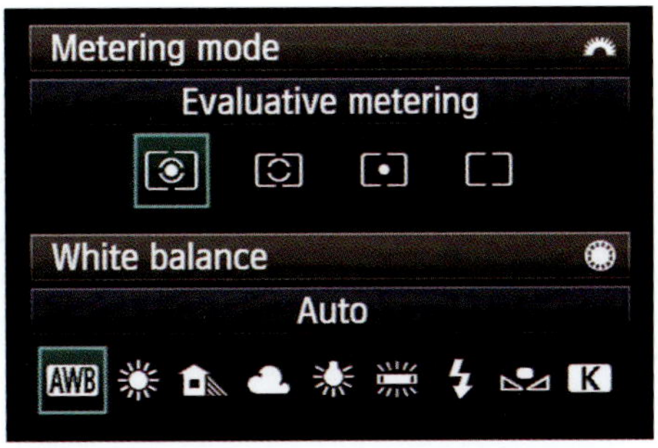

Figure 6-12: Or, access the metering mode from the Metering Mode Selection button.

TIP

You don't have to reevaluate the metering mode you're using unless you don't like the exposure the camera is setting. You'll know this when you review your photos. If you see that the exposure is off, you can adjust exposure with exposure compensation, ignore the standard exposure, and shoot in manual mode (with settings that produce the best photo, not the best exposure index), or change the metering mode to try to get the camera on the same wavelength as you are. Unless you're changing subjects and angles, or the lighting changes, after you find the right exposure (or metering mode), stick with it.

Setting the Shutter Speed, Aperture, and ISO

I made this section as short and simple as possible. You have two ways to set the exposure: Use the camera's buttons and dials or use the Quick Control screen.

Using dials and buttons

The 5D Mark III gives you control over the camera's exposure settings through the following: the Main dial, the Quick Control dial, and the ISO speed setting button. Table 6-1 summarizes the control that you should use in various exposure settings. Figure 6-13 shows them on the camera.

Table 6-1 Exposure Setting Controls by Shooting Mode

	Shutter speed	*Aperture*	*ISO*
P	Program shift with Main dial	Program shift with Main dial	ISO speed setting button
Tv	Main dial	N/A	ISO speed setting button

(continued)

Table 6-1 *(continued)*

	Shutter speed	*Aperture*	*ISO*
Av	N/A	Main dial	ISO speed setting button
M	Main dial	Quick Control dial	ISO speed setting button
B	N/A	Main dial	ISO speed setting button

Of course, you can customize this behavior. See Chapter 10 for more information on customizing controls to suit your style.

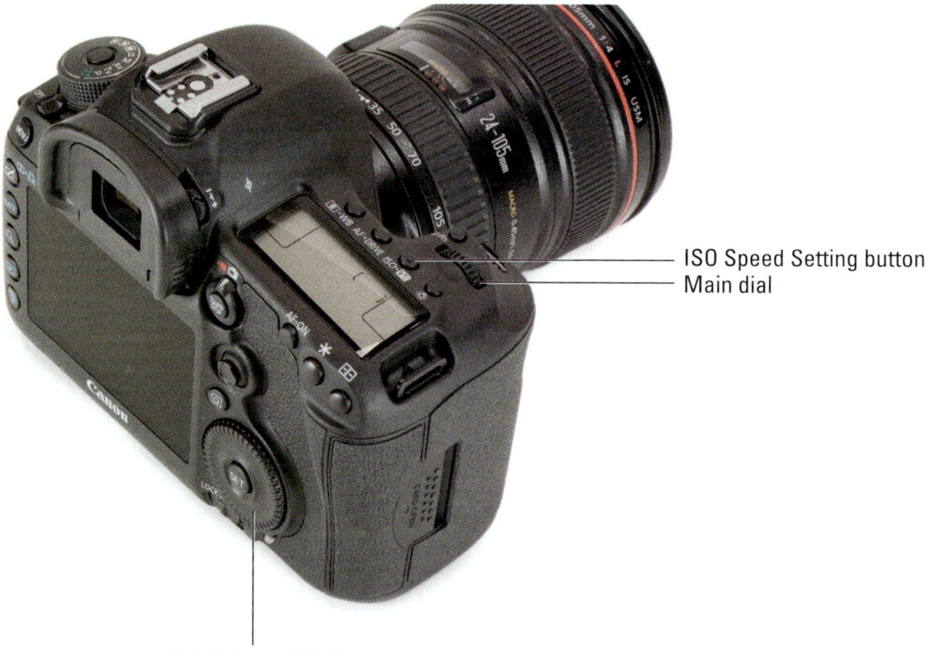

Figure 6-13: Use a combination of these controls to adjust exposure settings.

Using the Quick Control screen

The Quick Control screen is both easier and harder to use to adjust exposure settings than the camera's dials and buttons. The main difference involved in using physical controls is having a graphical interface in between you and what you want to do. That interface makes it easy to see what you're doing, but harder in that you must first enter Quick Control mode, highlight an exposure setting with the Multicontroller, and then either use the Quick Control dial to adjust the setting or press the Set button to display a full screen of information that enables you to adjust the setting.

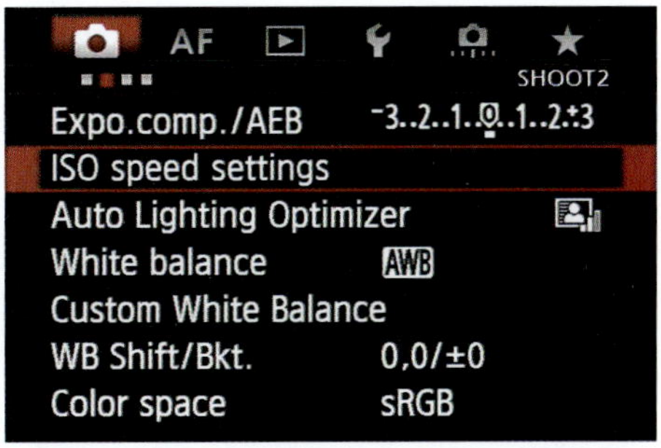

Figure 6-14: You can set and configure ISO speed from the menu.

Configuring ISO speed settings

You have the power to configure how ISO works on the 5D Mark III. Press the Menu button and navigate to Shooting Menu 2. Highlight ISO speed settings, as shown in Figure 6-14, and press the Set button.

The four choices (see Figure 6-15) are explained in the following list:

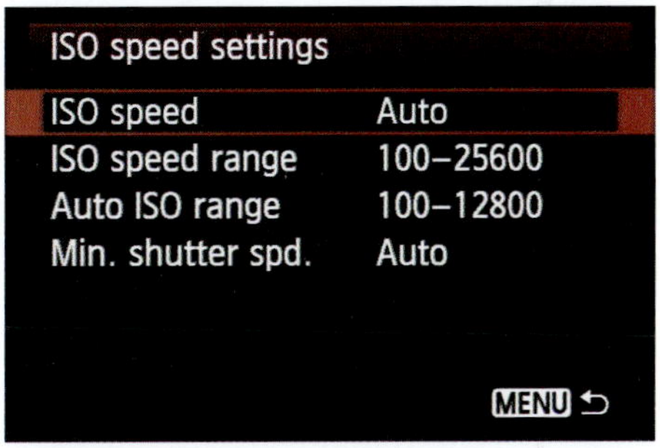

Figure 6-15: This is where you set minimum and maximum ISO speeds.

- **ISO Speed:** This is an alternative method of setting the ISO speed. If you're making other changes anyway, this option gives you the flexibility of setting the ISO now. See Figure 6-16.
- **ISO Speed Range:** This option (see Figure 6-17) controls the ISO range when you are setting the ISO manually. That's right: You can prevent yourself from setting the ISO too low or too high.
- **Auto ISO Range:** This option (see Figure 6-18) controls the ISO range when the ISO speed is set to Auto. Using this option is very effective when you don't want the camera to be able to set the ISO very high.

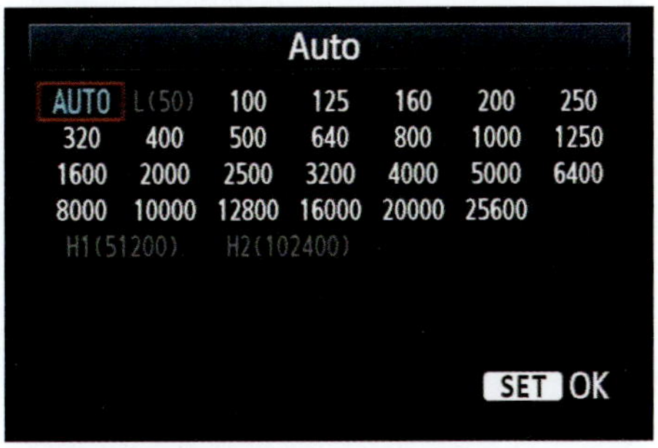

Figure 6-16: The ISO settings default to 1/3-stop increments.

- **Minimum Shutter Speed:** This last option (see Figure 6-19) enables you to set a minimum shutter speed when you set the ISO speed to Auto. To limit the chances of camera shake and motion blur, set the Minimum Shutter Speed higher.

Highlight an option and press the Set button to make changes.

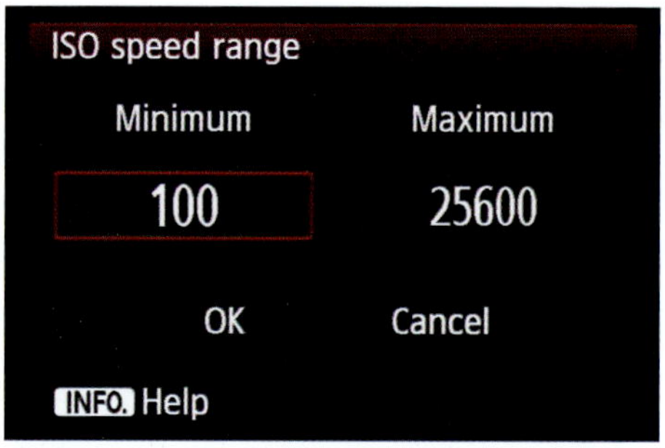

Figure 6-17: Think "manual" when configuring the ISO speed range.

When you use ISO Speed Range and Auto ISO Range, highlight the Minimum or Maximum ISO setting, press the Set button, and then use the Quick Control dial to change the value (see Figure 6-20). Press Set to lock the value in; then highlight OK and press the Set button to return to the main ISO menu. Highlight Cancel to return without saving your changes.

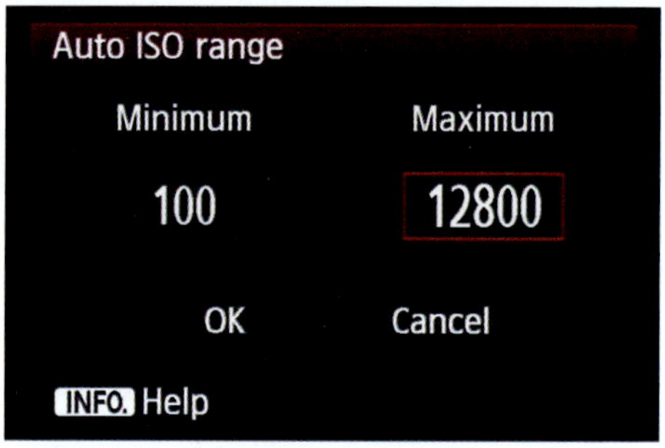

Figure 6-18: Auto ISO is configured independently of manual ISO speed range.

When you use ISO Speed and Minimum Shutter Speed, highlight your choice and press the Set button to lock in your change.

Locking the Autoexposure

Normally, after composing a scene, you press the Shutter button halfway to meter and focus and then press the Shutter button fully to take the photo. You frame, meter, and focus once.

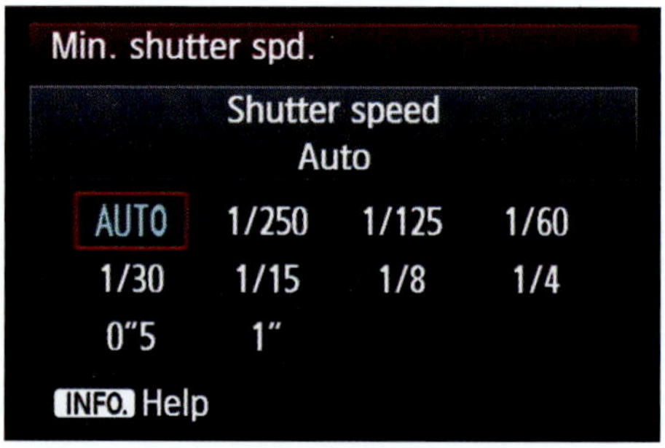

Figure 6-19: You can also set the Minimum Shutter Speed (when ISO is set to Auto) here.

You run into problems with this technique, however, when photographing high-contrast scenes in general and scenes with strong backlighting in particular. Bright areas dominate, pushing the exposure upward so that your photos don't get blown out. Darker areas, which often include your subject, will be underexposed as a result.

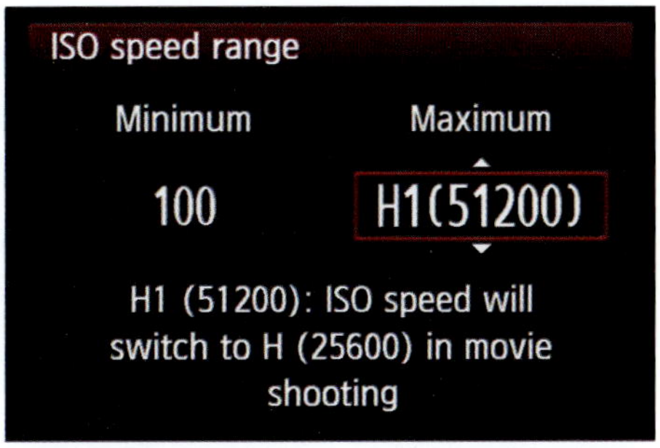

Figure 6-20: The triangles indicate that you can scroll up and down to set a new value.

One way around this problem is to determine the exposure based on the dark areas and then recompose and focus the scene. For this approach, you use *AE Lock*, or autoexposure lock. AE Lock gives you a fighting chance to take a good photo when the subject would otherwise be in shadow. (The other answer is to shoot manually: Meter the scene the way you want, dial in exposure settings including a manual ISO, recompose without changing the settings, and then take the photo.)

Here's how to use AE Lock:

1. **Point the camera at what you want to meter.**

   Depending on the metering mode and AF Point Selection method, you might use different areas to determine the exposure:

   - *Evaluative:* When the AF Point is automatically selected, the exposure is locked based on the AF Point that achieved focus. When you've selected the AF Point yourself (manually), the exposure is locked based on the point you chose.
   - *Partial, Spot, Center-Weighted Average:* The exposure is locked based on the center AF Point regardless of the AF point selection method.

   So if you want control over the specific point that AE lock uses, manually select the AF Point when in Evaluative metering mode, or switch to one of the other metering modes and center the area you want to meter in the viewfinder.

2. **Press the Shutter button halfway to focus (first time) and meter.**
3. **Press and release the AE Lock button (see Figure 6-21).**

   By default, you don't need to hold the button down as long as you don't take too much time. You can change this behavior, however, from Custom Function Menu 2, Custom Controls (see Chapter 10 for information on customizing controls). The other AE Lock behavior that you can assign to the AE Lock button is to lock the exposure until you press the button again.

4. **Release the Shutter button (very optional).**

   Release the Shutter button only if you've metered something that isn't necessarily going to be in the photo, or when what you're metering isn't the main subject and doesn't need to be in focus. This situation happens from time to time. You give yourself a chance to refocus when you finish composing the scene.

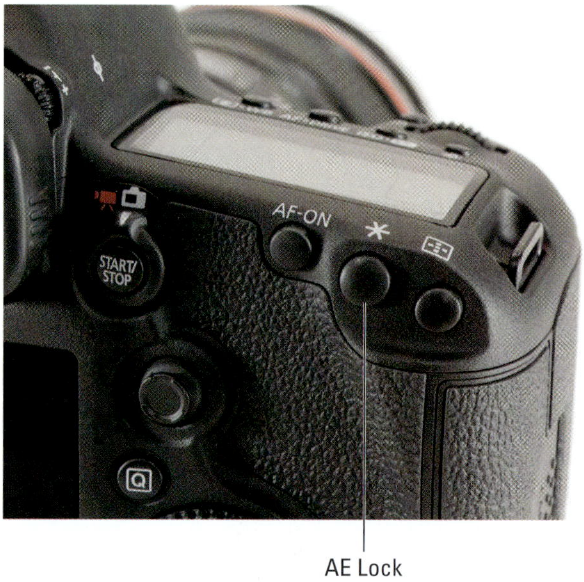

Figure 6-21: AE Lock locks the exposure so that you can recompose and refocus.

   If you're metering using a person's face (and you want that person to be in focus), you should keep pressing the Shutter button so that the person doesn't drop out of focus.

5. **Recompose.**
6. **Press the Shutter button halfway to focus (if necessary).**

   This step relates to Step 4. If you released the button, you have to refocus. If you didn't, skip this step.

7. **Press the Shutter button fully to take the photo.**

   Figure 6-22 shows a result of following the preceding steps. I took this photo of Anthony Wayne's statue looking up at a bright sky. To get any detail of the horse's head (which is what I focused on), I used AE Lock to meter on the dark horse body, locked the exposure in, and then recomposed on the head as you see here.

   Don't be surprised if skies or highlights are featureless when you use AE Lock. You're making the decision that getting a good exposure on what you want to take the photo of is more important than preserving details in highlights. In this case, it's a great trade-off, especially so because this is a black-and-white photo.

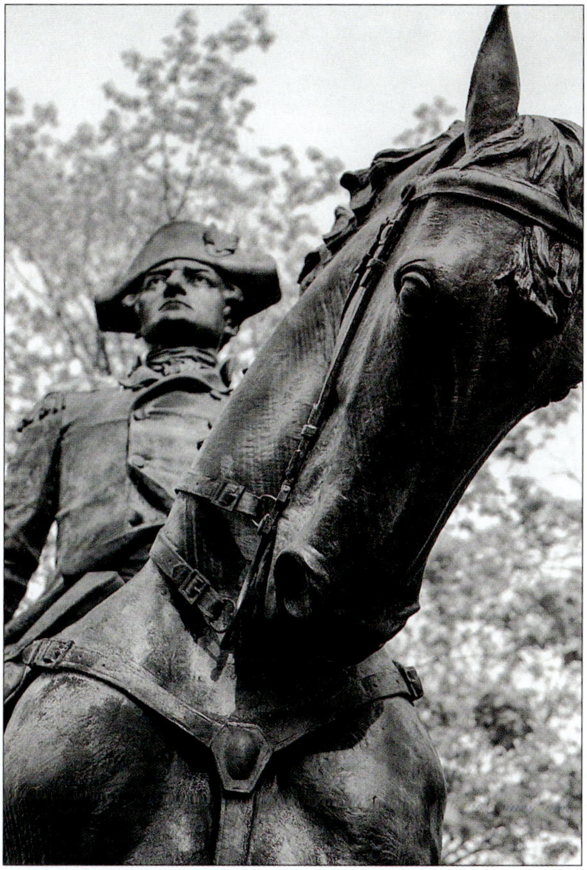

Figure 6-22: General Wayne endorses the use of AE Lock when the situation warrants.

Using the 5D's Exposure-Correction Tools

In addition to the normal controls over shutter speed, aperture, and ISO, your 5D Mark III offers a collection of tools that enable you to solve tricky exposure problems. The next few sections give you the lowdown on these features.

Overriding autoexposure results with Exposure Compensation

When you set your camera to the P, Tv, or Av shooting modes, you can enjoy the benefits of autoexposure support but retain some control over the final exposure. If you think that the image the camera produced is too dark or too light, you can use a feature known as *Exposure Compensation* to correct it.

Here are some details about it:

- Exposure compensation is stated in EV values, such as +2.0 EV. Possible values range from +5.0 EV to –5.0 EV.
- A setting of EV 0.0 results in no exposure adjustment.
- For a brighter image, you raise the EV value. The higher you go, the brighter the image becomes.
- For a darker image, you lower the EV value. The picture becomes progressively darker with each step down the EV scale.

Each full number on the EV scale represents an exposure shift of one *full stop.* By default, the exposure is adjusted in 1/3 stop increments, but you can change the adjustment to 1/2-stop increments if you want to shift the exposure in larger jumps. To do so, go to the Custom Function Menu 1 and change the Exposure level increments to 1/2-Stop. If you make this change, the exposure scale appears slightly different in the Shooting Information display and Live View display than you see it in this book. (Only one intermediate notch appears between each number on the meter instead of the usual two.) The viewfinder meter doesn't change, but the exposure level indicator appears as a double line if you set the Exposure Compensation value to a half-step value (+0.5, +1.5, and so on).

Exposure compensation is especially helpful when your subject is lighter or darker than an average scene. For example, take a look at the first image in Figure 6-23. The subject is clearly too dark. The lights in the foreground and background hijacked the camera's meter a bit, even though I am zoomed in pretty tightly. Dialing in a stop of positive exposure compensation resulted in a much better looking photo.

The only way to tell what you should do is to quickly review your photos. You don't have to microscopically examine every one, but get into the habit of checking general exposure often.

Sometimes you can cope with situations like this one by changing the metering mode setting, as discussed earlier in this chapter.

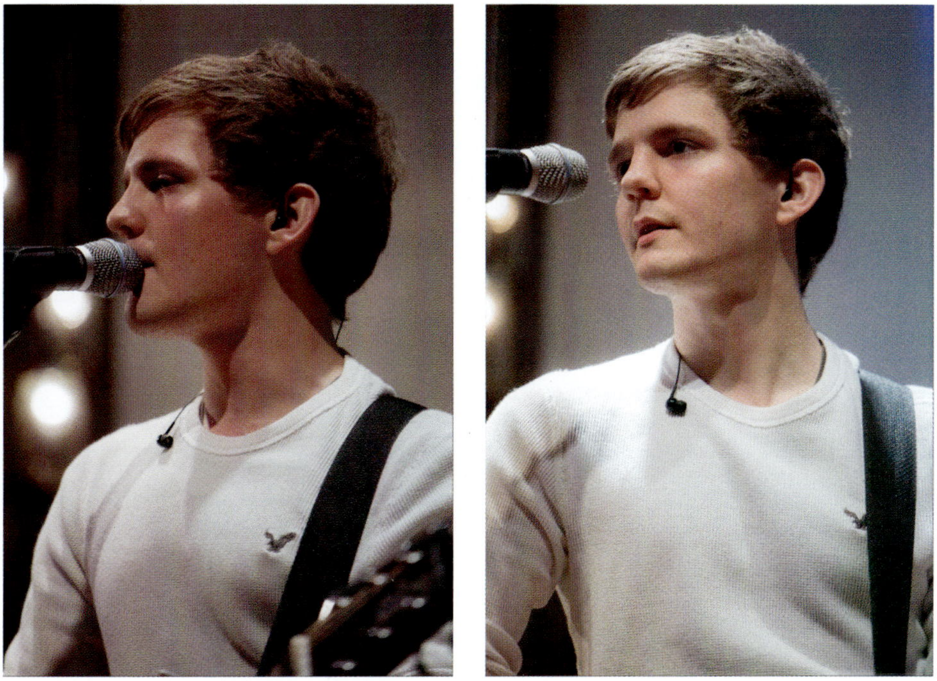

Figure 6-23: To lighten the scene, dial in a positive exposure compensation value.

In most cases, a two-stop Exposure Compensation range is more than enough; a setting beyond that is typically useful only for creating HDR (high dynamic range) images. If you find yourself needing more than two stops of compensation, revisit the exposure settings and try to correct the problem there.

Here's how to dial in Exposure Compensation:

- **Normal:** After you meter the scene, rotate the Quick Control dial to the left to lower the Exposure Compensation; dial to the right to raise it.
- **Quick Control screen:** When displaying the Quick Control screen, highlight the exposure scale and then rotate the Quick Control dial, as shown in Figure 6-24.

  Alternatively, press Set when the exposure scale is highlighted and then rotate the Quick Control dial. The screen shown in Figure 6-25 is a large visual helper. Press Set to finish.

- **Menu:** From the menu, navigate to Shooting Menu 2, highlight Exposure Compensation/ AEB, and press the Set button. Change the amount of compensation with the Quick Control dial. Press Set to finish.

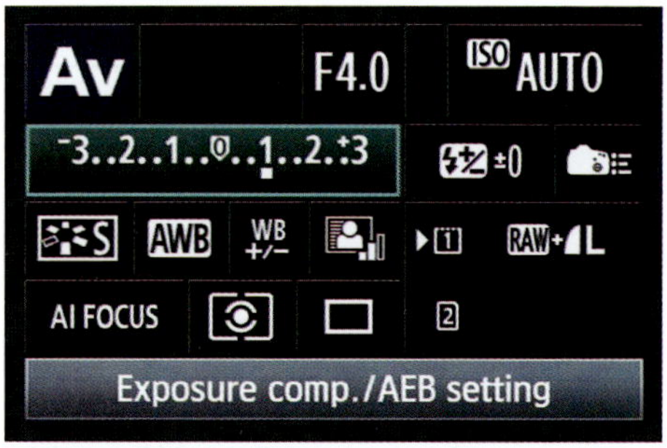

Figure 6-24: Dialing in positive Exposure Compensation in Quick Control mode.

Don't use the Main dial to attempt to set Exposure Compensation. It sets the Autoexposure Bracketing (AEB) distance.

Note that the viewfinder and top LCD panel display only +/3 stops of exposure compensation. You'll see small triangles at both ends of the scale to remind you that you exceeded the normal three-stop range of compensation. You *can* dial in more, but you have to count *clicks* or take a quick look at the main monitor to see what you're doing.

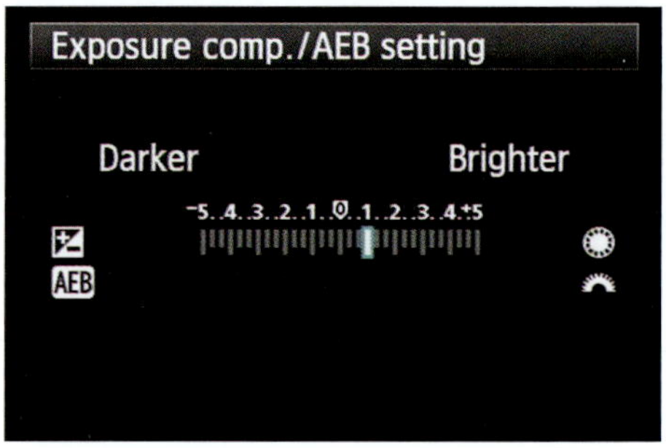

Figure 6-25: This scale goes to +/- 5.

How the camera arrives at the brighter or darker image you request depends on the exposure mode:

- **In Av (Aperture-Priority AE) mode:** The camera adjusts the shutter speed but leaves your selected aperture in force. Be sure to check the resulting shutter speed to make sure that it isn't so slow that camera shake or blur from moving objects is problematic. The camera will also adjust the ISO if you have it set to Auto.
- **In Tv (Shutter-Priority AE) mode:** The opposite occurs: The camera opens or stops down the aperture, leaving your selected shutter speed alone. ISO is also in play if it's set to Auto.
- **In M (Manual mode):** Just checking to see if you're awake. You can't dial in Exposure Compensation in Manual mode because you're responsible for the exposure settings. The Quick Control dial changes aperture in this instance.
- **In P (Programmed AE) mode:** The camera decides whether to adjust aperture, shutter speed, or both to accommodate the Exposure Compensation setting.

To keep the camera from changing the ISO when you dial in Exposure Compensation, set the ISO yourself.

Keep in mind, too, that the camera can adjust the aperture only so much, according to the aperture range of your lens. The range of shutter speeds is limited by the camera. So if you reach the end of those ranges, you have to compromise on either shutter speed or aperture, or adjust ISO.

A final, and critical, point about Exposure Compensation: Powering off the camera doesn't return you to a neutral setting (EV 0.0). The setting you last used remains in force until you change it.

Protecting highlights with Highlight Tone Priority

If you find yourself losing details in highlights, try enabling Highlight Tone Priority.

The minimum ISO is limited to ISO 200 for the process to work. The camera sneakily uses a lower ISO than the one you have set to underexpose the photo. This lower ISO preserves details in the highlights (theoretically). The camera then brightens the dark areas of the photo to bring them in line with the correct exposure. Your mileage may vary. Some complain that Highlight Tone Priority elevates noise in their photos. Others love it.

If you shoot RAW photos, enable Highlight Tone Priority with care. This is not a feature that affects only JPEGs. Your RAW photos are equally, and permanently, altered. It is not like the Auto Lighting Optimizer in this regard.

You can enable Highlight Tone Priority from Shooting Menu 3. If Highlight Tone Priority is enabled, Auto Lighting Optimizer is automatically disabled. As a reminder that Highlight Tone Priority is enabled, a D+ symbol appears near the ISO value in the Shooting Settings display, as shown in Figure 6-26. The same symbol appears near the ISO setting in the viewfinder and in the shooting data that appears onscreen in Live View mode and playback mode, as well as on the top LCD panel. (See Chapters 3 and 5 to find out more about Live View and picture playback.)

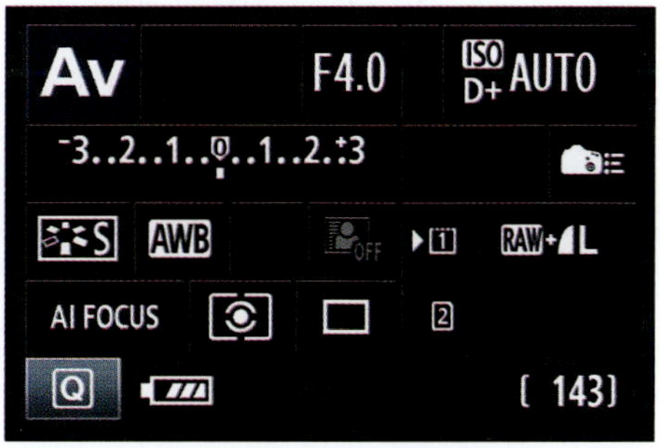

Figure 6-26: The D+ symbol beside the ISO indicates that Highlight Tone Priority is enabled.

Correcting brightness and contrast with Auto Lighting Optimizer

In contrast to Highlight Tone Priority, which concentrates on preserving highlight detail only, Auto Lighting Optimizer adjusts *both shadows and highlights* to improve the final image tonality. It is a processing technique applied to JPEGs, not RAW photos. So, whether you have it enabled in-camera or not, as long as you shoot RAW photos, you can experiment with different strengths in Digital Photo Professional.

Figure 6-27 shows a family portrait (using the 10-second timer) beside a river. In the first image, Auto Lighting Optimizer is off. The photo isn't bad, but the shadows are a bit dark. The second image shows what Auto Lighting Optimizer looks like when set to strong (for this image, that is; your mileage will vary from scene to scene and photo to photo). All the shadows are brightened without blowing out the highlights.

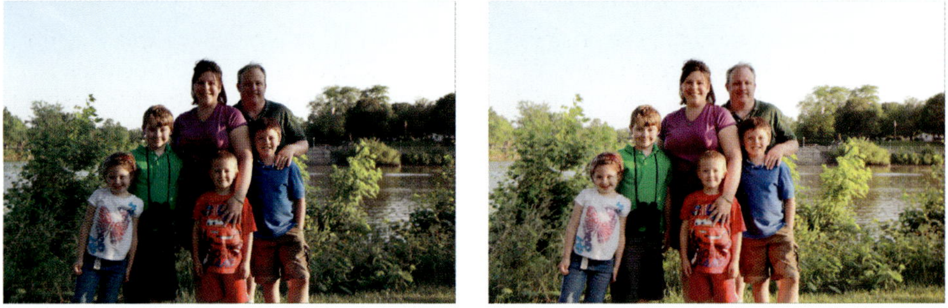

Figure 6-27: Sometimes natural lighting needs a little help.

By default, the camera applies Auto Lighting Optimizer at the Standard level. If you want to experiment with other settings, visit Shooting Menu 2 and select Auto Lighting Optimizer. There are four settings, as shown in Figure 6-28: Standard, which is the default level of correction; Strong; Low; and Disable (or Off). Highlight your preference and press Set again to lock the setting. The adjustment remains in force until you revisit the Shooting menu to change the setting.

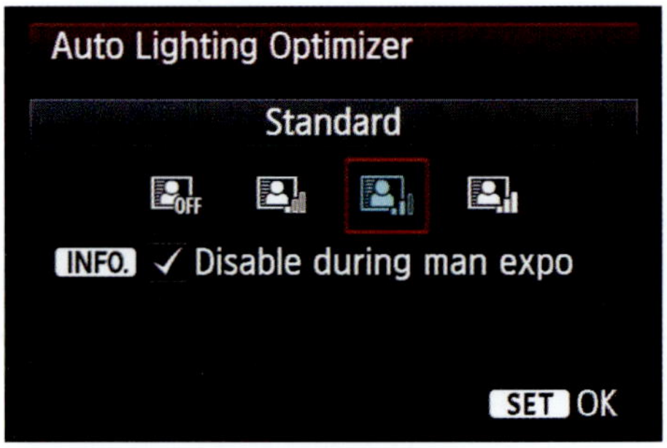

Figure 6-28: You can set the level of Auto Lighting Optimizer from Shooting Menu 2.

When in Scene Intelligent Auto mode, the filter is always applied at the Standard level. Notice that you have the option of disabling it when in manual mode.

You can also set the Auto Lighting Optimizer from the Quick Control screen. It is just above the drive mode icon.

Capturing More Dynamic Range

The world is a pretty dynamic place. The sun is an incredibly bright light source, and shadows are great at hiding things. When you put them together in the same photo, the camera has to choose to make one look good over the other. This dynamism has renewed interest in Auto Exposure Bracketing (AEB) for use with High Dynamic Range (HDR) photography and spurred developments such as the 5D Mark III's HDR mode.

Bracketing exposures automatically

Although now primarily for HDR photography, *Auto Exposure Bracketing* (AEB) began years ago on film cameras. Getting the right exposure was much trickier then, and you couldn't immediately play the photo back to inspect it. Shooting exposure brackets covered your exposure bases. You could take three photos and choose the best one when you developed the film. You can use it the same way today, but more people use bracketing for HDR photography.

Chapter 9 has more information about HDR. This section concentrates on using the AEB feature.

To shoot auto exposure brackets, follow these steps:

1. **Get your modes on.**

   I recommend setting the shooting mode to Aperture-Priority AE so that you can control the aperture. Maintaining a constant aperture across the brackets is important if you want the depth of field to be consistent.

   I also recommend setting the drive mode to Continuous. Doing so fires off the shots while you press the Shutter button. When drive mode is set to Single shot, you have to press the Shutter button repeatedly.

   Finally, you should probably set the image quality to RAW to make your source photos be of the highest quality possible. When processing in RAW software, you have finer control over tone with RAW photos than JPEGs (although JPEGs work just fine most of the time).

   If you have a flash attached, turn it off. AEB won't work.

2. **Press the Quick Control button and highlight the exposure scale, as shown in Figure 6-29.**

   Use the Multicontroller to change which function is highlighted.

   You can also configure AEB from Shooting Menu 2. Select Exposure Compensation/AEB and press the Set button to get to it.

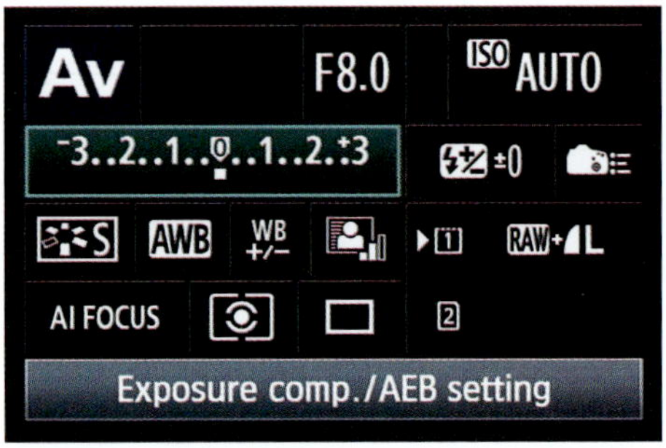

Figure 6-29: Highlight the Exposure Compensation/AEB area to dial in brackets.

3. **Rotate the Main dial to set the exposure difference.**

   As you rotate the Main dial clockwise, the exposure difference between brackets gets larger. You can set it to up to +/-3 EV, as shown in Figure 6-30. The greater the exposure difference between brackets, the larger the dynamic range you will capture.

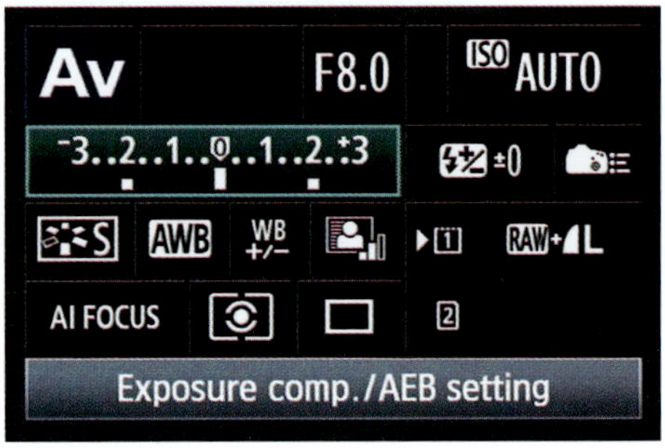

Figure 6-30: The brackets appear on the scale.

   If you want to shrink the distance, rotate the Main dial counterclockwise.

   By default, the 5D Mark III is set to shoot three brackets. Choose more brackets if the scene has high contrast and you want to capture an even large dynamic range. Change the number of brackets from the Custom Function Menu 1.

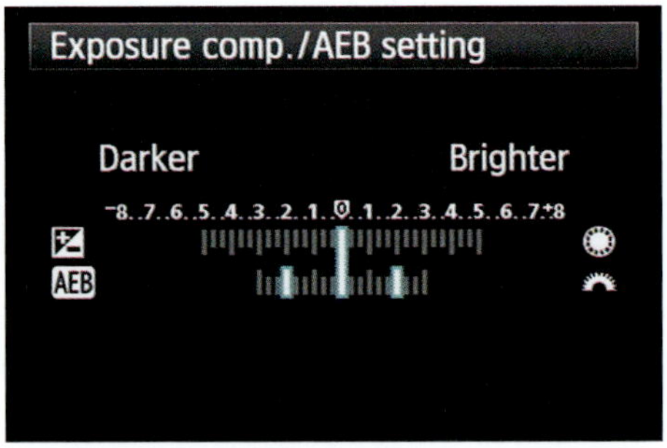

Figure 6-31: You can adjust the bracket distance and the exposure of the center bracket.

   You can also press the Set button to open the Exposure Compensation/AEB setting display, as shown in Figure 6-31.

   Spin the Quick Control dial to change the exposure of the center bracket. The other brackets will change with it.

4. **Frame and focus.**

5. **Start shooting.**

   The camera normally takes the photos in this order: spot on, under, and then over. You can change this order with the Bracketing sequence option in Custom Function Menu 1.

6. **Transfer your photos to a computer.**

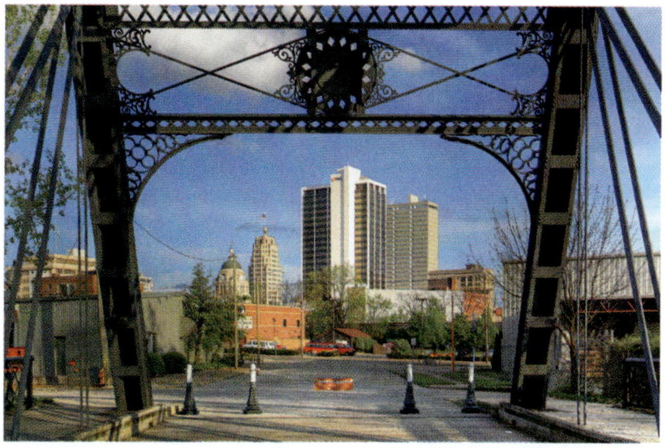

Figure 6-32: Exposure brackets expand the amount of dynamic range you can capture.

7. **Process the brackets in HDR software or choose the best single exposure.**

   I cover this part of the process briefly in Chapter 9. Figure 6-32 reveals the finished, tone-mapped image of a cityscape, looking out from a bridge. Three exposure brackets were used, each separated by 2.0 EV.

Having fun with HDR mode

HDR mode is another way to deal with high-contrast scenes that have a large dynamic range. Rather than shoot a single photo and try to save details (such as Highlight Tone Priority or Auto Lighting Optimizer), HDR mode shoots three photos with different exposure settings and merges them into a single JPEG.

To set up and use HDR mode, follow these steps:

1. **Set up the camera to take the shots you want.**

   This includes choosing a shooting mode and setting the applicable exposure settings.

2. **Press the Creative Photo button, highlight HDR mode (see Figure 6-33), and press the Set button.**

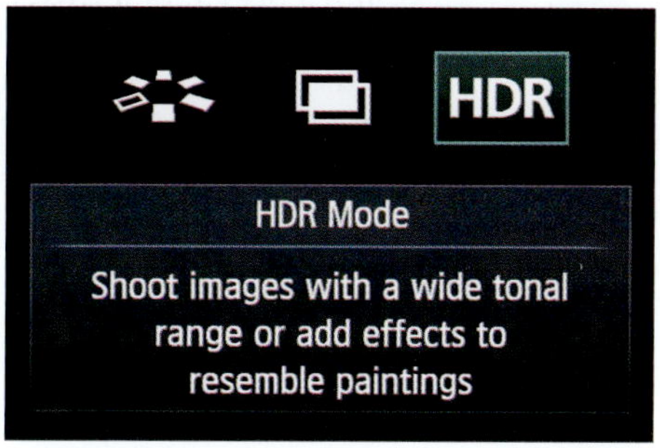

Figure 6-33: Press 3 for HDR.

   You can also press the Menu button and go to Shooting Menu 3.

3. **Configure HDR mode.**

   Highlight each option and press the Set button to access the settings. Choose a setting and press the Set button. The options are (see Figure 6-34) as follows:

   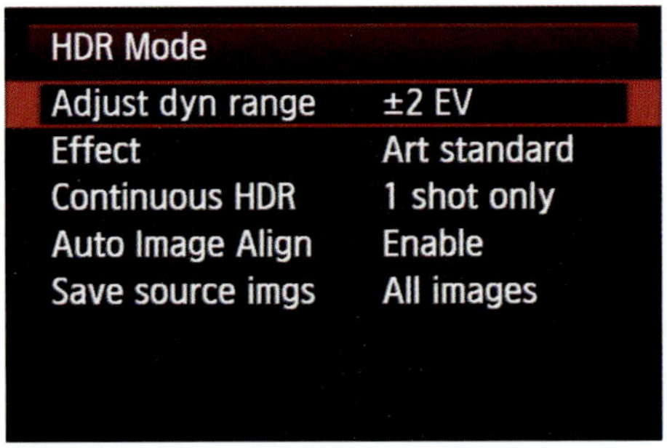

   Figure 6-34: Carefully Set HDR mode options.

   - *Adjust Dynamic Range:* Set to Disable HDR by default. To enable HDR, set to Auto or choose from one of the discrete EV ranges (from +/-1 EV to +/- 3 EV).
   - *Effect:* Select an effect. Options are Natural, Art Standard, Art Vivid, Art Bold, or Art Embossed
   - *Continuous HDR:* This is a neat option. Select 1 shot only if you want to shoot one HDR sequence and return to normal shooting. Set to Every shot if you want to continue to shoot HDR.
   - *Auto Image Align:* Set to Enable (best when shooting handheld) or disable (best when using a tripod).
   - *Save Source Images:* Select All Images if you want to save all the source images, including JPEGs and RAW. I highly recommend this setting because you can use software to create your own HDR images using the source photos later, in case you don't like the camera's result. Choose HDR Image only if you want the take-it-or-leave-it solution.

4. **Compose the scene.**

5. **Press the Shutter button halfway to focus and meter; then take the shot.**

   You don't need to hold down the Shutter button. The camera shoots continuously, regardless. Try to remain still and keep the camera steady as it shoots. If necessary, get a tripod.

Figure 6-35 shows the different effects in action. I like Art Vivid the most in this case.

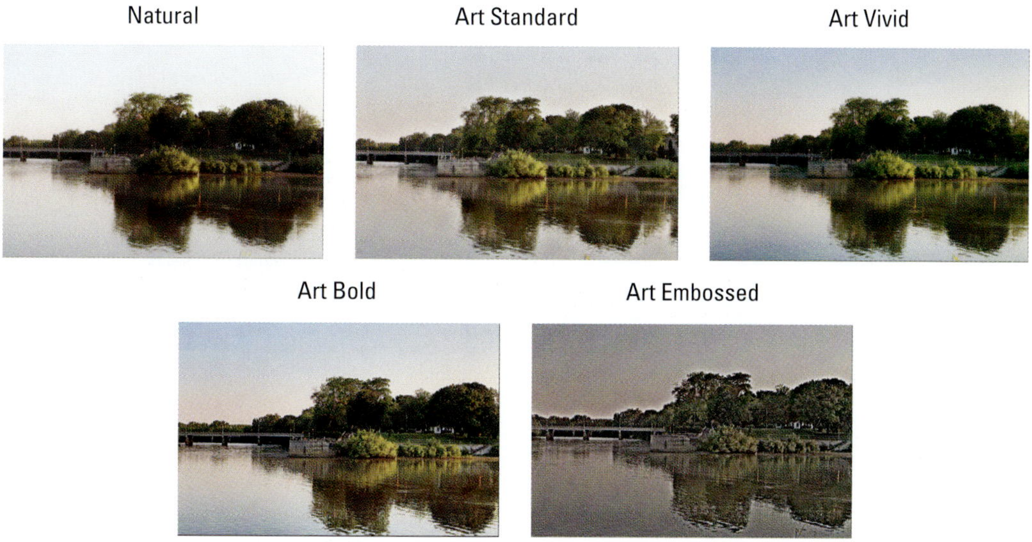

Figure 6-35: A river scene shot using the 5D Mark III's HDR mode.

Using the Flash in Advanced Shooting Modes

I would love to be able to devote more pages to using an external Speedlite with your 5D Mark III, but I can't. To have enough room for all the other important topics, I've had to limit the coverage of this topic to an overview.

Attaching an external Speedlite

Flash is a challenging aspect of photography. Sometimes, no amount of fiddling with shutter speed, aperture, and ISO produces a bright enough exposure — in which case you simply have to add more light.

The 5D Mark III, of course, doesn't come with a flash built in. You have to add it (see Figure 6-36).

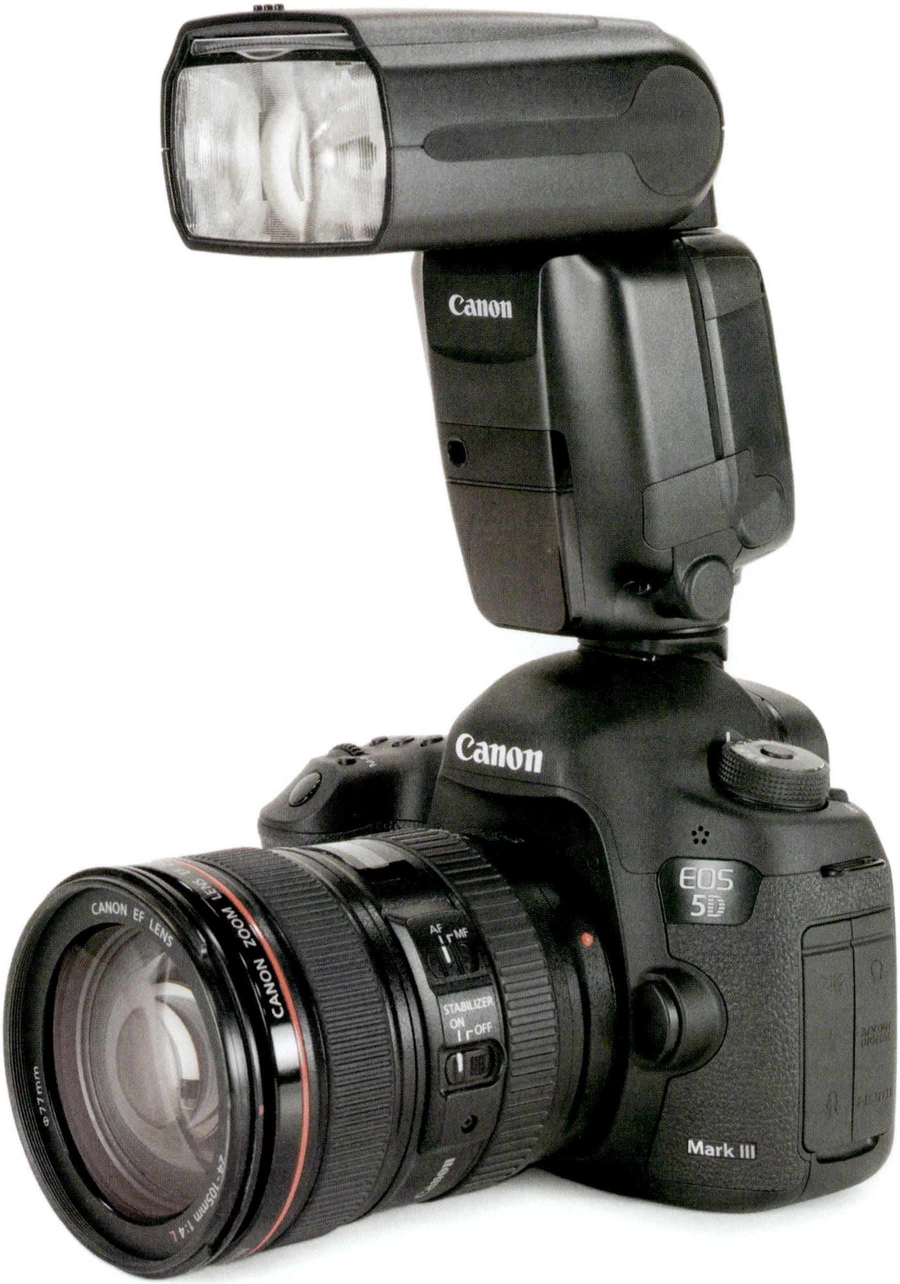

Figure 6-36: Add a Speedlite to look even more awesome.

Controlling the flash from the camera

To control the flash from the camera, navigate to Shooting Menu 1 and highlight External Speedlite control (see Figure 6-37).

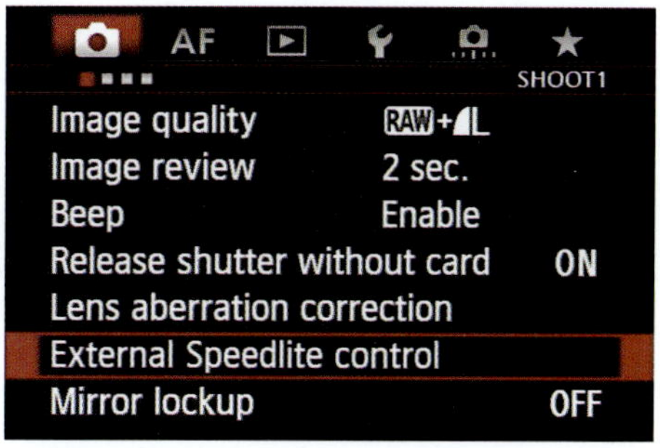

Figure 6-37: Because the camera has no built-in flash, you have to choose an External control.

Press the Set button to reveal the several options, which are as follows (see Figure 6-38):

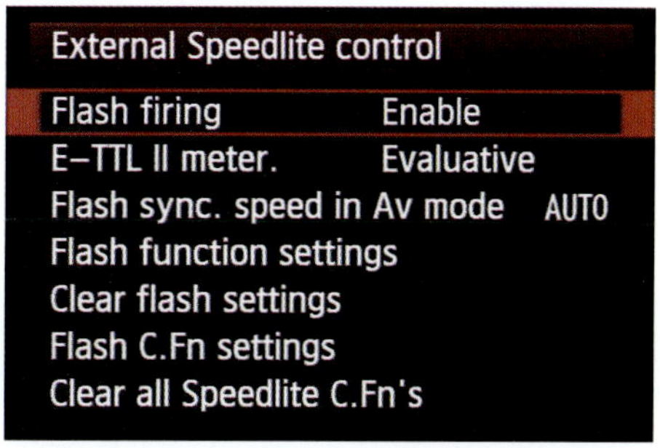

Figure 6-38: Just about everything you ever wanted to set on your Speedlite is here.

- **Flash Firing:** Enable or disable the flash.
- **E-TTL II Metering:** Evaluative (for normal exposures) or Average.
- **Flash Sync Speed in Av Mode:** Gives you three options for setting the flash sync speed in this shooting mode: Auto; 1/200 to 1/60 second (auto); or 1/200 second (fixed).
- **Flash Function settings:** Depends on the flash. In the case of the Speedlite 600EX-RT:
  - *Metering:* Options are ETTL-II, Manual, MULTI flash (stroboscopic), Auto External Flash Metering, or Manual External Flash Metering.
  - *Wireless:* Set to Off, Radio, or Optical.
  - *Flash Zoom:* Leave on Auto or set to a specific focal length.
  - *Synchronization:* Options are First-Curtain Synchronization (fire when the shutter opens, the default); Second-Curtain Synchronization (fire the flash just before the shutter closes); and High-Speed Synchronization (takes fast shutter speeds into account).
  - *Flash Exposure Compensation:* Dial in Flash Exposure Compensation. See the next section.
  - *Flash Exposure Bracketing:* Set distance between brackets.

- **Clear Flash Settings:** Yup. Clears them back to their default settings.
- **Flash Custom Function Settings:** The Speedlite 600EX-RT has 23 Custom Functions devoted solely to the flash. Right. Here are some examples of what they're for: Changing the distance indicator display from meters to feet; enabling auto zoom to match the camera sensor size; disabling the beep; changing how the light is distributed when the flash goes off (Standard, Guide Number Priority, or Even Coverage). If you're really that into controlling the flash, the Custom Functions will make a world of difference to you. All the nitty-gritty details can be found in the Speedlite manual.
- **Clear all Speedlite Custom Functions:** This option resets the Flash Custom Functions.

Adjusting flash power with Flash Exposure Compensation

TIP

When you shoot with a flash, the camera attempts to adjust the output as needed to produce a good exposure for the current lighting conditions. On some occasions, you may find that you want a little more or less light than the camera thinks is appropriate.

You can adjust the flash output by using the feature called Flash Exposure Compensation. Similar to Exposure Compensation (discussed earlier in this chapter), Flash Exposure Compensation affects the output level of the flash unit. Use Exposure Compensation to affect the brightness of the background in your flash photos. As with Exposure Compensation, Flash Exposure Compensation is stated in terms of EV *(exposure value)* numbers. A setting of 0.0 indicates no flash adjustment; you can increase the flash power to +3.0 or decrease it to –3.0.

Whichever direction you want to go with flash power, you have two ways to do so:

- **ISO Speed Setting/Flash Exposure Compensation button:** Press the Flash Exposure Compensation button and then dial in Flash Exposure Compensation by turning the Quick Control dial. This method is by far the fastest and easiest one.
- **Quick Control screen:** Press the Quick Control button to shift to the Quick Control mode. Highlight the Flash Exposure

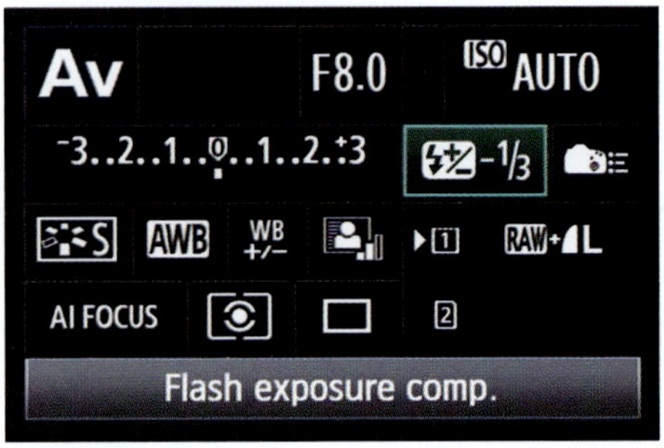

Figure 6-39: Another way to adjust flash power is via the Quick Control screen.

Compensation value, as shown in Figure 6-39. Rotate the Quick Control dial or the Main dial to raise or lower the amount of flash adjustment. Or, if you need more help, press Set to see the full-screen display. Make your adjustment; press Set when you finish. This method works well when you're already in Quick Control mode.

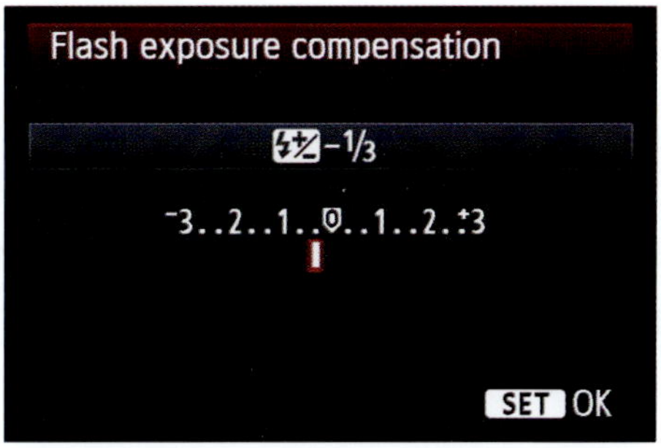

Figure 6-40: You can also change flash power by using the menus, but it's a tedious task.

- **Shooting Menu 1:** Navigate to this menu and highlight External Speedlite control. Select Flash Functions Settings and press Set. Highlight Flash Exposure Compensation and press Set. Dial in the amount of compensation you want (see Figure 6-40) and then press Set again. In other words, learn the Quick Control method and save yourself a bunch of button presses!

When flash compensation is in effect, the value appears on the Shooting Settings screen (refer to Figure 6-39 to see the icon in Quick Control mode). You see the same plus/minus flash symbol in the viewfinder and Live View display, although in both cases without the actual Flash Exposure Compensation value. If you change the Flash Exposure Compensation value to 0 (zero), the flash-power icon disappears from all the displays.

REMEMBER

As with exposure compensation, any flash-power adjustment you make remains in force until you reset the control, even if you turn off the camera. So be sure to check the setting before using your flash. Additionally, the Auto Lighting Optimizer feature, covered earlier in this chapter, can interfere with the effect produced by Flash Exposure Compensation, so you might want to disable it.

Locking the flash exposure

You might never notice it, but when you press the Shutter button to take a picture with flash enabled, the camera emits a brief *preflash* before the actual flash. This preflash is used to determine the proper flash power needed to expose the image.

TIP

Occasionally, the information that the camera collects from the preflash can be off target because of the assumptions the system makes about what area of the frame is likely to contain your subject. To address this problem, your camera has a feature called *Flash Exposure Lock,* or FE Lock. This tool enables you to set the flash power based on only the center of the frame.

To use FE Lock, point the camera at the subject, focus, and then press and release the M-Fn button. This fires a preflash and locks in the flash exposure.

The FE Lock symbol appears in the viewfinder (a flash symbol with the normal AE Lock asterisk). You can recompose and take the photo.

The flash exposure setting remains in force for several seconds, meaning that you can shoot a series of images using the same flash setting without firing another preflash at all.

REMEMBER

Unfortunately, FE Lock isn't available in Live View mode. If you want to use this feature, you must abandon Live View and use the viewfinder to frame your images.

7

Managing Focus and Depth of Field

In This Chapter

- Becoming acquainted with your focus roadmap
- Getting your AF mode on
- Ordering up a case of AI Servo AF
- Selecting an AF Area Selection mode
- Picking AF points
- Customizing yonder AF
- Pondering depth of field

Autofocus can sometimes act like an unruly puppy. You have to be able to control it to get the most out of it — but don't let the technical nature of most of this chapter scare you off. Even if you find the text a bit dry at times, I promise that it's worth it: There's no substitute for being able to focus on what you want. To ensure that you can do so, you must know about the different AF options and how to use them.

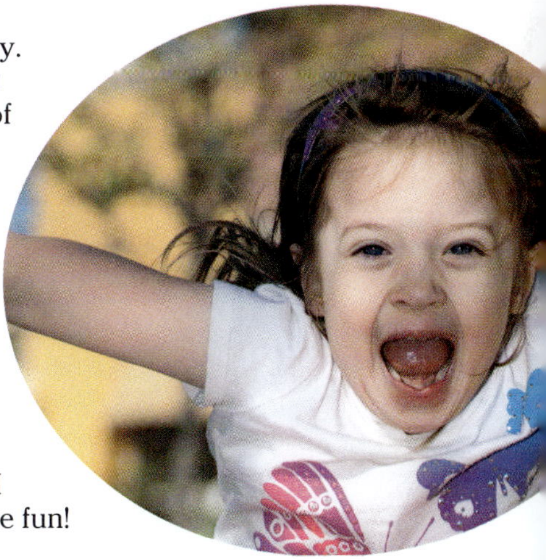

An artful photographer knows that focus means more than simply getting a sharp image of a subject. You also need to consider *depth of field,* or the distance over which objects remain sharply focused. I address that topic toward the end of the chapter. Have fun!

Reviewing Focus Fundamentals

This section covers the general path you should take to decide what focus mode to use on the 5D Mark III and understand what your options are. The decision points and branches are so numerous that it can be hard to cope with.

Use this section to get your head in the game. You may be able to settle on a few focusing strategies and not need to change them around that much. If you're in a lot of different situations and need to access the full power of the 5D Mark III, however, you should learn all the modes and options inside and out.

I explain many of the options in detail later in this chapter. Where I don't, I provide a reference to where you can find them.

Here, then, are steps that should help you get your focus on:

1. **Choose a focus mode.**

   Select one of two main focusing methods:

   - *Autofocus (AF):* Autofocusing is both easier and harder than manually focusing. When autofocus can focus on precisely what you want it to, you can trust that more often than manually focusing. Many more steps, however, are required to tweak AF to perform well in the specific situation you may be in.
   - *Manual Focus (MF):* Manually focusing is both easier and harder than autofocusing. It is far easier to configure (throw one switch and focus) but it is harder to nail the focus in many situations.

   See Chapter 1 for details and illustrations on choosing a focus mode as well as pointers for when you're manually focusing.

   If you choose to manually focus, you're done with these steps.

2. **Choose an AF mode.**

   If you choose to autofocus, select one of three AF modes:

   - *One-Shot AF:* The camera autofocuses once.
   - *AI Servo AF:* The camera continues to focus.
   - *AI Focus AF:* The camera can do both.

3. **If necessary, set AI Servo Characteristics.**

   If you chose AI Servo AF mode or are in AI Focus AF mode (which may engage AI Servo AF at any time), select (and optimize, if you want) a specific case that matches your subject as close as possible. The cases are as follows:

   - *Case 1:* Multipurpose
   - *Case 2:* Track subject and ignore obstacles
   - *Case 3:* Instantly focus on subjects when entering AF points
   - *Case 4:* Use for quickly accelerating/decelerating subjects
   - *Case 5:* Change direction erratically
   - *Case 6:* Change speed and direction erratically

   Although I have this step listed third, you can set the AI Servo Characteristics anytime before you start shooting.

4. **Choose an AF Area Selection mode.**

   Regardless of the AF mode you have chosen, you should choose an AF Area Selection mode. Your choice determines how the AF system looks for something to focus on.

   The selection modes are

   - *Single-Point Spot AF (Manual selection)*
   - *Single-Point AF (Manual selection)*
   - *AF Point Expansion (Manual selection)*
   - *AF Point Expansion (Manual selection, surrounding points)*
   - *Zone AF (Manual selection of zone)*
   - *61-Point Automatic Selection AF*

   You can group the modes into three categories. The first four fit into a single-point selection category. You select a single point and the camera uses it (or the points around it, in the case of expansion) to autofocus. Zone AF fits into its own category, as does 61-Point Automatic Selection. (See the upcoming section on choosing an AF area selection mode for more details.)

5. **If necessary, select an AF Area.**

   If you chose 61-Point Automatic Selection AF, ignore this step.

   Otherwise, select an AF point or zone.

So there you have it. The most complicated sequence is to select AF over MF, choose AI Servo AF, select an AI Servo AF case, configure it, set the AF Area Selection mode to something other than auto, and then select an AF point or zone.

You may need to return to any of these steps as you shoot to "rerack" your AF system. Be flexible. If something isn't working, analyze what the problem is and try to correct that first.

Selecting an AF Mode

Choosing the right AF mode depends on whether you need to continuously focus or not. It's that simple.

There are three AF modes. Two are diametric opposites, and the third combines features of the other two into a single mode:

- **One-Shot AF:** When you press the Shutter button halfway, the camera focuses once. Use for still subjects (you can't be moving, either).

  When the camera successfully focuses, it beeps, and the focus confirmation light comes on in the viewfinder and the AF point or points that achieved the focus are displayed (Chapter 3 illustrates this).

If the camera can't focus, the status indicator (see the small triangles beneath the focus confirmation light) blinks. Try again.

- **AI Servo AF:** When you press the Shutter button halfway, the camera focuses and then continues to focus as long as you hold the Shutter button halfway. Use when you're photographing moving subjects (or when you're moving around).

  Don't bother looking for the focus confirmation light when in AI Servo AF. It won't come on, even when the camera achieves focus.

- **AI Focus AF:** The camera initially focuses using One Shot AF. If the subject (or you) start moving, the camera will switch to AI Servo AF and track the target. Use when you are photographing a variety of subjects and don't want to continually switch modes yourself.

  If the camera is in AI Servo AF mode (after starting in AI Focus AF) when it achieves focus, you get a slight beep but no confirmation light.

To change AF modes, press the AF-Drive Mode button on top of the camera (see Figure 7-1) and cycle through the modes using the Main dial.

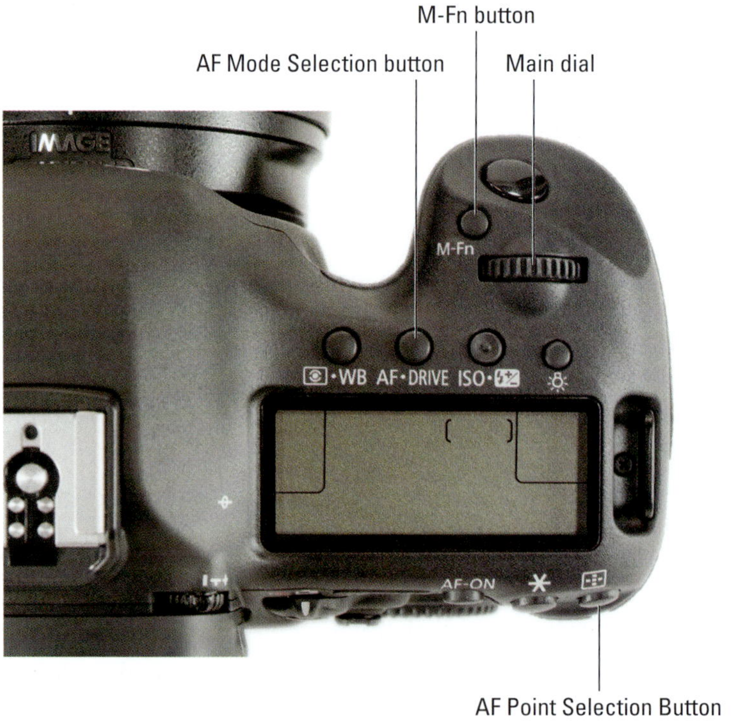

Figure 7-1: Important AF controls are located on the top-right of the camera.

You see the mode change on the top LCD panel, as shown in Figure 7-2.

You can also change modes using the Shooting Information (see Figure 7-3) and Quick Control screen.

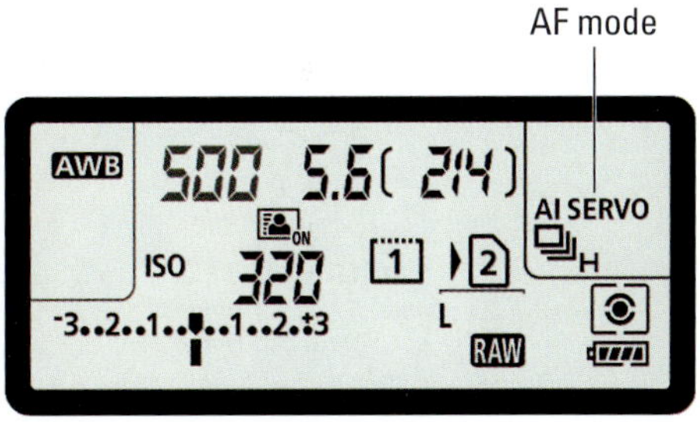

Figure 7-2: The LCD panel displays the focus mode.

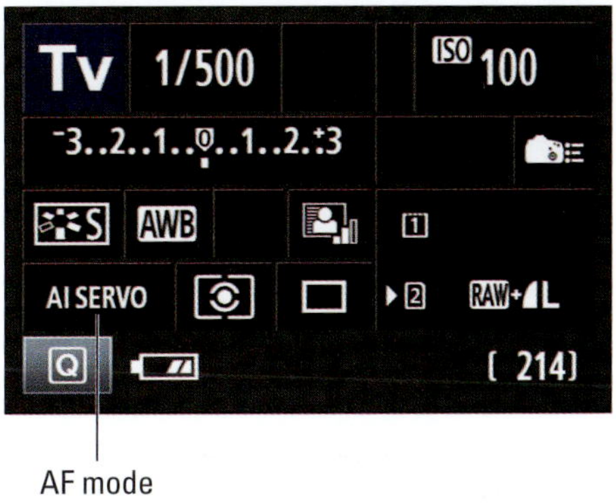

Figure 7-3: The displays on the back of the camera display the focus mode as well.

Choosing AI Servo AF Characteristics

Not all moving objects are the same. It makes sense, then, that some tricks for locking on and tracking one type of moving target might work for one object but not another. Canon has analyzed different types of movement and created six *cases* that you can choose from to govern how the AI Servo AF works.

Deciding on a case

There are six different AI Servo AF cases. They are organized into groups based on how closely you want to track the subject, how fast the subject accelerates or decelerates, and how fast the AF point should automatically switch to keep tracking it.

Here are the cases:

- **Case 1:** Case 1 is an all-purpose AI Servo AF setting. It tracks moving subjects in most situations. Change to another case when obstacles get in the way or when the subject's movement changes.

  Case 1 would be appropriate for this city bus (see Figure 7-4) I caught in action.

- **Case 2:** Think tennis or bowling, for example. When the player moves, with Case 2 the camera is less likely to focus on the wall behind or on the ball moving across the frame.

  Case 2 locks onto the subject, which makes it good for something like bowling (see Figure 7-5) so that the focus doesn't move to the back wall.

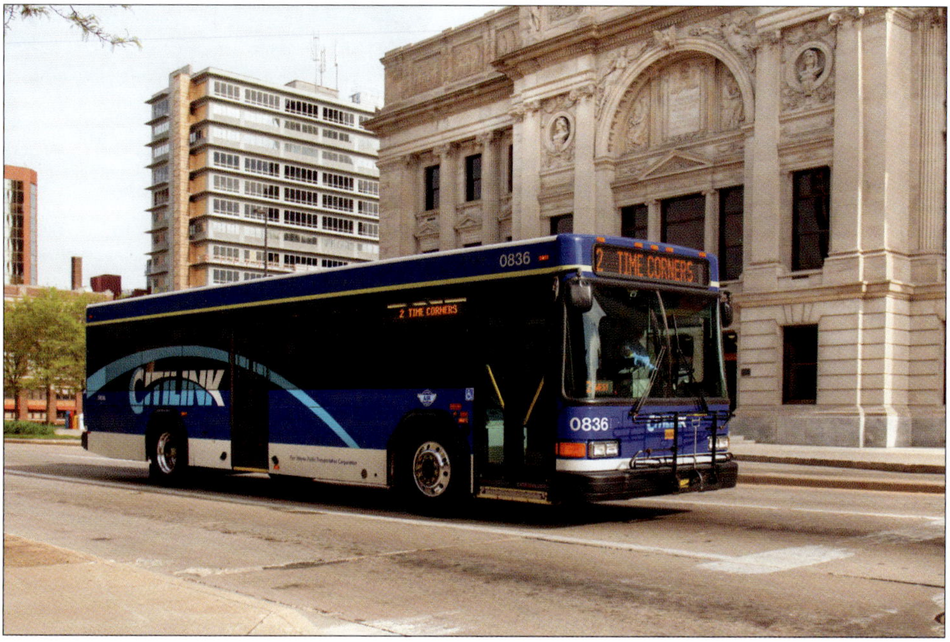

Figure 7-4: Capturing a moving bus with the all-purpose AI Servo AF case.

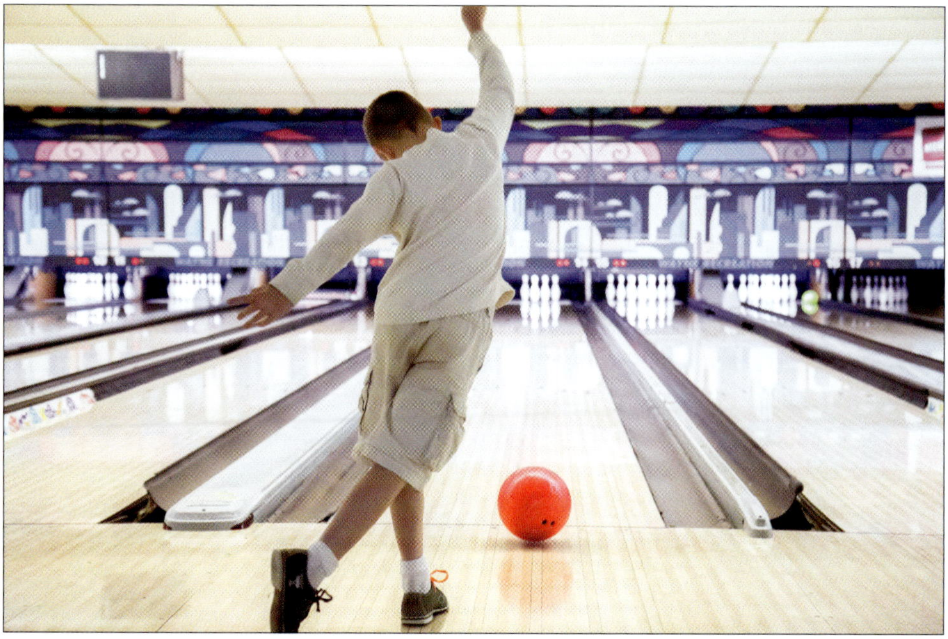

Figure 7-5: Locking on to the bowler.

- **Case 3:** Think cycling. When a rider suddenly enters the select AF point, the camera quickly focuses on them. It's easier to switch focus between participants using this case. Simply plop the AF area on top of the subject you want the camera to focus on.

  Figure 7-6 shows a boy riding toward me at breakneck speed. Normally, this scenario would be hard to track.

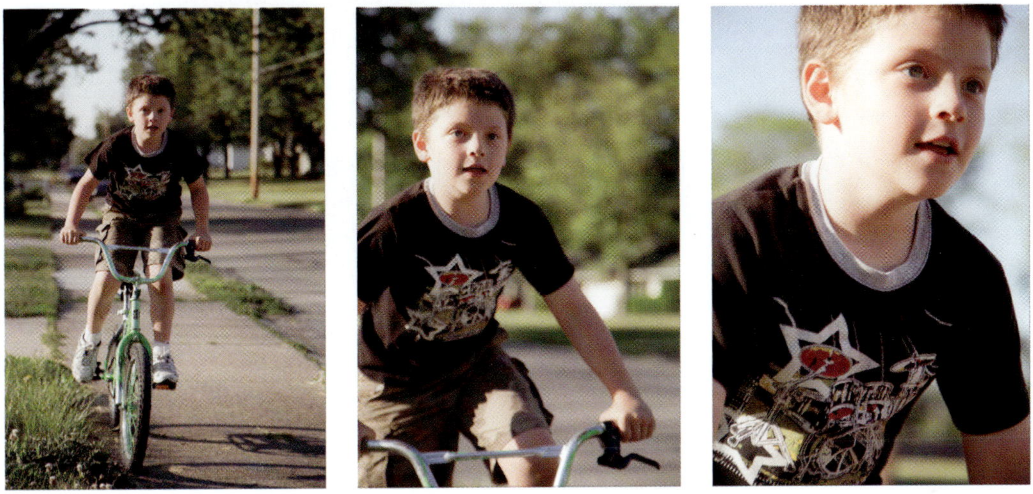

Figure 7-6: Tracking a bike rider.

- **Case 4:** In basketball, players run back and forth, quickly stopping and starting. Although Figure 7-7 doesn't show a basketball game, it illustrates a situation in which focus had to overcome and track a complete change of direction.
- **Case 5:** Figure skaters can quickly skate in new directions based on their routine. Case 5 is for movements that aren't as predictable as a line of cyclists. In Figure 7-8, I tracked a number of soaring buzzards. Their movement is remarkably skater-like.

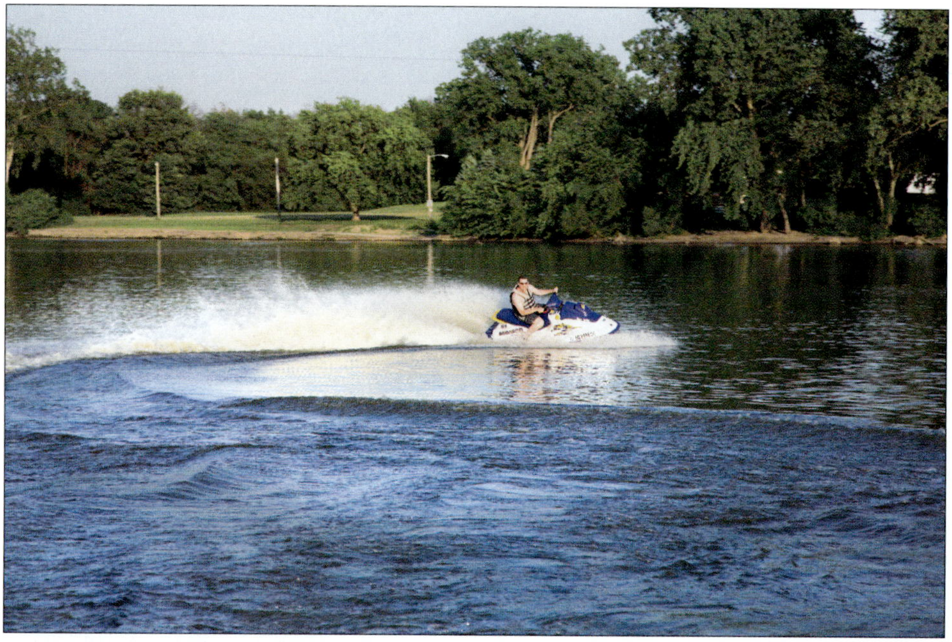

Figure 7-7: He's actually moving pretty fast.

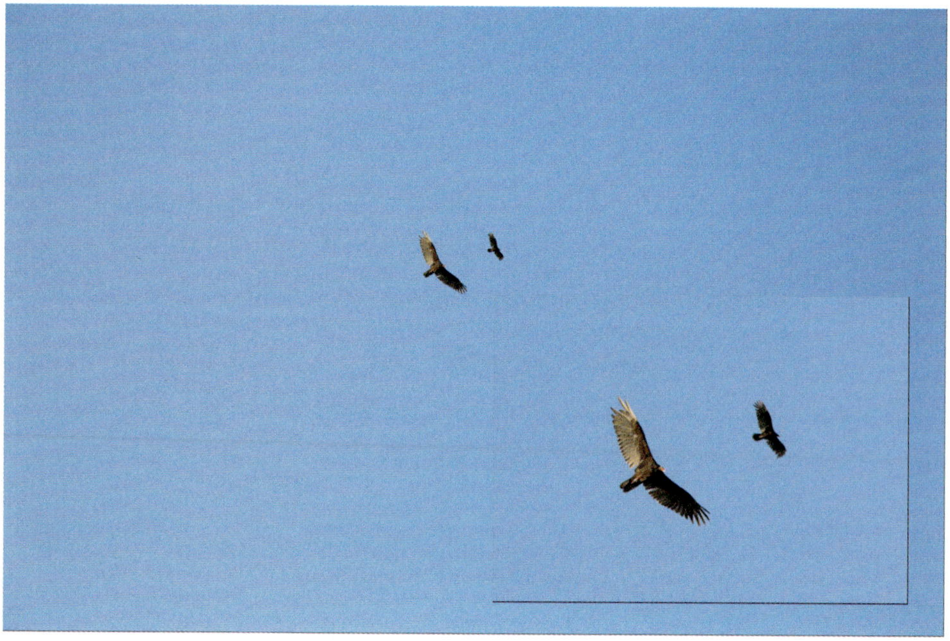

Figure 7-8: Soaring birds are fun to track.

- **Case 6:** Think UFOs. This case combines elements of Cases 4 and 5. The subject can quickly accelerate, decelerate, and change speed and direction erratically. Sounds like a close encounter to me.

  Finally, Figure 7-9 shows a girl leaping. I can't think of a better way to illustrate sudden changes of movement and direction than kids playing.

If you don't want to think in terms of sports or subjects, you can think in terms of the setting combinations that make each case different. Table 7-1 lists the default setting combinations by case. You can read about changing them in "Customizing the cases," later in this chapter.

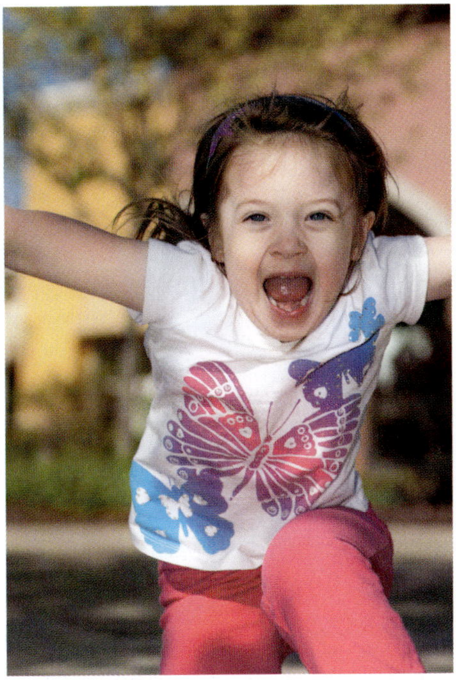

Figure 7-9: Boo!

Table 7-1 AI Servo AF Case Study

Case	*Tracking sensitivity*	*Accel/Decel Tracking*	*AF point auto switch*
1	Normal (0)	Steady (0)	Moderate (0)
2	Locked on (-1)	Steady (0)	Moderate (0)
3	Responsive (+1)	Sudden (+1)	Moderate (0)
4	Normal (0)	Sudden (+1)	Moderate (0)
5	Normal (0)	Steady (0)	Rapid (+1)
6	Normal (0)	Sudden (+1)	Rapid (+1)

Selecting an AI Servo AF case

To select an AI Servo AF case, press the Menu button and navigate to AF Menu 1. This entire page (see Figure 7-10) is devoted to the six cases. Use the Quick Control dial to highlight the case you want; then press the Set button to lock in your choice.

You have no other way to change the AI Servo case. You can't do it from the Quick Control screen or from any other button combination.

Customizing the cases

Each AI Servo AF case has three parameters that can be set to customize how the camera responds to movement, acceleration, and point switching:

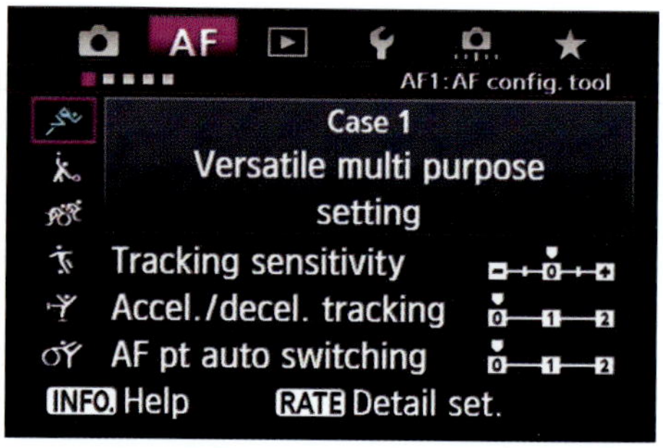

Figure 7-10: All six cases are on the first page of the AF menu.

- **Tracking Sensitivity:**
  Determines how tightly to lock onto a subject and resist changing the focus, even if something gets in the way or the subject moves out of the way (leaving the AF point empty and prone to focus on the background).

  The default is 0. Set to -2 to resist changing the focus. Set to +2 to be more responsive.

- **Acceleration/Deceleration Tracking:** Determines how steady the motion is. The default is 0. If the subject is prone to rapid acceleration or deceleration, set to +2.

- **AF Point Auto Switching:** Determines how quickly the camera will switch AF points (when set to anything but Single-Point AF or Single-Point Spot AF). The default is 0. Set to +1 or +2 to be able to handle erratic changes in direction.

To customize a case, follow these steps:

1. **Press the Menu button and navigate to AF Menu 1.**
2. **Highlight the case you want to modify; then press the Rate button.**

   You don't get to press Rate much. Make it count.

   The focus of attention switches to the settings, as shown in Figure 7-11.

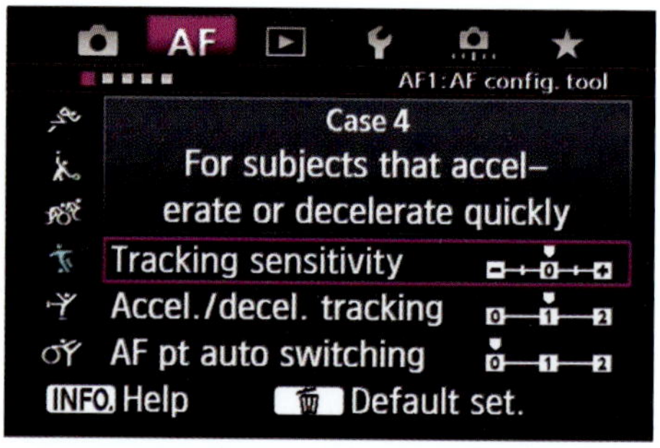

Figure 7-11: Look for the purple box, which highlights the active setting; press Info to edit.

3. **Use the Quick Control dial to highlight a setting; then press the Set button.**

4. **Use the Quick Control dial to change the setting, as shown in Figure 7-12.**

   The default setting is displayed as a faint marker. The new setting is shown with a bright white marker.

5. **Press the Set button to lock in the change.**
6. **Scroll to the other settings and change as desired.**
7. **When finished, press the Menu button.**

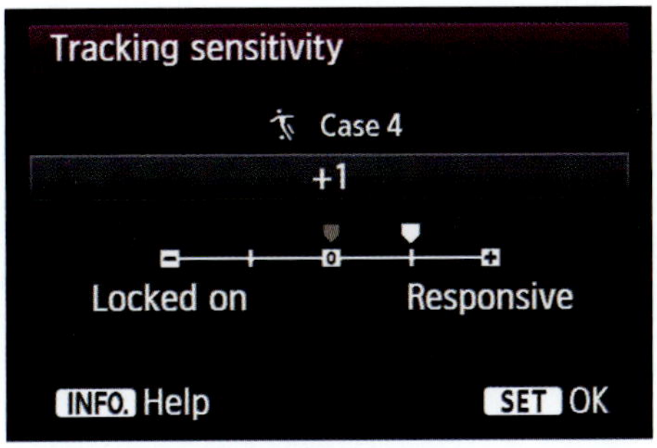

Figure 7-12: Being able to adjust these settings puts amazing flexibility at your fingertips.

TIP

You can't register the six cases to My Menu (see Chapter 11 for more information on My Menu). You can, however, register the three setting combinations: Tracking Sensitivity, Acceleration/Deceleration Tracking, and AF Point Auto Switching. Set My Menu to come up preselected (Display from My Menu), and you're set. You can quickly fine-tune the case you are using on the fly.

Choosing an AF Area Selection Mode

Right. It gets complicateder and complicateder. Seems like you're on Step 15 right now, doesn't it? If necessary, go back and review the first section in this chapter to see where selecting an AF Area Selection mode (but not the points themselves; that's next) fits in.

Deciding on a selection mode

The AF Area Selection modes have different characteristics from one another, as described in this section. Cross-reference those qualities with the type of photography you are shooting, as well as the possible motion of your subject, to choose the best mode to run with. Here are the six modes:

- **Single-Point Spot AF (Manual selection):** Single-Point Spot AF mode focuses using the inner element of a single AF point that you choose. Figure 7-13 shows this mode with the center AF point selected. The red area is where the focus is aimed. This mode has the most precision. Use it to focus on eyes or other small features of your subject. This mode works best for still subjects using One-Shot AF.

- **Single-Point AF (Manual selection):** Similar to the Single-Point Spot AF mode, but without the ultra precision. You select a single point, but instead of using a very small square as the AF point, a larger square is used as the AF point. Figure 7-14 shows this mode with the center AF point selected (compare the size of this point with that shown in Figure 7-13). This mode also works best for still subjects using One-Shot AF but can be used in AI Servo AF for easier-to-track subjects.

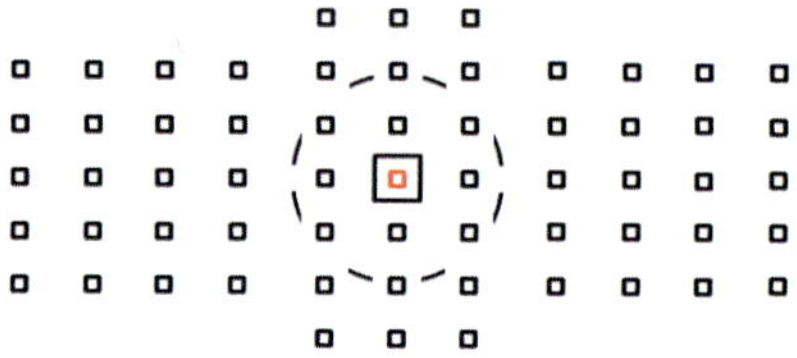

Figure 7-13: Single-Point Spot AF.

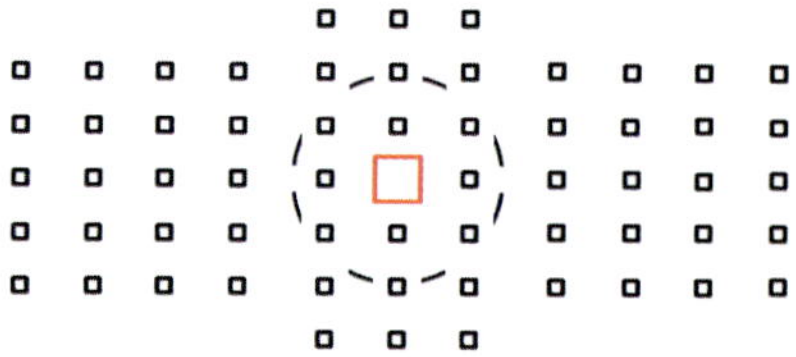

Figure 7-14: Single-point AF.

- **AF Point Expansion (Manual selection):** The first AF Point Expansion mode uses the AF point you select and the four points around it (up, down, left, and right). In Figure 7-15, the center point is selected. This mode is good for tracking moving subjects in AI Servo AF mode.

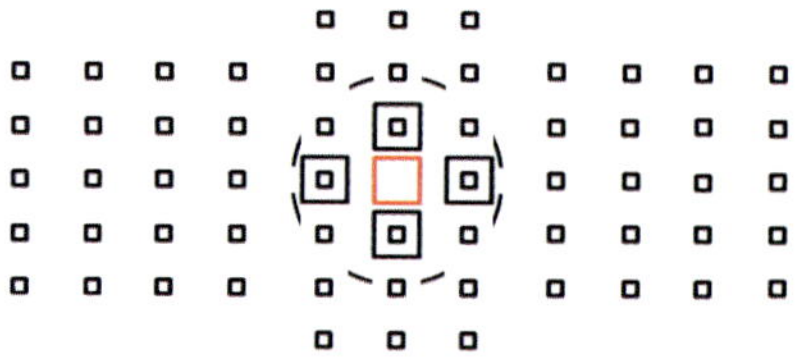

Figure 7-15: AF point expansion (four areas).

- **AF Point Expansion (Manual selection, surrounding points):** Another point expansion mode. This time, you get all eight surrounding points: up, down, left, right, and all the diagonals. Use this mode when you need more points to track the target, but realize that it is more susceptible to focus on other objects that stray into expanded AF points. Figure 7-16 shows this mode with all nine points displayed. The center point is in red.

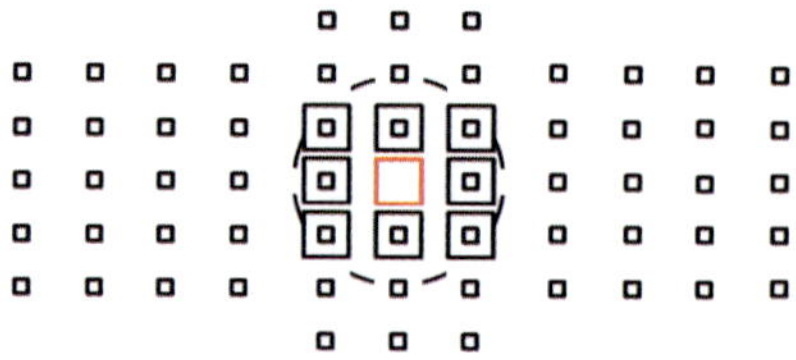

Figure 7-16: AF Point Expansion (eight points).

- **Zone AF (Manual selection of zone):** With Zone AF mode, the AF points are divided into nine zones. Each is three AF points high and either three (in the center) or four points (on the sides) wide. This mode is even better at tracking moving targets and getting that first focus lock-on. Again, though, because it uses more AF points, you could be locking on to the wrong thing. This mode is shown in Figure 7-17.

Figure 7-17: Zone AF.

- **61-Point Automatic Selection AF:** This is the ultimate automatic tracking mode. In One-Shot AF, you don't need to do a thing. The viewfinder begins with no AF points visible, as shown in the first image of Figure 7-18. The camera the AF points used to focus in the viewfinder. When shooting in AI Servo AF, however, you should manually select a single AF point (shown in red in the second image of Figure 7-18). The camera starts at the point you have identified and then selects the best AF points.

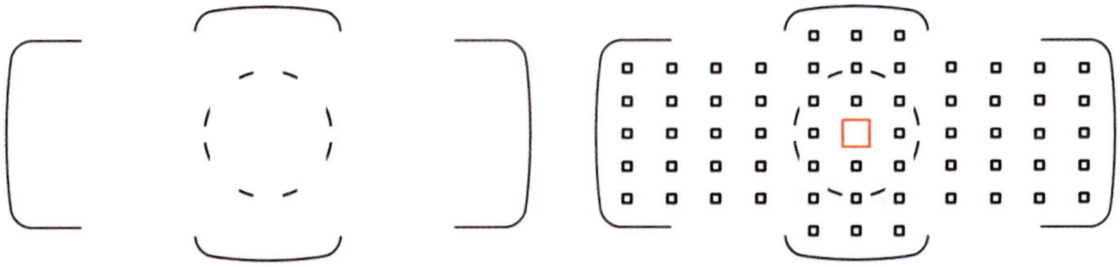

Figure 7-18: 61-Point Automatic Selection AF.

Choosing a selection mode

Choosing an AF Area Selection mode is easier than it sounds. To choose an AF Area Selection mode, follow these steps:

1. **Press the AF Point Selection button (refer to Figure 7-1).**
2. **Cycle though the modes by pressing the M-Fn button (also shown in Figure 7-1).**

   You should look through the viewfinder to see the modes as they are displayed unless you are shooting in Live View and using Quick mode. In that case, the modes are displayed on the monitor. (See Chapter 3 for more information on using Quick mode and shooting with Live View.)

   The AF points are highlighted in red in the viewfinder so that you can see them easier.

Unfortunately, you have to know the mode types to understand what you're doing. You have no other way to definitively tell what mode you have selected. See Figures 7-13 through 7-18 to review what the modes look like.

When you see the mode you want to use, stop pressing the M-Fn button.

To make things go faster, limit the number of AF selection modes that are available to you. Go to AF Menu 4, then choose the Select AF Area Selection Mode option.

3. **Select an AF point, if necessary.**

   I cover selecting an AF point in the next section.

Selecting Focus Points

Selecting a specific focus point is an important part of making the AF system work for you. You learn about the types of AF points the 5D Mark III has in this section, as well as how to choose a selection mode and AF points, if necessary.

About sensors and AF points

The newly designed 5D Mark III AF system is called a 61-Point High Density Reticular AF. It promises to capture fast-moving subjects dependably and accurately, far better than other AF systems. The 61 AF points have been concentrated in the middle of the frame, as opposed to being scattered all over. This concentration results in a high degree of precision and the ability to closely track moving subjects. The system also has 41 cross-type AF points, which improve accuracy and impart an ability to predict where the subject is going.

Although the AF points look the same in the viewfinder, the 5D Mark III has three different types of AF points, based on the sensor type and orientation at each position. They are

- **Linear pattern:** Linear pattern AF points are oriented either vertically or horizontally. They're most effective at detecting lines that cross their orientation. (A horizontally oriented sensor is adept at detecting vertical lines.) Every AF point in the 5D Mark III has at least one vertical focusing AF pattern point.
- **Cross-type pattern:** Cross pattern AF points are essentially two linear pattern sensors placed at the same spot, oriented at a 90-degree angle

to each other. One is horizontal and the other is vertical. Because they cover both directions, cross-type points are much better at detecting the details that make autofocus possible.

- **Dual cross-type pattern:** As you might imagine, dual cross-type pattern AF points have two sets of cross sensors oriented at an angle to each other, for a total of four linear sensors at each AF point location. You might call this overkill, if there were such a thing.

The 5D Mark III's AF sensor types are based on the aperture they were designed to work at, as follows:

- **f/2.8:** The highest precision sensor on the camera. Reserved for the dual cross-type AF points, which are oriented horizontally, vertically, and at angles.
- **f/4:** Also high-precision, but not as capable as the f/2.8 variety. These are oriented horizontally on the 5D Mark III.
- **f/5.6 horizontal:** Similar to the f/4 sensor in that they are horizontal, but more lenses can use them.
- **f/5.6 vertical:** f/5.6 horizontal sensors placed vertically. Every AF point on the camera has an f/5.6 vertical sensor.

When you combine these elements, you get four different types of AF points, as shown in this list:

- **Purple:** Dual cross-type point, comprised of f/2.8 diagonals and f/5.6 vertical and horizontal sensors.
- **Orange:** Cross-type, made of f/5.6 vertical and horizontal sensors.
- **Blue:** Cross-type, containing an f/4 horizontal and an f/5.6 vertical sensor.
- **Green:** Linear type (vertical), containing a single f/5.6 vertical sensor. This type of AF area blinks in the viewfinder when you are selecting an AF area (details on this later in this chapter, in "Selecting AF points"). The colors in the preceding list correspond to the AF areas in Figures 7-19 to 7-26. You'll need that information to decode the AF points for each group.

REMEMBER

The point of this section (you knew there had to be one) is that you should use your most capable sensor to do the heavy lifting. Try to use the dual cross-type AF points for the most precise focusing. They can detect and focus on lines much more reliably than, say, a single f/5.6 vertical sensor AF point.

Grouping lenses by AF points

The number of AF points you have at your disposal depends on the lens you have attached to your 5D Mark III. For organization's sake, Canon has segregated lenses into eight groups, named from A to H:

- **Group A:** This group has many L-series lenses. These lenses all have maximum apertures of f/2.8 or under.

  All 61 points are available. Five are precision dual cross (purples). The center columns in the outer banks (blue) combine f/4 horizontal and f/5.6 vertical AF patterns. The non-dual cross-type AF points in the center bank (orange) are cross-type f/5.6 vertical and horizontal patterns. The remainder (green) are f/5.6 vertical pattern points. See Figure 7-19.

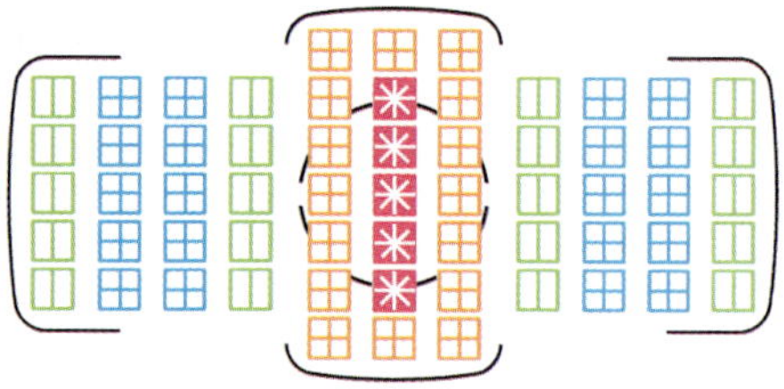

Figure 7-19: Group A has the most power.

- **Group B:** Group B consists of a handful of L-series lenses, with a few others thrown in for good measure. All have maximum apertures of f/2.8 or under.

  All 61 points are available. The only difference between Group B and Group A is that Group B has a single dual cross-type pattern AF area in the center (purple), as opposed to five dual cross-type pattern AF areas. The other dual cross-type pattern areas change to cross-type f/5.6 horizontal and vertical pattern (orange). See Figure 7-20.

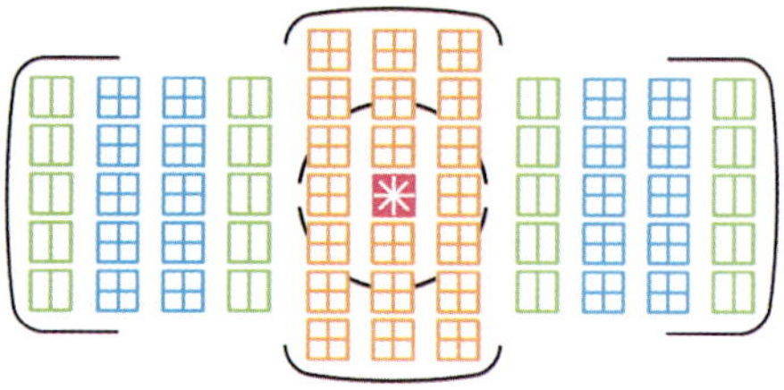

Figure 7-20: Group B is almost as effective as Group A.

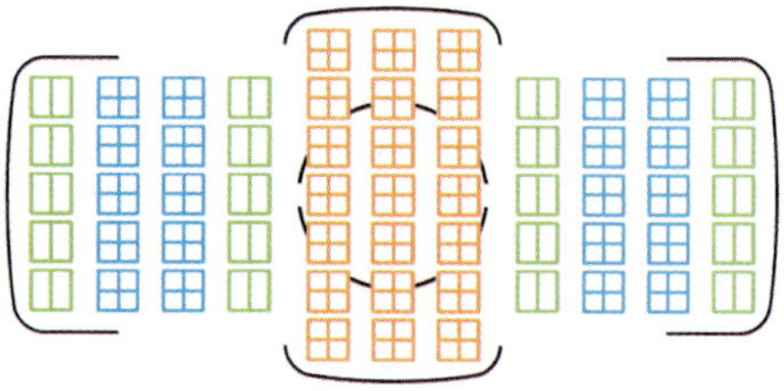

Figure 7-21: Group C has no dual cross-type areas.

- **Group C:** Group C has a mixture of L-series lenses and a few non L-series lenses whose maximum apertures are between f/4 and f/2.8 Now extenders come into the fray. Many Group A lenses with maximum apertures of f/2.8 or under fit into Group C when used with an extender.

  All 61 points are available. Group C differs from Group B in that the single dual cross-type pattern in the center changes to a cross-type f/5.6 horizontal and vertical pattern (orange). See Figure 7-21.

- **Group D:** Group D consists of a single lens at the moment, the EF28mm f/2.8.

  All 61 points are available. Group D is similar to Group B in the center of the viewfinder, but there are more simple f/5.6 vertical pattern AF points (green) in the outer banks. See Figure 7-22.

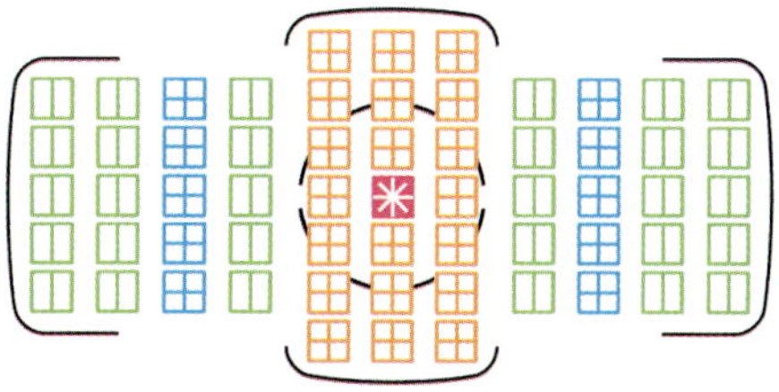

Figure 7-22: This is Group D.

- **Group E:** Group E has mostly non L-series lenses with maximum apertures between f/3.5 and f/5.6. Included are lenses with larger maximum apertures when used with extenders.

  All 61 points are available. Group E only has two types of AF points. Those in the center group are all cross-type f/5.6 horizontal and vertical pattern (orange). Those in the outer groups are f/5.6 vertical pattern AF points (green). See Figure 7-23.

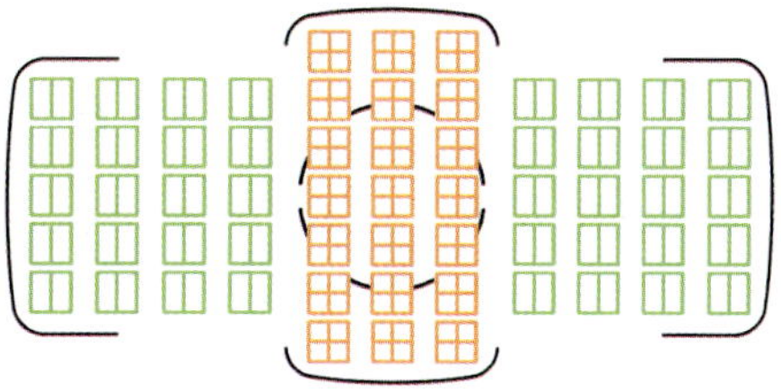

Figure 7-23: Group E has two types of AF areas.

- **Group F:** Group F consists of mostly non L-series zoom lenses with maximum apertures between f/3.5 and f/5.6. You start losing AF points at this stage. Group F has only 47. They are the same type as Group E, but this group has fewer of them. See Figure 7-24.

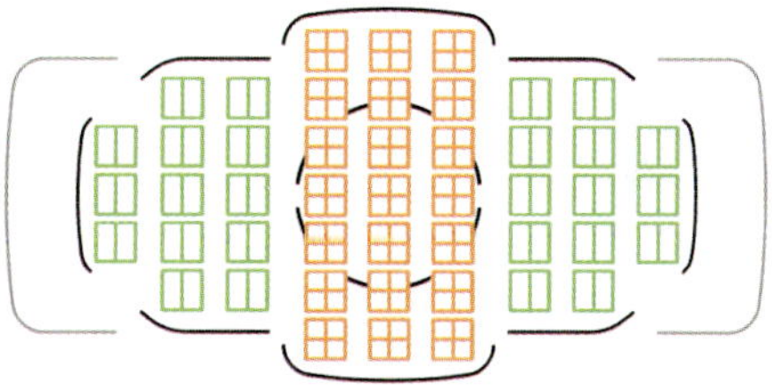

Figure 7-24: The numbers shrink starting with Group F.

- **Group G:** Group G consists of the 180mm macro lens, the 180mm macro lens with the 1.4 teleconverter, and a super-duper-ooper-schmooper 1200mm beast.

  Group G has 33 AF points. They are the same type as Group F, but there are fewer points in this group. See Figure 7-25.

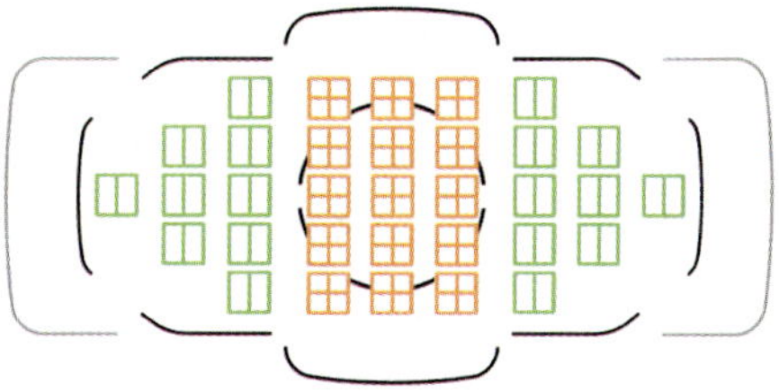

Figure 7-25: Further in Group G.

- **Group H:** Last, but not least, Group H has two lenses: both EF35-105mm f/4-f/5.6 (one has USM).

  Group H has a single cross-type f/5.6 horizontal and vertical pattern (orange) AF point in the center. See Figure 7-26.

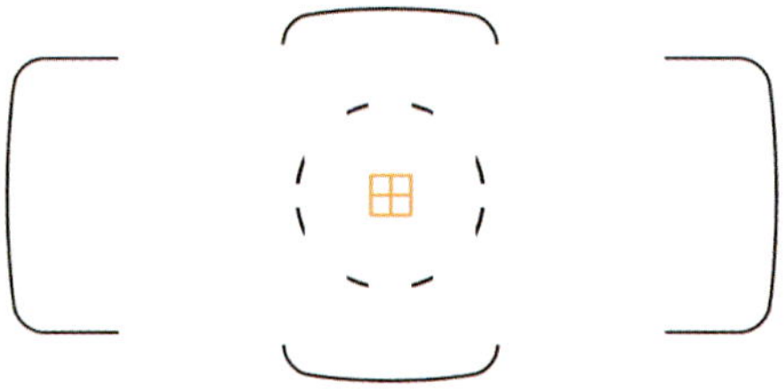

Figure 7-26: It's barebones for Group H.

TIP

To find out which group your lens belongs to, please consult the 5D Mark III manual.

Table 7-2 summarizes the number of points in each group and their type.

Table 7-2 AF Point Types by Group

Group	*Total AF Points*	*Dual Cross*	*Cross*	*Horizontal*
A	61	5	36	20
B	61	1	40	20
C	61	0	41	20
D	61	1	30	30
E	61	0	21	40
F	47	0	21	26
G	33	0	15	18
H	1	0	1	0

Selecting AF points

Here , finally, is the section on selecting AF points. Selecting these is actually easy when you know what you're doing.

1. **Select an AF Area Selection mode, if necessary.**

   See the steps in the "Choosing a selection mode" section, earlier in this chapter, for how to do this. To recap, press the AF Point Selection button and then press the M-Fn button to cycle through the modes.

   If you don't need to change the mode, simply press the AF Point Selection button (see Figure 7-27) and continue to the next step.

2. **Use the dials or Multicontroller to select the AF point.**

   The dials are actually pretty cool. Rotate the Main dial to move the AF area left or right. Rotate the Quick Control dial to move the AF point up or down.

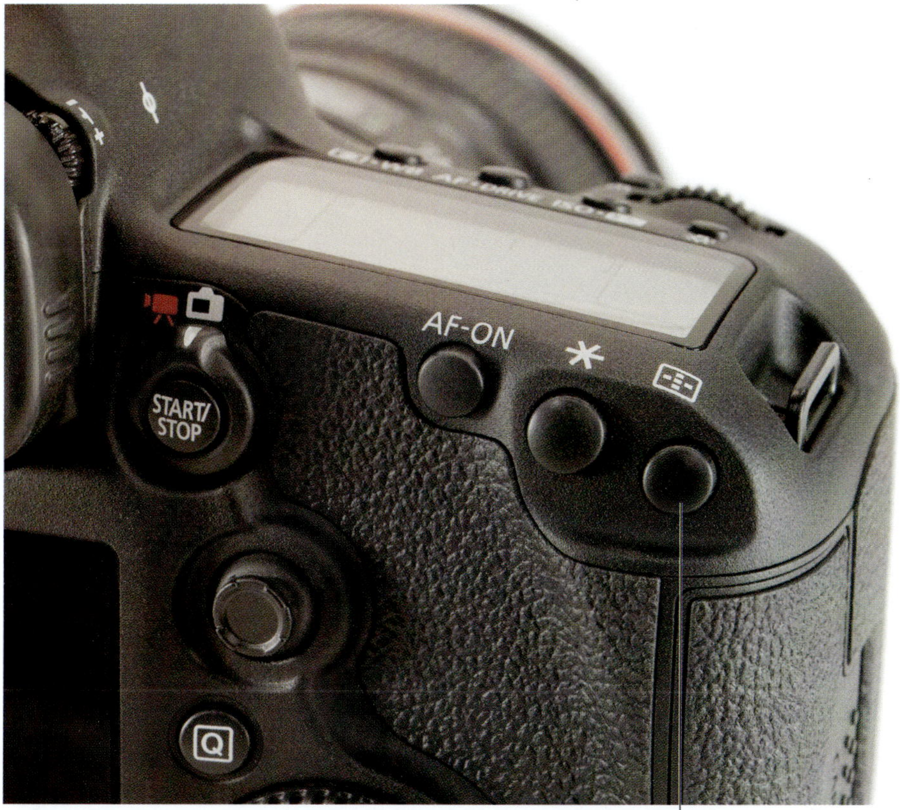

Figure 7-27: Press the AF Point Selection button to begin selecting AF points.

With a bit of practice, you can move the selected AF point around the viewfinder very quickly.

Or, use the Multicontroller to move the point around the viewfinder.

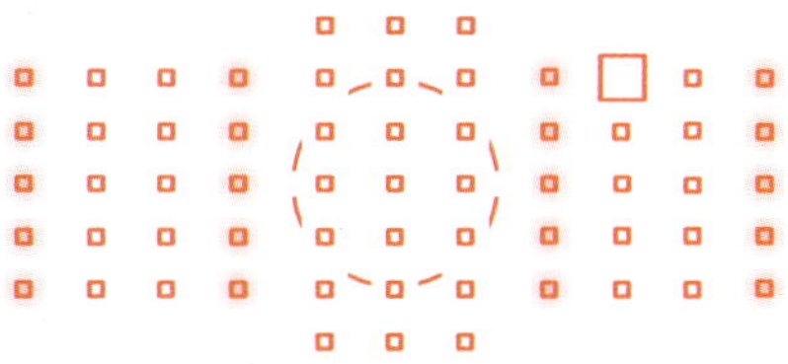

Figure 7-28: In this case (Single-point AF), the selected point is displayed as a large AF area.

The AF point you have selected is shown in the viewfinder, as in Figure 7-28. Those AF areas with a hint of shading in the figure blink in the viewfinder. In this case, the blinking areas are composed solely of f/5.6 vertical focusing sensors.

3. **Press the Shutter button halfway to focus.**

Using the AF-ON Button

If you're nervous about pressing the shutter halfway for fear that you'll accidentally take a photo (or several, if you're in High-Speed Continuous Drive mode), try the AF-ON button. (I use it all the time in the studio when I'm working with the camera on a tripod and need to quickly focus and meter without rattling one or more shots off.)

This button (see Figure 7-29) is located on the back of the camera, within easy reach of your right thumb when you're holding the camera and preparing to take photos. Simply press AF-ON to activate autofocus and have the camera meter the scene and set the exposure.

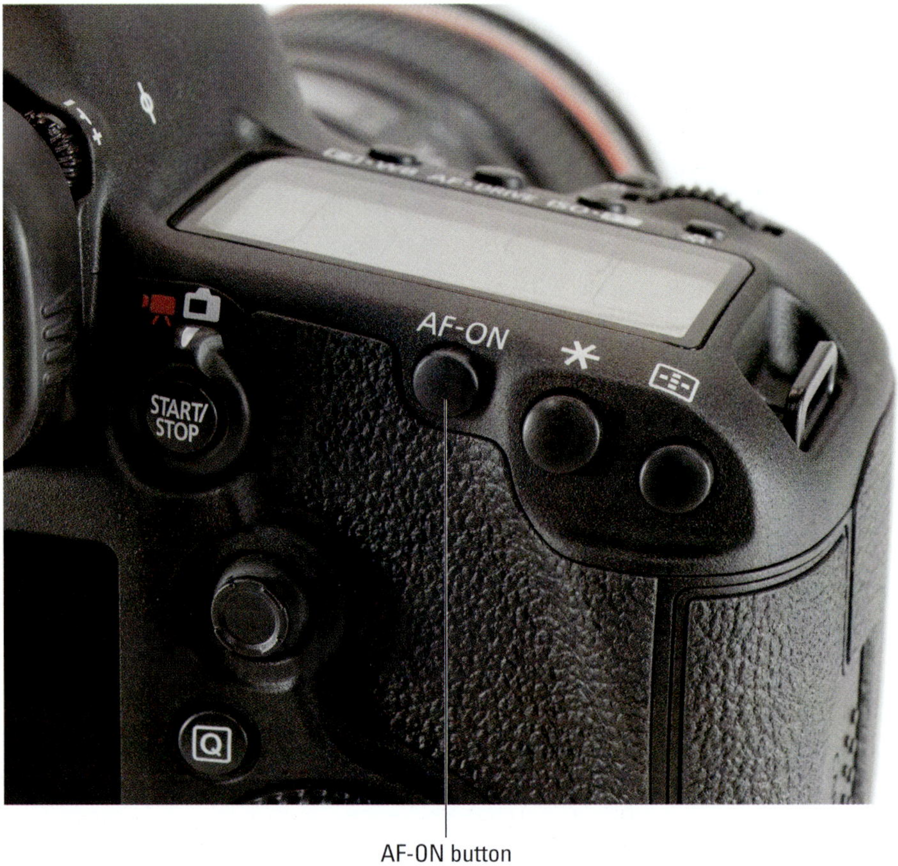

Figure 7-29: Use AF-ON to focus and meter without accidentally taking a photo.

This is a handy button, especially if you're using the Main dial to change exposure settings and you can't keep your index finger perfectly calibrated to press the Shutter button only halfway. Go ahead and press the AF-ON button for all you're worth, but your camera will never accidentally take a photo when you have the Shutter button pressed halfway.

Customizing AF

This section is a decidedly reference-ish look at the AF options in the menu. I don't explain it all in detail. However, I want to give you some inkling as to how much you can configure the AF system (as if it weren't obvious already) to match your style.

- **AF1 (AF configuration tool):** This menu has six cases for AI Servo AF. Each has different tracking and AF area sensitivities. These options are covered in this chapter.
- **AF2 (AI Servo):** The AI Servo menu has options that determine how the shutter is released for the first and subsequent photos. Both are covered in Chapter 11.
- **AF3 (One-Shot):** These options are related to One-Shot AF:
  - *USM Lens Electronic MF:* This option, covered in Chapter 11, enables you to choose how and when to enable the electronic focusing ring when in One Shot AF mode.
  - *AF-Assist Beam Firing:* Enables or disables the Speedlite AF-Assist beam if you have an external flash mounted to the camera.
  - *One-Shot AF Release Priority:* Enables you to set the priority for taking the photo when in One-Shot AF; that is, whether to favor taking the photo or getting the focus perfect.
- **AF4:** These options are related to different aspects of AF.
  - *Lens Drive when AF Impossible:* Tells the camera to stop trying to endlessly focus if it can't get it right the first time around. You should turn this option off when working with a telephoto lens.
  - *Selectable AF Point:* Enables you to change the number of manually selectable AF points (see Figure 7-30). Limiting the number you can use

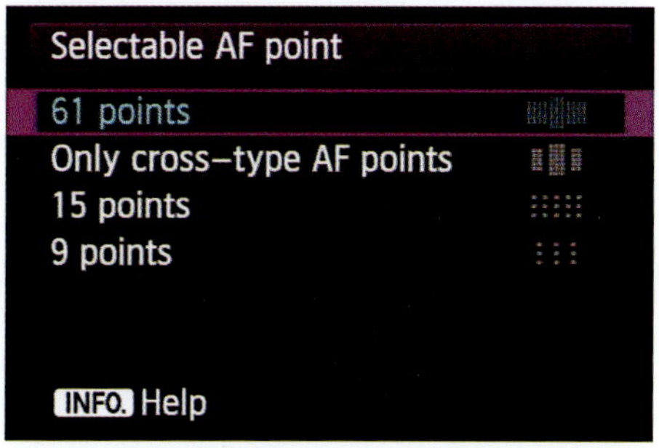

Figure 7-30: Customize how many AF points you can select.

can speed things up when you're frantically trying to set an AF point.

- *Select AF Area Selection Mode:* This option sets the type of AF Area Selection modes you have to cycle through when trying to set one. Toggle the ones you don't want to wade through, as shown in Figure 7-31.

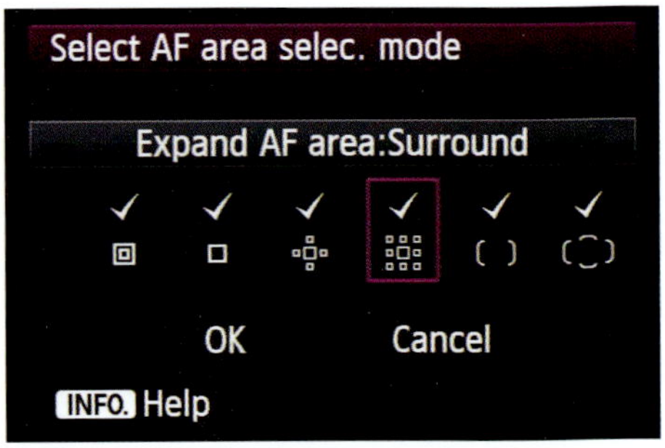

Figure 7-31: Customize which AF Area Selection modes you can select.

- *AF Area Selection Method:* This option changes the buttons you have to press to select an AF Area Selection method. The default is AF Point Selection button and then M-Fn. The other option uses the Main dial instead of the M-Fn button.
- *Orientation Linked AF Point:* By default, AF areas don't change based on how you hold the camera. In other words, when you select an AF point, it stays in place when you rotate the camera. If you like, you can enable Select Separate AF points, which separates selected AF areas by orientation. For instance, if you have a point selected on the far right of the viewfinder when holding the camera horizontally, you can have a different point selected (and in memory) for when you hold the camera vertically. The camera automatically switches. This is a pretty neat option.

- **AF5:** Another grab-bag of AF options.
  - *Manual AF Point Selection Pattern:* By default, you are stopped at the edge of the viewfinder when manually selecting an AF point. If you like, you can change that behavior so that you continuously scroll.
  - *AF Point Display during Focus:* This option enables you to configure what AF points are displayed when autofocusing. See Figure 7-32 for the different settings.

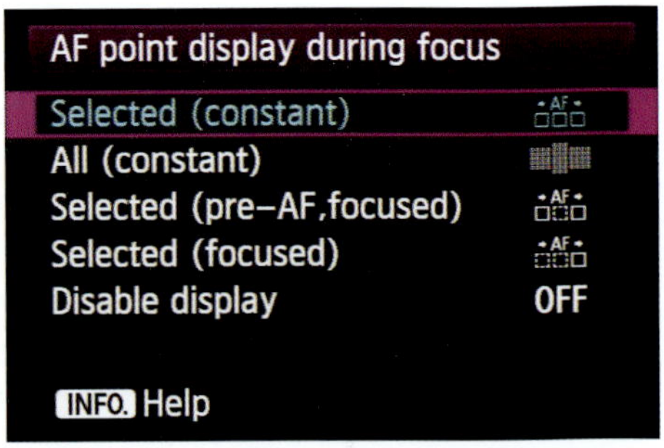

Figure 7-32: Customize what AF points are displayed when you are focusing.

- *VF Display Illumination:* Control whether the AF points light up in red at times.
- *AF Microadjustment:* This option, which enables you to adjust the camera's focus as a whole or by lens, is briefly covered in Chapter 11.

You have other ways to customize AF operation, namely by using Custom Controls (see Chapter 10).

Controlling Depth of Field

Depth of field is a mysterious name that refers to a straightforward photographic effect. The term refers to the depth of the area that looks like it's in focus. Depth of field is an astounding, important creative component of photography. On one hand, you can have the camera take photos in which almost everything looks like it's in focus. Landscapes are a good example. On the other hand, you can take pictures in which only a thin slice of the photo is sharp. Portraits and close-ups are good examples. Everything in front of and behind what you've focused on gets blurred — but it's not a *bad* out of focus. Depending on the lens, this area (called the *bokeh*) can be incredibly beautiful.

- **With a shallow (small) depth of field:** Only your subject and objects very close to it are sharp. Objects at a distance from the subject are blurry.
- **With a large depth of field:** The zone of sharp focus extends to include distant objects.

Figures 7-33 through 7-35 illustrate not only how thin you can make the depth of field but also the fact that you can move it back and forth.

- In Figure 7-33, the focus is on the black-and-white cat. The wooden cat to the right isn't that far away, but it's out of the depth of field. Still, you can make out some details of the wooden cat. The elephant in the background is almost unrecognizable.
- In Figure 7-34, the focus is on the wooden cat. The black-and-white cat is now partially blurred. Remember, something can be *in front of* your prime subject and be out of the depth of field. The elephant looks like an elephant now.
- In Figure 7-35, the elephant looks clear but the cats are blurred. Depth of field powerfully directs your attention.

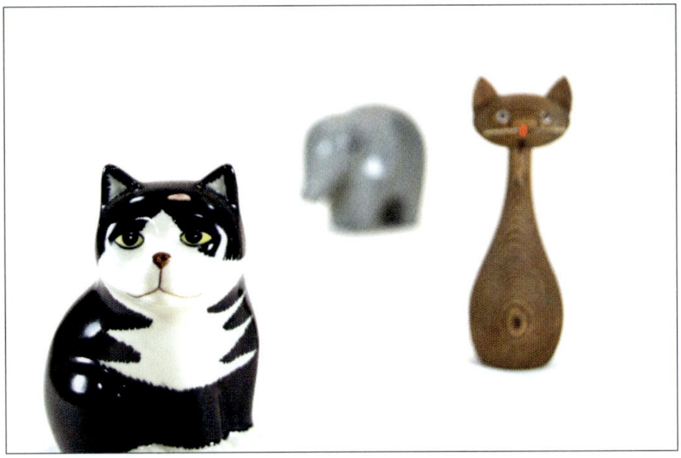

Figure 7-33: Focusing on the nearest object.

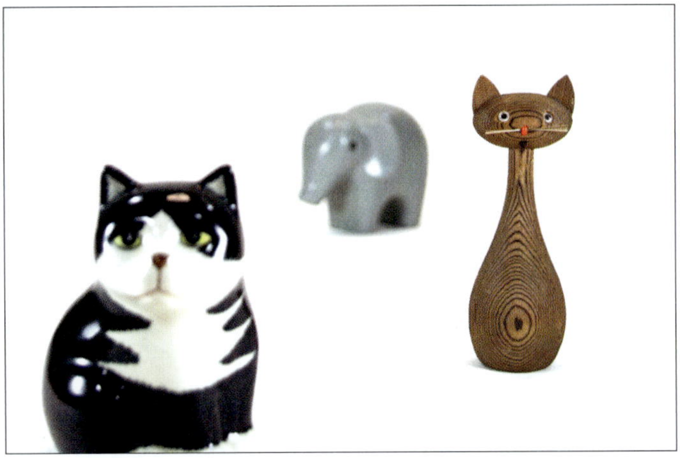

Figure 7-34: The depth of field is about a single cat wide.

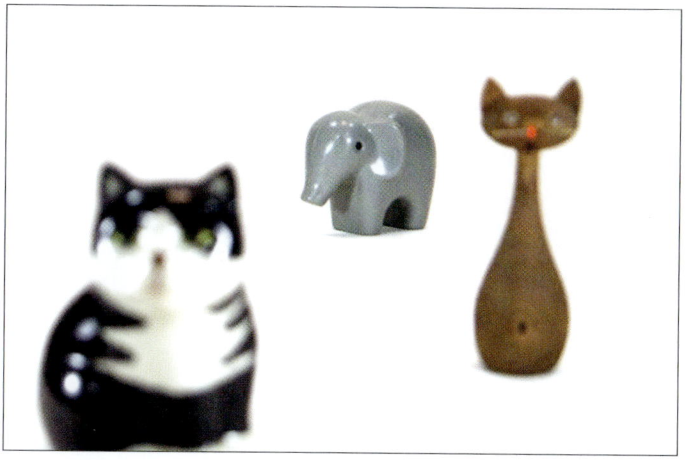

Figure 7-35: Managing the depth of field by focusing on the farthest object.

Controlling depth of field

So how do you adjust depth of field? You have these three points of control:

- **Aperture:** Very simply, the larger the aperture in the lens, the shallower the depth of field will be. Conversely, the smaller the aperture, the deeper the depth of field will be.

  Set the camera to Av mode and dial in the aperture that creates the depth of field you want.

- **Focal length:** The longer the focal length, the shallower the depth of field. By comparison, shorter focal lengths create wider depths of field.

  If you're shooting portraits, don't use a wide-angle lens if you want shallow depths of field. By the same token, wide-angle lenses work well for landscapes and help produce vast depths of field.

- **Distance:** Distance is the factor that everyone forgets about. When you're close to the subject, the depth of field is smaller than when you are far away.

Working with depth of field

Here are some pointers for working with depth of field:

- **Use Av or manual mode:** Choose Manual or Aperture Priority modes to gain maximum control over the depth of field.
- **Use Program Shift:** If you're in P mode and want a shallower depth of field, rotate the Main dial and choose an aperture-shutter speed combination with a larger aperture.
- **Shutter speed:** If you adjust aperture to affect depth of field, be sure to always keep an eye on shutter speed as well. To maintain the same exposure, shutter speed must change in tandem with aperture, and you may encounter a situation in which the shutter speed is too slow to permit holding a camera by hand. Lenses that offer optical image stabilization enable most people to manually hold the camera at slower shutter speeds than nonstabilized lenses permit, but double-check your results. You can also consider raising the ISO setting to make the image sensor more sensitive to light, but remember that higher ISO settings can produce noise. (Chapter 6 has details on ISO and noise.)
- **Depth of field preview:** Not sure which aperture setting you need to produce the depth of field you want? Good news: Your camera offers *depth of field preview,* which enables you to see in advance how the aperture affects the focus zone. Details on how to use this feature appear in the next section, "Checking depth of field."
- **Shallow and artistic:** In manual or Av modes, open the aperture (use a low f-number) and let the camera set the shutter speed and ISO. Step close and zoom in to the subject to make the depth of field even shallower.
- **Go deep:** In Manual or Av modes, close the aperture down (to between f/8 and f/22). Use a wider-angle lens (35mm or less) and step back from the subject.

Checking depth of field

When you look through your viewfinder and press the Shutter button halfway, you can see only a partial indication of the depth of field that your current camera settings will produce. You can see the effect of focal length and the camera-to-subject distance, but because the aperture doesn't actually stop-down to the selected aperture until you take the picture, the viewfinder doesn't show you how that setting will affect depth of field.

The Depth-of-Field Preview button, however, does enable you to preview the depth of field, including how the aperture will affect it, before you take the photo. The button, labeled in Figure 7-36, is on the front of the camera. Reach around with your right ring finger or pinky to press it after you have focused.

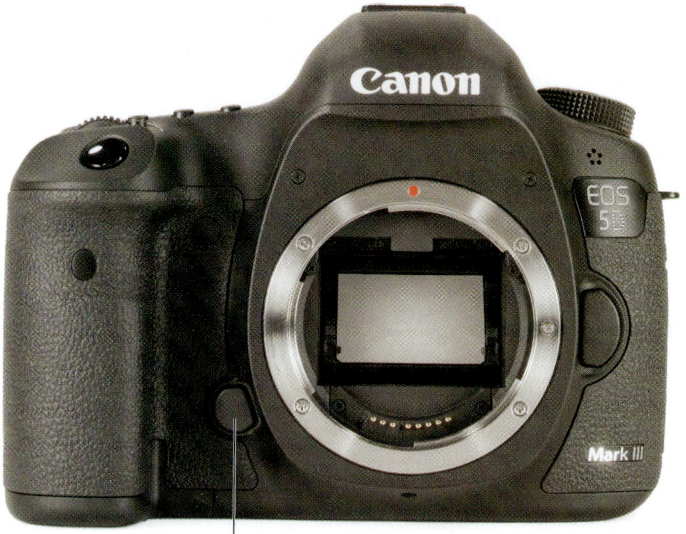

Figure 7-36: Press here to preview the depth of field.

REMEMBER

Checking the depth of field is most effective when the aperture is set smaller than the maximum aperture of the lens. This is because the camera meters and focuses at the lens' maximum aperture. In effect, maximum-aperture preview is *always on*. When you have the lens set to a smaller aperture and press the Depth-of-Field Preview button, the lens quickly stops down for the preview. If you're quiet, you can hear it.

8

Designing with White Balance, Color, and Style

In This Chapter

- Understanding white balance
- Setting the white balance
- Creating a custom white balance
- Deciding on a color space
- Using Picture Styles

Photography is a whole lot of fun for so many different reasons. This chapter dives into the topic of color, explaining such concepts as *white balance* (a feature that compensates for the varying color casts created by different light sources) and *color space* (an option that determines how the colors in your photos should be rendered). I conclude with a discussion of Picture Styles, which are processing options built right into the camera.

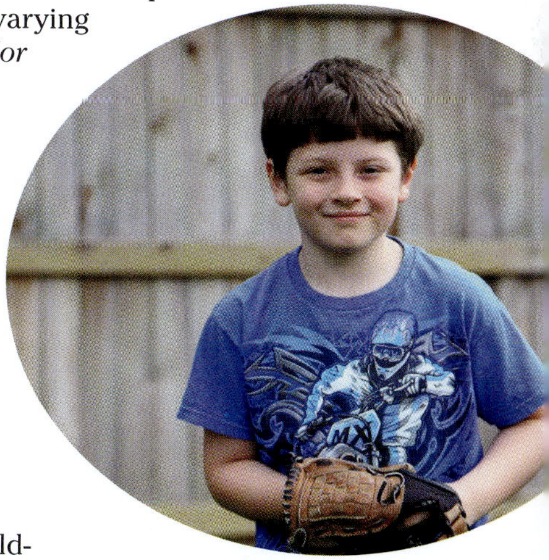

That's a lot. It's important. When you begin to fine-tune your photos by paying attention to white balance, you have expanded your horizons as a photographer. That's a good thing!

Shedding Light on White Balance

Every light source emits a particular color cast. The old-fashioned fluorescent lights found in most public restrooms, for example, put out a bluish-green light, which is why our reflections in the mirrors in those restrooms always look so sickly. And if you think that your beloved looks especially attractive by candlelight, you aren't imagining things: Candlelight casts a warm, yellow-red glow that's flattering to the skin.

Science-y types measure the color of light, officially known as *color temperature,* on the Kelvin scale, which is named after its creator. You can see an illustration of the Kelvin scale in Figure 8-1.

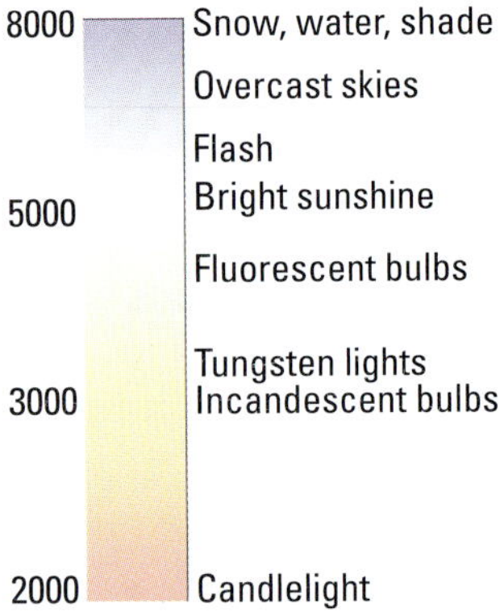

Figure 8-1: Each light source emits a specific color.

Most of us don't notice these fluctuating colors of light because our eyes automatically compensate for them. Except in extreme lighting conditions, a white tablecloth appears white to us no matter whether we view it by candlelight, fluorescent light, or regular house lights.

Similarly, a digital camera compensates for different colors of light through a feature known as *white balancing.* Simply put, white balancing neutralizes light so that whites are always white, which in turn ensures that other colors are rendered accurately. Your camera's Automatic White Balance setting, which carries the label AWB, tackles this process remarkably well in most situations.

In some lighting conditions, though, the AWB adjustment doesn't quite do the trick, resulting in an unwanted color cast like the one you see in the left image in Figure 8-2. If you compare the Auto setting versus Daylight, you can see that the fence turns from a bland gray to a warmer wood color, as it should be. In this case, the Auto setting turns skin color too blue. The Daylight setting corrects that.

Some problems are more severe. The photo in Figure 8-3 reveals a white balance problem that can't be fixed by selecting one of the presets. Nor can it be fixed by selecting the color temperature manually. This exact white balance is in between everything you can select using these methods. To fix problems like this, use White Balance Shift to enter a correction after you take a few test shots and examine them. You should be on the lookout for situations like this in which you need to fine tune the white balance.

The next section first explains precisely how to make a simple white balance correction and then explores some advanced white balance features.

(The good news is that if you shoot in RAW, you can make all white balance corrections after the fact, from the comfort of your computer. Try to get as close as you can on location, but don't fret if you can't nail it.)

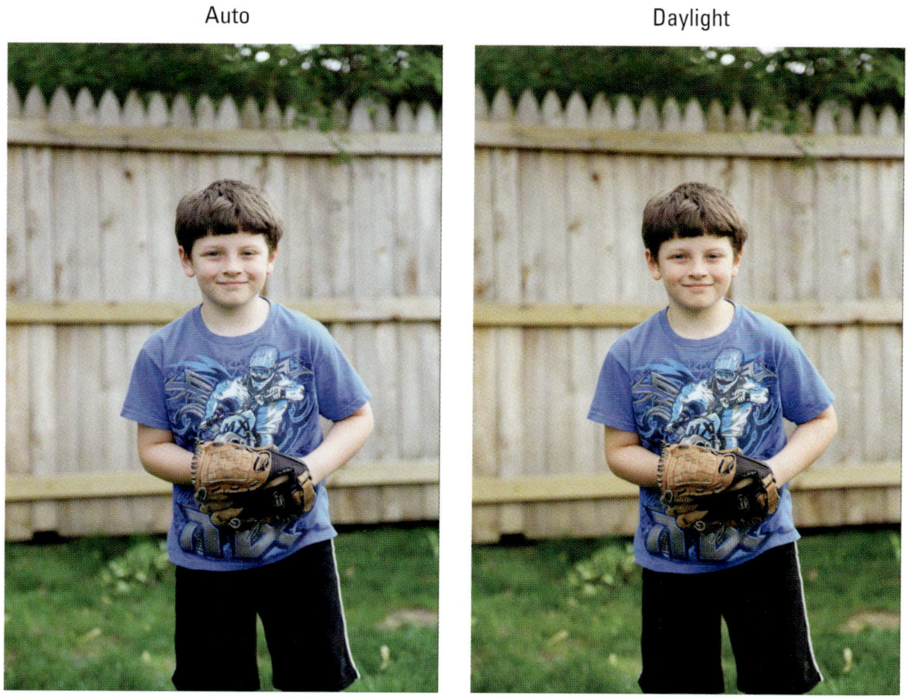

Figure 8-2: Auto White Balance doesn't always get it totally right (left). In this case, Daylight works best (right).

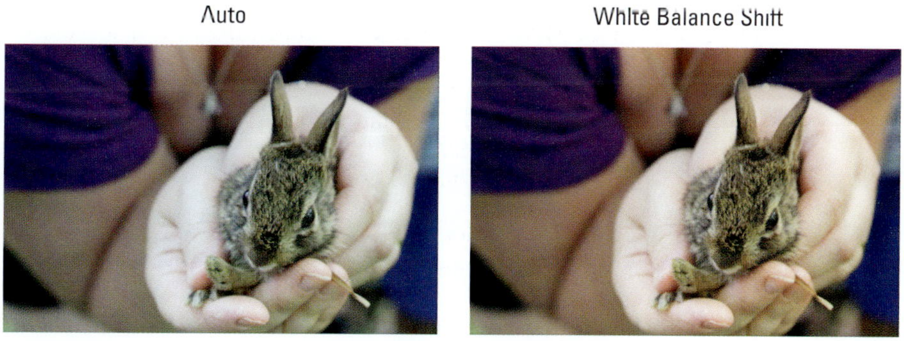

Figure 8-3: Use White Balance Shift to quickly remove a color cast.

Changing the White Balance setting

WARNING!

Unfortunately, you can't change the White Balance selection in Scene Intelligent Auto. So, if you spy color problems when playing back photos, switch to P, Tv, Av, M, B, or a Custom Shooting mode. You also can select the White Balance setting when shooting movies in these more advanced modes.

You can use any of the following methods to adjust the white balance:

- **Metering Mode Selection/White Balance Selection button:** If the Shooting settings screen is visible on the LCD monitor (or the Quick Control screen), press this button (it's the leftmost button beyond the top LCD panel) to open the screen shown in Figure 8-4. Change the white balance by spinning the Quick Control dial and pressing Set to lock it in.

  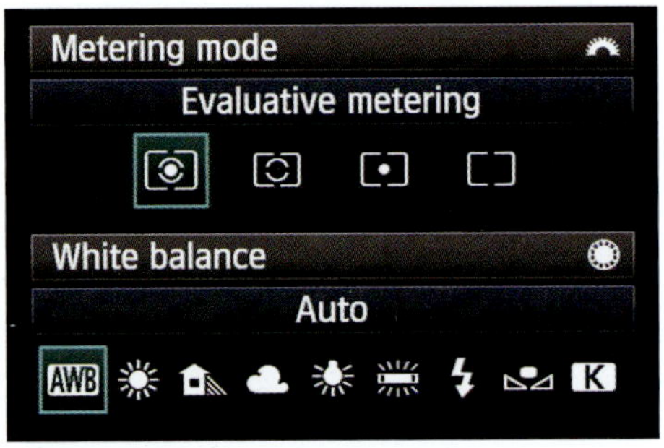

  Figure 8-4: Don't forget about the buttons on top of the camera; they're useful.

  If the Shooting settings display is not present, press the Info button until you see it. See Chapter 1 for more information on the Shooting settings display.

- **Quick Control screen:** Press the Quick Control button to bring up the Quick Control screen. Then highlight the White Balance icon, found at the spot shown in Figure 8-5. The selected setting appears at the bottom of the screen, and you can then rotate the Main dial or Quick Control dial to cycle through the various options.

  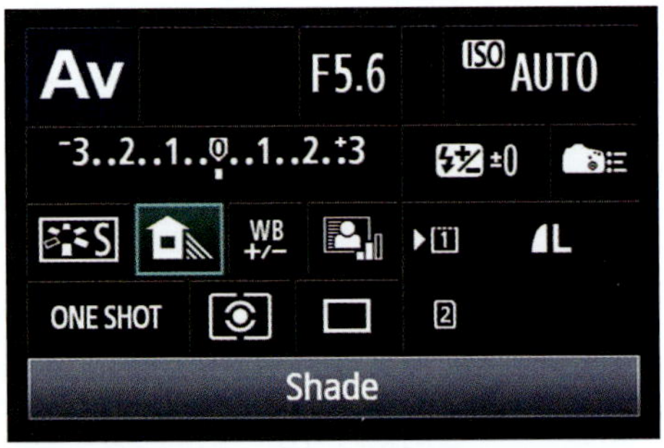

  Figure 8-5: You can adjust the White Balance setting from the Quick Control screen.

  If you want to see all settings at one time, press Set with the White Balance setting highlighted instead of rotating a dial. The screen shown in Figure 8-6 appears. Highlight your choice and press the Set button.

  On this screen, as in the Shooting settings and Quick Control displays, the various White Balance settings are represented by the icons listed in Table 8-1. You don't need to memorize them, however, because as you scroll through the list of options, the name of the selected setting appears on the screen. For most settings, the camera also displays the approximate Kelvin temperature (K) of the selected light source, as shown in the figure. (Refer to Figure 8-1 for a look at the Kelvin scale.)

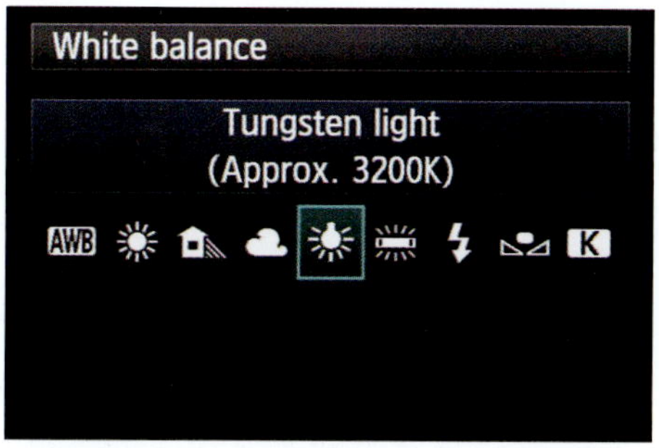

Figure 8-6: View White Balance settings full screen.

If the scene is lit by several sources, choose the setting that corresponds to the strongest one. The Tungsten Light setting is usually best for shooting scenes lit by regular incandescent household bulbs. Use the White Fluorescent setting when the scene is lit by fluorescent bulbs, provided that the bulbs are "Cool White" and in the range of 4,000 degrees Kelvin. However, you can't always use the White Fluorescent setting, even in rooms with fluorescent lights. If you have trouble, your best bet is to create a custom White Balance setting that's precisely tuned to the light. See the upcoming section "Setting the white balance temperature" for details.

- **Shooting Menu 2:** Press Menu, go to Shooting Menu 2, and select White Balance. Press Set and then choose settings, which are identical to those on the Quick Control screen. Highlight the setting you want to use and press Set.

Your selected White Balance setting remains in force until you change it again. To avoid accidentally using an incorrect setting later, you may want to get in the habit of resetting the option to the automatic setting (AWB) after you finish shooting whatever subject it was that caused you to switch to manual White Balance mode.

Table 8-1 White Balance Settings

Symbol	*Setting*
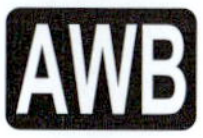	Auto
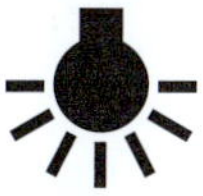	Daylight
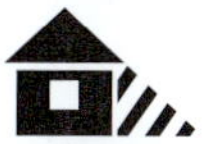	Shade
	Cloudy

(continued)

Table 8-1 *(continued)*

Symbol	*Setting*
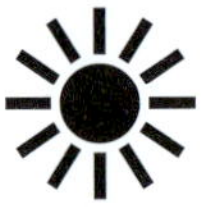	Tungsten light
	White Fluorescent light
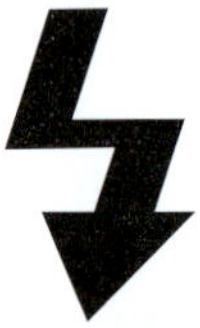	Flash
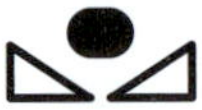	Custom
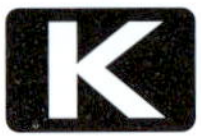	Color temp (in degrees Kelvin)

Setting the White Balance temperature

Although the 5D Mark III has a number of good White Balance presets, you also can set the white balance to a specific color temperature. Access the White Balance settings as in the previous section and then select Color Temp. With Color Temp highlighted (see Figure 8-7), scroll through temperatures by using the Main dial. Each click changes the color temperature by 100° Kelvin. The overall range runs from 2500–10000°.

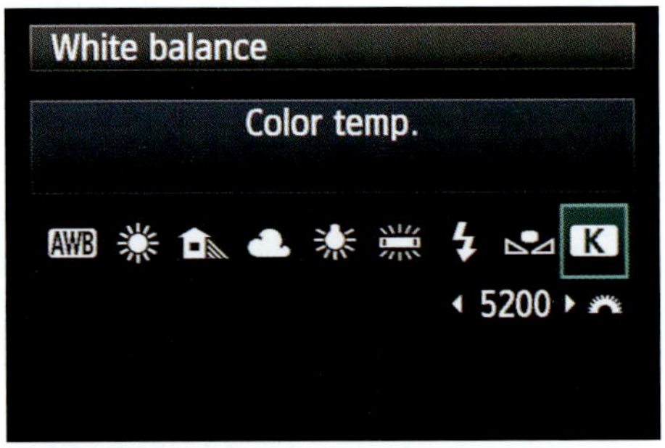

Figure 8-7: Set the temperature directly using the Main dial.

Creating a custom White Balance setting

If none of the preset White Balance options produces the right amount of color correction, you can create your own, custom setting. To use this technique, you need a piece of card stock that's either neutral gray (18 percent reflectance) or absolute white — not eggshell white, sand white, or any other close-but-not-perfect white. (You can buy reference cards made just for this purpose in many camera stores for less than $20.)

Position the reference card so that it receives the same lighting you'll use for your photo. Then follow these steps:

1. **Set the camera Aperture-Priority AE Shooting mode.**

   You can choose anything but Scene Intelligent Auto. Do yourself a favor, though, and choose an autoexposure mode. That makes setting the standard exposure (0.0) easy.

2. **Set the White Balance setting to Auto, as described in the earlier section "Changing the white balance setting."**

3. **Set the camera to Manual focus and then focus on your reference card.**

   You can check Chapter 1 for details on manual focusing if you need help.

4. **Frame the shot so that your reference card fills the center area of the viewfinder.**

   In other words, make sure that at least the center autofocus point and the surrounding circle — the *spot metering circle* — cover the reference card. (Feel free to shoot for overkill.)

5. **Make sure that the exposure settings are correct.**

   Press the shutter button halfway or check exposure. In M mode, make sure that the exposure indicator is at the midway point of the exposure meter. In other modes, a blinking aperture or shutter speed value indicates an exposure problem. If necessary, adjust ISO, aperture, or shutter speed to fix the problem; Chapter 6 explains how.

6. **Take the picture of your reference card.**

   You'll tell the camera to use this picture to establish a custom White Balance setting in the following steps.

7. **Display Shooting Menu 2 and highlight Custom White Balance, as shown in Figure 8-8.**

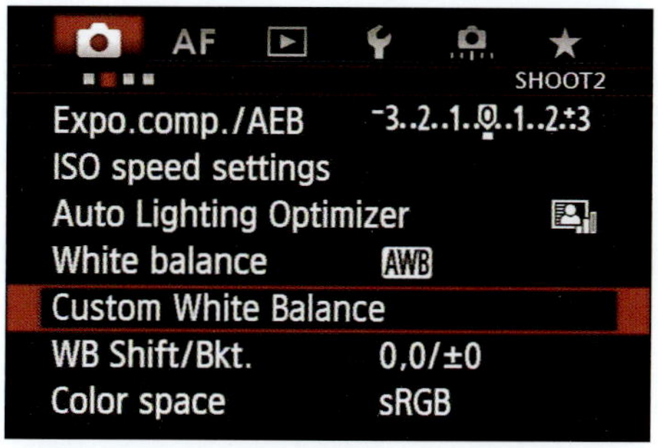

Figure 8-8: Create a custom White Balance setting from Shooting Menu 2.

8. **Press Set.**

   You see the screen shown in Figure 8-9. The image you just captured should appear in the display. If not, turn the Quick Control dial to scroll to the image.

9. **Press Set to select the displayed image as the basis for your custom White Balance reference.**

   A message is displayed, asking you to confirm that you want the camera to use the image to create the custom White Balance setting.

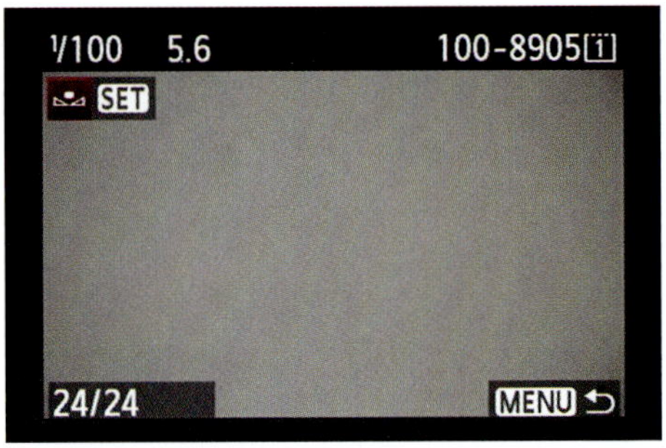

Figure 8-9: Use white or a neutral gray card.

10. **Highlight OK and then press Set.**

    You see a message telling you that the new setting is now stored, as shown in Figure 8-10, and reminding you to set the white balance to Custom (which is the small icon).

11. **Press Set one more time to finalize the custom setting.**

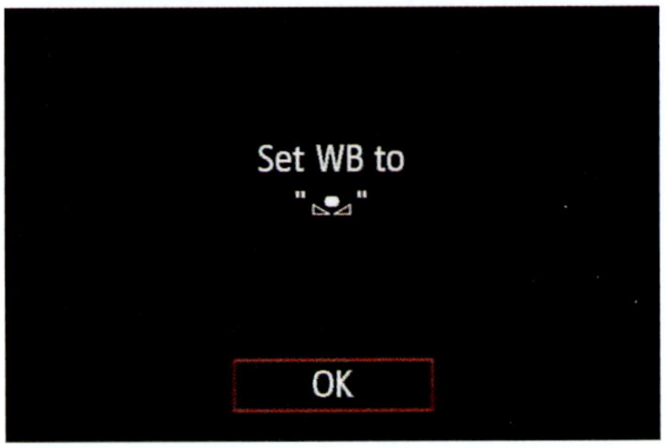

Figure 8-10: After measuring, don't forget to set the white balance to the Custom setting.

Your custom White Balance setting remains stored until the next time you work your way through these steps. Anytime you're shooting in the same lighting conditions and want to apply the same white balance correction, just access the White Balance settings and then select the Custom option.

Correcting the white balance

If the white balance that you have chosen needs tweaking, you can use White Balance Shift to correct the color tone. The result is similar to applying a traditional color filter to your lens.

To access the White Balance Shift option, follow these steps:

1. **Display Shooting Menu 2 and highlight WB Shift/Bracket, as shown in Figure 8-11.**

   You can't be in Scene Intelligent Auto mode.

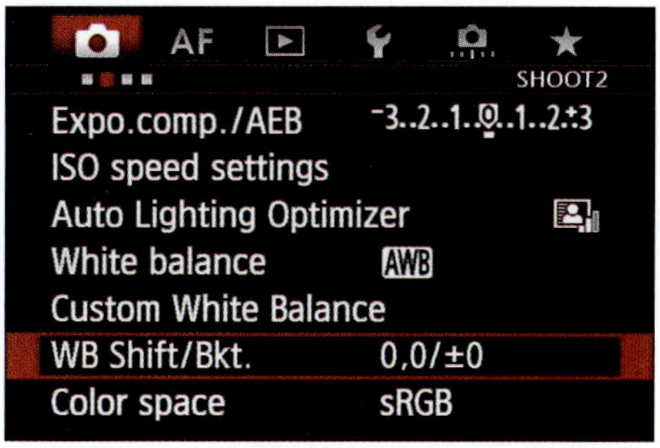

Figure 8-11: White Balance Shift offers another way to control colors.

2. **Press Set.**

   The screen changes to show a grid that's oriented around two main color pairs: green and magenta (represented by the G and M labels) and blue and amber (represented by B and A). The small white square indicates the amount of white balance correction, or *shift.* When the square is dead center in the grid, as in the figure, no shift is applied.

3. **Use the Multicontroller to move the square marker in the direction of the shift you want to achieve.**

   As you do, the Shift area of the display tells the amount of color bias you selected. For example, in Figure 8-12, the shift is four levels toward amber and two toward magenta.

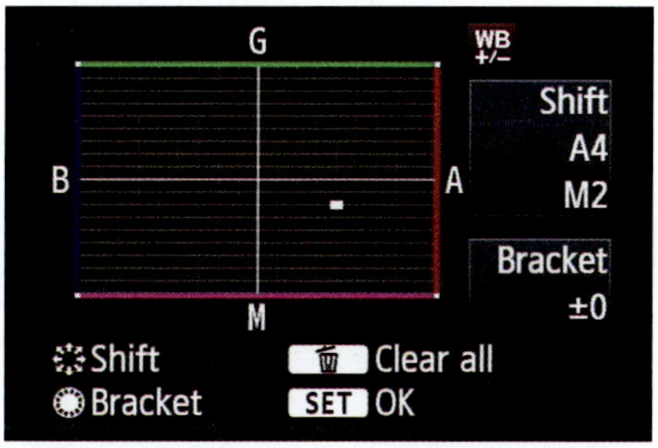

Figure 8-12: Use the Multicontroller to move the marker and shift white balance.

   If you're familiar with traditional lens filters, you may know that the density of a filter, which determines the degree of color correction it provides, is measured in *mireds* (pronounced "*my*-reds"). The white balance grid is designed around this system: Moving the marker one level is the equivalent of adding a filter with a density of five mireds.

4. **Press Set to apply the change and return to the menu.**

   After you apply White Balance Shift, the White Balance Correction icon appears in the Shooting Settings display, as shown in Figure 8-13. The icon reminds you that White Balance Shift is being applied. The same symbol appears in the top LCD panel, and you will get a warning symbol in the viewfinder.

   You can see the exact shift values in Shooting Menu 2 and in the Camera Settings display.

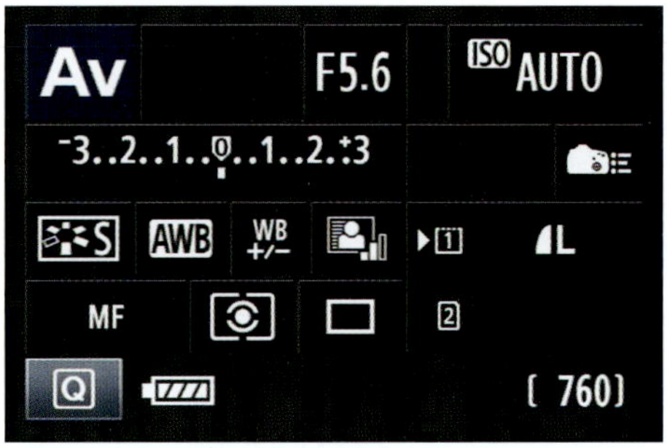

Figure 8-13: Look for the White Balance Correction symbol (to the right of AWB).

WARNING!

Your adjustment remains in force for all shooting modes except Scene Intelligent Auto until you change it. The correction is applied no matter which White Balance setting you choose. Check the monitor or viewfinder before your next shoot; otherwise, you may forget to adjust the white balance for the current light.

5. **To cancel White Balance Correction, repeat Steps 1–3, press the Erase button to clear all the settings, and then press Set.**

   Alternatively, use the Multicontroller to move the marker back to the center of the grid. Be sure that both values in the Shift area of the display are set to 0.

TIP

Many film photography enthusiasts place colored filters on their lenses to warm or cool their images. Portrait photographers, for example, often add a warming filter to give skin tones a healthy, golden glow. You can mimic the effects of these filters by fine-tuning your camera's White Balance settings as just described. Experiment with shifting the white balance a tad toward amber and magenta for a warming effect or toward blue and green for a cooling effect.

Shooting white balance brackets

Chapter 6 introduces you to your camera's Automatic Exposure Bracketing, which enables you to easily record the same image at three different exposure settings. Similarly, you can take advantage of automatic White Balance Bracketing. With this feature, the camera records the same image three times, using a slightly different white balance adjustment for each one.

This feature is especially helpful when you're shooting in varying light sources, such as a mix of fluorescent light, daylight, and flash. Bracketing the shots increases the odds that the color rendition of at least one of the shots will be to your liking.

REMEMBER

Hare are some notes about this feature:

- If you shoot and process your own RAW photos, you can ignore this section and set the white balance yourself in software. That's one of the main benefits of shooting RAW photos.
- Because the camera records three images each time you press the Shutter button, using White Balance Bracketing reduces the maximum capture speed that's possible when you use the Continuous shooting mode. See Chapter 2 for more about Continuous mode. Of course, recording three images instead of one also eats up more space on your memory card.
- The White Balance Bracketing feature is designed around the same grid used for White Balance Correction, explained in the preceding section. As a reminder, the grid is based on two color pairs: green/magenta and blue/amber.
- When White Balance Bracketing is enabled, the camera always records the center bracket first. Then it records blue/magenta brackets. It finishes with amber/green brackets. In the case of two brackets, it first records the bracket with a blue/magenta bias and then the photo with an amber/green bias. You can view the shift applied to each photo in photo playback. Press the Info button to show the Shooting Information or Histogram displays. The shift is located on line three.
- The number of bracketed shots is set in Custom Function: Number of Bracketed Shots. The options are 3 (the default), 2, 5, or 7.

To enable White Balance Bracketing, follow these steps:

1. **Display Shooting Menu 2 and highlight WB Shift/Bracket.**

   You can't shoot white balance brackets in Scene Intelligent Auto mode.

2. **Press Set to display the grid.**

   The screen is the same one you see when you use the White Balance Correction feature, explained in the preceding section.

3. **Rotate the Quick Control dial to set the amount of the bracketing shift.**

Rotate the dial as follows to specify whether you want the bracketing to be applied across the horizontal axis (blue to amber) or the vertical axis (green to magenta).

- *Blue to amber bracketing:* Rotate the dial right.
- *Green to magenta bracketing:* Rotate the dial left.

As you rotate the dial, markers appear on the grid, indicating the amount of shift that will be applied to your bracketed images (see Figure 8-14). You can apply a maximum shift of plus or minus three levels of adjustment. If you need more, add brackets.

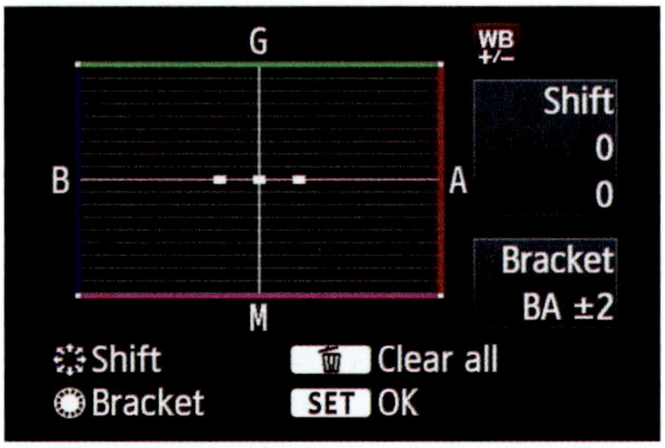

Figure 8-14: The markers indicate the shift that will be applied to each bracket.

4. **Apply a correction, if desired.**

   TIP: If you want to get truly fancy, you can combine White Balance Bracketing with White Balance Shift. To set the amount of White Balance Shift, press the Multicontroller to move the square markers around the grid. See Figure 8-15.

5. **Press Set to apply your changes and return to the menu.**

   The White Balance symbol on the Shooting Information display, the Quick Control screens, and the top LCD panel blinks when you have enabled White Balance Bracketing.

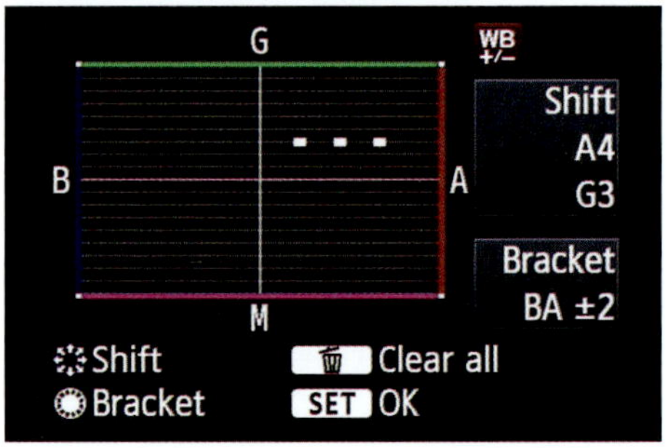

Figure 8-15: You can also shift the brackets around the screen.

REMEMBER: The bracketing setting remains in effect until you turn off the camera. You can also cancel bracketing by revisiting the grid screen shown earlier and either rotating the Main dial until you see only a single grid marker or pressing the Erase button. Then press Set to officially turn off bracketing.

Choosing a Color Space

Digital cameras assign a color space to every photo you take. The color space, in essence, defines the range of colors that your photo is squeezed into. Defining the range of colors is necessary because monitors can't possibly display every conceivable color. Nor can printers. We must agree to limit what is expected and possible.

When it comes to choosing a color space, you have a choice between sRGB and Adobe RGB:

- **sRGB:** sRGB defines a smaller color space than Adobe RGB but is more widely accepted. In fact, sRGB is the de facto standard. It is so ubiquitous that devices with no color management capabilities at all assume that all colors are defined in sRGB and reproduce sRGB photos perfectly. The same devices will not reproduce a photo in the Adobe RGB color space correctly. I recommend assigning this color space to your photos.
- **Adobe RGB:** Adobe RGB defines a larger color space than sRGB but is less widely implemented. The danger of using Adobe RGB is that you may be viewing or editing colors on your system that cannot be displayed or printed correctly by others. If you work in an environment that is tightly color managed, you may be able to take advantage of Adobe RGB's greater color range.

To set the color space, press the Menu button and navigate to Shooting Menu 2. Look for the Color Space option. Highlight it, press the Set button, and make your choice.

In the end, which option is right for you depends on what you do with your photos and where you intend to use them. I prefer sRGB to Adobe RGB, despite its limitations, because I want to view the same color space from beginning to end. To be honest, I don't think many people could tell which color profile a photo is using without performing a carefully prepared test viewing with the photos displayed side by side on a system that is set up to work in Adobe RGB.

REMEMBER

This Color Space choice applies only when you are not in Scene Intelligent Auto Shooting mode. In Scene Intelligent Auto Shooting mode, the camera automatically selects sRGB as the color space. Also, your Color Space selection is applied to only your JPEG images; with RAW captures, decisions on color space happen in your image editing software, not in the camera.

TIP

After you transfer pictures to your computer, you can tell whether you captured an image in the Adobe RGB color space by looking at its filename. Adobe RGB images start with an underscore. Those captured in sRGB do not.

Exploring Picture Styles

The 5D Mark III has a number of Picture Styles that you can use to process your photos in-camera. Each predefined style has different color, saturation contrast, and sharpening settings. You can tweak existing styles or create your own.

The camera offers the following seven Picture Styles:

- **Auto:** In this case, the camera applies the photo style (but not monochrome) that it considers appropriate to the scene. Mileage may vary from photo to photo.
- **Standard:** The default setting, this option promises sharp images with good contrast and strong colors.
- **Portrait:** This mode reduces sharpening slightly (compared to Standard) to soften skin textures.
- **Landscape:** In a nod to landscape photography, this Picture Style emphasizes greens and blues and amps up color saturation and sharpness, resulting in bolder images.
- **Neutral:** Use the Neutral style if you want to edit your photos yourself. The colors are subdued but natural.
- **Faithful:** The Faithful style is designed to render colors as closely as possible to how your eye perceives them in the daylight.
- **Monochrome:** This setting produces black-and-white photos. You can also apply four different filters (yellow, orange, red, and green) and four different toning effects (sepia, blue, purple, and green).
- **User Defined 1 to 3:** You have three spaces to save your own styles. After you create them, select them here.

Figure 8-16 shows four of the Picture Styles in action: Standard, Portrait, Landscape, and Monochrome. As you can see, except for Monochrome, the differences are subtle, but not without merit. The girls' faces are warmer in Landscape than in the other two color styles. They *do* look a bit softer in Portrait. The carrots are more saturated in Standard and Landscape.

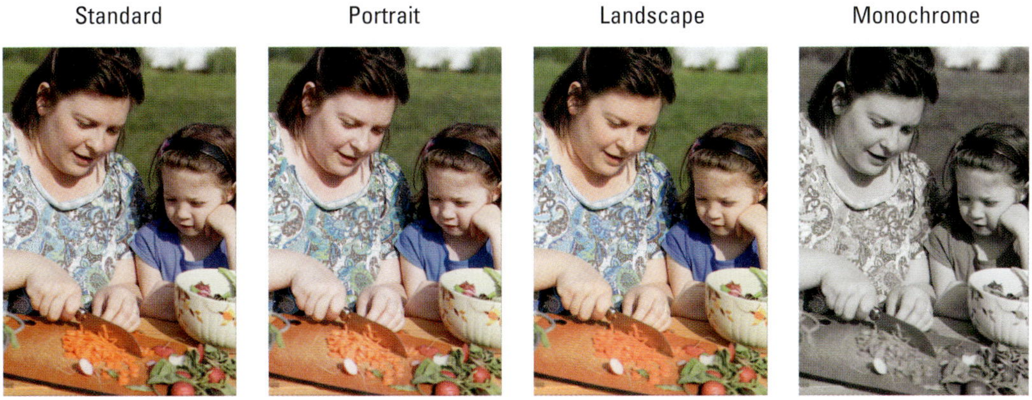

Figure 8-16: Outdoor cooking is a blast!

Picture Styles are applied to both RAW and JPEGs. With RAW photos, the style changes the internal JPEG thumbnail. When you process the photo, you can change or remove the style. With JPEGs, the styles are not reversible.

For still photography, you can select a Picture Style in three ways:

- **Creative Photo button:** Press the Creative Photo button to open the screen shown in Figure 8-17. Highlight Picture Style and press the Set button.
- **Quick Control screen:** Press the Quick Control button to open the Quick Controls screen. Highlight the current Picture Style (see Figure 8-18) and then spin the Quick Control dial or Main dial to change styles.

  If you want to see all available styles, just press Set to display the Picture Style screen.

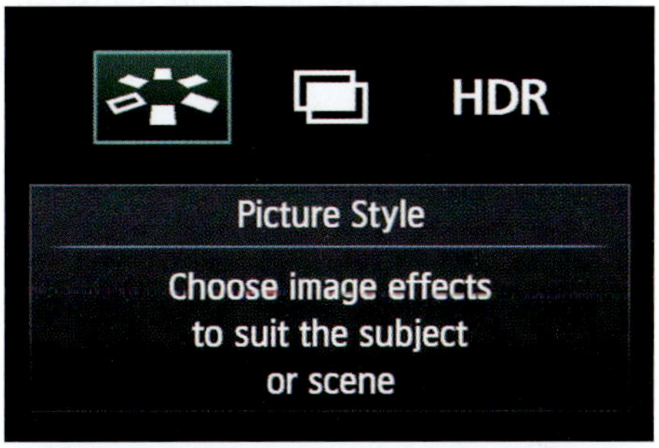

Figure 8-17: Select Picture Style from this screen.

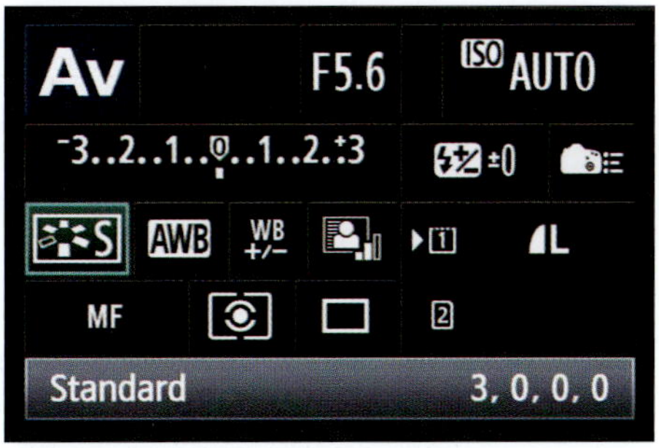

Figure 8-18: The current style is set to Standard.

- **Shooting Menu 3:** Select the Picture Style option and press Set to display a menu full of all the styles (see Figure 8-19). Highlight your choice and press Set again.

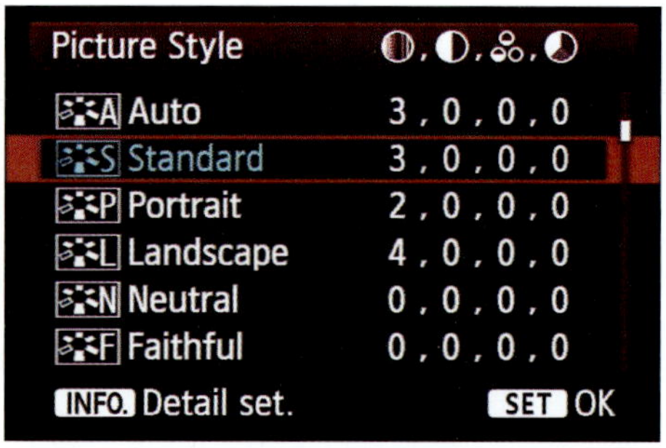

Figure 8-19: This screen displays details of all the presets and allows you to select them.

The numbers you see along with the style name represent the four characteristics applied by the style: Sharpness, Contrast, Saturation, and Color Tone. Sharpness values range from 0 to 7; the higher the value, the more sharpening is applied. At 0, no sharpening is applied. The other values range from –4 to +4. They are initially set to 0, which represents the default setting for the selected Picture Style. Press the Info button to alter the parameters. Highlight each one, press the Set button, and then spin the Quick Control dial to change the setting (see Figure 8-20). The bright white triangle shows the current value. The shaded triangle is the default setting.

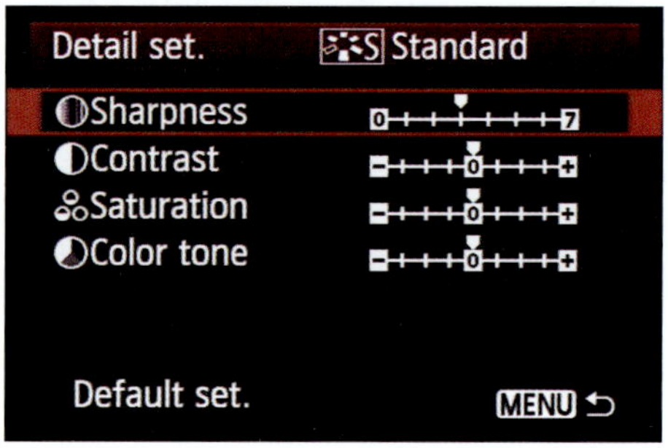

Figure 8-20: Tweak the presets to your liking.

When shooting in Live View or when recording movies, select a Picture Style from Shooting Menu 2 or by pressing the Creative Photo button. You can't change the Picture Style in Quick Control mode.

In general, you're better off shooting in RAW and then making similar adjustments on a picture-by-picture basis in your RAW processor. You can, if you like, assign a Picture Style to your RAW files in Canon Digital Photo Professional (which comes free with the camera) and then compare how each one affects the image.

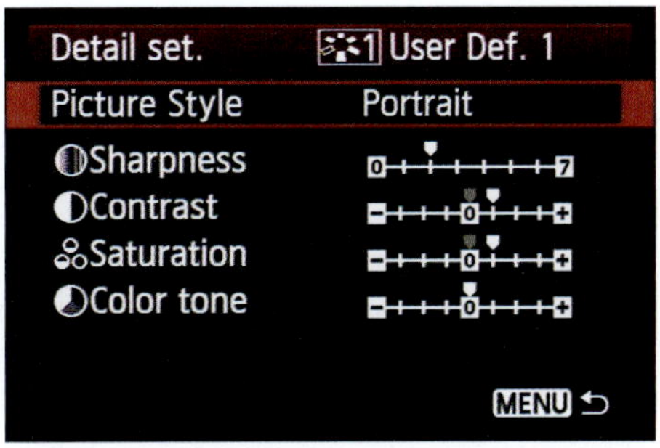

Figure 8-21: Save your favorite tweaks as a User Defined preset.

If you want to shoot JPEG only and don't plan on editing anything in software, Picture Styles are the best way for you to control the photo's appearance. I heartily recommend playing around with the Standard, Portrait, Landscape, and Monochrome styles to find your preferred look. When you do, select a User Defined style, choose an existing style to base it on, and then make your adjustments. Figure 8-21 shows what the Detail setting screen looks like. Notice that the base style is listed above the Sharpness setting. User Defined styles are erased when you clear all the camera's settings.

Also, for über geeks (you know who you are), the CD accompanying your camera includes a software package named — are you ready? — Picture Style Editor, in which you can create and save Picture Style files to your heart's content.

9

Putting It All Together

In This Chapter

- Following a shooting strategy
- Shooting great portraits
- Capturing breathtaking landscapes
- Freezing sports and action
- Shooting in a small studio
- Trying out High Dynamic Range (HDR) photography

Earlier chapters of this book cover the details of the EOS 5D Mark III, describing how the various controls affect exposure, picture quality, focus, color, and the like. This chapter pulls together all that information to help you set up your camera for different types of photography.

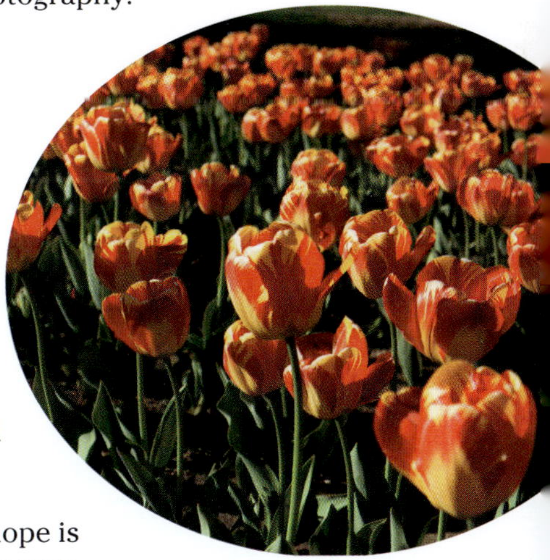

The first few pages offer a quick summary of critical settings that should serve you well in a variety of general situations. Following that, I offer guidance on developing a shooting strategy as well as on which settings to use for portraits, action shots, landscapes, close-ups, and so forth.

Although I offer specific recommendations in this chapter, I want to stress that no one "right way" exists to shoot a portrait, a landscape, or whatever. The ultimate test is whether the photo effectively communicates to the viewer. Although there are valid reasons why portraits tend to be shot similarly, don't be afraid to wander off on your own, tweaking this exposure setting or adjusting that focus control. My hope is that you'll discover your own creative vision along the way.

Solid Settings for All Occasions

It pays to know what settings you should use in general situations. Table 9-1 lists the recommended settings, when you should change them, and what chapter to turn to for more detailed information.

Use these recipes for taking good photos in most situations (the *most* part is key; they are not intended to be practical in *all* situations). Try them and learn when and where to make your own. The rest of the chapter talks about how best to shoot specific types of subjects.

Table 9-1 Settings Cheat Sheet

Option	*Recommended Setting*	*See This Chapter*
Shooting mode	Action: Tv Others: Av	2
Image quality	Large/Fine (JPEG) or Medium/Fine (JPEG) RAW or M-RAW	2
Drive mode	Action: Continuous All others: Single	2
ISO	Outside: 100 or lower Inside: 800 or lower(elevate when necessary)	6
Metering mode	Evaluative	6
AF mode	AI Focus	7
AF Point Selection mode	Auto	7
White balance	Auto	8
Picture Style	Standard	8

Many of the options listed in Table 9-1 have a corresponding button on the camera. Figure 9-1 shows the top of the camera, where the metering mode, white balance, AF mode, drive mode, and ISO buttons are located. Use the Mode dial to set the shooting mode and the Creative Photo button to set the Picture Style. Press the AF Point Selection button to set the AF point selection mode with the M-Fn button.

In addition to the buttons, you can use the Quick Control screen to quickly change most settings.

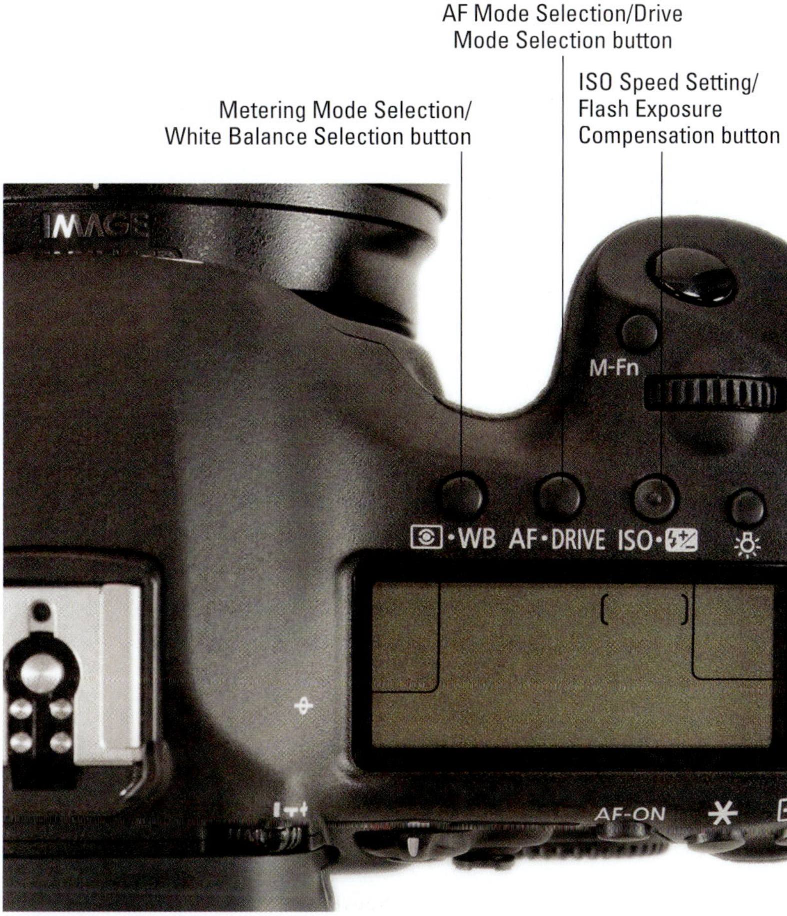

Figure 9-1: Despite advances in software, buttons are incredible things.

Developing a Shooting Strategy

Successful photo shoots (even if you're just enjoying a walk down the street) depend, in part, on good preparation. Preparation helps you get your money's worth out of the camera and not waste your time. Every shot counts, even bad ones (they are a great learning experience, but you can't make a living off of bad photos).

TIP

Having a routine will help you keep the camera configured properly. It lessens the chances of forgetting which settings you changed and need to change back.

Prepare before the shoot

Commit some prep time to the following before you go out with your camera:

- *Battery:* Batteries are the life blood of digital SLRs.

  TIP

  Buy more than one battery if you shoot a lot. Maybe several. Always have one in the charger so that you can pop a fresh battery in the camera at a moment's notice. If you go on a trip, take the charger(s) with you. If you're using an external flash, take extra batteries with you.

  If you shoot in a studio, consider getting the AC Adapter AC-E6 and DC Coupler DR-E6 and running the camera using wall power.

  If you like the convenience of being able to buy more batteries on location, consider fitting your 5D Mark III with the BG-E11 Battery Grip and fitting it with the GMB-E11A Battery Magazine filled with AA batteries.

- *Lenses:* Clean your lens before packing. Don't wait until you're on location where it might be windy, dusty, or wet. Make sure that the lens caps (front and rear, if applicable) are on securely.
- *Memory cards:* Have at least one backup. If you expect to shoot a lot, especially if using rapid-fire continuous shooting or brackets for High Dynamic Range Photography, buy more than one extra. Make sure that all photos and movies are transferred to your computer; then format the memory cards using your camera before you pack them.

  TIP

  If you shoot movies, consider buying several extra cards. You may even want to keep your photos and HD movies on separate cards.

- *Camera settings:* It's frustrating when you have the camera set up to shoot action shots one day and accidentally leave things that way when you go out to shoot landscapes. It's even more frustrating when your camera is set up to save JPEGs and you find out too late that you forgot to change your setting to include RAW.

  Take advantage of the Custom Shooting modes (see Chapter 10) to store different settings and be able to recall them later. By doing so, you don't have to reset the camera every time you turn around (although that's not a bad idea).

- *Packing list:* Whether you have a physical list or one in your head, know what goes in your camera bag and check that everything is there before you leave.
- *Set general goals:* Have a good general idea of what you want to accomplish. Categorize these ideas into camera-oriented groupings such as wide-angle landscapes, the sunset, close-ups, action shots, portraits, or casual shots of the family. Having categories helps you stay focused.

- *Get set up:* When you get to where you're shooting (whether that's outside your door or across town), get set up before you start worrying about subjects and exposure. Get your camera out, put the lens on (if necessary), make any other connections (such as flash or tripod), turn the power on, and check the battery power. Double-check to make sure that your memory card(s) are inserted and empty.

Establish specific goals for the shoot

Now that you are on location and have unpacked, take the general ideas you developed earlier and get specific. The following questions are examples of what you might ask yourself:

- What about this event or location do I want to showcase?
- What angle looks best?
- Where is the light coming from?
- Will focusing be a challenge?

When setting specific goals, be flexible. You might set out with a particular idea in mind, only to find that your idea isn't possible because of the lighting or weather. Or you may realize something about the scene that you didn't know beforehand and decide that another goal will likely produce better results. These situations happen to me all the time.

Configure the camera

Now configure the camera.

- **Set the shooting mode:** Probably the first camera-related decision you should make is what shooting mode to use. Set it from the Mode dial (see Figure 9-2). Refer to Table 9-1 and the following sections for help choosing.
    - *Aperture-Priority AE:* If you entered Av mode, set the aperture now using the Main dial.
    - *Shutter-Priority AE:* If you entered Tv mode, set a shutter speed now using the Main dial.

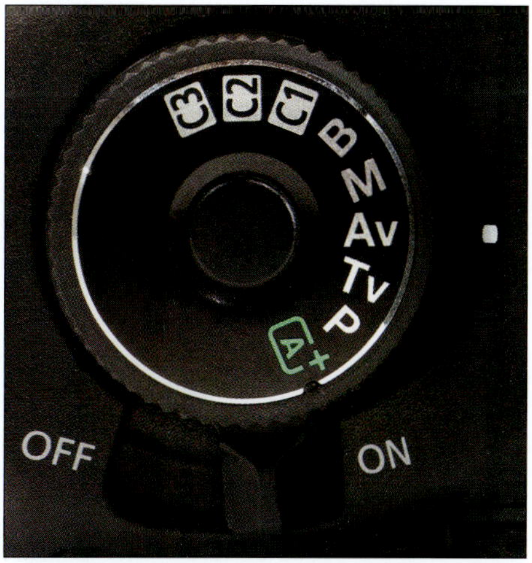

Figure 9-2: To turn, remember to press and hold the Mode dial release button.

- *Manual:* Set something. Aperture, shutter speed. Your call.
- *Program AE:* If you like, you can change the program (this is known as *Program Shift*), but you must first meter, focus, and be ready to take the photo. Changing the program comes later.
- *Custom Shooting mode:* If you've already created a Custom Shooting mode, you've already done much of the work of configuring the camera. That's why they are so powerful. Simply dial in the Custovm Shooting mode of your choice on the Mode dial and then dial in a primary exposure setting (aperture or shutter speed). See Chapter 10 for more information on setting up Custom Shooting modes.

You can always change the shooting mode or the combination of exposure settings you initially set. They aren't set in stone!

- **Flash:** Power on and configure the flash, if necessary. See Chapter 7 for more information on using an external Speedlite with the 5D Mark III.
- **Shooting Information screen:** Have a quick look at the Shooting Information screen (Figure 9-3) to check things like noise reduction settings, filename, and free space on your cards.

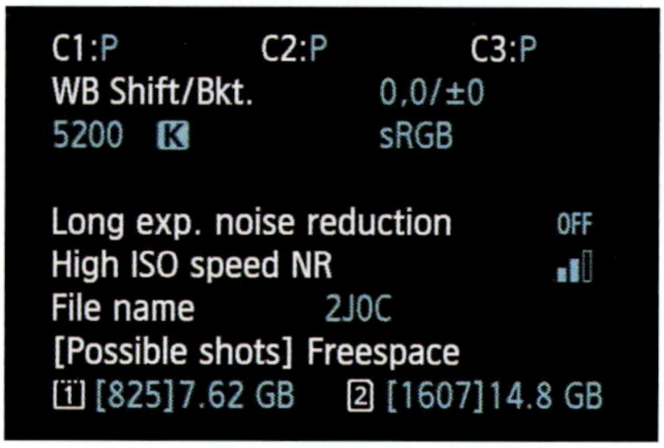

Figure 9-3: One-stop shopping for several important camera settings.

- **Menus:** If necessary (which often means that you aren't using a Custom Shooting mode), browse through the menu and look for critical items that you can't set from the Quick Control screen. These fall into two categories:
  - *Normal stuff:* Look at the settings for Image Review, Beep, Mirror Lockup, ISO Speed Range, Color Space (see Figure 9-4), noise reduction, Grid Display, and so forth. Chapter 2 explains numerous general setup features.
  - *Custom Functions:* Skip over to the Custom Functions menu and make sure that critical

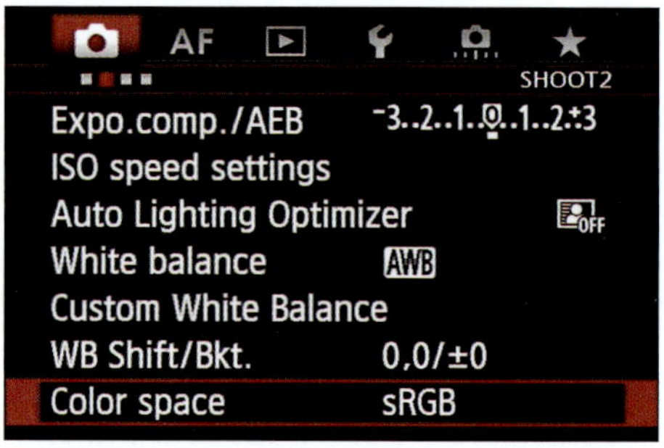

Figure 9-4: Check settings such as Color Space before shooting.

settings are to your liking. Enable or disable Safety Shift, add cropping information, change the number of bracketed shots when using the AEB feature (see Figure 9-5), and so forth. Reset Custom Functions if necessary. See Chapter 10 for more information on Custom Functions.

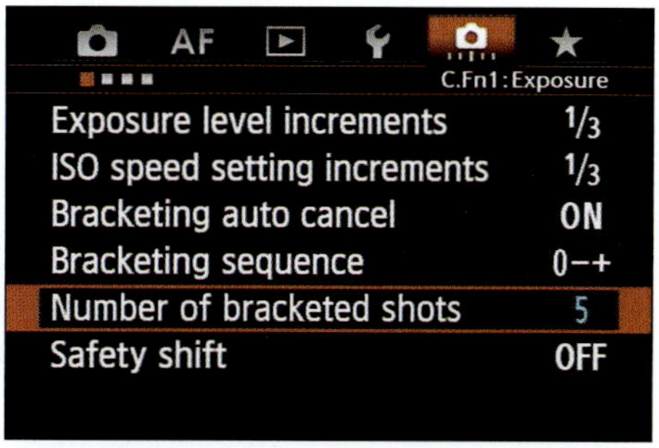

Figure 9-5: Check Custom Functions as well.

- **Quick Control screen:** Press the Quick Control button and have a look at the Quick Control screen (see Figure 9-6). Scan it to double-check that the settings are correct:

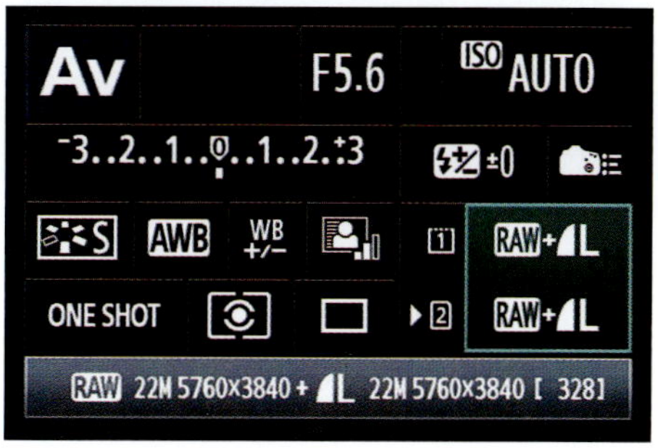

Figure 9-6: Check important shooting settings from the Quick Control screen.

  - *Shooting mode:* Check.
  - *Shutter Speed/Aperture:* Check and set.
  - *ISO Speed:* Check.
  - *Bracketing:* Turn off, if necessary.
  - *Exposure Compensation:* Reset to 0 EV, if necessary.
  - *Flash Compensation:* Reset to 0 EV, if necessary.
  - *Custom Controls:* Check, if needed. This is one Custom Function that you can set from the Quick Control screen.
  - *Picture Style:* Check and reset, if necessary.
  - *White Balance/White Balance Correction:* Check and remove, if necessary.
  - *Auto Lighting Optimizer:* Check and configure, if necessary.
  - *Focus mode:* Check.
  - *Metering mode:* Check.
  - *Drive mode:* Check and set.
  - *Memory Card:* Check which card is active. Swap, if necessary. If desired, set up Record Function.
  - *Image Quality:* Check and double-check the Image Quality setting at which you are recording.

- **Live View:** Configure Live View, if desired. See Chapter 3 for more information on using Live View.
- **Movies:** Configure the camera for Movies, if desired. See Chapter 4 for more information on shooting movies.

Configure the lens

Always, and I mean always, confirm manual versus autofocus:

- **Auto:** Set the Focus Mode switch on the lens to AF.
- **Manual:** Set the Focus Mode switch on the lens to MF.

You can easily switch to MF and then completely forget about it (see Figure 9-7). If you don't make a habit of checking the focus mode every time you pick up the camera, you can get caught up in the action and miss it. At some point, you realize (with luck, sooner rather than later) that the last 30 shots you have taken are out of focus. Ouch!

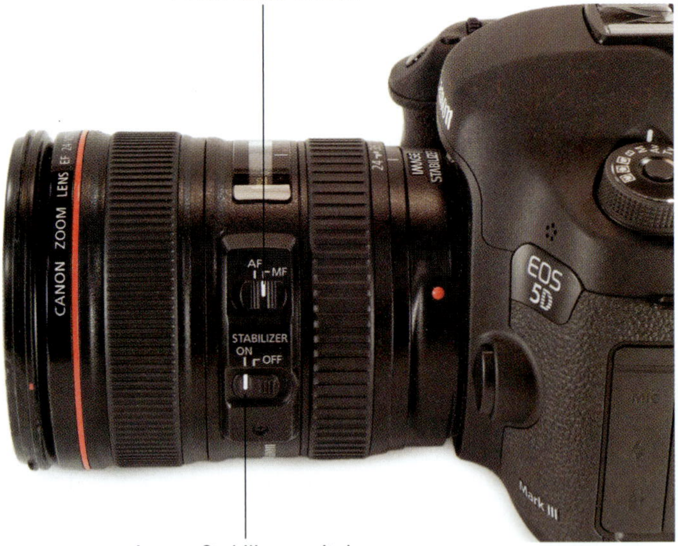

Figure 9-7: Check the focus mode and whether Stabilization is on.

If your lens has IS, set Stabilization to On to enable it (see Figure 9-7). This is helpful if shooting handheld. You can turn it off if you're using a tripod.

Configure autofocus

If you're using autofocus, set up an initial AF Area Selection Mode (press the AF Point Selection button and then choose a mode by pressing the M-Fn button):

- Single-Point Spot AF (Manual selection)
- Single-Point AF (Manual selection)
- AF Point Expansion (Manual selection)
- AF Point Expansion (Manual selection, surrounding points)
- Zone AF (Manual selection of zone)
- 61-Point Automatic Selection AF

After selecting the selection mode, set the area, if necessary. (Press the AF Point Selection button and then select an AF point with the Multicontroller or Quick Control dial.)

If you need to track moving subjects, set the AI Servo AF Characteristics from AF Menu 1:

- **Case 1:** Multipurpose
- **Case 2:** Track subject and ignore obstacles
- **Case 3:** Instant focus on subjects when entering AF points
- **Case 4:** Use for quickly accelerating/decelerating subjects
- **Case 5:** Change direction erratically
- **Case 6:** Change speed and direction erratically

If all this sounds like Greek to you, turn to Chapter 7 and have a read about autofocus. There's a lot to it.

Frame, meter, and autofocus

Frame the scene through the viewfinder or, if you're using Live View, from the monitor. Press the Shutter button halfway to initiate metering and establish autofocus. Don't stab at the button; press it smoothly. Know how much more pressure causes the camera to take a photo. If you're focusing manually, use the focus ring to dial in a rough focus.

If you use a remote shutter release, there may be a tangible tactile difference when pressing it, compared to the Shutter button on the camera. It might feel stiffer, looser, or different in other ways. Know your equipment and what to expect.

Fine-tune the composition

Zoom in or out, if necessary. If you are using a prime lens, physically move toward or away from your subject. Check the background to make sure that it's as photogenic as possible.

Adjust exposure and shoot

At this point in your shooting strategy, you need to

1. **Make any changes to the main exposure settings.**

   Those settings include ISO, shutter speed, and aperture.

2. **Press the Shutter button fully to take the photo.**

3. **Review your photo.**

   If necessary, press the Playback button. Check to see that it's framed and well lit (see Figure 9-8). Magnify the photo and more closely inspect the focus (see Figure 9-9). If necessary, use the Multicontroller to pan around and look at different areas.

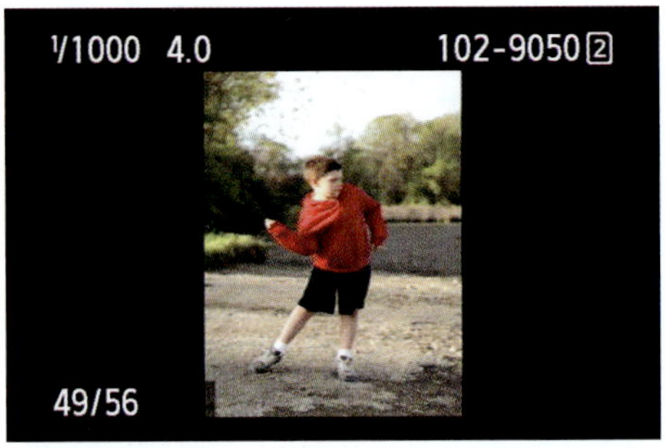

Figure 9-8: Check composition, color, and exposure using the whole photo.

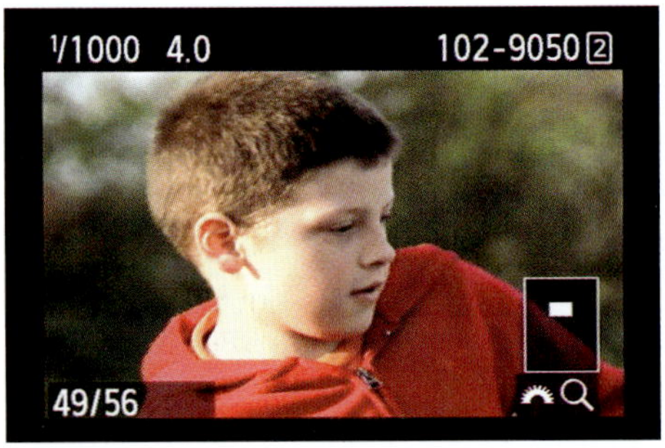

Figure 9-9: Magnify to check focus and other details.

Correct problems

REMEMBER

Correcting problems is an important step. If you identify problems when you review a shot, make the changes to the camera (if possible) to correct them.

For example, you might be taking a portrait of someone with strong backlighting. If you left the metering mode set to Evaluative, the light may overpower the person's face and leave her in shadow. Change the metering mode to Center-weighted, Partial, or Spot to see whether you can get the camera to correctly expose her face. You might also need to use the

Exposure Compensation button, or change the flash intensity by using Flash Compensation. If the problem lies with you, such as a tilted photo, note what you did and correct it in the next photo.

When reviewing for problems, you're looking to solve the following general issues:

- **Composition:** Look for anything that's out of level, is badly positioned, includes a distracting background, and so forth.
- **Exposure:** The exposure should not be too bright or too dark; be on the lookout for blown highlights; look for important details.
- **Focus:** The focus should be sharp; check the depth of field to ensure that it's as you intended.
- **Color:** Check to see whether the colors look natural and well balanced. If you have applied a Picture Style, evaluate the photo to make sure it's what you wanted.
- **Subject-related:** Look for open eyes and whether you want someone looking away or at the camera. Check expressions to see whether they convey the emotion you want to showcase.

Perfecting Portraits

A *portrait* is a photo in which the subject takes center stage. In other words, the subject dominates the frame and is the reason you're taking the photo. The setting may be casual or formal, and the photo may be planned or taken at the spur of the moment. Portraits isolate the subject from the background by almost always limiting the depth of field. This keeps the subject in sharp focus while softening the background.

Portraits are one of the most rewarding styles of photography because they're about people. You'll never run out of interesting people to photograph.

My photos in this section represent a casual approach to portraiture. If you want to shoot formal portraits in a studio or on location, you have to adjust your style accordingly.

Figure 9-10 is a portrait that was processed in black and white. The shelving in the background of a gourmet cookware store helps make this an awesome portrait!

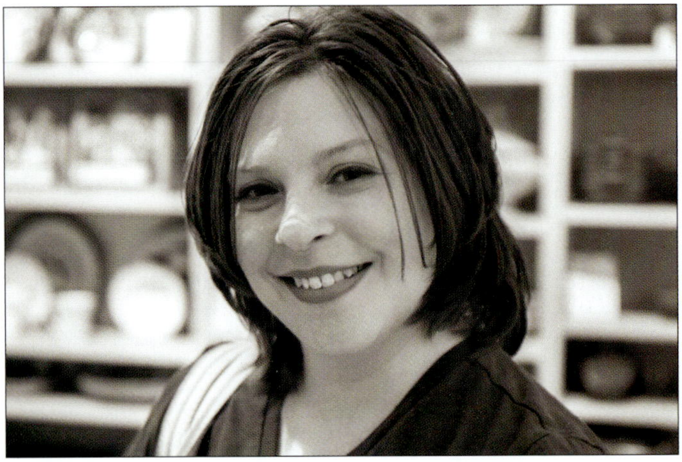

Figure 9-10: Black-and-white portraits are captivating.

Key camera settings

With portraits, it's all about creating a nice *bokeh* (that soft background I refer to earlier in the chapter). To create a bokeh, choose a shooting mode that enables you to control the aperture. For the most part, that is Aperture-Priority AE, although you can use Manual (for more control over the camera) or Program AE (for less control).

TIP

Be careful when using a lens with a maximum aperture in the range of f/1.4 to f/2.8. If you open the lens and get too close, the depth of field may be too small. You might find yourself in a situation in which the freckle on someone's face is in focus but the hair follicle just behind it is out of focus. Heavens to Betsy, stop down (a fancy way of saying "choose a smaller aperture") and step back.

Because of shallow depth of field, precise focus is often very important. Manual works well. If you're using autofocus, set to One-Shot AF and choose an appropriate AF Area Selection mode. I use Single-Point AF most often, which enables me to manually select the exact AF point I want to use. Single-Point Spot AF gives you even more precision than Single-Point AF because it uses the smaller center square of the AF area instead of the larger outer square. If you don't need that level of control, 61-Point Automatic Selection AF works very well unless you're dealing with intervening objects. You don't benefit more by choosing AF Point Expansion (either mode) or Zone AF unless you're shooting a moving subject. (Chapter 7 explains all the focus modes and how to use them.)

When you shoot portraits with a flash, be careful not to brighten the subject's face too much. This issue seems to arise most often indoors, but not exclusively. To guard against an overpowering flash, bounce the flash (that is, rotate the flash head so that it shoots toward the ceiling, which bounces the light off the ceiling rather than your subject), use a lighting modifier (such as a diffuser, umbrella, or soft box), or do both. You can also dial in negative Flash Exposure Compensation.

I use a flash for portraits outside all the time, in the form of fill flash. The fill flash keeps people's faces bright when they would ordinarily be in shadow. Figure 9-11 illustrates this technique in action. The sun is somewhat overhead, shining from my left. The flash helped brighten the subject's face and keep the tone relatively even. I used high-speed sync because the aperture was open pretty wide (f/3.5) and the sun was bright. The shutter speed needed to be 1/1000 second to compensate. (Chapter 7 has more information on flash.)

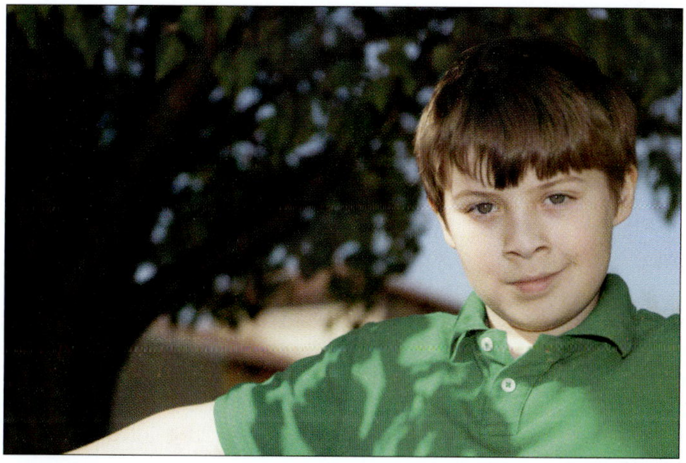

Figure 9-11: Use a flash even when outside. This one takes advantage of high-speed sync.

Keep an eye on shutter speed. If it drops too low, you won't get a good sharp photo, either because you're moving and shooting handheld or the subject isn't quite still.

All other settings are optional, within certain limits. Try to keep the noise to a minimum by using a low ISO, although you may have to raise it when shooting indoors or in dim light to guarantee a reasonable shutter speed. Use a focal length from standard range (50mm) upward to help limit the depth of field. Wide-angle lenses (or focal lengths, should you be using a zoom lens) are less suitable because they shoot expansive depths of field. They also add more distortion to the photo than other lenses do, which doesn't look as good when photographing a person. Likewise, choose the metering method that works best given your lighting situation.

Pointers galore

TIP

Although I encourage you to find your own style, here are some general suggestions when shooting portraits:

- **Get close:** Don't be afraid to zoom in or get closer to your subject. You don't have to do this for every photo, but getting closer places the focus of attention squarely on the subject and removes distractions.
- **Don't get too close:** However, don't zoom in so close that your portrait feels like a passport or driver's license photo. Give your subject room to breathe and show a little background.
- **Vary your height:** When photographing kids, kneel down and get on their level. The same thing goes for pets.
- **Background:** What's happening in the background? Nothing ruins a good portrait faster than a messy room, power lines, or other distractions. If working inside is too restrictive, go outside and stand your subject in front of a nice bush or fence, or go to a park or other scenic location. The possibilities are endless.

Goodbye, City Life: Shooting Landscapes

Landscape photos can take your breath away with their sense of depth and breadth, not to mention color (color is lovely, but is not required) and detail. Figure 9-12 shows the sun setting past a river in Ohio. I wanted to convey the sense of distance to the horizon as well as the great colors of the sunset, but also the interesting foreground detail.

Key camera settings

When shooting landscapes, you're most concerned with enlarging the depth of field. Choose a shooting mode that enables you to control the aperture. That will be Aperture-Priority AE most of the time, although, as when shooting portraits, you can use Manual or Program AE (making sure to shift the program to a suitable aperture). Set the aperture to f/8 for starters. Stop down to f/16 (or even a smaller aperture) when necessary.

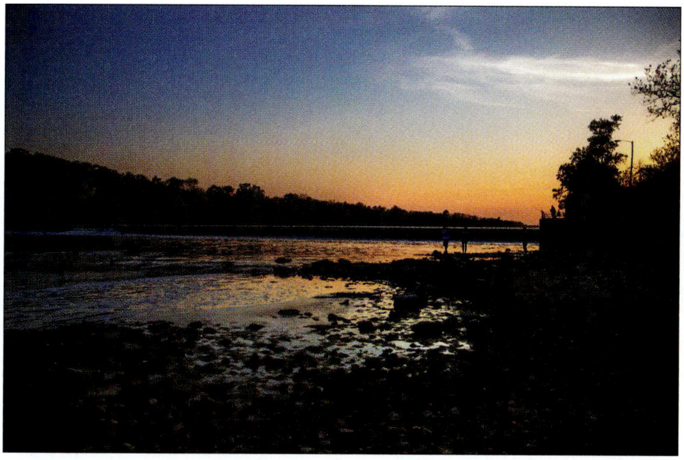

Figure 9-12: A tranquil sunset by a river.

Figure 9-13 is a classic landscape shot, showing the fields of northeast Indiana. The key elements in this photo are the depth of field and feeling of expansiveness. A small aperture (f/8) puts the corn and the barn in focus, whereas the framing emphasizes the open spaces.

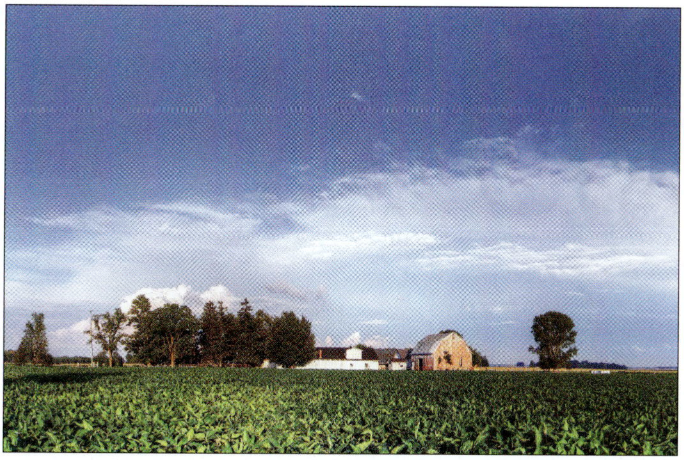

Figure 9-13: Farmland in America's midwest.

Choose a wide-angle lens or set the focal length of your zoom lens to wide-angle territory (40mm or so, and under). If you don't have a lens capable of wide angles, try shooting frames of a panorama and stitching them together using Photoshop or other, panorama-dedicated software.

You should also consider investing in some extra gear. A good tripod and head will help you take longer exposures without shaking the camera around. A remote switch or wireless remote permits you to take your hands off the camera. Filters can help control exposure (either ND or ND Grad filters) and color, as well as create other special effects.

Rarely do you need to raise ISO when shooting landscapes. Put it at 100 (you can go as low as 50 on the 5D Mark III if you set new ISO limits) and don't let it rise unless you have no choice.

The other camera settings can vary.

Pointers galore

Landscapes are fun to shoot. When you go out to shoot them, keep these tips in mind:

- **Think front to back:** One goal of landscape photos, barring exceptions for creative framing and subjects, is to emphasize the size of the scene. Help yourself out by framing the scene with space from the foreground to the background.
- **Focus on foreground:** At times, you can shoot very effective landscapes by focusing on something in the foreground. In Figure 9-14, for example, I focus on the flowering tree. The river isn't the main object in the photos, but it's still very important. It contributes to the feeling of space and depth.
- **Time:** The time of day matters. You get more aesthetically pleasing results right after sunrise or an hour or so before sunset. These times are called the *golden hour* because the light is softer and prettier.

  During these hours, the light hits the sides of buildings and trees. Shooting away from the sun means that shadows are cast away from you. The light is really nice: softer than at midday and more appealing.
- **Direction:** Think whether you'll be shooting into, away from, or across from the sun. Direction, along with time, determines whether some of your landscape will be in shadow, silhouetted, or brightly lit.
- **Weather:** Landscapes in particular benefit from how the changing weather changes the scene. Not every season will produce a photo with the same look. Snow, rain, heat, fall colors, wind, and other factors all affect your photos in different ways.

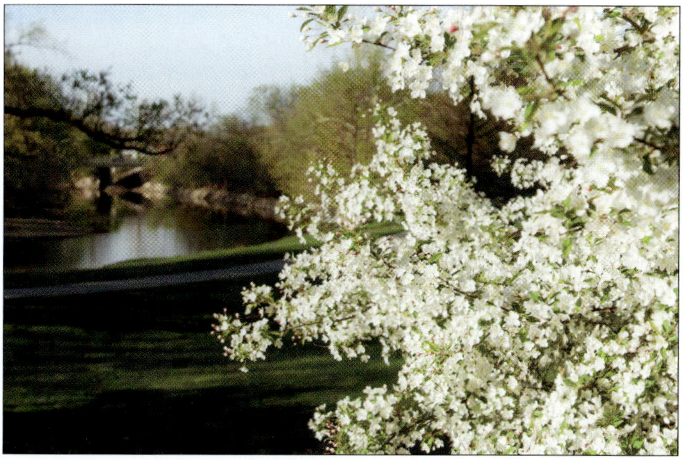

Figure 9-14: Although expansive, the focus is on the foreground in this landscape.

- **Wide angle works best:** Don't zoom in when shooting landscapes. In fact, zoom out as far as you can.
- **Clouds:** When possible, shoot landscapes when the skies are partly cloudy (not hazy or overcast, though). Clouds often make the sky more interesting
- **Sunsets:** Sunsets are a subset of landscape photography. They're challenging because of the bright sun, which tends to cast everything in silhouette.

Give Me Park Avenue: Shooting in the City

Cityscapes, buildings, and other facets of civilization can be just as compelling as landscapes and nature. Most times, your goal should be to take photos with a good depth of field and low noise level that show off the building, city, or activity in question. Figure 9-15 shows a classic city shot of Detroit's Renaissance Center taken from several blocks away on Brush Street. The buildings in the foreground act like canyon walls as they lead your eye to the main subject. The depth of field provided by an aperture of f/8 ensures that everything looks sharp and clear. The light was bright enough to allow an ISO of 100 and a shutter speed of 1/60 second — perfect for handheld photography.

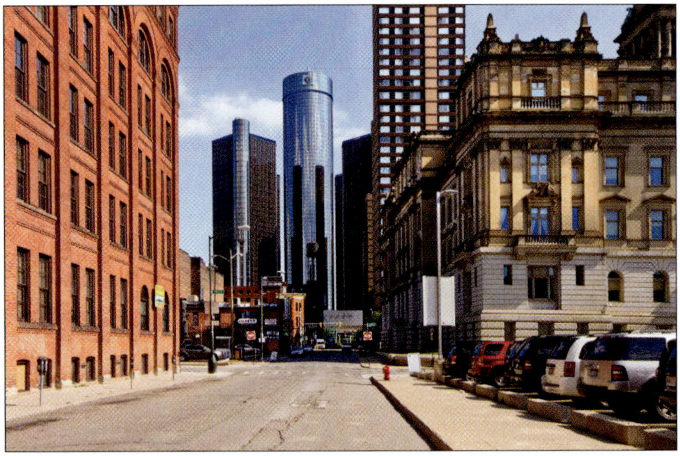

Figure 9-15: Some cityscapes evoke the same feelings as landscapes.

Key camera settings

Set your camera up much as you would for landscape photography (Av, M, or P shooting modes). Your goal is to control the aperture, which helps determine the depth of field. As with landscapes, wide-angle lenses work wonders in the city. You need the extra field of view that wide-angle lenses provide to fit large, tall buildings (or the entire skyline) in your frame. In contrast to shooting landscapes, though, you'll often be able to get much closer to your subject when in the city. When you're that close to large buildings, using a wide-angle lens is almost a necessity.

As with landscapes, try to keep ISO low. ISO will climb, however, when you take photos at night. You may also need to raise it because of motion in the scene, which will push shutter speed. Counteract the effect or faster shutter speeds on exposure by raising the ISO.

Pointers galore

You have many ways available to shoot cities and buildings. Although no one recipe satisfies all circumstances, keep these tips in mind:

- **Looking at:** When you're featuring a tall building and you're far enough away, you can shoot more or less directly at it. The building will look natural. Foreground objects, such as the trees at the bottom and top right of the scene, help frame the building and give a feeling of the distance.

- **Looking up:** Sometimes, even when you're using a wide-angle lens, you're so close to a building that you have to look up. Doing so often introduces vertical distortion in the photo. In other words, the building seems to lean away from you. You can sometimes fix these problems when they aren't too pronounced, but more often than not, the cure looks worse than the original. Figure 9-16 shows a shot in which I'm looking up at the War Memorial Coliseum in the town where I live. Although the distortion is apparent when you're looking for it, it seems to work in this photo.

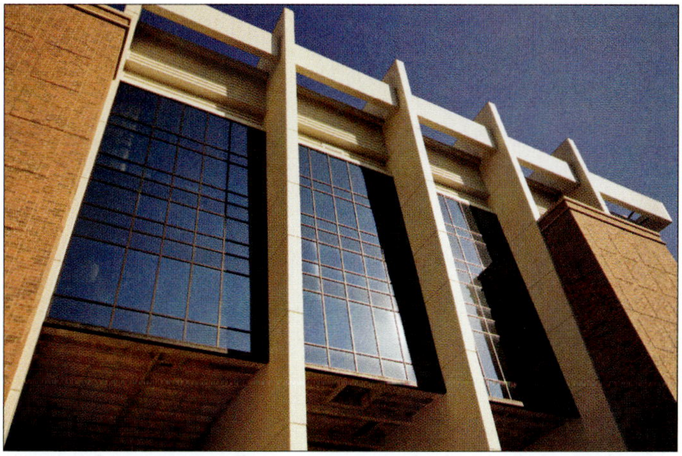

Figure 9-16: Looking up is sometimes necessary to capture tall buildings when close by.

- **Get out and walk:** Park your car (or get off the train) and walk around town. Cities are alive. People go about their business. Cars drive to and fro. Sometimes the scene is frantic and busy. At other times, as Figure 9-17 shows, the atmosphere is calm. You never know what you'll find, and walking is often the best way to discover the best shots.
- **Night scenes:** Cities and buildings are fun to photograph at night. Choose buildings with interesting light sources, spotlights, or street lights. Use a tripod when you can, which lets you lengthen shutter speed without blurring. Use a small aperture (on the order of f/22) to create star effects in bright lights.
- **Sometimes bigger isn't better:** As Figure 9-18 shows, not every city scene has to be large. After taking several conventional shots of the ivy-covered building, I realized that I had some great shots to take close in.

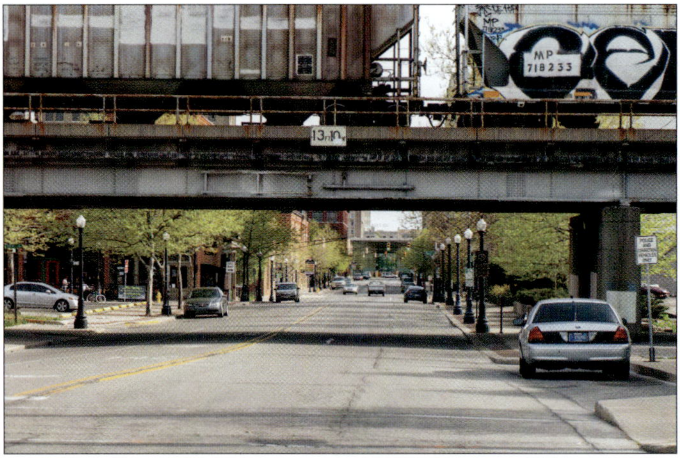

Figure 9-17: Walking is great exercise and good for photography.

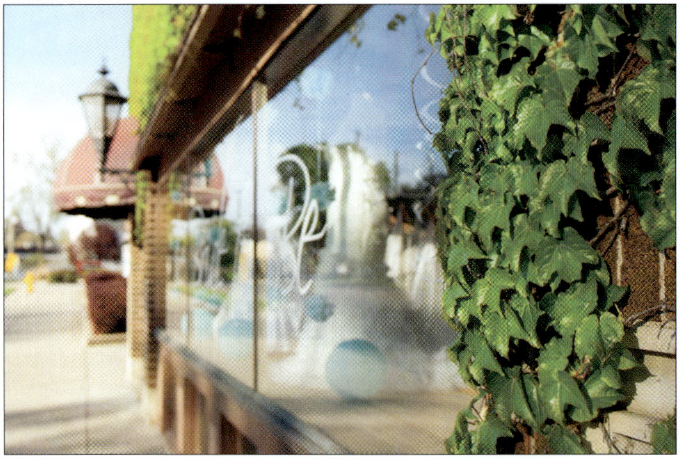

Figure 9-18: Look for unconventional angles in the city.

Shooting Freeze-Frame Moments

Action shots are all about shutter speed and getting the right focus. Your subjects are moving, sometimes rapidly, in or across your field of view, toward or away from you. No matter how you slice it, your goal is to capture moving objects quickly and clearly. Figure 9-19 shows a classic sports action shot of someone playing basketball. He's moving across my field of view. The ball is moving. His hands are moving. To have any chance of freezing him in place, the shutter speed had to be fast. In this case, that was 1/500 second.

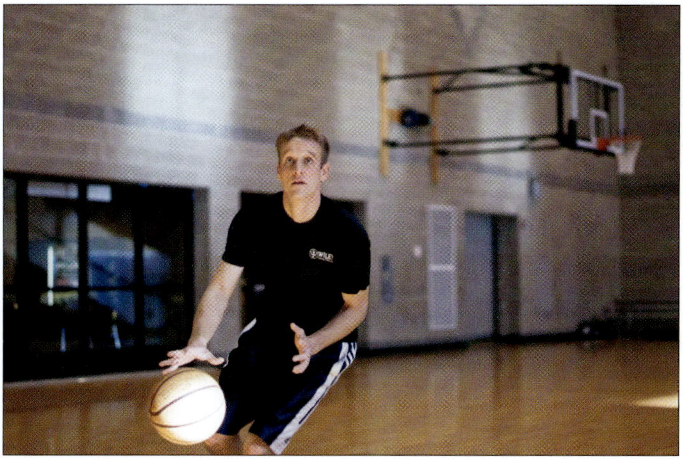

Figure 9-19: Pay attention to shutter speed when capturing action.

Key camera settings

To capture action, first set the camera up so that you can control the shutter speed. You should almost always choose the Shutter-Priority AE Shooting mode (Tv), although Manual also works.

In general, 1/250 to 1/500 second is fast enough to capture most action, but you may have to select a faster speed, depending on the lighting and action. If the subject is moving across your field of view, expect motion blur if you're not shooting with a fast enough shutter speed. Motion blur can be appealing at times. If the subject is moving toward or away from you, he will look out of focus if the shutter speed is too slow.

On bright days with a wide aperture, you may have to shoot at 1/1000 second or faster. Of course, if you have the light, the 5D Mark III can reach 1/8000 second. That's fast.

When shooting action shots in dimmer lighting, expect the ISO to climb. You may set it there yourself or rely on the Auto setting to take care of it.

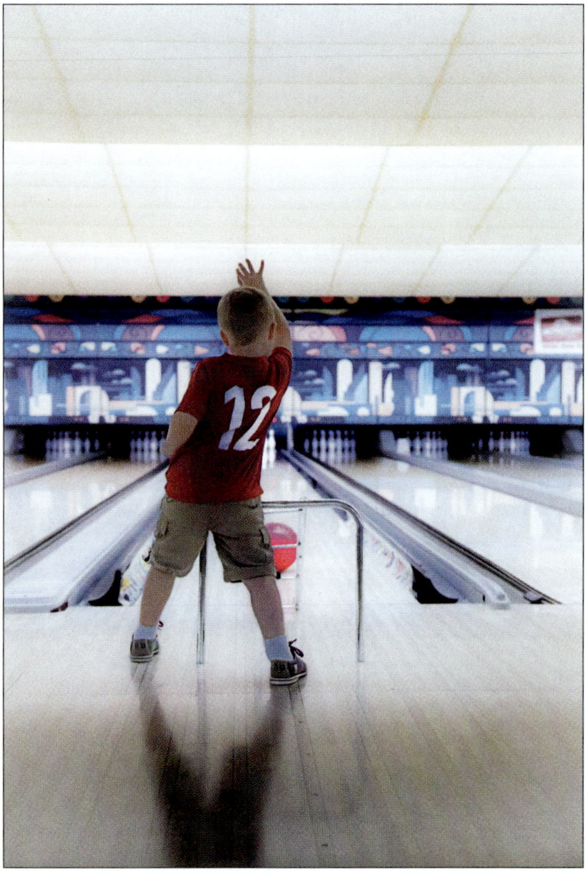

Figure 9-20: When the lighting stinks, ISO often rises to let you get fast shutter speeds.

Figure 9-20 shows the balancing act of ISO versus shutter speed and aperture in action. In this case, I couldn't do anything about the lighting in this bowling alley. The lanes were fairly bright, but the spot where the subject stood was much darker. To be able to capture a subject in action at 1/250 second, I had to set the ISO to 12800. If I'd had a faster lens (The 24-105mm f/4L is limited to f/4), I could have traded a few stops of aperture for ISO. The 5D Mark III is such a good camera, however, that the noise level is reasonable even at 12800.

The other critical camera setting when you're shooting fast-moving action is the autofocus mode. Although you can choose to manually focus, it's very hard to do. Autofocus is actually more reliable, especially when shooting at a distance from the action. Set the mode to AI Servo AF and fine-tune it to match the situation you're in. (In other words, choose the right case number.) The case enables the camera to track the target and continually updates the focus. See Chapter 7 for detailed information on the 5D Mark III's autofocus system.

Use fill flash when necessary. Be aware that you'll run up against the camera's *sync speed* — the fastest speed at which you can set the shutter and use the flash unless you enable high-speed sync on the flash. The 5D Mark III's sync speed is 1/200 second. If you set your 600EX Speedlite to

High-Speed Sync, you can shoot with shutter speeds up to the camera's maximum, 1/8000 second.

Finally, set the drive mode to Continuous if you want to capture a sequence of action shots. Continuous mode can be very effective. You can choose the best one or create a montage using a handful of key frames.

Pointers galore

Here are some pointers to help make your action shots even better:

- **Brighter is better:** Because of the premium that sports and action photography place on fast shutter speeds, the brighter the scene, the better. You'll often find the best conditions during bright days.

  Another advantage of a very bright scene is that you can be in a different shooting mode and not worry directly about the shutter speed (see Figure 9-21). When I shot this figure, the camera was in Aperture-Priority AE mode, and I could think in terms of setting a nice depth of field without worrying about whether the shutter speed would be fast enough to capture the action. After the first few test shots, it was obvious that I had room to spare. The shutter speed here is 1/800 second and the ISO is a paltry 100. Tons of overhead.

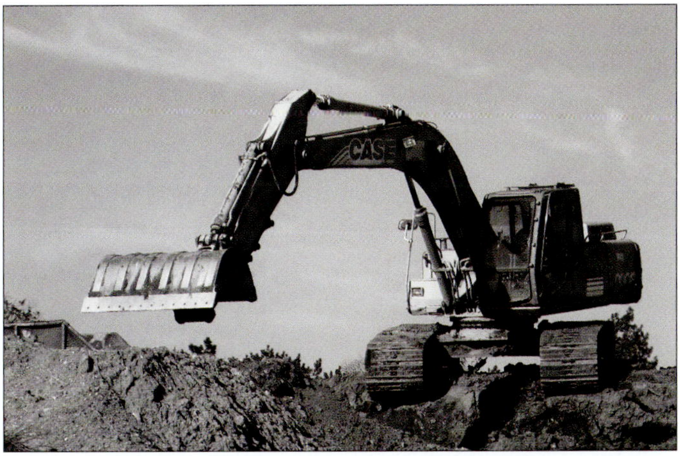

Figure 9-21: Bright scenes almost always make it easier.

- **Fast is relative:** You don't have to dial in shutter speeds of 1/2000 second or faster to catch all the action. You may want a bit of motion blur in some photos. At other times, you may want to completely freeze the action.
- **Not just sports:** Action isn't limited to sports. You can photograph kids, pets, people, and anything else that's moving when you don't want excessive blurring. Photographing musicians is one such activity. In Figure 9-22, I was present at a rehearsal and was able to get close to the action. I set the camera to Shutter-Priority AE mode and dialed in 1/250 second to keep motion-blurring to a minimum. I opened the lens up to f/4 and elevated the ISO to 1250 to increase the exposure.

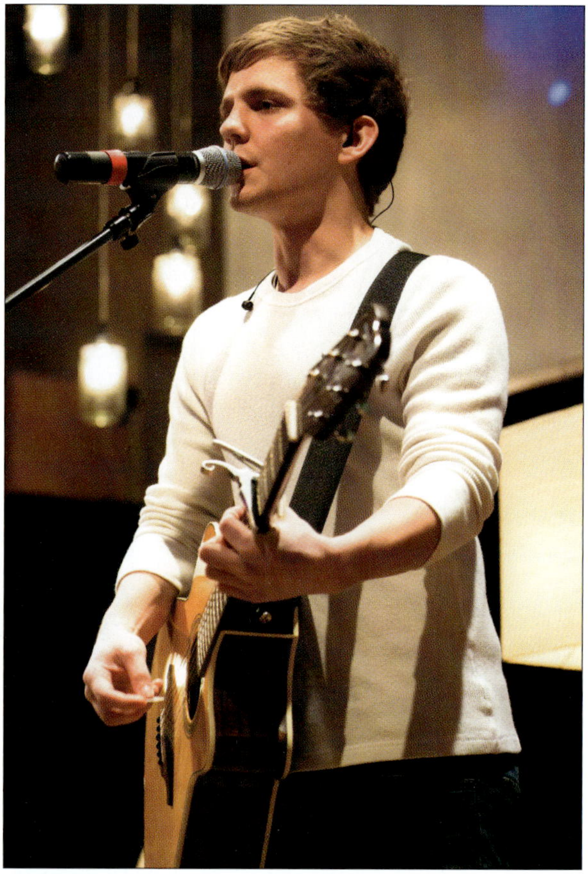

Figure 9-22: Don't just think sport; action includes a lot of things.

Tabletop Studio Photography

Setting up a tabletop studio is easier than you might think. All you need is some space in your house, apartment, church, place of business, school, or tree house (joke) that you can control. It could be a corner of your basement or an entire loft. The point is to be able to devote the space to setting up and photographing small-scale subjects, such as the rabbits in Figure 9-23. It helps if you have total control over the lighting, but that isn't absolutely necessary. You can work with what you have.

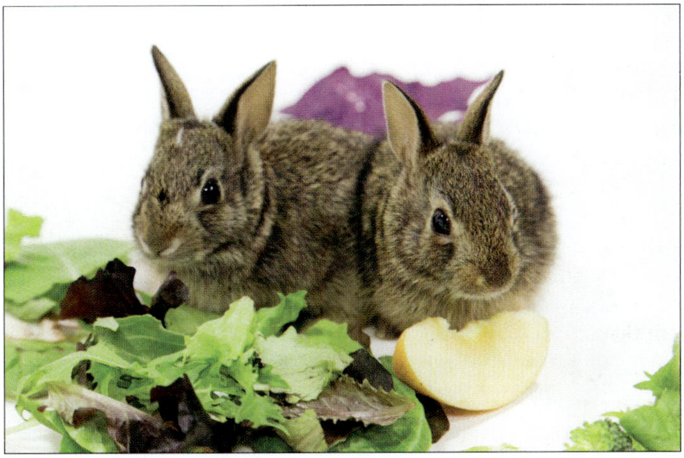

Figure 9-23: Rabbits are loads of fun.

Key camera settings

I like working in manual mode (including taking the ISO off of Auto) when photographing small-scale subjects. Manual mode lets me set the exposure the way I want it, rather than according to the camera's meter.

Pay attention to your depth of field when working very closely with subjects. Apertures that you would normally use to create larger depths of field, f/8 being a prime example, suddenly produce much smaller depths of field. Apertures that you might use when shooting portraits (under f/5.6, for example) create microscopic depths of field. When photographing cameras and many other objects, I set the aperture to f/16 or smaller.

Set ISO to 100 or lower and don't raise it.

Use a tripod and a remote, and consider enabling Mirror lockup to limit camera shake. Shutter speed is not a problem unless you're photographing something that moves.

Consider using Live View and magnifying the screen so that you can focus precisely. I prefer manual focus.

Off-camera flash (indeed, any sort of external lighting, whether it's continuous or strobe) works very well in this type of setup. You can achieve some truly creative effects that way.

Pointers galore

Try these pointers on for size:

- **Take test shots:** Always take test shots! The reason is next.
- **Review your photos:** Always review your photos! Analyze them to check composition, focus, color, and exposure. Examine the histogram so that you know how far you can push the exposure. I know exactly what I want in my studio shots from looking at the histogram.
- **Control lighting:** Because you're in a studio, you control the lighting. If you have more multiple flashes, set them up to work from different angles. I prefer a number of continuous lights. Collectively, they are very bright, and I can position them where I want them.
- **Use modifiers:** Soften your flash or continuous lights with soft boxes, umbrellas, or other modifiers. Diffused light casts softer, less obtrusive shadows. If you want the opposite (for a creative effect), you can remove all diffusers and even add snoots and grids.
- **The background is important:** Your background doesn't have to be anything fancy, but it should look nice. I use a lot of plain-white or black backgrounds. They are great for isolating cameras and other objects.

Exploring HDR Photography

I can't show you all the ins and outs of High Dynamic Range (HDR) photography. However, I can relay enough about it so that you can decide whether it's something you want to try. HDR photography is very rewarding and no more difficult than the other types of photography after you get the hang of it.

TECHNICAL STUFF

HDR is a type of photography that uses more than one photograph to push the light-capturing capability of the camera beyond what is possible in a single photograph. These additional photos are called *exposure brackets*. The bracketed photos are framed identically (or nearly so) but exposed differently. The most common practice is to take three photos: one underexposed, one correctly exposed, and one overexposed. That's why they are called *exposure* brackets. You "bracket" the ideal exposure with other photos. Figure 9-24 shows three exposure brackets of a single scene.

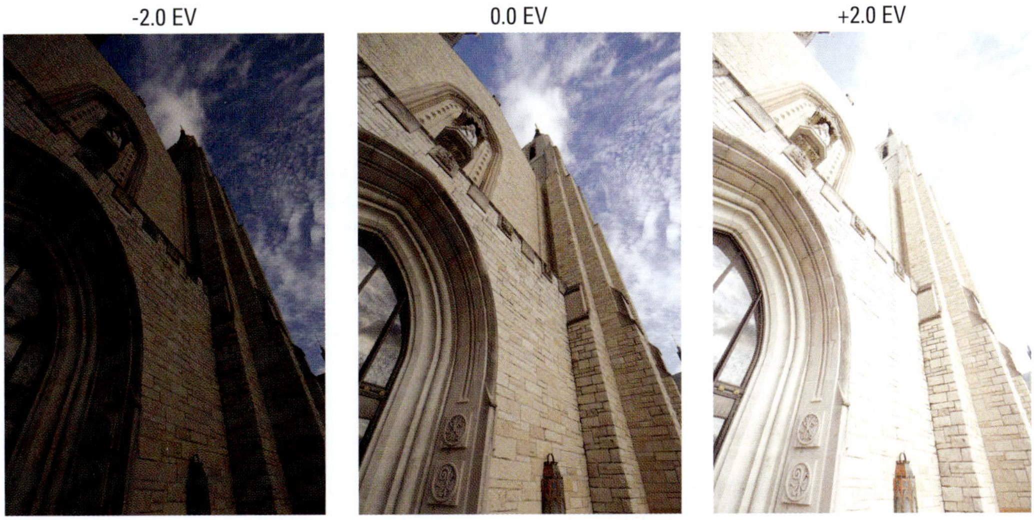

Figure 9-24: HDR uses exposure brackets to capture more detail than one photo can.

After the brackets are photographed, you use special HDR software to combine them into an HDR image, which you convert to a TIFF or JPEG. That process is called *tone mapping* and is similar in theory to converting a RAW photo into a JPEG or TIFF. You're able to change the relative brightness, darkness, and detail across the scene. In the end, you wind up with one photograph that was created with light captured by three or more photos. Figure 9-25 shows a finished HDR image.

TIP

Photomatix Pro (`www.hdrsoft.com`) is one of the leading HDR applications available today. Photoshop, by Adobe, is capable of merging exposure brackets into a single high-bit-depth image that you process and is often preferred by those looking for a more natural result.

REMEMBER

The 5D Mark III has a few automated processes that take multiple exposures for HDR. In HDR mode (accessed by pressing the Creative Photo button), the camera shoots the exposures and does the tone mapping for you. When using Auto Exposure Bracketing (set primarily from the Quick Control screen), the camera shoots the brackets automatically, but you have to do the HDR processing yourself after you download the photos. See Chapter 6 for more information on how to use the 5D Mark III's HDR capabilities.

You can also shoot exposure brackets in manual mode by setting the aperture and then adjusting the shutter speed by regular increments. You're the one who has to make the adjustments, take the photos, and process them later.

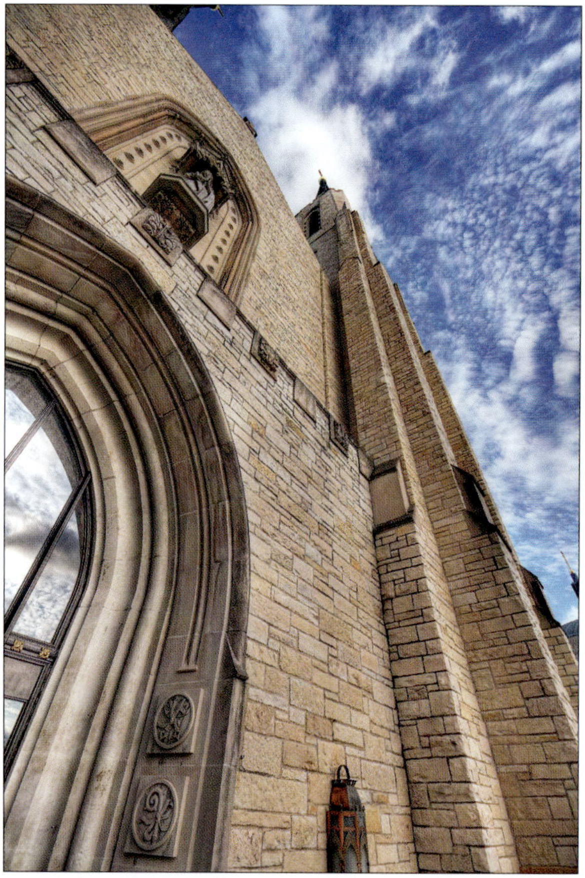

Figure 9-25: The final result combines exposure data not available from one photo.

Dial "F" for Fun

Photography can be a lot of fun, especially if you seek different types of photos and different ways to take them. Try these scenes and suggestions on for size:

- **Concert photography:** Treating concert photography almost like sports and action is necessary because the artists are almost always in motion. They sing, jump around, and play the guitar, bass, drums, or piano. Set the camera to Shutter-Priority AE or manual mode and dial in a reasonably fast shutter speed (1/250 second; take test shots to see whether you need a faster one or can slow it down).

  The problem is, the lighting doesn't always make it easy for you to set a fast shutter speed. Even bright spots may not be bright enough to shoot at 1/250 second or faster without raising the ISO. Take a fast lens (under f/4.0 if you can) and be prepared for high ISOs.

  I shot Figure 9-26 at 1/250 second, f/4.0, and ISO 12800.

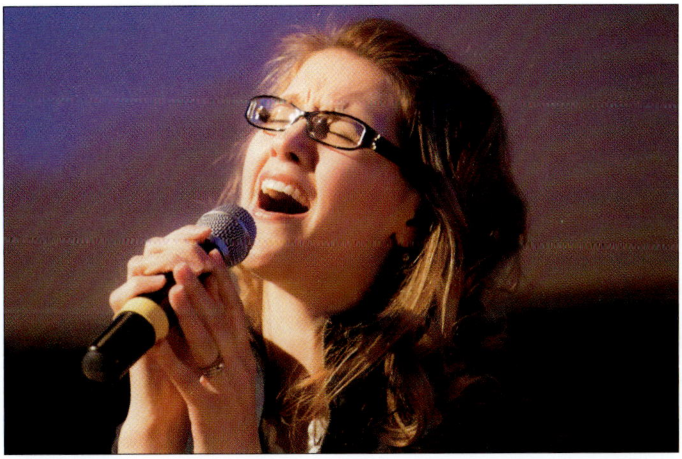

Figure 9-26: Focus on shutter speed when shooting concerts so that the artists aren't all blurred.

I prefer manual focus so that I have complete control. I don't have to worry about what the camera is doing or what it might focus on that way. However, if you can't see well enough to focus manually, you should switch to autofocus. Whether you use One-Shot AF or AI Servo AF depends on how much tracking you need to do. If the artist is standing in one spot, you should be okay with the former.

- **Keep shooting:** I love taking photos of motorcycles. Figure 9-27 shows one in a parking lot that I snapped after a shoot one day, with quite unexpectedly nice results. Treat shots like this as portraits and look for the best angle from which to approach the subject.

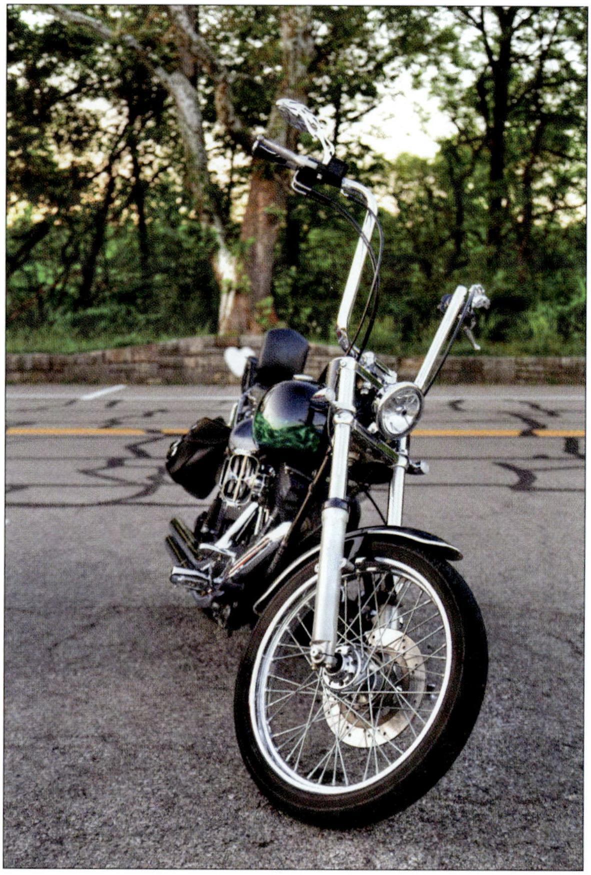

Figure 9-27: I dig those ape-hanger handlebars.

- **Flash for white balance:** When you don't have control over the lighting and you are inside, use a flash for exposure *and* to help with white balance. In Figure 9-28, the subject is perusing colorful cookware on the shelf. The room behind her is very warm and imparts a yellow color cast on just about everything. The flash lit her nicely with a clean white light.

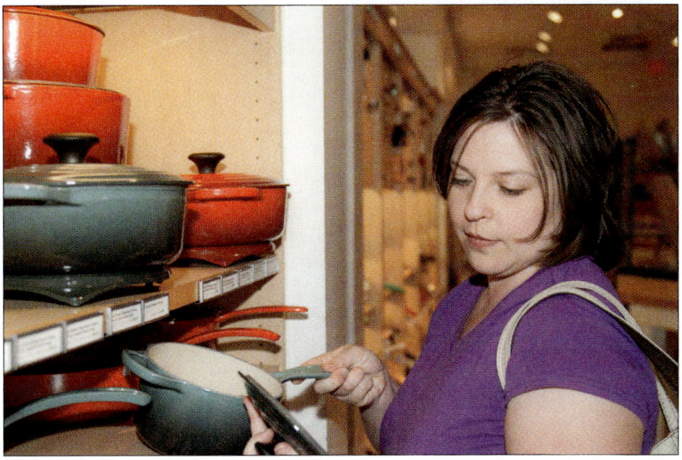

Figure 9-28: Can I help you, ma'am?

- **Working with kids:** Working with kids is challenging but rewarding. When casually shooting, set up your camera as you would when shooting sports and action. Children are, after all, in continuous motion. When you can get them to stay still for a moment, shoot as you would a portrait.

  It always helps to give them something to do because they find posing for pictures frustratingly boring. The kids in Figure 9-29 are balancing and walking along a short wall.

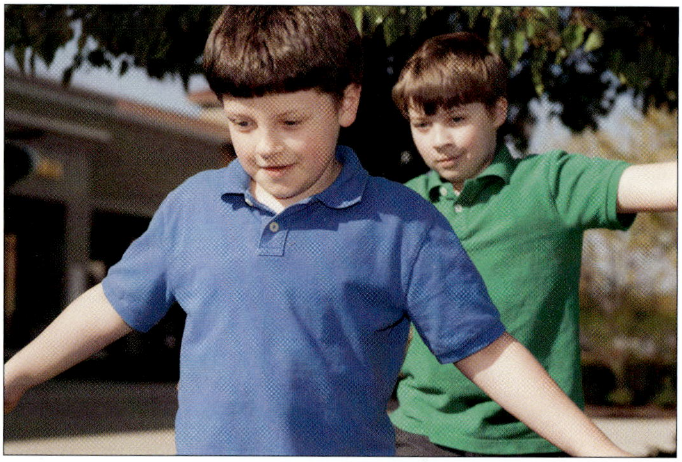

Figure 9-29: Give kids something to do and then photograph them doing it.

- **Be ready for anything:** My family took a road trip to visit some old cemeteries where many of my wife's ancestors are buried. We were standing in a cemetery when an airplane suddenly flew over. It returned a few minutes later, this time just above the trees (see Figure 9-30). I was able to capture it with a 1/1000 second shutter speed and an aperture of f/8 using AI Servo AF to track the plane.

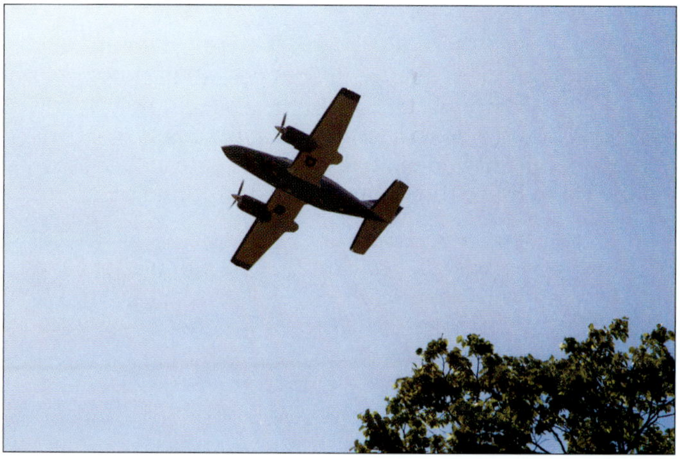

Figure 9-30: Sometimes your subjects appear out of thin air.

- **Really, be ready for anything:** I was out taking photos when I ran across another photographer taking wedding shots. He had the bride, groom, and their attendants on a photogenic bridge. I walked up and asked him if I could unobtrusively take a few shots of him in action (and some of the wedding party). He said yes, and this (see Figure 9-31) is one of the results. I used One-Shot AF and chose the specific AF Point using Single-Point AF (Manual selection) to keep the photographer in focus.

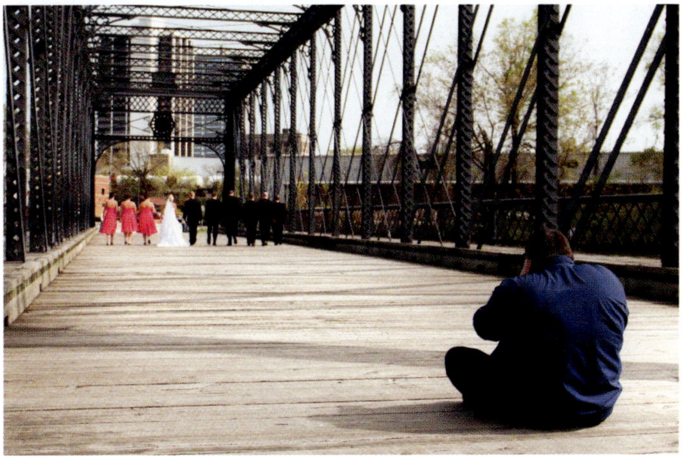

Figure 9-31: Another photographer in action.

- **Using the background and foreground:** In Figure 9-32, I used the background to make the tree in the foreground much more interesting. Believe me, I've taken a lot of boring photos of trees. They look beautiful in person, but that doesn't always translate into a good photo. The challenge is to make the photo interesting while capturing something of what you see.
- **Splash and spray:** Getting into the action makes for dynamic photos. I took this photo (see Figure 9-33) of the James Scott Memorial Fountain on Belle Isle, near Detroit. When shooting toward the sun, keep the aperture small.

WARNING!

Don't let the camera get too wet. A few drops won't hurt it (the 5D Mark III is supposed to be weather resistant), but dousing it may.

- **The more the merrier:** I love flowers. In Figure 9-34, I got down to shoot across the top of this bed of tulips. This was also shot very close to sunset, so the light is hitting the flowers almost directly from the left. I used my closeness and a wide aperture to limit the depth of field to about a flower's width. Although one flower can make a great photo, if you can take a shot of an entire flower bed, the result can be even more captivating.

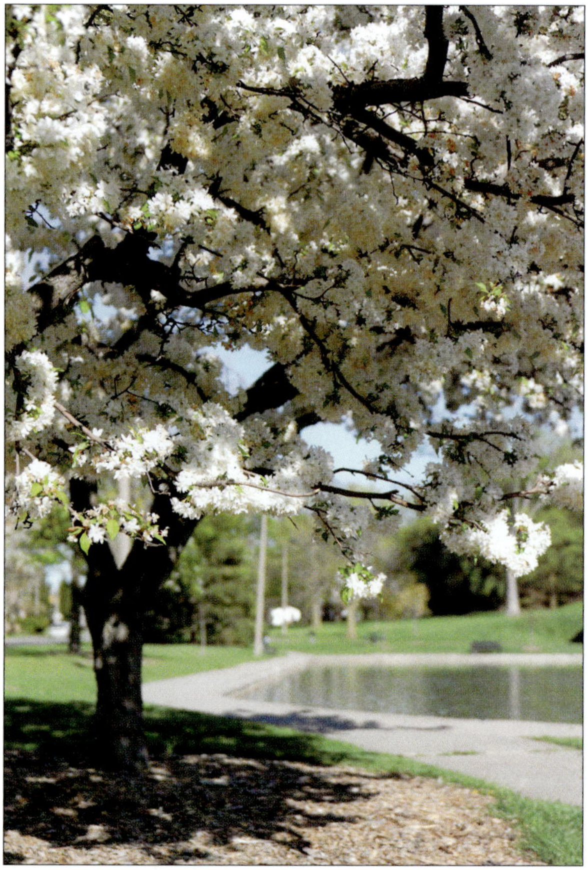

Figure 9-32: The expansive background makes the tree in the foreground stand out more.

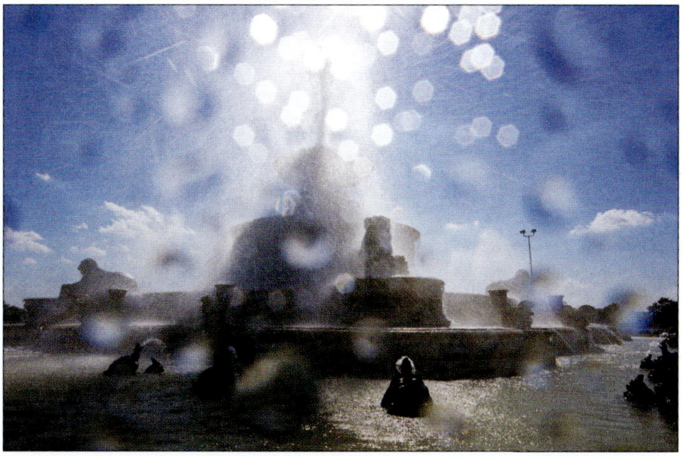

Figure 9-33: The splashing water adds energy to this photo of a fountain.

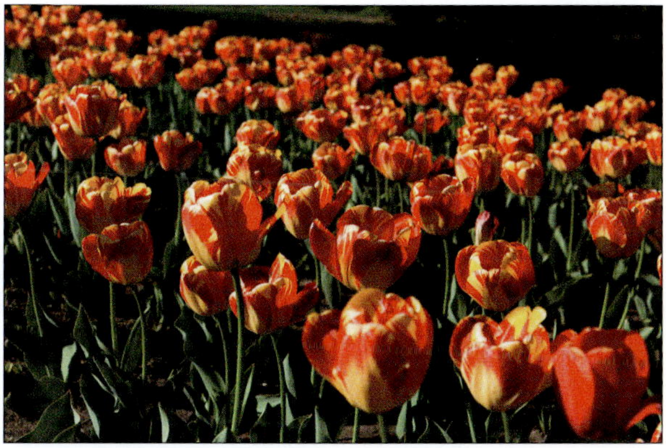

Figure 9-34: There's something magical about an entire bed of beautiful flowers.

Part IV

The Part of Tens

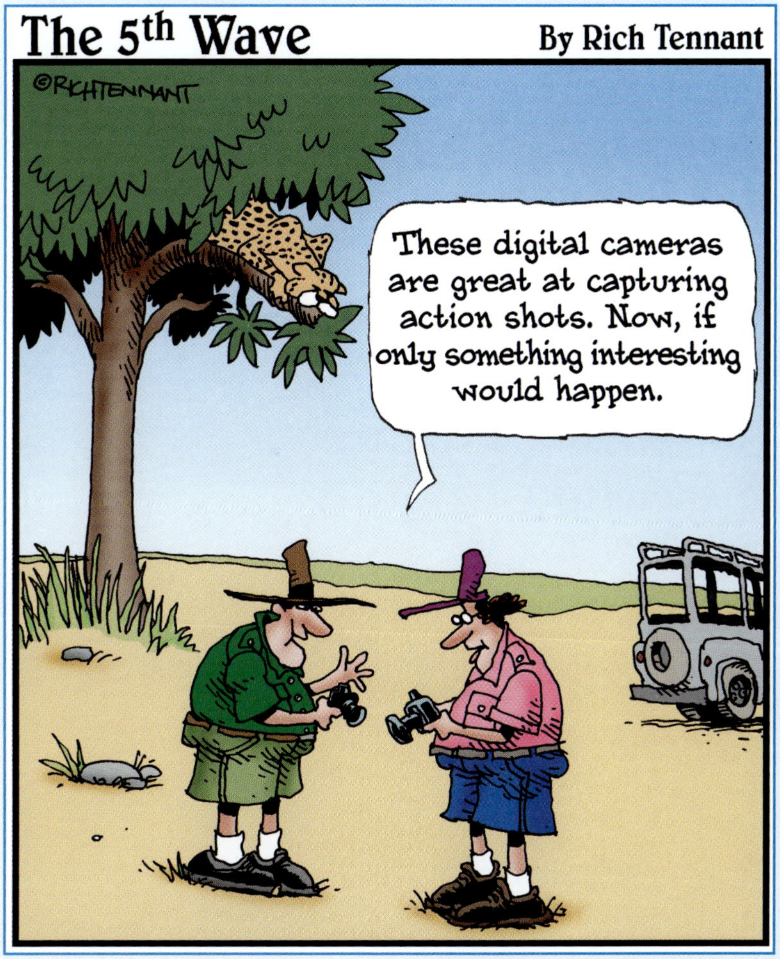

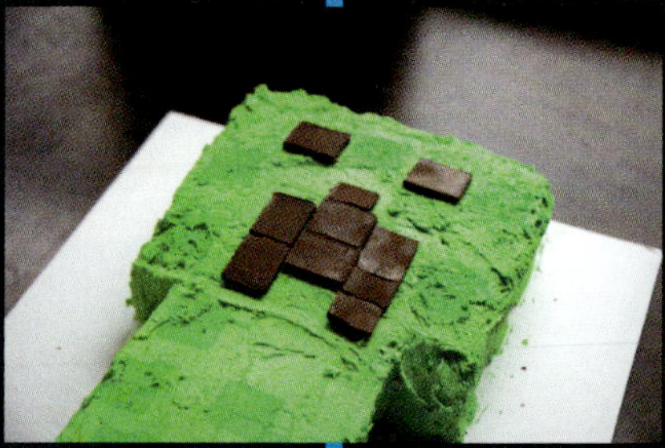

In the *For Dummies* tradition, this part of the book contains additional tidbits of information presented in the always popular Top Ten list format.

Chapter 10 covers lots of cools ways to customize your 5D Mark III, such as registering your own shooting modes and customizing controls and which displays appear on the back LCD monitor. Following that, Chapter 11 introduces you to several awesome (but optional) features, such as working with dual memory cards, adding copyright information, and calibrating the camera's autofocus system.

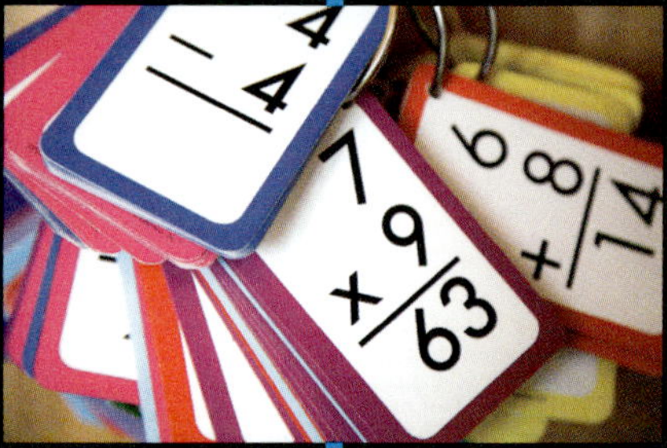

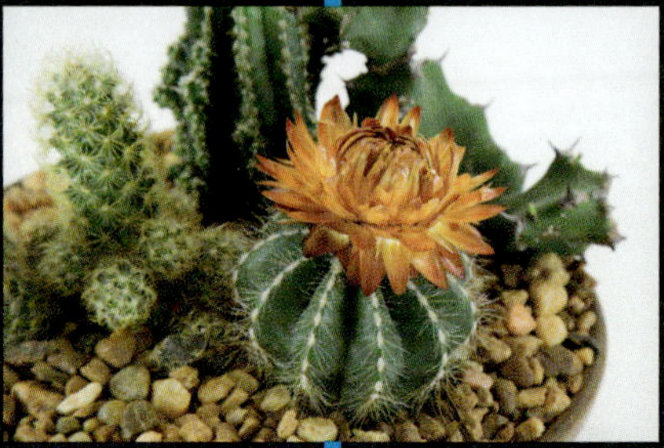

10

Ten Ways to Customize Your Camera

In This Chapter

- Customizing Custom Functions
- Creating your own camera menu
- Reassigning camera controls
- Changing how files are named and numbered
- Creating your own shooting modes
- Working with custom folders
- Changing dial directions
- Customizing displays

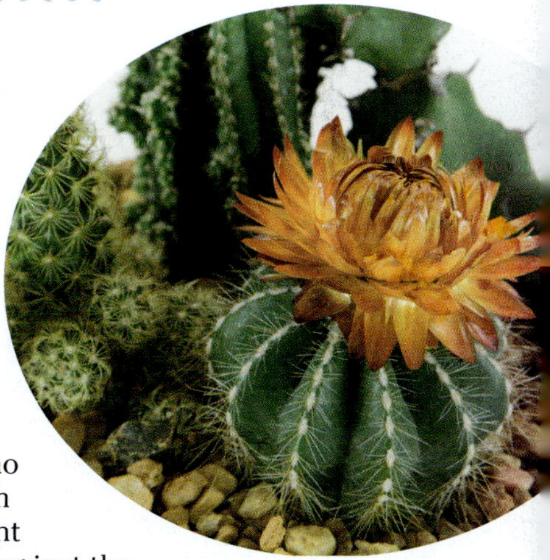

Whereas the rest of the book covers how to use your 5D Mark III, this chapter points you in the right direction if you want to customize it to suit your own needs. You have numerous options to consider. You can create your own camera menu and folders, as well as change how files are named and numbered. You can also work with Custom Functions, create your own menu, customize controls, and create your own shooting modes.

These features may come in handy only for certain users, on certain occasions. Still, they're included at no extra charge with your camera, so check 'em out when you have a few spare moments. Who knows? You might discover a bonus feature that's a hidden gem, providing just the solution you need for one of your photography problems.

Custom Function, What's Your Function?

Several features covered in this book mention *Custom Functions,* which are more advanced options grouped together in the camera's menu system. On the 5D Mark III, Canon groups Custom Functions into four categories:

- **C.Fn 1 (Exposure):** Includes Exposure Level Increments, ISO Speed Setting Increments, Bracketing Auto Cancel, Bracketing Sequence, Number of Bracketed Shots, and Safety Shift.
- **C.Fn 2 (Display/Operation):** Includes Warnings in Viewfinder, LV Shooting Area Display, Dial Direction During Tv/Av Multi Function Lock, and Custom Controls.
- **C.Fn 3 (Others):** Includes Add Cropping Information and Default Erase Option.
- **C.Fn 4 (Clear):** Only one this time: Clear All Custom Functions. It works for all Custom Functions except Custom Controls, which must be reset by itself.

The Canon EOS 7D Custom Functions are almost identical to the 5D Mark III, but if you're upgrading from the Canon EOS 5D Mark II, you'll notice several changes. If you are using both cameras, you'll have to get used to these differences. Many Custom Functions don't work in Movie mode, and a few don't work when you're using Live View (namely, Warnings in Viewfinder and the Default Erase option).

To access the Custom Functions, make sure that you're not in Scene Intelligent Auto shooting mode; then press the Menu button. Rotate the Main dial or use the Multicontroller to navigate left or right until you find the Custom Function menus (see Figure 10-1).

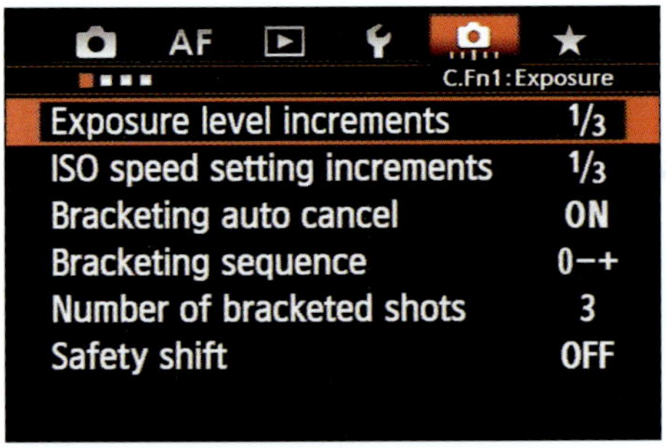

Figure 10-1: Use Custom Functions to customize your camera.

Consider registering your favorite Custom Functions, perhaps one or two that you use all the time, in My Menu (shown in the "Creating Your Own Camera Menu" section, later in this chapter). You can access them, in addition to all the other items you have saved in My Menu, faster than if they were spread out all over the menu system.

Adding Copyright Information to Your Photos

Your 5D Mark III can store your personal copyright information as part of a picture file's *metadata* — the extra data that contains helpful bits of information such as the aperture, shutter speed, ISO, date, and time. Including a copyright notice is a reasonable first step to take if you want to prevent anyone from using your pictures without your permission. Anyone who views your picture in a program that can display metadata will see your copyright notice and know who owns the rights to the picture.

REMEMBER: You cannot set copyright information when in Scene Intelligent Auto mode, but it will still be attached to each photo.

To enter information, go to Setup Menu 4 and look for the Copyright Information option. Follow the screens to enter your name and other information. The display then changes to a data-entry screen, as shown in Figure 10-2. You have 63 characters to work with.

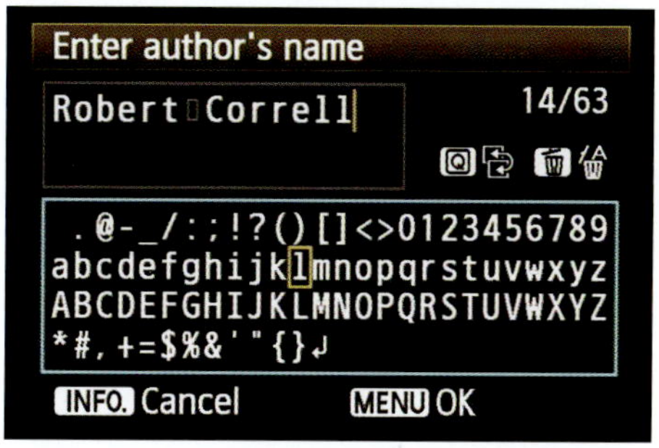

Figure 10-2: Enter the copyright information that you want tagged to your images.

To check the accuracy of your data, select Display Copyright Info and press Set. You should see a screen similar to Figure 10-3.

TIP: Disable copyright tagging later, if desired (for example, when someone else is using the camera), by selecting the Delete Copyright Information option.

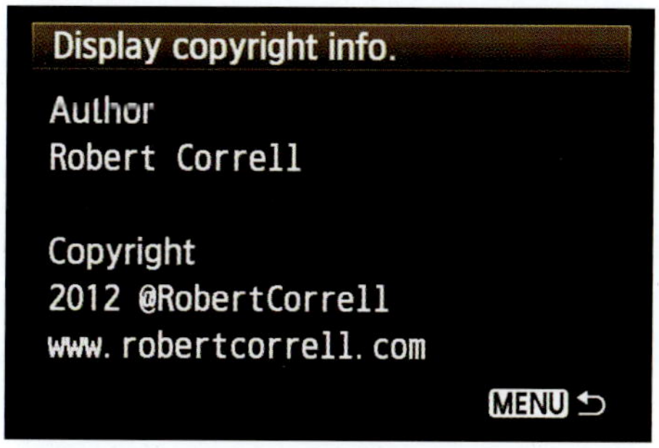

Figure 10-3: Check to make sure that you spelled your name correctly.

Creating Your Own Camera Menu

The 5D Mark III enables you to create (when not in Scene Intelligent Auto mode) your own custom menu containing up to six items from the camera's other menus. Customizing a menu speeds the process of finding your favorite menu options. Figure 10-4 shows a typical custom list of menu items that you can store in My Menu.

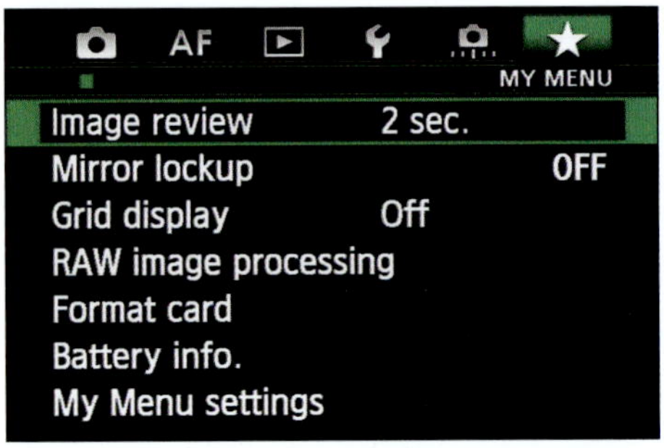

Figure 10-4: Group your favorite menu items.

To create your own menu, go to the My Menu menu and select the My Menu Settings option. On the My Menu Settings screen that opens, select Register to My Menu. A scrolling list appears, containing every item on the camera's other menus. Simply highlight them and press the Set button.

The list items are organized in the order they appear in the camera's menu but are not identified by their menu category. In other words, you can't know that Multi Function Lock belongs in the Custom Function menu unless you know it already.

After creating your menu, you can further customize and manage it by following these suggestions (they are all located in the My Menu Settings screen):

- **Give your menu priority.** You can tell the camera to automatically display your menu anytime you press the Menu button. To do so, select the Display From My Menu option.
- **Change the order of the list of menu items.** Select the Sort option to move a menu item up or down in the list.
- **Delete menu items.** To delete one or more items, select Delete Item/Items.

Creating Custom Shooting Modes

It's hard to miss the Custom Shooting Modes (C1, C2, and C3) on the Main dial. With three out of nine modes devoted to the Custom modes, they take up a third of the space on the dial, as shown in Figure 10-5. With the Custom Shooting Modes, you set the shooting mode, shutter speed, metering mode, and so forth, and then save — *register*, in Canon lingo — those settings. Later, when you're out shooting, recall those settings in an instant from the Mode dial, which is faster and less annoying than having to reset all those modes again.

Custom shooting modes

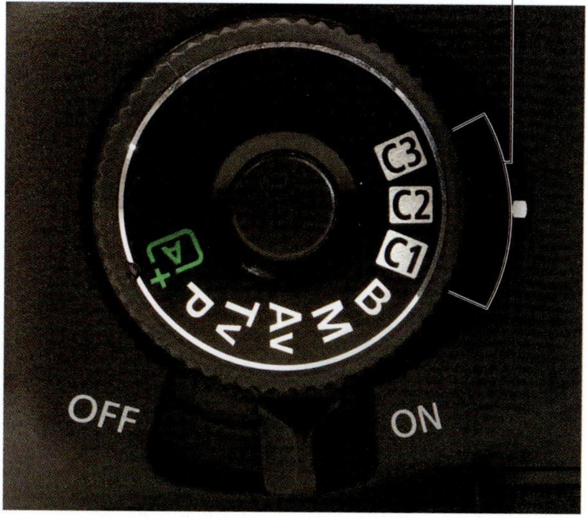

Figure 10-5: The Custom Shooting Modes on the Mode dial.

To register your settings in a Custom Shooting Mode, set up your camera the way you want it, starting with the shooting mode (except Scene Intelligent Auto). Next, configure your camera according to the menu options you want to include. See Table 10-1 for a list of menu options that you can save in a Custom Shooting Mode.

Table 10-1 Menu Options Stored in Custom Shooting Modes

Menus	*What You Can Save*
Shooting Menu 1–5	All options except Dust Delete Data (Shooting 3)
AF Menu 1–5	All options except AF Microadjustment (AF5)
Playback Menu 1–2	Only Slide show and Image jump with Main dial
Playback Menu 3	All except Control over HDMI
Setup Menu 1	File Numbering, Auto rotate, and Eye-Fi settings only
Setup Menu 2	All except Date/Time, Language, and GPS device settings
Setup Menu 3	All except Video system, Battery info, and Communication settings
Setup Menu 4	Nope, nada, nothing
Custom Functions Menu	All except Warnings in the viewfinder and Clear All Custom Functions (CF 4)
My Menu	None

Return to Setup Menu 4 and select Custom Shooting Mode (C1-C3) to register the settings. You can also clear the settings, which returns the custom mode to its default settings, and set the camera to automatically update your mode as you use it.

When you want to use your custom settings, select C1, C2, or C3 from the Mode dial (see Chapter 1 for more information about the Mode dial) and start taking pictures. Couldn't be easier!

Customizing Camera Buttons and Dials

One of the cooler things about modern digital SLRs is that the engineers on the sixty-third floor have realized that people like to customize what buttons do. It's a real leap of courage for them, I'm sure, to allow us to turn their well-crafted Depth-of-Field Preview button into a Viewfinder Electronic Level button. But that's exactly what you can do. The following list summarizes all the possible combinations.

- **Shutter button (half-press):** Metering and AF Start (default), Metering Start, AE Lock (when held)
- **AF-ON button:** Metering and AF Start (default), AE Lock, AF Stop, FE Lock, AE Lock (hold), Off (disabled)
- **AE Lock button:** AE Lock (default), Metering and AF Start, AF Stop, FE Lock, AE Lock (hold), Off (disabled)

- **DOF preview button:** Depth-of-Field Preview (default), AF Stop, AE Lock, Switch AF Mode (One-Shot AF to AI Servo AF), IS Start, Switch to Registered AF Function (assigns select AF characteristics such as AF Area Selection mode, tracking sensitivity, and so forth, to the button), One-Touch Image Quality Setting (fast switching between different image qualities), One-Touch Image Quality Setting (hold), FE Lock, VF Electronic Level, Switch to Registered AF Point, AE Lock (hold), Off (disabled)
- **Lens AF stop button:** AF Stop (default), Metering and AF Start, AE Lock, Switch AF Mode (One-Shot AF to AI Servo AF), IS Start, Switch to Registered AF Function (assigns select AF characteristics such as AF Area Selection mode, tracking sensitivity, and so forth, to the button), AE Lock (hold), Switch to Registered AF Point
- **Multi-function button:** FE Lock (default), AE Lock, One-Touch Image Quality Setting (fast switching between different image qualities), One-Touch Image Quality Setting (hold), VF Electronic Level, AE Lock (hold)
- **Set button:** Off (disabled, default), Image Quality, Picture Style, Menu, Playback, Zoom (press Set and turn the Main dial), ISO (press and hold Set and then turn the Main dial)
- **Main dial:** Tv (shutter speed in M mode, default), Av (aperture in M mode)
- **Quick Control dial:** Av (aperture in M mode, default), Tv (shutter speed in M mode, default), AF Point Direct Selection, ISO (turn during metering)
- **Multicontroller:** Off (disabled, default), AF Point Direct Selection

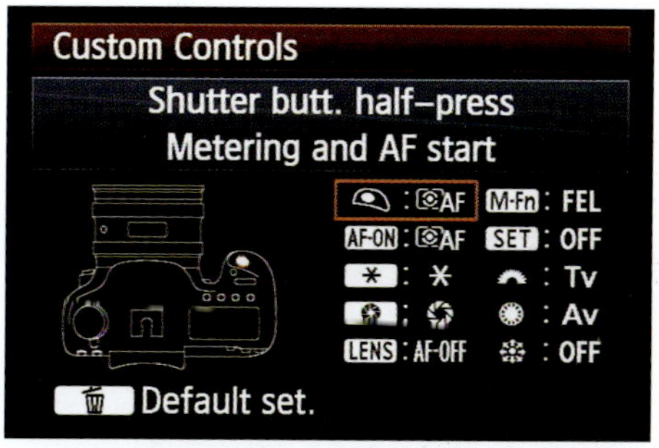

Figure 10-6: This looks promising.

To customize the controls, make your way over to the Custom Function Menu 2. Selecting the Custom Controls option changes the display to that shown in Figure 10-6.

Highlight the control of your choice, press the Set button, and then highlight a new function of your choice, as shown in Figure 10-7.

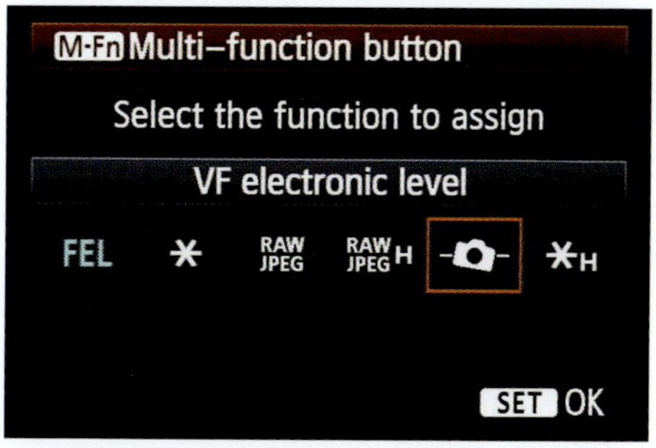

Figure 10-7: Your options are clearly displayed for each control.

TIP: Don't be afraid of messing things up. You can always return and press the Erase button to return everything to the default.

Creating and Using Folders

Custom folders are a feature that you might find helpful when you want to separate and organize shots while you shoot. The applicable menu is called Record Function+Card/Folder Select and is located in Setup Menu 1. The detailed options are shown in Figure 10-8. Select Folder and press the Set button to create and select folders.

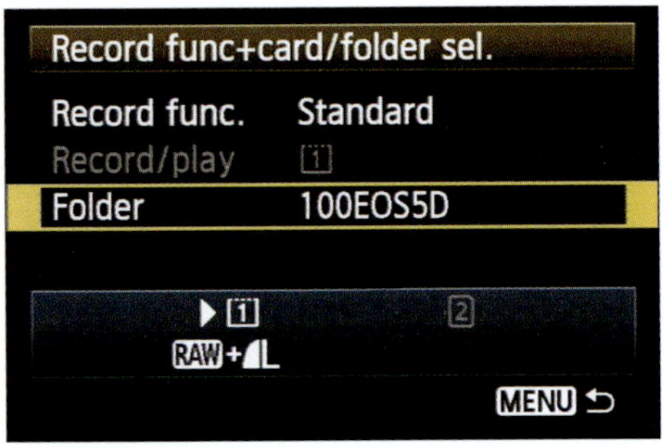

Figure 10-8: Select the folder to create or switch.

REMEMBER

If you have more than one memory card in the camera, select the one you want to work with first.

Changing How Files Are Named and Numbered

I have great news for tweak-heads everywhere. You can change how images are named and numbered on the 5D Mark III. You have three name prefixes to choose from, and you can edit two of them. Here, in brief, are the three prefixes:

- **Factory default:** Canon sets a four-character alphanumeric prefix at the factory that is theoretically unique to your camera. For example, my camera puts 2JOC in front of the number. Love it or hate it, you can't change this.
- **User Setting 1:** Register your own four-character alphanumeric prefix. The default is IMG_ (yes, you can change the underscore character).
- **User Setting 2:** Register your own three-character alphanumeric prefix (which turns into a four-character prefix when the camera adds the last character). The default is IMG plus an image size identifier (L, M, and S for Large, Medium or Small; T for S2 JPEG; U for S3 JPEG).

Select the prefix you want to use (or edit the two User Setting prefixes) from the File Name option in Setup Menu 1. Figure 10-9 shows the display. When editing one of the two User Settings, you enter text in much the same way as you enter copyright information (shown earlier in this chapter).

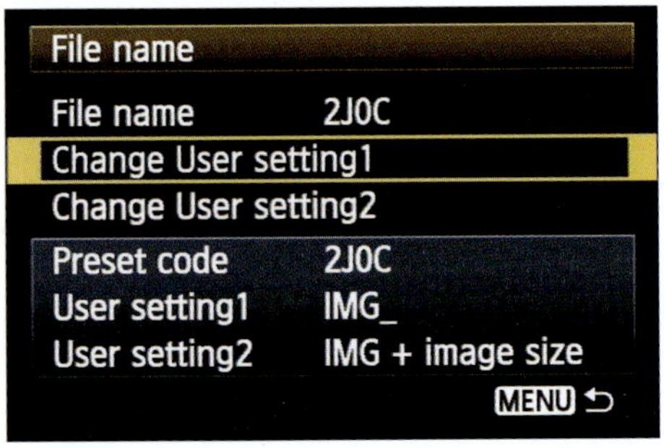

Figure 10-9: Of the three prefixes, you can change the bottom two.

In terms of numbering, you have fewer options. You can change how the number (from 0001 to 9999) is assigned and when to reset the count to 0000. You change the File Numbering option from Setup Menu 1. Here are the options:

- **Continuous:** Files are numbered from 0001 to 9999 regardless of the folder or card being used. This is the default setting and works pretty well. Its main advantage is that it won't create fifteen photos with the same filename and number.
- **Auto Reset:** This method resets the file number to 0001 every time you replace the memory card, create a folder, or switch the target card that the camera uses.
- **Manual Reset:** Select this option to create a new folder and start the file numbering over at 0001. You can't bypass the folder business. The camera creates a new folder to protect the other photos on the card.

Reversing the Main Dial Direction

The Main dial has directionality when you're in Tv (Shutter-Priority AE) or Av (Aperture-Priority AE) mode. Turn it one way and the numbers go up; turn it the other way and the numbers go down.

If you want the numbers to go the other direction when you rotate the Main dial, set Dial Direction During Tv/Av (found in Custom Function Menu 2) to Reverse Direction.

Adding Cropping Information to Photos

When shooting in Live View mode (see Chapter 3), you can assign cropping information to photos and preview them on the LCD monitor. It works like "try before you buy." The camera takes a photo with a traditional 3:2 aspect ratio and adds the cropping information to the file's metadata. *It doesn't actually crop it.* You can change your mind about how you want to crop the photo later if you use Canon's Digital Photo Professional (DPP). Your mileage may vary in other applications; many simply crop the photo.

Figure 10-10 shows a photo in DPP. The full photo is presented as a smallish thumbnail to the left. The cropped photo appears in the main window.

To add cropping information, choose the Add Cropping Information option from Custom Function Menu 3 and select an aspect ratio.

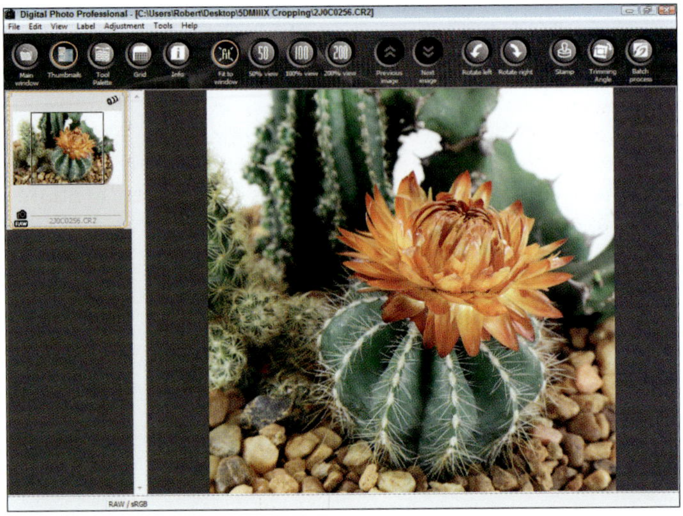

Figure 10-10: DPP shows you the cropped image and lets you change it.

Customizing Info Button Display Options

The Info button is versatile, but it can be frustrating to have to keep pressing the button like a hungry rat in a maze when all you want to do is look at a single page. So what's an impatient photographer to do? Limit the pages that can be displayed. Choose the Info Button Display Options option from Setup Menu 3 and then configure the displays you want to see (see Figure 10-11). Refer to Chapter 1 for information on the individual displays.

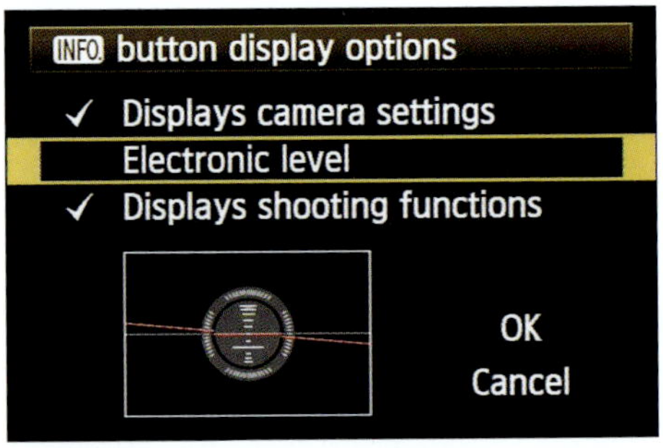

Figure 10-11: Deselect any items you don't want to see.

You can't deselect everything; at least one option must remain selected. When you're finished, make sure to highlight OK and press Set.

Customizing Auto Power Off Options

Your 5D Mark III saves power by taking a coffee break every minute as long as you aren't pressing buttons. To change the amount of time the camera waits to power down, select the Auto Power Off option from Setup Menu 2. Choose a new time (from 1 to 30 minutes) or disable the feature. No matter what setting you choose, the LCD monitor powers down after 30 minutes of inactivity to save power.

TIP

To wake up the camera, press a button. I like pressing Menu or AF-ON because I can't accidentally take a photo.

11

Ten Cool Features Worth Investigating

In This Chapter

- Registering automatic dust deletion data
- Using the electronic level
- Working with dual memory cards
- Enabling Safety Shift to make sure the camera can set the right exposure
- Using an Eye-Fi memory card
- Calibrating autofocus

The 5D Mark III has a ton of interesting features and capabilities. Although the major ones have been covered in the rest of the book, the camera has enough "leftovers" to cover in an entire book. I can't do that here, of course, but I can tip you off to some interesting features that you can investigate on your own time.

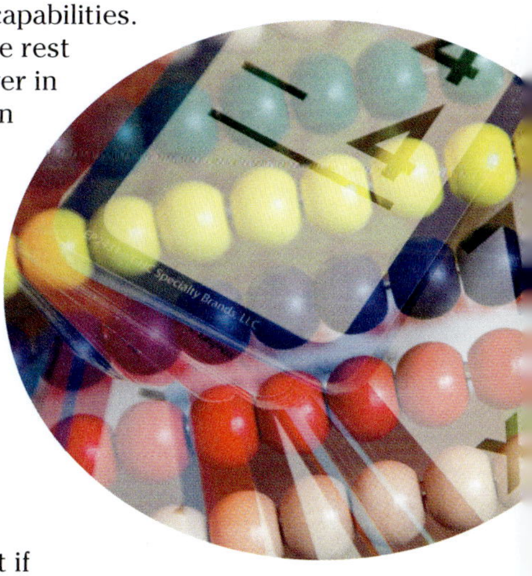

Most features' options described in this chapter are available or configurable only when you are *not* in the Scene Intelligent Auto shooting mode. Shooting with more than one memory card is the exception.

All Your Dust Are Belong to Us

The automated sensor cleaning normally is all that's necessary to keep the 5D Mark III sensor dust free. But if you notice small spots appearing consistently on your photos and movies, you might have a dust problem.

Until you can have the camera cleaned, try the automatic dust removal filter, which is located in Shooting Menu 3. When enabled, this option creates a Dust Delete Data file that you can apply in Digital Photo Professional (DPP).

The data is attached to every subsequent image (that's right, both JPEG and RAW photos), regardless of the shooting mode you're using.

TIP

If you don't use DPP, don't bother recording Dust Delete Data. You'll have to remove dust spots yourself in whatever software you prefer to use.

To clean a photo, open it in DPP and select the Stamp tool. Your photo appears in an editing window; click the Apply Dust Delete Data button to start the automated dust-busting feature. The program's manual, provided on one of the CDs that ship with your camera, offers details about this process; look for the Help entry related to using the Copy Stamp tool or Dust Delete Data.

(If the heading of this section confuses you, Google "all your base are belong to us." Read the wiki article and watch the videos on YouTube.)

Becoming One with the Level

TIP

When you need assistance keeping the camera level, use the 5D Mark III's built-in electronic level. Turn it on by pressing the Info button with your left thumb until the level shows up full-sized on the LCD monitor.

If the camera is tilted left or right, a long green line turns orange and the outer sections tilt to show you the camera's current orientation. A gray artificial horizon line is revealed underneath. The center of the level shows you whether you're tilting the camera from front to back (or vice versa). It's smaller than the horizontal component and can be a bit harder to line up.

If you need to compose the scene at the same time you're leveling, you can choose one of these two methods:

- **Live View level:** When in Live View mode, press the Info button until you see the level. Although it is smaller than the level that takes up the entire LCD monitor, it is useful and works the same way.
- **Viewfinder level:** Although it is disabled by default, the electronic level in the viewfinder can be activated after you assign a button to the feature. (See Chapter 10 for information on customizing the camera's controls.) When you activate the viewfinder level, a red grid lights up and the AF points form the electronic level (see Figure 11-1).

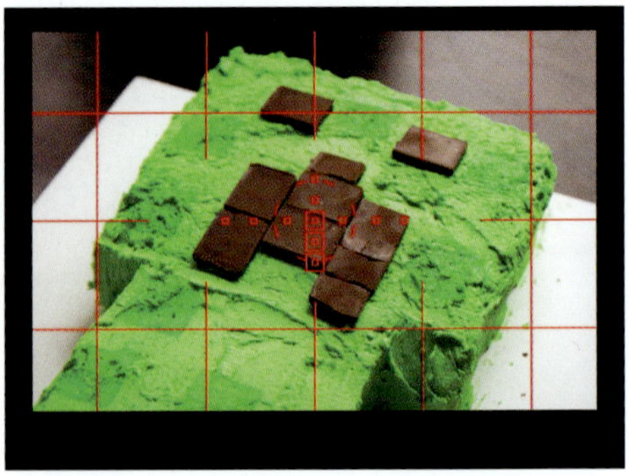

Figure 11-1: Looking down on a Creeper cake through the viewfinder.

"Dual"ing Memory Cards

One of the best optional features of the 5D Mark III is that you can have a Compact Flash (CF) and Secure Digital (SD) card inserted and record to one or both at the same time. To configure the camera to use multiple cards, visit the Record Function+Card/Folder Select option in Setup Menu 1. Here are the Record function options:

- **Standard:** When more than one card is in the camera, you should manually select which card you want to record to (and manually do the switching later). The camera defaults to standard mode and will record to Card 1 if you do nothing.
- **Auto Switch Card:** When this option is selected, the camera automatically switches memory cards when the card it is recording to becomes full.

  TIP: This is my go-to setting when I use two cards because I don't have to look down and deal with a "Card Full" message.
- **Record Separately:** This option enables you to record to both cards simultaneously. Also, you can set the image quality for the photos stored to each card independently. To do so, first select the memory card and then set the recording quality, as described in Chapter 2.
- **Record to Multiple:** This option stores the same photo to both cards. Think of it as a master and alternative (to hand to someone) or backup copy.

To switch cards, select the Record/Play option, press Set, and choose the card you want to record to or play back from.

It's often quicker to use the Quick Control screen to change cards. Press the Quick Control button, highlight the memory cards, and then spin the Main dial to change the selected card (see Figure 11-2). Pressing Set with the cards highlighted on the Quick Control screen brings up more options. Press the Quick Control button or the Shutter button halfway to lock in your choice and get back to shooting.

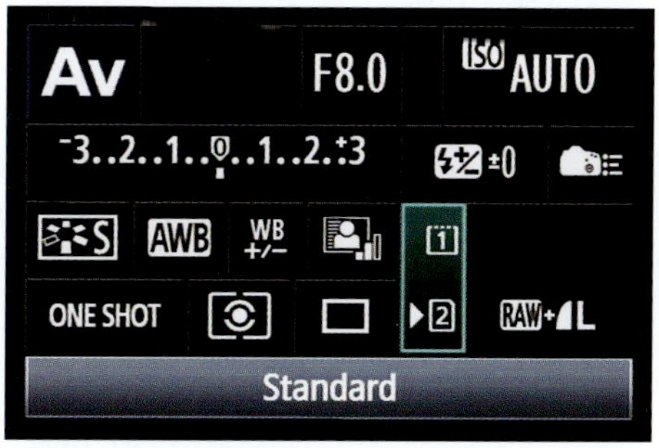

Figure 11-2: You can quickly change cards from the Quick Control screen.

You see the cards displayed on the top LCD panel, as shown in Figure 11-3. The one you are recording to is identified by an arrow. The photo size and quality are also displayed.

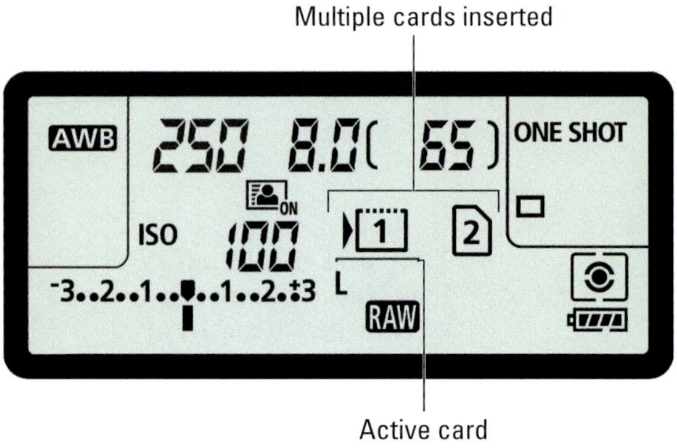

Figure 11-3: The LCD panel nicely summarizes all the card information.

TIP

If you're ever confused as to which card you're referring to, the Compact Flash card icon looks like a photo in Landscape orientation. The Secure Digital card icon looks like a photo in Portrait orientation (and has a clipped corner).

Playing It Safe with Safety Shift

By enabling the Safety Shift option, you give your 5D Mark III permission to change the shutter speed, aperture, or ISO that you have chosen so that you can get the shot with the right exposure. It's an exposure setting override that allows the camera to change your settings when it can't reach the standard exposure solution any other way.

To use this feature, enable Safety Shift from Custom Function Menu 1. You can customize Safety Shift as follows:

- **Off:** This is the default setting. Enable Safety Shift by selecting either of the following two options.
- **Shutter Speed/Aperture (Tv/Av):** Selecting this option limits Safety Shift to Shutter-Priority AE (Tv) and Aperture-Priority AE (Av) modes.

  If necessary, the camera will change the aperture if in Av mode, or change the shutter speed if you are in Tv shooting mode.
- **ISO Speed (ISO):** The ISO option enables Safety Shift using ISO in Shutter-Priority AE (Tv), Aperture-Priority AE (Av), or Program AE shooting modes. This feature differs from ISO Auto in that Safety Shift overrides your manual ISO setting. You don't need to enable it if you use ISO Auto.

I Spy an Eye-Fi Memory Card

Your 5D Mark III is compatible with *Eye-Fi cards*, which are memory cards that wirelessly transfer photos and movies from your camera to a computer. That sounds great, but consider a few realities before jumping into the Eye-Fi pool:

- **Time and trouble:** It takes more time, trouble, and money to buy an Eye-Fi card compared to a standard memory card for your camera. You have to get the right one, install Eye-Fi software on your computer, and register for a free Eye-Fi account.
- **Battery power:** When you're transferring photos from your camera to a computer, you're draining the battery.
- **Speed:** Eye-Fi transfer speeds, although not as slow smoke signals, aren't as fast as a card reader or a USB connection.

By default, Eye-Fi is disabled. When you put in a card for the first time, the icon on the display on the back LCD monitor shows Off. You can enable Eye-Fi from Setup Menu 1.

You have to control the card's transfer settings from within the Eye-Fi Center on your computer. Check your Eye-Fi documentation for more information on setting up and configuring Eye-Fi.

WARNING!

Not all Eye-Fi cards transfer RAW photos. If you need one that does, read the fine print and make sure to get the right one.

Shooting Multiple-Exposure Exposures

The 5D Mark III has a robust multiple-exposure routine that enables you to merge from two to nine exposures into one image. It's fun and might just break you out of a shooting rut.

Although you have several settings to choose from when shooting multiple exposures on the 5D Mark III, the real challenge is experimenting with different scenes to come up with something that effectively takes advantage of merging multiple exposures. Figure 11-4 is an example of a dual exposure shot with the control method set to Average, followed by Bright and then Dark.

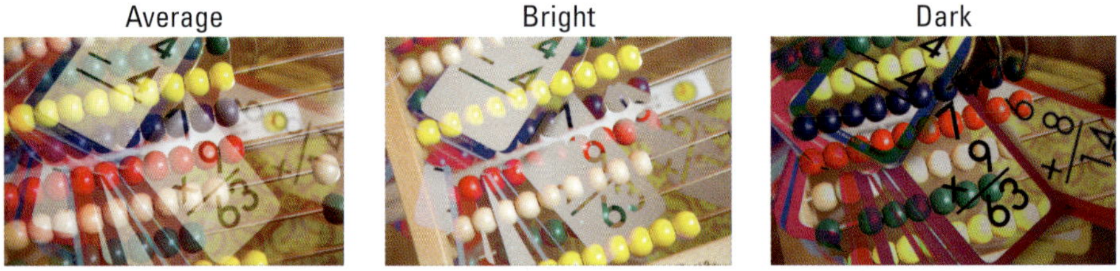

Figure 11-4: Different methods produce very different results.

Enable Multiple Exposure shooting by pressing the Creative Photo button. Figure 11-5 shows the options.

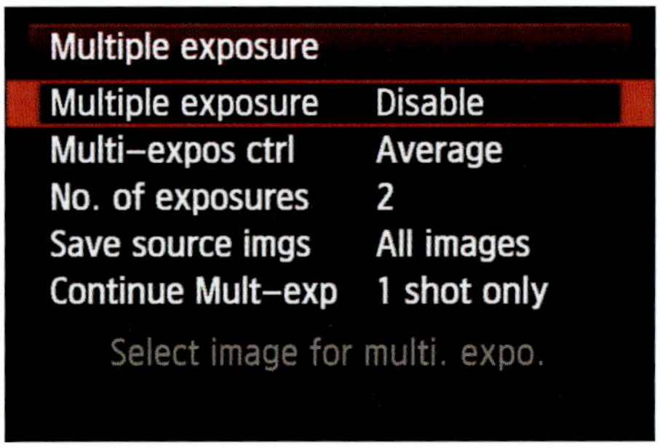

Figure 11-5: Change options from the Multiple Exposure screen.

Navigating with GPS

Although a Global Positioning System (GPS) receiver is not built into the 5D Mark III, you can connect a GPS receiver to your camera and receive positioning data.

Canon's new GPS receiver, the GP-E2, is exactly what you need to get started. The external unit is powered by a single AA battery and can be mounted on the camera's hot shoe. Data is transferred between the camera and GPS receiver through the hot shoe or, optionally, a cable connected to the camera's USB port. When connected to your camera, the GP-E2 provides latitude, longitude, altitude, direction (from its digital compass), and time information to your camera, which is then embedded in each photo's EXIF data.

To set up GPS on the 5D Mark III, attach the GPS receiver to your camera and turn it on. Next, press the Menu button and navigate to Setup Menu 2. Highlight the GPS Device Settings option (which appears only if you have the GPS receiver attached) and press the Set button.

Introducing Wireless Flash

Working with wireless flash — which you do by mounting your Speedlite off-camera and using some form of optical or radio trigger to fire it — is very liberating. You can position your light source (indeed, sources) where you want it or them, not where the camera is. That opens up a world of creativity, as shown in Figure 11-6. You can put a flash to the side, to the rear, beneath, above, or, within some limits, just about anywhere that strikes your fancy.

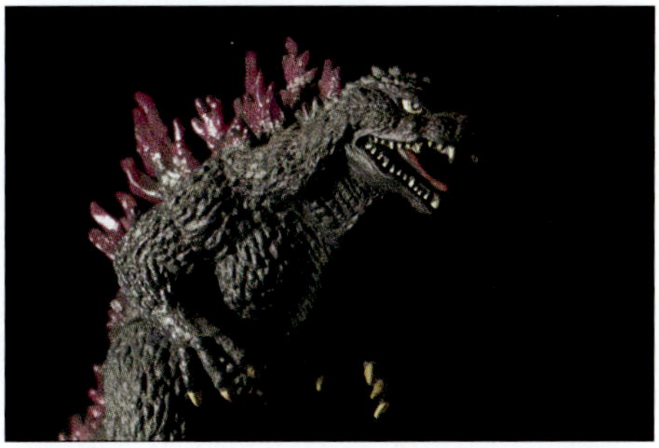

Figure 11-6: The flash was set up low and to the left of the figure.

The problem with wireless flash is that the 5D Mark III doesn't have a built-in flash (or a suitable substitute) with which to trigger an external unit. That puts a crimp in things. To shoot wireless flash, you have to attach something (often called the master) to your camera to trigger the other flashes (called slaves).

You have two basic options:

- **Mount a master flash:** Attach a Speedlite to the camera's hot shoe and use it as the master flash. It will trigger slave units via an optical burst (which is limiting because of line-of-sight considerations) or radio signal (which provides more flexibility and range because of the nature of radio). Of course, the method you use — radio or optical — depends on the exact gear you have. Canon's new Speedlite 600EX-RT is just the ticket, offering both radio and optical triggering.
- **Mount a transmitter:** Attach a compatible transmitter to the camera, such as the Canon ST-E3-RT Speedlite Transmitter (see Figure 11-7). The ST-E3-RT works like a master flash but doesn't flash; it only transmits radio signals. It works much the same as a master flash, but again, it doesn't flash.

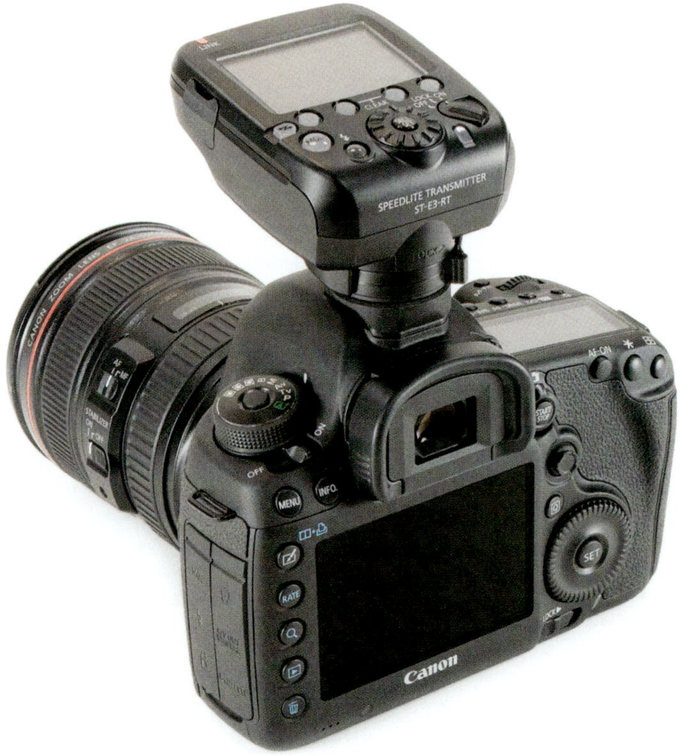

Figure 11-7: The ST-E3-RT is one way of enabling wireless flash.

In either case, you can configure the unit by visiting the External Speedlite Control option in Shooting Menu 1 and enabling Wireless Transmission (see Figure 11-8).

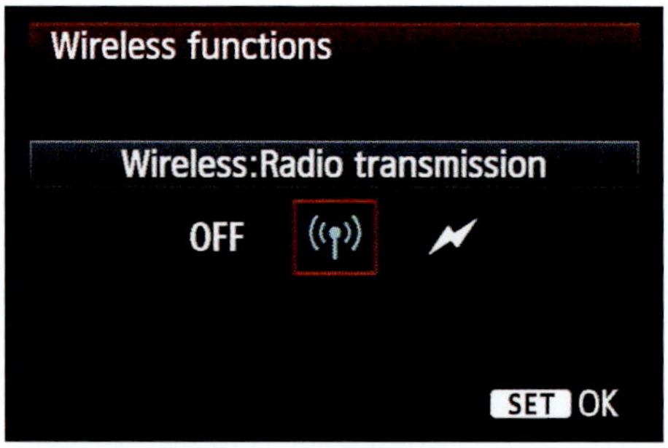

Figure 11-8: Setting the 600EX-RT to wireless radio.

Using Mirror Lockup

When you take a photo using the viewfinder (not Live View, nor can you be shooting movies) the 5D Mark III's mirror flips up and clunks out of the way of the camera's sensor. This can, unfortunately, cause the camera to shake. Taking photos with a shaking camera is never a good idea.

You can't remove this type of shake by using a tripod because you're not the one shaking. The problem is internal to the camera. To minimize it, enable Mirror Lockup from Shooting Menu 1. You see the Mirror Lockup icon appear in the top LCD panel (see Figure 11-9). This helpful reminder makes it easy to confirm whether Mirror Lockup is enabled with a quick glance to the top of the camera.

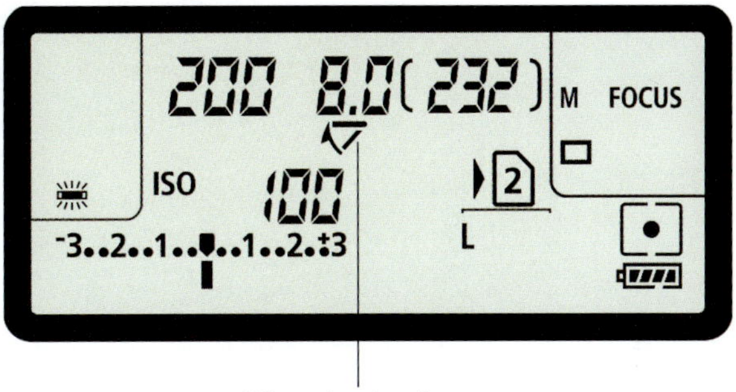

Figure 11-9: Another handy reminder.

In contrast to other cameras you may be used to using, when shooting with Mirror Lockup enabled on the 5D Mark III, you must press the Shutter button twice. That's right: The first press locks the mirror; the second takes the photo.

You hear the mirror swinging up and locking out of the way after the first press. In fact, it sounds like you just took a photo. Don't be fooled by this sound! You have one more press to go. The Mirror Lockup icon blinks on the LCD panel to remind you.

Plugging into Some Brainiac AF Features

As you can tell from Chapter 7, the 5D Mark III has a ton of autofocus (AF) features. I pulled some of the more esoteric options out and have put them in this chapter. Give these AF features a look-see when you have some time.

AF

- **AI Servo AF First Image Priority:** Located in AF Menu 3 and shown in Figure 11-10. When in AI Servo mode, this option determines how the shutter is released for the first photo. It has three settings:

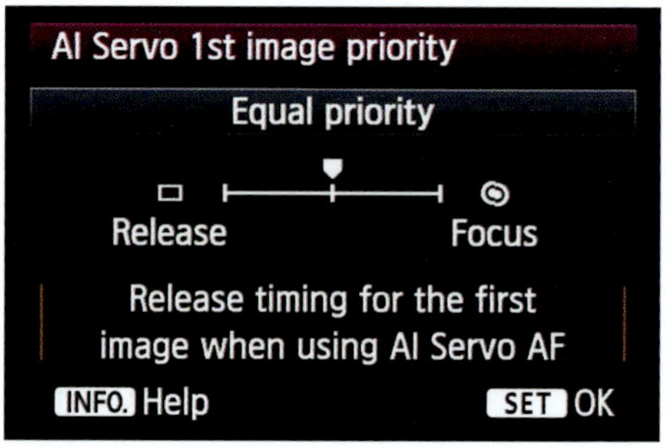

Figure 11-10: Setting the AI Servo First Image Priority.

  - *Equal Priority:* Focus and shutter release have the same priority.
  - *Release Priority:* This option gives greater importance to release than to focus. The camera lets you start your series of shots even if you're not in focus. Use this option if you find that you're missing a lot of shots because the camera is slightly out of focus and you can't get it to start taking photos.
  - *Focus Priority:* By choosing this option, you're saying that focus is the most important element. The camera doesn't release the shutter unless focus is achieved. You may miss some shots, but the first one should be in focus.

AF

- **AI Servo AF Second Image Priority:** Located in AF Menu 3 and shown in Figure 11-11. This option enables you to set the priority for the following shots when you are in AI Servo AF mode. This option has three settings:

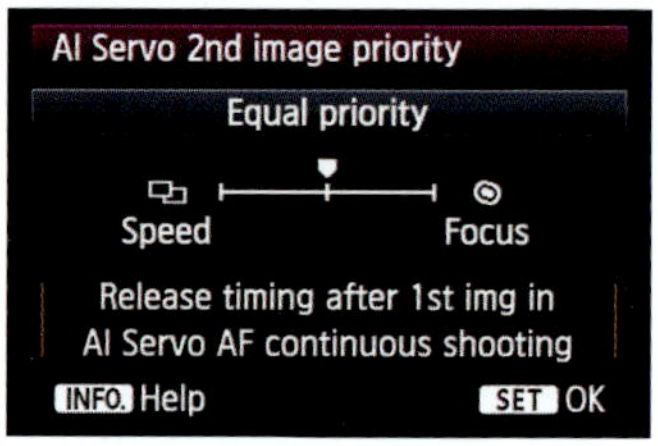

Figure 11-11: Setting the AI Servo second (and following) image priority.

  - *Equal Priority:* Focusing and release are given equal priority here.
  - *Shooting Speed Priority:* You've got the pedal to the metal with this setting, and you're not interested in slowing down. Select it if you want to continue shooting no matter what. Focus? What focus?
  - *Focus Priority:* You're in focus lock-down with this setting. The camera doesn't continue unless you're in focus. (You had better be in focus.)

AF

- **USM Len Electronic MF:** Located in AF Menu 4. If you have a lens with an electronic focusing ring (sometimes referred to as electronic manual focus), you can choose how and when you want to enable the electronic focusing ring when in One Shot AF mode. (See Chapter 7 for more information on AF modes.)

If you're somewhat confused (but not deliriously out of it), I don't blame you. Most lenses don't have an electronic focusing ring. When you manually focus with a traditional focus ring, you rely on a direct mechanical connection between your fingers and the focus elements of the lens.

Not so with a lens equipped with an electronic focusing ring. When you turn the electronic focusing ring, sensors detect how far you turn the ring and send a signal to the focus motor, which then focuses the lens.

In this case, you're not directly connected to the focus elements of the lens. You can confirm this fact by trying to focus when the camera is off (do me a favor and switch to manual focus on the lens, just to be safe). If you can't focus this way, your lens has an electronic focus ring. (The specific Canon lenses that currently apply are listed in the 5D Mark III manual.)

You can choose the following: Enable After One-Shot AF (the default, which enables manual electronic focusing after you press the Shutter button halfway to autofocus); Disable After One-Shot AF; or Disable in AF Mode.

- **AF Microadjustment:** Located in AF Menu 5. Consider microadjusting the AF point of focus when you need focus perfection and the lens is a bit off. It might be autofocusing in front of (called front focus) or behind (called back focus) where you intend.

Before you jump into it, read the disclaimer first.

Canon warns that this adjustment is not normally required and that performing it may prevent the lens from focusing. Canon also reminds you that the AF point of focus will vary based on a number of different factors, which means that you may not be able to adjust the focus to your liking. What's more, you will probably have to repeat the process, you know, in case it's a tad more humid from one day to the next. Take note of the warnings and proceed at your own risk.

You can make two types of adjustments from the AF Microadjustment option:

  - *All By Same Amount:* If you seem to be out of focus by the same amount regardless of whether you're using your prized L-series zoom lens, try adjusting the autofocus for all lenses. You should also think about taking your camera to an authorized service center or getting your eyes checked.

  - *Adjust By Lens:* You may also correct the focal point for individual lenses (the camera stores adjustments for up to 40 lenses). This is, not surprisingly, a very powerful option. Most often, you'll use it if you have a specific lens that always focuses in front of or behind where you intend. Although you can send the lens in for servicing, this option is cheaper and gets you back to being productive very quickly.

Index

• Numerics •

• A •

• B •

• C •

• D •

• F •

G

H

I

• J •

• K •

• L •

• N •

• O •

• P •

• Q •

• R •

• S •

• T •

• U •

• V •

W

Z

Notes

Notes

Notes

Math & Science

Algebra I For Dummies, 2nd Edition
978-0-470-55964-2

Biology For Dummies, 2nd Edition
978-0-470-59875-7

Chemistry For Dummies, 2nd Edition
978-1-1180-0730-3

Geometry For Dummies, 2nd Edition
978-0-470-08946-0

Pre-Algebra Essentials For Dummies
978-0-470-61838-7

Microsoft Office

Excel 2010 For Dummies
978-0-470-48953-6

Office 2010 All-in-One For Dummies
978-0-470-49748-7

Office 2011 for Mac For Dummies
978-0-470-87869-9

Word 2010 For Dummies
978-0-470-48772-3

Music

Guitar For Dummies, 2nd Edition
978-0-7645-9904-0

Clarinet For Dummies
978-0-470-58477-4

iPod & iTunes For Dummies, 9th Edition
978-1-118-13060-5

Pets

Cats For Dummies, 2nd Edition
978-0-7645-5275-5

Dogs All-in One For Dummies
978-0470-52978-2

Saltwater Aquariums For Dummies
978-0-470-06805-2

Religion & Inspiration

The Bible For Dummies
978-0-7645-5296-0

Catholicism For Dummies, 2nd Edition
978-1-118-07778-8

Spirituality For Dummies, 2nd Edition
978-0-470-19142-2

Self-Help & Relationships

Happiness For Dummies
978-0-470-28171-0

Overcoming Anxiety For Dummies, 2nd Edition
978-0-470-57441-6

Seniors

Crosswords For Seniors For Dummies
978-0-470-49157-7

iPad 2 For Seniors For Dummies, 3rd Edition
978-1-118-17678-8

Laptops & Tablets For Seniors For Dummies, 2nd Edition
978-1-118-09596-6

Smartphones & Tablets

BlackBerry For Dummies, 5th Edition
978-1-118-10035-6

Droid X2 For Dummies
978-1-118-14864-8

HTC ThunderBolt For Dummies
978-1-118-07601-9

MOTOROLA XOOM For Dummies
978-1-118-08835-7

Sports

Basketball For Dummies, 3rd Edition
978-1-118-07374-2

Football For Dummies, 2nd Edition
978-1-118-01261-1

Golf For Dummies, 4th Edition
978-0-470-88279-5

Test Prep

ACT For Dummies, 5th Edition
978-1-118-01259-8

ASVAB For Dummies, 3rd Edition
978-0-470-63760-9

The GRE Test For Dummies, 7th Edition
978-0-470-00919-2

Police Officer Exam For Dummies
978-0-470-88724-0

Series 7 Exam For Dummies
978-0-470-09932-2

Web Development

HTML, CSS, & XHTML For Dummies, 7th Edition
978-0-470-91659-9

Drupal For Dummies, 2nd Edition
978-1-118-08348-2

Windows 7

Windows 7 For Dummies
978-0-470-49743-2

Windows 7 For Dummies, Book + DVD Bundle
978-0-470-52398-8

Windows 7 All-in-One For Dummies
978-0-470-48763-1

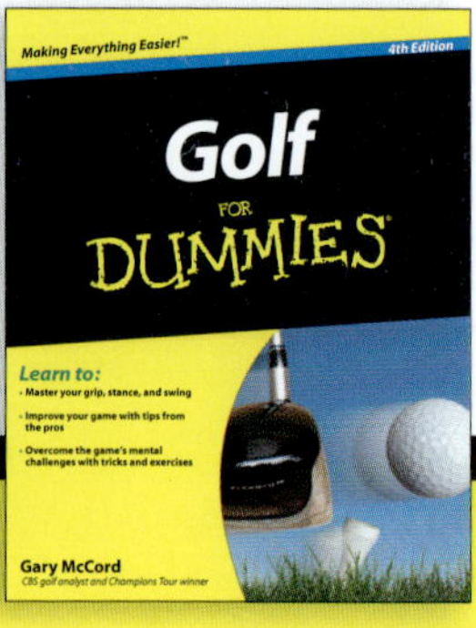

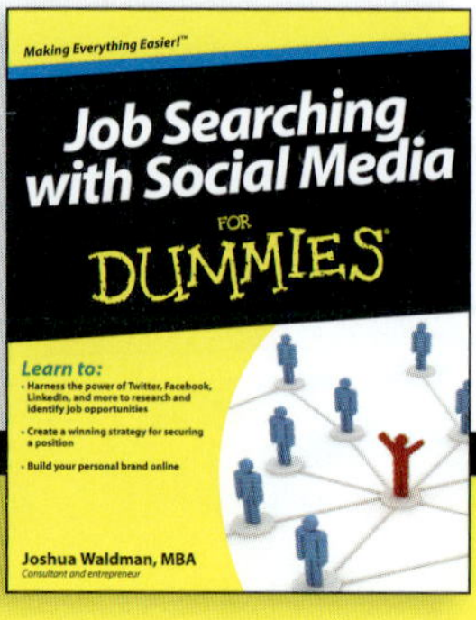

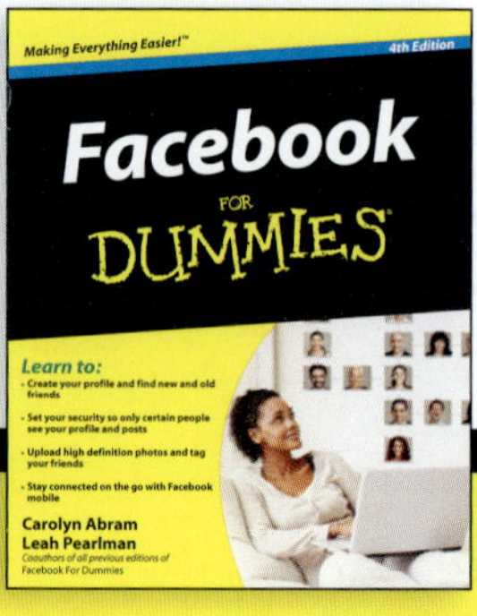

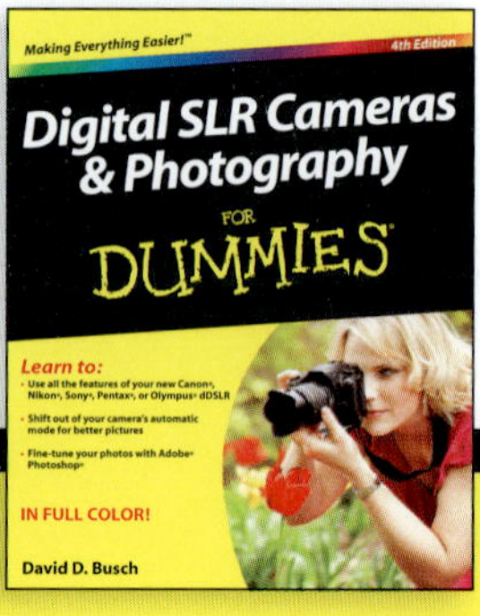

Available wherever books are sold. For more information or to order direct: U.S. customers visit www.dummies.com or call 1-877-762-297
U.K. customers visit www.wileyeurope.com or call (0) 1243 843291. Canadian customers visit www.wiley.ca or call 1-800-567-4797.
Connect with us online at www.facebook.com/fordummies or @fordummies

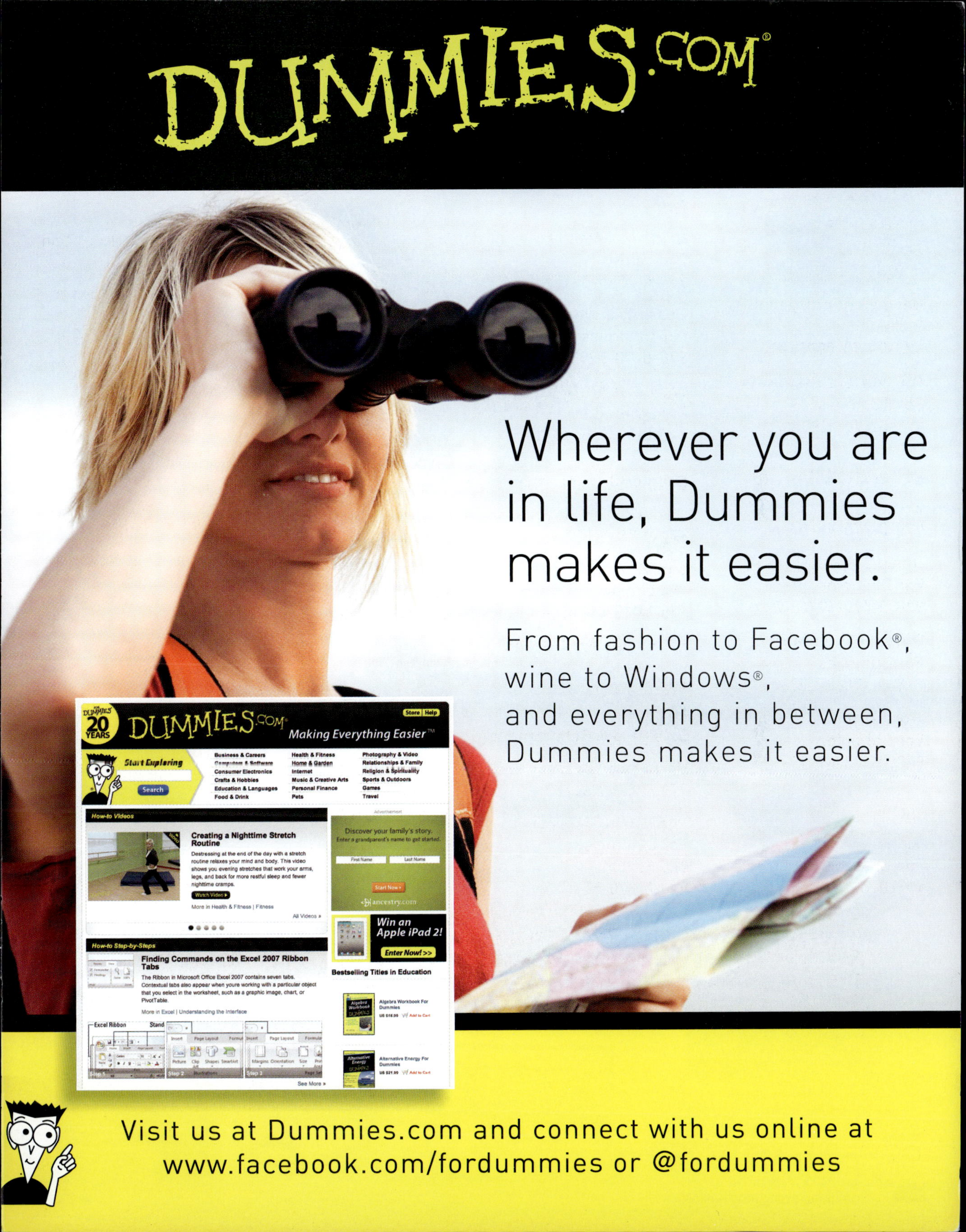
DUMMIES.COM®
Wherever you are in life, Dummies makes it easier.
From fashion to Facebook®, wine to Windows®, and everything in between, Dummies makes it easier.
DUMMIES.COM
Making Everything Easier™
Start Exploring
Search
How-to Videos
Creating a Nighttime Stretch Routine
How-to Step-by-Steps
Finding Commands on the Excel 2007 Ribbon Tabs
Win an Apple iPad 2!
Enter Now! >>
Bestselling Titles in Education
Visit us at Dummies.com and connect with us online at www.facebook.com/fordummies or @fordummies